Competitiveness and the Value of Intangible Assets

"L'essentiel est invisible pour les yeux"

Antoine de SAINT-EXUPÉRY, *Le Petit Prince*
© Éditions GALLIMARD
Avec l'aimable autorisation de la succession SAINT-EXUPÉRY
et des Éditions GALLIMARD

Competitiveness and the Value of Intangible Assets

Edited by

Pierre Buigues
Head of Unit, European Commission, Belgium

Alexis Jacquemin
*Chief Advisor, European Commission
and Professor of Economics,
Université Catholique de Louvain, Belgium*

Jean-François Marchipont
Director, European Commission, Belgium

Preface by
Romano Prodi
President, European Commission, Belgium

Edward Elgar
Cheltenham, UK • Northampton, MA, USA

© Pierre Buigues, Alexis Jacquemin and Jean-François Marchipont, 2000

All rights reserved. No part of this publication may be reproduced, stored in a retrieval system or transmitted in any form or by any means, electronic, mechanical or photocopying, recording, or otherwise without the prior permission of the publisher.

Published by
Edward Elgar Publishing Limited
Glensanda House
Montpellier Parade
Cheltenham
Glos GL50 1UA
UK

Edward Elgar Publishing, Inc.
136 West Street
Suite 202
Northampton
Massachusetts 01060
USA

A catalogue record for this book
is available from the British Library

Library of Congress Cataloguing in Publication Data

Competitiveness and the value of intangible assets / edited by Pierre Buiges [i.e. Buigues], Alexis Jacquemin, Jean-François Marchipont.
 "Proceedings of the conference on 'Intangible Assets and the Competitiveness of the European Economy', held in Louvain-la-Neuve on 29–30 April 1999".
 Includes bibliographical references and index.
 1. Information technology—Economic aspects—European Union countries—Congresses. 2. Technological innovations—Economic aspects—European Union countries—Congresses. 3. Business networks—European Union countries—Congresses. 4. Intellectual capital—European Union countries—Congresses. 5. Human capital—European Union countries—Congresses. 6. Competition, International—Congresses.
 I. Buigues, P. II. Jacquemin, Alex. III. Marchipont, Jean-François, 1951–

HC240.9.I55 C65 2000
338.6'048—dc21

99–045192

ISBN 1 84064 391 9
Printed and bound in Great Britain by MPG Books Ltd, Bodmin, Cornwall

Contents

LIST OF FIGURES	viii
LIST OF TABLES	x
LIST OF CONTRIBUTORS	xiii
PREFACE	xv
FOREWORD	xvii
ACKNOWLEDGEMENTS	xix

PART I   INTANGIBLES: A GENERAL FRAMEWORK

1. Intellectual Capital: Economic Theory and Analysis
   Jorgen Mortensen   3

2. Intangible Resources and Competitiveness:
   Towards a Dynamic View of Corporate Performance
   Ahmed Bounfour   17

3. Making Intangibles Visible: The Value, the Efficiency
   and the Economic Consequences of Knowledge
   Gunnar Eliasson   42

4. Accounting for Intangibles: Issues and Prospects
   Graham Vickery   72

PART II	INTANGIBLES: IMPACT ON SECTORS AND ENTERPRISES	
5.	The Adaptive Capacity of the Firm as a Key to European Competitiveness John Kay	103
6.	Intangible Assets and the Competitiveness of European Industries Michael Peneder	117
7.	Intangible Assets and Service Sectors: The Challenges of Service Industries Ian Miles and Mark Tomlinson	154
8.	Discussion Lionel Fontagné	187
9.	Tangible and Intangible Investment and Economic Performance: Evidence from Company Accounts Mary O'Mahony and Michela Vecchi	199
10.	Research and Development, Innovation and Corporate Performance in the Chemical Industry: A Case Study Alfonso Gambardella, Walter García-Fontes and Gérald Petit	228
11.	Discussion Christian Huveneers	251
PART III	INTANGIBLES: ANALYSIS OF INPUTS	
12.	Human Capital Stock and Productivity: The Case of Dutch Manufacturing Firms Martin Boon	259

13.	**Patents and Trademarks as Indicators of International Competitiveness: The VAR versus the Hysteresis Approach** **Wim Meeusen and Glenn Rayp**	273
14.	**Research and Development as a Source of Technological Change** **Dominique Guellec**	297
15.	**Education and Information Society** **Jacques Lesourne**	309
16.	**Discussion** **Elisabeth Waelbroeck-Rocha**	316
17.	**Conclusion** **Pierre Buigues, Alexis Jacquemin and Jean-François Marchipont**	320

INDEX   331

List of Figures

2.1	Four dimensions of competitiveness	27
2.2	Intellectual capital is at the heart of the MIR scope	28
2.3	The three types of value within companies	28
2.4	Internal processes for value-added services	30
2.5	The architecture of management of intangible resources (MIR)	36
4.1	Investment in tangibles and knowledge-related intangibles	74
4.2	Knowledge-based industry and services	77
4.3	Exports in high-technology industries	78
4.4	ICTs	79
4.5	Human resources	80
6.1	Intangible assets and competitive strategy: deviation of mean number of entries (%)	123
6.2	Unit values in EU trade: 1997 in ECU per kg	129
6.3	Standard deviation of unit values in the EU 1996	131
6.4	Aggregate labour productivity: EU-Japan-USA 1997 in 1000 ECU	136
6.5	Intangibles and labour productivity: factor intensities, shares of skilled labour	141
6.6	The dynamics of value added shares in the EU15, Japan and the USA	143
6.7	Relative similarity in value added shares across industries 1997: labour skills	146
6.8	Mapping European specialisation (I): value added shares by skill types 1997	146
6.9	Relative similarity in value added shares across industry types: factor inputs	149
6.10	Value added shares by skill types and factor inputs 1997	150

List of Figures

7.1	A classification and impressionistic mapping of services	161
7.2	Service 'clusters' from UK IO data: overlapping clusters in services	172
7.3	Selected services' technology related expenditures	179
7.4	Classification of innovation stances of Italian services from innovation survey data	180
9.1	Advertising expenditure and R&D expenditure as a proportion of GDP in the five countries	201
10.1	Chemical industry indicators, EU	230

List of Tables

1.1	Capital stock and capital/output ratio in the United States 1929-1990	8
2.1	Examples of intangible resources considered in the resource and capabilities views	22
2.2	Examples of companies implementing an approach for Intellectual Capital and Knowledge Management	24
2.3	Elements of Intellectual Capital – example of a taxonomy used	25
2.4	Example of calculation of present performance indicators, for three dimensions of competitiveness	32
2.5	Estimation of 10 major intangible assets for an SME	34
3.1	The statistical accounts of the knowledge-based information economy	51
3.2	Actors in the competence bloc	55
3.3	The complete balance sheet of a firm (9 and 17 Swedish firms)	61
4.1	Nature of intangible assets recognised: early 1990s	93
4.2	Measurement of research and development	94
6.1	Non-parametric tests for significant differences in unit values 1997: factor inputs	133
6.2	Non-parametric tests for significant differences in unit values 1997: skill types	134
6.3	Non-parametric tests for significant differences in labour productivity and wages 1997: factor inputs	137
6.4	Non-parametric tests for significant differences in labour productivity and wages: skill types	138
6.5	Value added shares in total manufacturing 1997 (%): skill types	144

List of Tables

6.6	Value added shares in total manufacturing 1997 (%): factor inputs	147
7.1	Occupations in UK services, 1991, OECD dataset	163
7.2	Services in UK ranked by HSWC intensity	164
7.3	Three countries' data on the share of high-skilled employees in the workforce of service sectors	165
7.4	Services' use of intermediate services and labour, UK 1990	168
7.5	'Clusters' of services from factor analysis 1990	171
7.6	OECD data on services' share of business R&D expenditures, c 1993	174
7.7	UK services technology activities, CIS2 data (1997)	177
7.8	Employment by non-national enterprises in EU services (%)	184
8.1	Average technological intensity for major industrialised countries (%), 1990-93	191
8.2	Share of high tech products (OECD-Eurostat list) in EU15 trade by NACE three-digit position, 1996	192
8.3	Revealed comparative advantage by technological level and by position on the quality ladder, Germany and United Kingdom, 1996	196
9.1	Pooled regressions with interactive dummies (base category: United States)	211
9.2	Pooled regressions with manufacturing and non-manufacturing dummies (base category: non-manufacturing)	212
9.3	Profitability rate regression (base category: United States)	214
9.4	Profitability ratio in the manufacturing and non-manufacturing sector	215
9.5	The chemical sector	216
9.6	Econometric results: machinery sector	218
9.7	Econometric results: business services	219
9.A.1	Econometric results: panel methods	226
9.A.2	Econometric results: GMM estimation	227

List of Tables

10.1	Firms with highest 1996 market values	234
10.2	Average annual growth rate of sales 1990-96 (%), by sector	235
10.3	Average profitability 1996 (%), by sector and origin of firm	235
10.4	Average stock of patent by firm, by sector	236
10.5	Average R&D intensities (1990-1996), by sector	237
10.6	External growth strategies (average numbers by firm, 1990-96), by sector	238
10.7	Definition of variables used in the regressions	239
10.8	Market value in chemicals, 1990-1996 – OLS	242
10.9	TFP in chemicals, 1991-1996 – OLS	245
10.10	Net profits over sales in chemicals, 1991-1996 – OLS	247
12.1	Summary statistics	263
12.2	Estimates of the gross output elasticity with respect to human capital	268
12.3	Estimates of the value added elasticity with respect to human capital	269
13.1	Export-shares, relative unit labour cost, relative R&D intensities, patent shares and trademark shares in manufacturing industry in twelve OECD countries	281
13.2	Results of the co-integration analysis of eleven OECD countries	286
13.3	Long-run competitiveness (C) and labour cost (W) equations for seven OECD countries	287
13.4	First difference regression results for OECD export shares (1970-1995)	292
13.A.1	Results of the (Augmented) Dickey-Fuller unit root tests	295
14.1	Growth of R&D expenditures in the business sector: average annual growth rate at 1990 GDP prices	299
14.2	Estimated results	301
14.3	Average results from available estimates of internal rate of return to R&D at the industry level	306
17.1	Tangible versus intangible activities and market structure	323

List of Contributors

BOON, Martin	*Statistics Netherlands, Division Research and Development, Voorburg.*
BOUNFOUR, Ahmed	*Scientific Director of RCS Conseil (Research on Competitiveness Strategies) Paris*
BUIGUES, Pierre	*Head of Unit, European Commission*
ELIASSON, Gunnar	*Professor, KTH (Kungl Tekniska Högskolan), Stockholm*
FONTAGNÉ, Lionel	*Professor, University Paris-I (TEAM-CNRS), Paris*
GAMBARDELLA, Alfonso	*Professor of Economics and Management, University of Urbino, Italy*
GARCÍA-FONTES, Walter	*Professor of Applied Economics, Departament d'Economia i Empresa, Universitat Pompeu Fabra, Barcelona*
GUELLEC, Dominique	*Administrator, OECD, Paris*
HUVENEERS, Christian	*Professor, UCL, Louvain-la-Neuve*
JACQUEMIN, Alexis	*Chief Adviser, European Commission and Professor, UCL, Louvain-la-Neuve*
KAY, John	*Director, London Economics, London*
LESOURNE, Jacques	*Economist, former Director of* Le Monde, *Paris*
MARCHIPONT, Jean-François	*Director, European Commission*
MEEUSEN, Wim	*Professor, University of Antwerp (RUCA)*
MILES, Ian	*Professor and CoDirector, PREST and CRIC (Centre for Research on Innovation and Competition), University of Manchester*
MORTENSEN, Jorgen	*Independent consultant and Senior Research Fellow, Centre for European Policy Studies, Brussels*

O'MAHONY, Mary	*National Institute of Economic and Social Research, London*
PENEDER, Michael	*WIFO, Vienna*
PETIT, Gérald	*Administrator, European Commission*
RAYP, Glenn	*University of Ghent*
TOMLINSON, Mark	*Research Fellow, CRIC (Centre for Research on Innovation and Competition), University of Manchester*
VECCHI, Michela	*National Institute of Economic and Social Research, London*
VICKERY, Graham	*Principal Administrator, OECD, Paris*
WAELBROECK-ROCHA, Elisabeth	*Chief European Economist, Standard & Poor's DRI, Brussels*

Preface
by Romano Prodi
President of the Commission of the European Communities

New forms of economic organisation are emerging from the new developments in technology. The new technology has expanded our capacity to analyse and exchange information and accelerated the shift from manufacturing to services.

The part which the so-called "intangibles" play in this process is gaining increasing recognition.

Intangible assets are a factor of growing importance in boosting corporate competitiveness and economic performance. In the last twenty years there has been a shift from competitive advantage based on size and power to competitive advantage based on the assimilation of knowledge. These intangibles include not only R&D but also human capital, innovation in products and in organisation, trademarks and patents, networking and software.

At the same time, intangible investments are increasingly generating economic growth and jobs. In fact, since the 1990s, the US economy has benefited greatly from faster application of new technology and the USA is now clearly the most successful country in the world in making the transition to a new knowledge-based economy.

A priority for Europe, then, is to move faster in expanding its capacity to benefit from these new opportunities.

The EU has laid the foundations for future success with the single market and the euro. The new "e-Europe Initiative", designed to speed up Europe's transformation into a genuine information society, sets ambitious objectives. The first target is to help Europe "bring every citizen, home and school, every business and administration into the digital age and online". The second is to "create a digitally literate Europe, supported by an entrepreneurial culture ready to finance and develop new ideas", and the third is to "ensure the whole process is socially inclusive, builds consumer trust and strengthens social cohesion".

This is the first step the EU must take if it is to cope successfully with the new challenges.

Highlighting, as it does, the increasing importance of intangibles and their future implications, this book, which is the fruit of high-level scientific research, will enable the reader to "grasp the intangible", while opening up crucial new prospects for Community policies.

Foreword

Intangible assets need analysing to identify the effects they are having on competitiveness, growth, productivity and microeconomic performance.

Their implications for the "rules of the game" will also need to be looked at. Some economists fear that the possession of knowledge will create a society of "winner-takes-all" markets, and that concentration will accentuate market dominance, with a small number of global players controlling standards, brands and processes of innovation. Others maintain that the knowledge-based economy will create a field of opportunities for new entrants where no one can expect to enjoy control of the markets in which they operate.

In practice, the new forms of technology, especially data-transmission technology, are closing the gap between consumers and the latest developments on the technology front. In traditional industrial structures, R&D is the first step in the value-added chain which runs through from the manufacturing processes, along the distribution channels, to the final consumers. In the knowledge-based economy, the different links in the chain are disappearing and the Internet is set to close the gap between knowledge producers and consumers.

As a contribution to this complex debate, the value of this book is that it first of all presents an extensive collection of empirical studies based on rigorous methodologies, and then draws the policy implications at the European level.

The book is structured in four parts. The first part seeks to inculcate a better understanding of the importance of intangible investment at the macroeconomic level, and points to some gaps in the present accounting framework.

Part two assesses the economic impact of intangible assets, presenting two empirical exercises designed to gauge the detailed effects of intangible investment on the performance of particular sectors and companies. By means of rigorous statistical analysis, it tests various hypotheses as to the possible causal link between the type of investment made and the performance which countries achieve, culminating in a tentative assessment of how far the European Union lags behind Japan and the USA in fast-moving branches of the economy, where intangible investment is of primary importance.

In part three, the author describes and discusses some major case studies of intangible assets, involving human capital, R&D and innovation, patents and trademarks, and information technology.

The fourth and last part of the book attempts to draw some policy implications from the preceding discussions, especially looking towards the future of industrial policy in Europe against the background of a fast-growing information society.

Acknowledgements

This book documents the proceedings of the conference on 'Intangible Assets and the Competitiveness of the European Economy', held in Louvain-la-Neuve on 29-30 April 1999.

The studies presented at the Conference were funded and monitored by the European Commission's Directorate General for Research and Development, the Directorate General for Industry* and the Forward Studies Unit.

We are grateful to the Catholic University of Louvain (UCL) for providing excellent conference facilities. The support of Christian Huveneers, Professor at UCL, and of Cia Rosenqvist, was very useful. We also express our gratitude to Gérald Petit, administrator at the Directorate General for Industry, and to Montse Berges, whose competence and hard work were of crucial importance in the coordination and production of our book. We would also like to mention the attention to detail made by Alison Edwards, from E. Elgar Publishing Ltd., for the irreproachable meticulousness of her work.

We are also grateful to Jorma Routti, Director General in charge of research and development, who delivered the Opening Address.

---

* As of September 1999, the services of the Directorate General for Industry are part of the Enterprise Directorate General.

PART I

INTANGIBLES: A GENERAL FRAMEWORK

1. Intellectual Capital: Economic Theory and Analysis
Jorgen Mortensen

Competitiveness and "the new economy"

The concept of "The New Economy" is frequently referred to in the specialised press. This, however, is a very general label on a number of features of the economic performance of the leading economies. Furthermore, there is hardly agreement as to how much of recent developments are really new. In addition, different, albeit not mutually exclusive, aspects of these developments are emphasised by different researchers and experts:

- The revolution in *information technology*;
- The rising importance of *knowledge*;
- The changing patterns of *resource management* at the level of firms;
- The emergence of *innovation* as the principal determinant of competitiveness.

However, whether the economic and sociological developments are viewed through the "filter" of the "information society", "the knowledge-based economy", "the network society" or "innovation" there is evidently a large common ground. This common ground we may, to simplify matters, characterise as the increasing importance of *"intellectual capital"* in the determination of national economic performance or enterprise competitiveness.

The concept of "information society" is most directly related to the emergence of the microchip and the huge reduction in the cost of data processing and transmission. Nevertheless, the most striking feature of recent developments is perhaps the speed with which the technological revolution has been followed closely by a change in behaviour and patterns of work of large segments of the population in the advanced and less advanced economies. It is thus the interaction between technology and culture that has entailed the emergence of the "knowledge society".

Although the importance of knowledge has been recognised for centuries, the technological revolution has, in fact, opened new possibilities for managing knowledge and, notably, for moving from a static to a dynamic approach to knowledge: the information society is rapidly also becoming a "learning society". The "learning society" is one where firms and institutions actively, through training and explicit codification and storing of competence, influence their "intellectual capital" (human capital and organisational competence).

Firms on the leading edge of the information society, therefore, search for new ways of managing the inter-personal relations both within the firm and between the firm and clients and suppliers. They tend to move away from the vertical hierarchical command structures towards flatter decentralised (neuronal) structure in which each element is perceived as part of a "network". Some firms even go as far as to argue that the management of inter-personal relations is the condition for success as a business and therefore is the main task of management. All firms on the leading edge, however, put increasing emphasis on the reciprocal links with suppliers and clients.

However, few would deny that today "innovation" is the motor of competitiveness. The promotion of the capacity to *innovate,* that is, to invent new products or processes, is and must be the main purpose of investments in training, changes in organisational structures and R&D. Innovation is at the origin of the emergence of the information society. In return, the emergence of the information society has seriously enhanced both the scope and the need for innovation in order to compete in the global, liberalised market.

Intellectual capital formation: theory and practice

i.   Sources of economic growth and productivity

Classical economic theory, on which much of current economic theory remains founded, considered essentially three factors of production: land, labour and capital. Each of those had its own dimension: land was a stock, labour a flow (input), and capital was money capital in the form of a stock of capital goods. The concept of capital as an "advance" of money was taken to its extreme by Von Böhm-Bawerk who coined the notion of "*Umwegsproduktion*". The view of the stock of capital as an advance of money was rejected by Clark and Wicksteed, arguing that (fixed) capital was a factor of production on an equal footing with land and labour. The distinction between monetary capital and fixed capital has, however, throughout the history of economic analysis been blurred by the fact that at the macroeconomic level the stock of fixed capital unavoidably must be expressed as an aggregate in monetary terms, that is as a "value". The same is, and for the same reasons, the case for the aggregate output of the production process while the input of labour at least in the majority of cases is measured as hours or man-years worked. Consequently, a "production function", while being in essence an expression of the relation between material input of labour and capital, in practice takes the form of a relation between (three) variables of which at least two are expressed in monetary terms.

The path-breaking Harrod-Domar model saw output as being mainly determined by the amount of capital utilised in the production process and introduced the "capital/output ratio" as the key constant in economic growth. The later "neo-classical growth model" (formulated initially by Solow) dropped the assumption of a linear relation between fixed capital and output by introducing the input of labour explicitly into the production function with a scope for substitution between capital and labour (measured in hours or man-years).

This analysis of the relation between factor use and output was initially largely based on a production function including capital and labour and allowing for substitution between the two factors of production presented in 1928 in an article by Cobb and Douglas. Subsequently the implications and limitations of this approach were made evident and a series of alternatives proposed by a number of researchers. Nevertheless the analysis of the relation between factor use and output has been a staple of economic analysis for the whole post-war period, with the development of a branch of quantitative analysis of the growth process commonly known as "growth accounting".

Growth accounting, which aims at explaining the growth of productivity, was initiated essentially by Denison in 1962. When investigating the sources of growth in the United States from 1909 to 1958 he concluded that the knowledge, skill and energy of labour were important determinants of economic growth. Subsequent analysis by, notably, Kendrick, Jorgenson and Griliches, has aimed by and large at identifying the contribution of various, mainly "intangible", factors to the overall growth in productivity, in this context defined as the combined productivity of capital and labour, generally called "total factor productivity". As recognised by Denison himself, growth accounting by definition cannot take appropriate account of the interaction among determinants and does not involve a "controlled experiment". The underlying causal relationships in the "black box", consequently, can only be approximated by detailed, careful classification of the ingredients in the production function.

The measurement of "input" of labour input in terms of hours or man-years has for a long time been accepted intuitively as the relevant statistic. However, the pooling together of man-years of an unskilled youngster and an engineer with a diploma from a leading institute of technology and several decades of professional experience from the point of view of economic analysis does not make more sense than to add pears and apples together in one set. In fact, by failing to make a distinction between different categories of labour input, the early production function simply assumed away an aggregation problem of the same fundamental nature as for the stock of fixed capital or output.

The mere fact of constructing and estimating a "production function" in which output and the capital stock were calculated as weighted indices of the constituent elements while the input of labour was considered to be homogeneous and uni-dimensional resulted in a "residual" between the growth in output and the growth of input: the rise in the "quality" of labour input came back into analysis as a rise in "productivity". However, as has been again and again stressed, notably, by Dale Jorgenson,[1] a part of the "unexplained" residual in estimated productions functions would disappear if the input of labour were appropriately defined with due account taken of the level of education, skill and knowledge.

A residual, nevertheless, remains and, in the (relatively few) estimates based on very long time series for the United States, shows a marked tendency to rise through time: according to estimates prepared by David and Abramovitz,[2] the part of the rise in output per unit of labour input which could be explained by an increase in the input of capital per unit of labour (capital intensity), during most of the twentieth century was only

---

[1] See, for example, Jorgenson's speech to the Conference on Service Sector Productivity and the Productivity Paradox, Centre for the Study of Living Standards, Ottawa, 11-12 April 1997.

[2] M. Abramovitz and Paul A. David: Economic Growth in the U.S., in *Employment and Growth in the Knowledge-based Economy*, OECD, 1996.

between a half and a third of the level estimated for the nineteenth century.

During several decades a considerable amount of research has attempted to explain this residual (technological progress or productivity) by introducing various additional assumptions concerning the nature of innovation (embodied or disembodied technical change, etc.). This research has on the whole concluded that the residual could, as argued by Jorgenson, be attributed to improvements in "intellectual capital", that is, a number of factors which, in fact, constitute the main characteristics of the "knowledge society". This led leading researchers in the field to conclude that the "residual", in fact, was not an "unexplained" aspect of economic growth but essentially a result of a gap in the understanding of the growth process and in the availability of data. The measurement problem, thus, arises from the failure of most economists to make a clear distinction between "productivity growth" and "technological change". The solution to this measurement problem would lie in the introduction of a much broader concept of investment, including investment in R&D, in the creation of ideas, in training and education, etc.

The solution to this apparent paradox from a conceptual point of view would appear to be found in a considerable broadening of the ancient concept of capital formation to include also investment spending on education, training, research and development, software design, marketing and, even, certain kinds of expenditure on reorganisation of production and marketing aimed at making more efficient use of technology. Indeed, expenditure should be, in this perspective, considered as "investment" spending which is not directly related to current operations but constitutes a commitment of resources to ensure the survival of the firm beyond the current period.

Estimates, notably by J.W. Kendrick, of the total amount of "intangible" investment in the United States during this century, in fact, show a pronounced increase, reflecting in particular the important rise in resources devoted to education, training and R&D. The rise in intangible investment has, then, translated into a substantial rise in the stock of intangible capital. Furthermore, during the first half of the present century the relative prices of conventional tangible capital goods – at least those that have been used as deflators to create constant-price estimates of the capital stock – were rising more rapidly than the prices of consumer goods and real wages. This, and the shorter and shortening service lives of tangible reproducible assets, especially in comparison with the assumed longevity of educational and training investment embodied in the labour force, have also contributed to the differentially rapid growth of the intangible component of the total capital stock.[3]

The estimates prepared by Kendrick and reproduced by Abramovitz and David and reordered somewhat by the author, presented in Table 1.1, show that the share of conventional tangible capital in the total stock of capital in the U.S. economy fell from 65% in 1929 to 46.5% in 1990. Correspondingly, the share of non-conventional, non-tangible capital rose from some 35% in 1929 to 53.5% in 1990. Consequently, by 1990 the total estimated value of immaterial capital was higher than that of tangible fixed capital.

Table 1.1: Capital stock and capital/output ratio in the United States 1929-1990

	1929	1948	1973	1990
Share of total capital stock, %				
Conventional tangible capital	65.1	57.8	50.2	46.5
Non-conventional, non-tangible capital	34.9	42.2	49.8	53.5
Capital/GDP ratio				
Conventional capital/GDP	7.39	6.25	5.35	5.85
Intangible capital/GDP	3.95	4.57	5.30	6.73
Total capital stock/GDP	11.35	10.82	10.65	12.58

Source: J.W. Kendrick: *Total Capital and Economic Growth* as quoted in Moses Abramovitz and Paul A. David: Technological Change and the Rise of Intangible Investments: The US Economy's Growth-Path in the Twentieth Century, in *Employment and Growth in the Knowledge-based Economy*, OECD 1996. Calculations by the author.

A striking conclusion emerging from these estimates is the sharp decline in the conventionally defined capital/output ratio from 7.4 in 1929 to 5.4 in 1973. However, this decline was largely compensated by a pronounced rise in the ratio of intangible capital to GDP, from about 4 in 1929 to 5.3 in 1973. The overall capital/output ratio consequently declined only moderately from 1929 to 1948 and even less from 1948 to 1973. Since 1973, furthermore, the conventionally defined capital/output ratio increased somewhat while the ratio of intangible capital to output rose strongly, resulting in a steep rise in the overall capital/output ratio, to a level preceding that of 1929.

Although the estimates compiled by other researchers may differ somewhat from those presented above, the broad conclusions in most cases are consistent with Kendrick's results: in the most advanced

---

[3] See Abramovitz and David, op. cit., p. 41.

industrial economy, the United States, the economic weight and impact of intellectual capital now exceeds that of tangible capital. Furthermore, as already stressed above, even the conventional hardware incorporates an increasing amount of (embodied) intangible goods such as, for example, incarnated software.

These findings thus shed new light on a policy issue which was a concern for policy makers on both sides of the Atlantic during the 1970s and 1980s: the decline in fixed capital formation in proportion to GDP. In fact, in a context of the emerging "knowledge economy" and changes in the nature of competition, enterprises have not reduced the overall capital formation but rather shifted more and more resources into investment in intangibles. Since investment in intangibles from the point of view of accounting is normally not considered as "capital formation", this change in behaviour of firms and managers for a long time went unnoticed by academics and policy makers, resulting possibly in certain countries and periods in certain failures and mistakes in the design of economic policy.

More recently a number of researchers, notably Romer, Lucas and Barro, have, however, argued that knowledge accumulation, while being an essential feature of economic growth, cannot be analysed only as an independent factor of production. This approach, under the name of *endogenous growth theory*, consequently aims at identifying and analysing the reciprocity between tangible and intangible capital formation and the interaction between public policy and the market.

ii. Theory of human capital formation

The rise of the knowledge society can be considered a quantum jump in a long history of development of human skills and know-how. In fact, two centuries ago, Adam Smith, in *The Wealth of Nations,* underlined that improvement of workers' skills was a fundamental source of economic progress. He also stressed that investment in human capital and skills affects personal incomes and the structure of wages. Attempts to quantify the actuarial value of a person's knowledge and skills were made by Lotka (1880-1949) and J.R. Walsh. Frank Knight (1885-1962) was probably one of the first to argue that improvements in the stock of intellectual capital might allow an economy to overcome the (classical) law of diminishing returns. Conceptual analysis of the impact of intellectual capital has accelerated considerably since the Second World War.

In parallel with the analysis of the sources of economic growth an important strand of economic theory has, in fact, focussed directly on investment in and the stock of *human capital*, that is, the knowledge, skills and mobility of individuals. This strand of research took as the starting point the impact on life-cycle income and income distribution of investment in education and training. An article by J. Mincer in 1958 may constitute the first step towards the elaboration of a theory of investment in human capital. However, the principal contribution was made by Gary Becker in 1962 (a contribution to an NBER conference) and, notably, in 1964, in a seminal volume: *Human Capital: A Theoretical and Empirical Analysis with Special Reference to Education.* Fritz Machlup, also in 1962, presented a first comprehensive review (but without a theoretical discussion) of "The Production and Distribution of Knowledge in the United States". A further step was taken in 1969, by T.W. Schultz, in "Investment in Human Capital", in E.S. Phelps (ed.) *The Goal of Economic Growth.*

Gary Becker's initial formalisation of a theory of human capital formation undertook a brief formulation of a theory of investment in education with the aim of providing a conceptual framework for an estimation of the rate of return on college and high-school education in the United States. As stated in the first edition of his work (p. 30 in the 3rd edn), this general analysis would offer a unified explanation of a wide range of empirical phenomena that had either been given ad hoc interpretations or had confused investigators. The main thrust of the theory developed by Becker was, indeed, to apply elements of microeconomic theory to the decision making by individuals, families and the authorities concerning investment in education and training. The second strand of research then provided comprehensive quantitative evidence and verification of the basic conceptual framework.

The formalisation of a conceptual framework for human capital formation elaborated by Gary Becker encompasses a number of different aspects of the approach of individuals and families to the question of education and accumulation of knowledge. The third edition, thus, includes the development of a framework for the analysis of the effects on earnings of, and the rate of return on, investment in human capital. With respect to the effect on earnings, different models are developed for "on-the-job training", schooling, the development of other kinds of knowledge and, somewhat unexpectedly, the effects of investing in emotional and physical health. The rate of return on investment in human capital is then analysed from different points of view: relation between earnings, costs and rate of return, the incentives to invest. The risk and "liquidity" of human capital and the relation between capital markets and knowledge are covered in special sections.

A second, and important, part of this seminal book is then devoted to a comprehensive analysis of empirical research on different categories of investment in knowledge, such as:

- Rates of return from college education
- Rates of return from high school education
- The relation between age, earnings, wealth and human capital

The main conclusion drawn from this empirical analysis is that the general theory of human capital formation developed by Becker helps to explain such diverse phenomena as inter-personal and inter-area differences in earnings, the shape of age-earnings profiles and the effects of specialisation on skill.

It also shows, however, that some investments in human capital do not affect earnings because costs are paid and returns are collected not by the persons involved but by the firm, industries or countries employing them. These investments, which Becker calls "specific" investments, range from hiring costs to executive training and are of considerable importance. They also help to explain the fact that unemployment on the whole is greater among unskilled than among skilled workers, since more specific capital is invested in the latter and employers have a special incentive to continue to have them on the payroll.

According to Becker the huge differences in productivity levels between countries are largely related to the accumulation of knowledge and the maintenance of health. The concept of investment in human capital can be considered simply as a way to organise and analyse these basic truths.

In the third edition of this book, published in 1993, Becker added an important analysis of *economy-wide changes* providing a link between the analysis of human capital formation contained in the earlier versions and the macroeconomic analysis of sources of economic growth. Becker, in particular, formulates a formal model explaining the change in per capita income in the economy as a function of (i) the growth of human capital, (ii) the growth in technology, and (iii) the decline in co-ordination costs.

One of the most important conclusions of this analysis is that growth in knowledge is closely connected with investments in new technologies and basic research. Analysing the interaction between the division of labour, the accumulation of knowledge and economic growth, Becker states that "knowledge is not subject to diminishing returns in the same obvious ways as physical capital because greater knowledge raises the productivity of further investment in knowledge".[4] Becker, nevertheless, argues that, as knowledge continues to grow, limited human capacities tend to make it harder to pack more knowledge into a person without running into diminishing returns.

In the conventional neo-classical model autonomous technological progress offsets the diminishing returns to a higher capital-labour ratio. In Becker's model, the induced expansion in the *division of labour* accompanying human capital formation raises the marginal product of additional knowledge. Thus, due to the effects of specialisation, the total elasticity of output with respect to human capital is higher than the elasticity calculated individually for each "team member". Greater specialisation, thus, enables workers to absorb knowledge more easily, offsetting to some extent the tendency towards diminishing returns from the accumulation of knowledge for the individual. Increasing co-ordination costs may however, to some extent compensate for this effect.[5]

Without presenting a formal conceptual framework, Fritz Machlup, in the late 1970s and early 1980s prepared, in three volumes, a comprehensive, indeed unique, assessment of many different aspects of the knowledge economy, including a review of the formalisation of conceptual frameworks presented by other authors. The third volume, in particular, published only after his death in 1983, contained a detailed discussion of "education production functions" and constitutes an indispensable complement to the more formal approach by Becker.

In recent years a considerable amount of conceptual and quantitative research has been undertaken in the field of human capital formation. A good overview of the state of the art in this field was provided at an OECD Conference on *Employment and Growth in the Knowledge-based Economy* held in Copenhagen in November 1994.

iii. Research and development, technology and innovation

A third strand of research, mainly in the form of applied economic theory, has dealt directly with the patterns of technological development, the classification of activities, assessment of different aspects of the innovation process, etc.

---

[4] Gary Becker: *Human Capital*, 3rd edn. p. 312.
[5] Becker, op. cit., p. 312.

Whereas Schumpeter had already emphasised technical progress and innovation as the main factors of "creative destruction", many OECD member countries took steps, in the 1960s and 1970s, to formulate and implement policies in favour of R&D and, notably, the application of the results of scientific research. Seeking to harmonise the approach to R&D policies and data collection, the OECD, consequently, in June 1963 held a meeting of national experts on research and development and with their assistance prepared a first version on *Proposed Standard Practice for Surveys of Research and Development* (the Frascati Manual). This manual (now in a fifth edition) consequently constitutes an important step in the direction of providing a harmonised approach to the collection and interpretation of data on R&D from the input side.

Soon it became clear, however, that the evaluation of R&D could not rely only on data on expenditure on activities classified as such or the share of staff devoted to R&D. There was a perceived need to provide some common standards for evaluating the results (the output) of research activities and, indeed, of all categories of intellectual capital formation. A first attempt at setting standards was made by the publication, in 1987, of an OECD report on *Evaluation of Research*. A further step was taken by the preparation, in 1996, of an OECD report on *Measuring What People Know* (by Riel Miller of the OECD Secretariat). A manual on guidelines for collecting and interpreting innovation data prepared by the OECD and Eurostat in common was published in a first version in 1992 and in a new version in 1997.

In parallel the OECD, as indicated in the preceding section, in 1988 launched a major programme aimed at formulating an integrated approach to technological, economic and social issues (The Technology/Economy Programme, or TEP). The reports prepared in the framework of this programme provide an opportunity to examine the consequences of the qualitative changes in the knowledge intensity of production of goods and services, the role of intangibles in the economy, the forms of organisation and the management of firms.

iv.   *Accounting for and reporting on intellectual capital*

From the beginning of the growth accounting exercises in the 1960s it has been recognised that conventional accounts and statistical data could provide only scant and incomplete evidence of the presence of "intangibles". Firstly, there was a perceived need to distinguish more clearly between, on one side, investment in (expenditure on) intangibles and, on the other, the resulting improvement in the *stock of intellectual capital*. Secondly, the classifications utilised in national and business accounts in general did not allow a separate identification of investment in intangibles. Thirdly, the general failure to distinguish between "services" and "intangibles" creates a fundamental problem of perception and taxonomy in the analysis of economic performance. While there is broad recognition that intellectual capital formation has become a decisive factor of economic growth and welfare, our knowledge of the process has, therefore, remained elusive, subjective and scattered.

The very fact that intangibles are only incompletely revealed in available statistical data and company accounting and reporting, furthermore, may be at the origin of several potential distortions of resource allocation and policy making:

- Capital markets – in part due to prudential rules and regulations – still put an excessive emphasis on fixed capital: intellectual capital can rarely be recognised as collateral for bank loans and the cost of capital is frequently higher for companies relying heavily on intellectual capital.
- The widely applied mandatory expending of investment in intangibles is the cause of under-reporting of profits in early-stage companies and overstatement of profits in the later phase of exploitation of intangible assets. This will strengthen the hands of managers and insiders, in possession of efficient information, but weaken the position of shareholders and increase the volatility of share prices.
- Even inside companies insufficient information on the level and evolution of intellectual capital may create the risk of distortion of management decisions and formulation of an adequate company strategy.
- Overemphasis on fixed investment and inadequate reporting of intangible investment and intellectual capital may be a source of distortions of public policy, for example on taxation of company profits, rules of depreciation of different kinds of capital, etc.

There is, therefore, a large and increasing need for improving insight into the role of intangibles in the economy by generating new indicators at all levels of decision making and economic analysis.

In growth accounting the response has in general, as indicated above, been to move beyond the original elementary definition of capital and labour as homogeneous entities. In its place has been introduced a detailed classification of capital by category and vintage and of labour by level of education and skill and to take account of hours worked etc. This analysis has, however, not involved modification of the traditional statistical data but has mainly relied on the search for additional indicators, frequently through ad hoc surveys or education statistics, etc.

In fact, the accountants, whether in national or business accounting, have been very reluctant to fundamentally reform the basic principles of accounting as practised throughout most of the twentieth century. Indeed, as argued by senior accountants throughout the industrial countries, there has been a broad consensus in the profession that the purpose of company balance sheets cannot and should not be to show the *market value* of a company as a going concern. The aim should be to provide a record of transactions and an evaluation of individual, identifiable and separable assets according to their market value if detached from the reporting company. The accounting profession has, consequently, refused to extend the concept of assets to include the estimated value of a company's "organisational competence" or its command of the human capital invested in the staff members, etc.

At the level of the enterprises a number of firms in the early 1990s took steps to improve their insight into the management and development of intellectual capital. Certain companies took the initiative to publish their findings in regular annual or ad hoc reports and thereby contributed to giving a more concrete and operational thrust to the debate. The experience gained at the level of business management and institutional investors, including new methods of reporting to and interfacing with capital markets, at the end of the 1990s constituted a most fertile ground for the development of a new approach to the compilation of indicators on various aspects of "intangibles".

References

Abramovitz, M. and David, Paul A.: Economic Growth in the U.S., in *Employment and Growth in the Knowledge-based Economy*, OECD, 1996.

Becker, G. (1962), *Investment in Human Capital, A Theoretical Analysis in Investment in Human Beings*, NBER Special Conference, Supplement to Journal of Political Economy, October.

Clark, J.B. (1997), *Concerning the Nature of Capital: a Reply*, Quarterly Journal of Economics, May, pp.526-53.

Cobb, C.W. and Douglas, P.H. (1928), *A Theory of Production*, American Economic Review, March.

Denison, E.F. (1962), *The Sources of Economic Growth in the United States and the Alternatives Before Us*, Committee for Economic Development 1962 and "Why Growth Rates Differ: Postwar Experience in Nine Western Countries", Brookings Institution 1967. See also "Accounting for Slower Economic Growth: The United States in the 1970s", Brookings Institution, 1979.

Griliches, Z. (1984) *Research and Development, Patents and Productivity*, Chicago University Press.

Jorgenson, D. (1997), "Computers and Productivity", speech at the Conference on Service Sector Productivity and the Productivity Paradox, Centre for the Study of Living Standards, Canada, 1997 (available at the web site of CSLS).

Jorgenson, D. (1963), *Capital Theory and Investment Behaviour*, American Economic Review, 29.

Kendrick, J. (1961), *Productivity Trends in the United States*, Princeton Press.

Kendrick, J. (1994), *Total Capital and Economic Growth*, Atlantic Economic Journal, Vol 22.

Machlup, F. (1984), *The Economics of Information and Human Capital*, Vol. III of *Knowledge: Its Creation, Distribution, and Economic Significance*, Princeton.

Miller, R. (1996), *Measuring What People Know*, OECD.

OECD (1996), *Employment and Growth in the Knowledge-based Economy*, OECD Documents.

OECD (1993), *Proposed Standard Practice for Surveys of Research and Experimental Development: The Frascati Manual*.

Romer, P.M. (1989), *Human Capital and Growth: Theory and Evidence*, NBER Working Paper N° 3173.

Schultz, T.W. (1969), *Investment in Human Capital* in Phelps, E.S. (ed.) *The Goal of Economic Growth*, Norton New York.

Von Böhm-Bawerk, E. (1991), *Positive Theory of Capital*, Macmillan.

2. Intangible Resources and Competitiveness: Towards a Dynamic View of Corporate Performance
Ahmed Bounfour

During the 1980s, competitiveness emerged as a major problematic issue for public policy support, and for corporate behaviour in the market place. For horizontal policies (such as the Single Market programme), as well as for vertical policies, such as Research and Development (R&D) support, strengthening the competitiveness of participating organisations is ever more clearly emphasised as the ultimate goal to be achieved. For corporate behaviour itself, the main question debated by researchers, analysts and managers is related to the source of value creation and growth.

The objective of this chapter is to consider the problem of intangible assets building and management as a central issue for corporate competitiveness. The chapter will then

1. examine first of all how the problematic of competitiveness has been considered by the literature, especially by stressing the growing importance of intangible resources as key determining factors;
2. review how the problem of competitiveness and intangible resources is dealt with in operational terms;
3. suggest ways of developing a dynamic practical approach- the *IC-dVal* (Intellectual Capital-dynamic Value) approach to Intangibles within organisations.

1. The emerging role of intangible resources in corporate competitiveness

Empirical analyses as well as the review of the economic and strategic literature converge to the necessity of considering intangible resources as the main source of value creation, and corporate competitiveness.

Different reasons explain the growing interest of researchers and practitioners in this issue of intangibles. At least five reasons justify such an interest:[1]

- *the rapid growth of services activities,* as they now contribute to more than 75% of GDP in more of the advanced economies;
- *the dematerialisation of manufacturing activities*, as most of them now invest more in developing, distributing and marketing, and managing products than in manufacturing them;
- *the industrialisation of services activities*: these activities are registering a deep change in their mode of production and valorisation, which could be summarised in few words: the necessity of continuously creating value for clients, but also for internal resources. In organisational terms, such a requirement attests for the necessity in these organisations to shift from the "profession libérale" mode of production to a real "industrialised" one (Bounfour, 1987);
- *the recognition of knowledge as the main source of competitive advantage.* We will not discuss here the specific status of knowledge within organisations, especially its intrinsic characteristics in comparison to information (this has been largely debated in the organisation science literature).[2] What has to be underlined here concerns the great interest of managers in maximising knowledge's value within organisations, whether it is in 'individual heads', or stored somewhere, while at the same time, they look to make organisations the least dependent upon individuals' knowledge (this is the main reason for the development of what is now named Structural Capital in IC literature). From the analytical point of view, this problematic is now completely revised thanks to new stimulating approaches such as those developed in evolutionary (Nelson and Winter, 1982) or knowledge management perspectives (Nonaka, 1994; Nonaka and Takeuchi, 1995). The new information

---

[1] For a general review of the importance of intangibles to organisations' management see: Bounfour, 1998. See also Bounfour, forthcoming.

[2] See for instance the works by Machlup (1980).

and communication technologies are naturally very important supports to new approaches development and implementation;
- *the disequilibrium between market value and book value for most listed companies.* It is now largely recognised that balance sheets provide less and less a fair picture of companies' value. This is particularly true for high tech established companies (for Microsoft the ratio between MV and BV is estimated at around 12 to 13). But more importantly, especially in a very services oriented economy, the physical paradigm is no longer adapted to the measurement of corporate assets;
- *recent researches and surveys have demonstrated the role of intangibles* in corporate competitiveness (PIMS Associates, 1994; RCS Conseil, 1998),[3] at individual company level, but also when cooperative programmes are considered, such as those carried out at the European level. This is more and more clearly demonstrated in R&D programmes' evaluations (Eureka and ESPRIT);[4]
- *the question of value creation.* This criterion is now predominant in measuring corporate performance. Hence the importance of developing and implementing adapted tools for identification and assessment of sources of value within companies as well as outside them.

Taking into account all these elements - and as far as corporate competitiveness is concerned, it appears that we still need a structured theoretical and empirical framework in order to deal with these multidimensional issues. Indeed, important theoretical problems are still open (Clement et al. 1998), even if different frameworks could be considered (Ducharme, 1998). Here, we will only consider recent developments in strategic literature, in order to see how the problematic of intangibles can be dealt with in a *dynamic way*.

Intangible resources in the strategic literature

The work of Porter (1980, 1985, 1990) has contributed to the definition and implementation of an interesting analytical framework from which to

---

[3] See also sectoral papers presented at Louvain-la-Neuve Symposium, and published in this volume.
[4] This is one of the main interim results of an on-going evaluation we are carrying out for the EC DG XIII, on the impact of ESPRIT on industrial competitiveness (in association with Institut für Wirtschaftsforschung (IFO) and Policy Research in Engineering, Science and Technology. (PREST)).

consider competitiveness. The concept of competitive advantage is at the heart of such a development, on the basis of an analysis of the dynamic of competitive forces within market structures. However, Porter's model of the 1980s is now largely challenged by new approaches to competitiveness, especially those focusing on resources - mainly those of an intangible nature - as a main source of competitive advantage.

Indeed, during recent years different approaches have been developed, focusing on corporate intangible resources, competences and capabilities as the main lever creating competitive advantage. In opposition to Porter's view, these approaches, taking into account the fact that differences of performance are more important within individual industries than between industries, consider that such differences are to be attributed to the type of combination of resources, mainly intangibles, developed by firms, rather than to industry structures. The strategic approach developed includes different analyses that explicitly stress the importance of intangible resources (assets) as a lever for competitive advantage. Within this approach, we can include different types of works:

- Approaches based on core intellectual and services competencies (Quinn, 1992);
- Approaches based on resources (the Resource-based View) (Barney, 1991; Penrose, 1959; Wenerfelt, 1984, 1989; Dierickx et Cool, 1989; Grant, 1991, 1996; Itami and Roehl, 1987; Itami, 1989; Peteraf, 1993, among others) and intangible resources (Bounfour, 1995, 1998a; Hall, 1993);
- Approaches based on core competences (Prahalad and Hamel, 1990);
- Approaches based on knowledge creation dynamics (Nonaka, 1994; Nonaka and Takeuchi, 1995);
- Approaches based on competences as 'organisational routines' (around the work of Nelson and Winter, 1982).

All these approaches can be considered as contributions to the foundation of a strategic paradigm for intangibles.

The Resource-based view

The resource-based view (RBV) of the firm is built upon seminal ideas developed by Penrose (1959), who considered that what was really determinant for industry's structure was the resources possessed by the firm. Looking at firms in terms of their resources naturally leads to a radical shift from the traditional product/market structure paradigm.

There is no unanimity among researchers about the nature and number of items to be considered. Wenerfelt (1984: 172), defined resource as "any thing which could be thought of as a strength or weakness of a given firm. More formally, a firm's resources at a given time could be defined as those (tangible and intangible) assets which are tied semipermanently to the firm ... Examples of resources are: brand names, in-house knowledge of technology, employment of skilled personnel, trade contacts, machinery, efficient procedures, capital, etc.". Among the questions considered here: 'under what circumstances will a resource lead to high returns over longer period of time'. Porter's five competitive forces (Porter, 1980) are used here, but from the resources point of view and not from the product point of view. Also, and by analogy, Wenerfelt considers the interest for firms in developing competitive advantages in terms of resources (including by building barriers to entry for intangibles and not solely for products). For instance, with regards to the bargaining power of suppliers and buyers, as well as the threat posed by substitute resources, different statements could be established: if the production of a critical resource is controlled by a monopolistic group, then it will, ceteris paribus, reduce the amount of returns available to the users of this resource (a patent holder versus its licence holder, a good advertising agency versus its client).

Dierckx and Cool (1989) stress the importance of building a coherent policy for accumulating strategic intangible assets, especially those of a non-tradable nature (reputation, quality, etc.). In their view "a key dimension of strategic formulation may be identified as the task of making appropriate choices about strategic expenditures (advertising spending, R&D outlays, etc.) with a view to accumulating required resources and skills (brand loyalty, technological expertise, etc.). In other words, appropriate time paths of relevant flow variables must be chosen to build required asset stocks. Critical or strategic asset stocks are those assets which are non-tradable, non-imitable and non-substituable" (p. 1506). Sustainability of a firm's position for a specific asset will then depend on how easily it can be replicated. Different characteristics are therefore to be considered with regards to this problem of sustainability: time compression diseconomies, asset mass efficiencies, interconnectedness of asset stocks, asset erosion and causal ambiguity.

Barney (1991), on the other hand, considers only three resources: physical resources, human resources and organisational resources. Finally, Grant (1991) considers the following resources: financial resources, physical resources, human resources, technological resources, reputation and organisational resources. Resources are considered as specific to companies and so non-tradable, non-imitable and non-transferable. Corporate strategy is mainly influenced by the stock of resources available at any particular time.

Grant differentiates between resources and capabilities: resources are "input to the production process" and constitute the basis for analysis, whereas capabilities refer to "the capacity of a combination of resources to carry out specific tasks or activities". Therefore, capabilities (or competences) are at the basis of establishing competitive advantage. This notion of capability is similar to that of "core competency" developed by Prahalad and Hamel (1990), on the basis of the analysis of Nippon Electric Corporations's (NEC) success factors in information technology and semiconductors, in comparison with its main competitors (GTE in particular). It can also be related to the concept of "core services competences" suggested by Quinn (1992).

Table 2.1: Examples of intangible resources considered in the resource and capabilities views

The Resource-based View			Dynamic Capabilities View
Barney	**Grant**	**Wenerfelt**	**Teece, Pisano and Shuen**
• Physical resources • Human resources • Organisational resources	• Financial resources • Technological resources • Reputation • Organisational resources	• Fixed assets (plants, equipment,…) • Blue Prints (patents, brands, reputation) • Culture: team effects, routines, collective know-how	• Resources as specific assets difficult to imitate • Organisational routines/competences • Core competences • Dynamic capabilities: the firm's ability to integrate and reconfigure internal and external competences to address rapidly changing environment • Products: the final goods and services based on the firms competences

Sources: Barney (1991);Grant (1991); Wenerfelt (1989); Teece, Pisano and Shuen (1997).

In operational terms, this approach suggests that the notion of capability could be defined from a functional perspective (R&D, production, information systems). The most important thing here is the ability of a company to integrate individual competences. If McDonalds has strong distinctive competences in product development, market research and human resources management, its worldwide success is mainly explained by its capacity to integrate these basic competences.

But, as such, resources are not productive. Porter (1994: 446) points to the fact that resources have a value only because they allow companies to carry out activities. It is the latter that are the real sources of competitive advantage. They have to be combined in order to generate distinctive competences.

These recent developments in strategic literature underline the importance of resources and internal firm competences as the main lever for competitive advantage. According to these approaches, firms are invited to focus their strategies more on the development of such key resources and competences, than on industrial structure analysis and product market positioning. Put differently, valorising intangible resources appears as the most important source of long-term competitiveness.

The resource-based view, despite its broad nature, has a simple message for long-term performance: companies have to be approached as a portfolio of resources, tangibles and, more importantly, intangibles. It is these resources that allow the development of competences and therefore the establishment of a sustainable competitive position in the market place. This approach seems most suited to the knowledge economy: resources and competences are still "hidden values" not sufficiently valorised in the market place.

The main arguments from this literature review then are the following:

- a firm's performance is mainly influenced by its endowment of resources, rather than by its industry's structure;
- firms are heterogeneous with respect to their resources/capabilities endowments;
- building (critical) resources may take time;
- firms may lack the organisational capabilities needed to develop new competences;
- some assets are non-tradable: for instance tacit knowledge or reputation;
- a dynamic and consistent view of intangibles should be developed;
- efficient processes have to be implemented, especially those dedicated to combining intangible resources;
- a competitive strategy has then to be built on firms' distinctive resources and capabilities.

2. Emerging practices on reporting and management of intangibles

On-going practices of measuring and valorising intangibles can be split into two types, with a certain overlapping: those related to knowledge management (KM) practices and those putting more emphasis on intellectual capital (IC) measurement and processes of development. In fact, these two practices address the same reality. However, the dominant initiators are slightly different for each of these practices: KM is primarily developed around information technologies resources, whereas IC is more the field of intervention for accounting firms and general management organisations.

Table 2.2: Examples of companies implementing an approach for IC and KM

• ABB	Conglomerate, Swiss-Sweden
• ATP	Pension services, Denmark
• Celemi	Training tools, Sweden
• Coloplast	Nursing and hospital services, Denmark
• Luftarstverket	Airport Operator, Sweden
• Amphion	Consultant services, Denmark
• Arthur Andersen	Consultant services, USA
• Booz Allen & Hamilton	Consultant services, USA
• Consultus	Consultant services, Sweden
• Ernst & Young	Consultant services, USA
• McKinsey	Consultant services, USA
• PLS Consultus	Consultant services, Denmark
• Ramboll	Engineering and consulting services, Denmark
• CIBC	Financial services, Canada
• Royal Bank	Financial services
• Skandia	Financial services, Sweden
• Sparbanken	Financial service, Sweden
• SparekassenBordJylland	Financial services, Denmark
• Dow Chemical	High tech knowledge based organisations, USA
• Hewlett Packard	High tech knowledge based organisations, USA
• Hughes Space and Communications	High tech knowledge based organisations, USA
• Merck	High tech knowledge based organisations,
• Nova Care	High tech knowledge based organisations
• Microsoft	Software and IT Services, USA
• Siemens, Germany	Electrical and Electronics products and services, Germany
• Electricité de France	Electrical supply, France
• Framatome	Nuclear reactor manufacturing, France
• Société Européenne de Propulsion	Space propulsion, France
• Chevron	Chemical and energy company, USA
• WM Data	IT consulting, Sweden
• TELIA	Telecommunications, Sweden

Source: Business Intelligence (1998), IFAC (1998), Danish Agency for Trade and Industry (1999), Lokken et al. (1997), Mouritsen (1998), Sveiby (1997), Miscellaneous.

These innovative practices are mainly initiated by three sectors of activities: high-tech industries (telecom, aerospace, nuclear industries), financial services and business services (Table 2.2). This number is growing exponentially, if we consider the contiguous thematic of knowledge management. However, this picture could be misleading, since some 'traditional' industries, such as the automotive industry, contribute considerably to developing new managerial and organisational practices (the *lean production* concept; see for instance, Womack et al., 1990), already adopted by other sectors of activities. Indeed, all the sectors of activities are deeply concerned by the problematic of managing (and not only measuring) these intangible resources.

The balanced scorecard approach (Kaplan and Norton, 1992, 1993, 1996a, 1996b) was used as a methodological framework for the most mediatised case studies (Skandia, Dow Chemical). Different categories of intellectual capital and related indicators of performance have been defined (Brooking, 1996; Edvinsson and Malone, 1997, IFAC, 1998, Stewart, 1997; Sveiby, 1997). Whatever the taxonomy used, most of the implemented approaches are centred on processes of value creation.

Table 2.3: Elements of Intellectual Capital - example of a taxonomy used

Human Capital	Customer (relational Capital)
• Know-how • Education • Vocational qualification • Work-related knowledge • Occupational assessments • Psychometric assessments • Work related competencies • Entrepreneurial elan, innovativeness, proactive and reactive abilities, changeability	• Brands • Customers • Customers loyalty • Company names • Backlog orders • Distribution channels • Business collaborations • Licensing agreements • Favourable contracts • Franchising agreements
Organisational (structural)Capital	
Intellectual Property	**Infrastructure Assets**
• Patents • Copyrights • Design rights • Trade secrets • Trademarks • Service Marks	• Management philosophy • Corporate culture • Management processes • Information systems • Networking systems • Financial relations

Source: IFAC (1998: 7). A typology adapted from SMAC.

In terms of operational tools, most of those resorted to are developed around specific components of IC: human capital, customer capital, innovation capital, processes capital, etc. (Table 2.3 illustrates most of the taxonomies used). For each of these components, specific indicators of performance are suggested. The basic idea here is to develop a sort of dual accounting approach on intangibles, which may take the form of publishing an IC report (such as that published for several years by Skandia), besides the traditional financial report.

From the organisational point of view, behind these practices lies a strong invitation towards the adoption of a *stakeholder approach* within organisations, with a specific focus on human dimension.[5] In fact, the human dimension of organisation's immateriality is probably becoming one of the most critical issues for organisations' management and competitive positioning. This is already recognised by numerous researchers and analysts (Pfeffer, 1991, 1994). This will naturally bring to the fore important stakes for human capital management and valorisation. One of the most important at this level concerns the problematic of implementing real efficient 'rewarding systems', over a long period.

3. Towards a dynamic approach of corporate competitiveness

Building competitive advantages from intangibles is fundamentally a problem of combining these resources in a very distinctive (and necessarily specific) way by organisations. In other words, the problem is that of defining a dynamic approach to corporate competitiveness on the basis of implementing efficient organisational processes that can be defined as *"the way things are done in the firm, or what might be referred to as its routines or patterns of current practices and learning"* (Teece et al., 1997).

In analytical terms, and as far as performance is concerned, four important and interrelated dimensions of competitiveness, appear as important (Figure 2.1):

- *Resources as inputs* (R&D investment, technology acquisition, etc.). The main point to be addressed here will consist of identifying critical intangible resources and how the level and mode of exploitation of these resources could be improved by the adoption of specific processes;

---

[5] For a review of the literature on human resources reporting and accounting, see Johanson et al. (1998).

- *Intangible assets building*. These can be built by combining these resources and can lead to specific outcomes such as knowledge, patents, brand names, reputation, networks, routines, etc. For these, specific indicators can be used and defined.
- *Management of process change*. This is one of the most important levers for implementing a dynamic view of organisational change. Practical aspects on this dimension will be detailed in the following section.
- *Development of competitive advantage*, at the microeconomic level. This is the most classical level of competitiveness analysis: the output level (products, economic performance).

By integrating these four dimensions (and not solely the last one), the problem of competitiveness appears as a complex one, and not to be concentrated on only short-term market shares and profits assessments.

Figure 2.1: Four dimensions of competitiveness

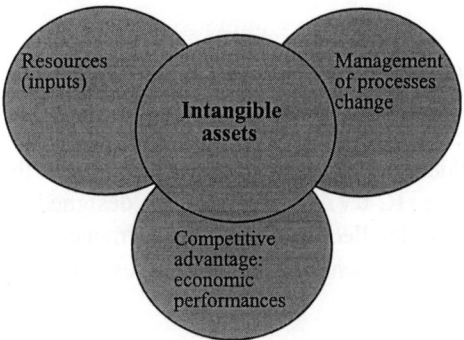

Processes into practice for Intellectual Capital building and valorisation

From these developments, it appears necessary to develop a specific research field: the management of intangible resources (MIR). Its aim is to maximise the value created by companies, by articulating these three components around intellectual capital building: *resources and competences*, *functions* and *processes* (Figure 2.2).

Figure 2.2: Intellectual capital is at the heart of the MIR scope

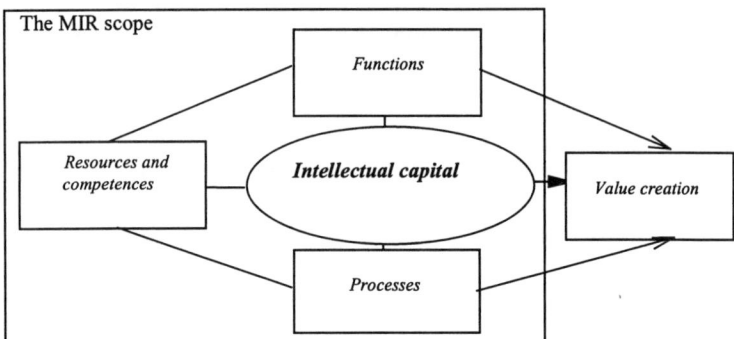

Following developments will concentrate on showing how specific processes could be implemented within organisations in order to maximise the value created in a dynamic perspective. This will be presented around a simple approach, namely: the *IC-dVAL* - intellectual capital - dynamic value - approach.

Developing value from intellectual capital: the IC-dVAL approach

From a stakeholder approach, three types of values have to be integrated in a consistent way: the shareholders value, the customers value, and the internal value (Figure 2.3). The IC-dVAL approach is designed to identify and measure organisations' intellectual capital performance in a dynamic way, by searching for an alignment between processes dedicated to these three values' creation.

Figure 2.3: The three types of value within companies

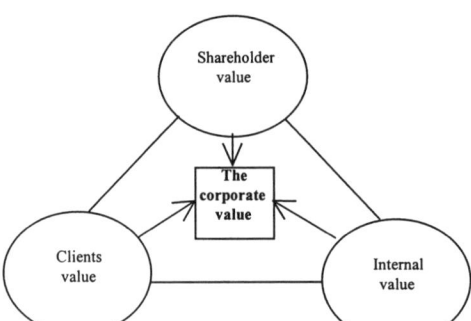

Five steps

In a practical way, five steps have to be followed to build a dynamic approach to IC within companies:

1. First of all, determining the key processes for each of the components of the value, within each of the corporate's activities (if they are many);
2. Benchmarking corporate performance with those companies best in class, for most of these processes, and quantifying its positioning via an ad hoc index. Benchmarking is now a classical exercise for measuring relative performance. Stewart (1997: 243-246) suggested an interesting approach, by resorting to specific metrics (market-to-book ratio, customer capital measures, structural capital measures, human capital measures);
3. Benchmarking corporate performance with those best in class, for most of the activities processes, and quantifying its positioning via an ad hoc index;
4. Evaluating the corporate overall performance, on the basis of its positioning for all the considered activities. This will be done by calculating an overall ratio: the corporate IC performance index;
5. Calculating the overall intellectual capital value for the whole company.

1. Identification of critical processes

A process could be defined as a set of homogeneous routines designed for the completion of specific value functionalities. In operational terms, these processes are defined in generic terms, for each of the sources of value within companies, with a necessary adaptation to specific sectors and activities (manufacturing, service). Internal processes are split here into two groups: value processes and resources and competences processes.

30 *Intangibles: A General Framework*

Figure 2.4: Internal processes for value-added services

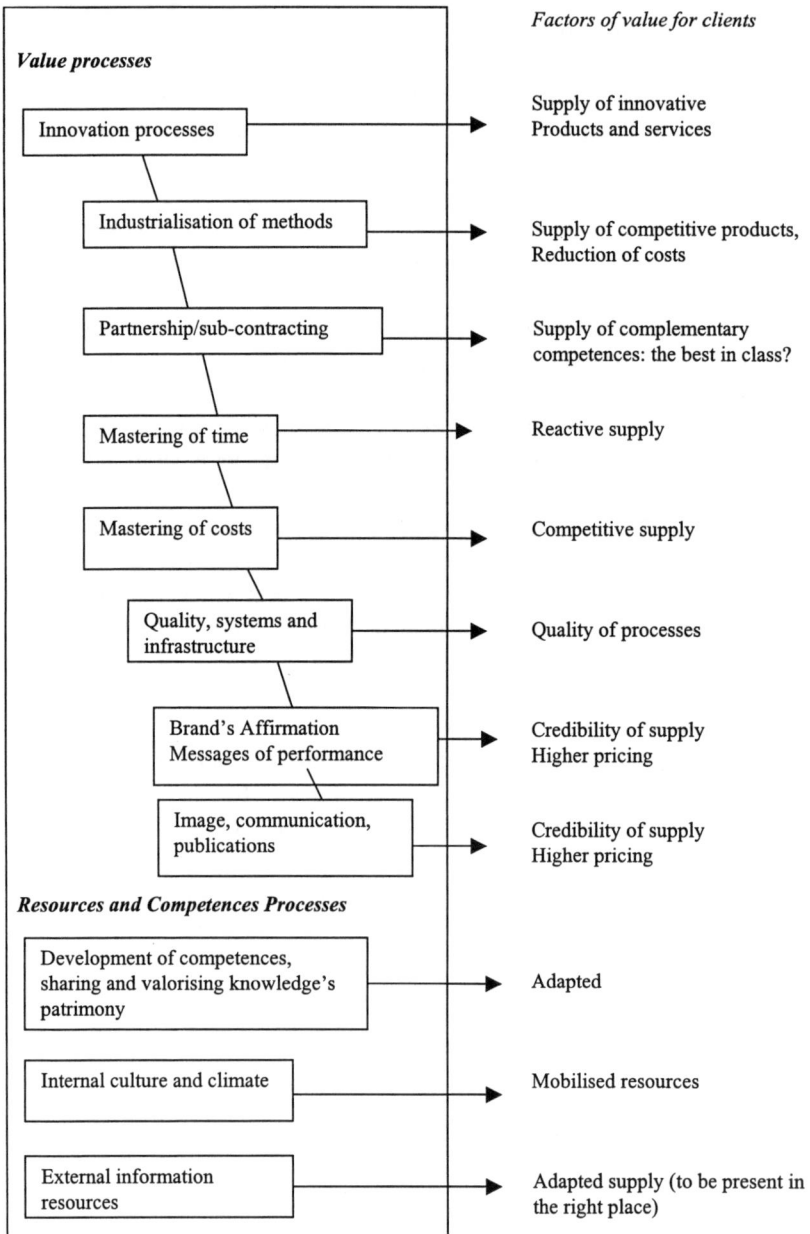

Figure 2.4 illustrates the type of processes in services industries (here internal processes). Research we have conducted recently on the basis of this framework for an important European services group, showed its weak positioning for most of the processes distinguished, especially those of an internal nature (industrialisation of methods, capitalisation of knowledge, etc.). This weak positioning naturally resulted in an insufficient creation of value, in comparison to those best in class, and therefore weak value indicators for most processes.

2. *Benchmarking corporate performance*

After the identification of key processes, the organisation is now in a position to benchmark its performances with those best in class. As has been underlined, this comparative analysis is conducted at the level of processes for each of the four components of value and for each of the corporate activities. At the outcome, we should arrive at an overall performance ratio for the whole organisation.

3. *Measuring corporate performance: from processes to corporate overall value*

On the basis of the indicators for key processes already calculated, it is now possible to proceed to the calculation of the corporate performance for intellectual capital.

The equation for calculating the corporate overall value indicator (CVI) can be established on the basis of the following steps:

- calculation of activities value indicators as follows:

(1)
weighted processes value indicators
=
activities value indicators

- calculation of the corporate overall value indicator as follows:

(2)
weighted activities value indicators
=
the corporate overall value indicator

Table 2.4 illustrates the overall approach for calculating these metrics, for an SME (small and medium-sized enterprises). We can see that in the case of this company, the overall value indicator is, on average, 0.80, which represents the present performance of the company for three

dimensions of competitiveness: resources and competences, processes and outputs. Now, we have to consider the problem of calculating the dynamic value of intellectual capital for this company, that is the expectations for rent generation, on the basis of the fourth component of competitiveness: intangible assets.

Table 2.4: *Example of calculation of present performance indicators, for three dimensions of competitiveness*

Dimension of Competitiveness	Key Items	Benchmarking Firm's Position (100 = the best in Class)
Resources and competences	• Investment in physical resources (e.g. equipment, buildings)	90
	• Investment in R&D or innovation	90
	• Investment in human resources	85
	• The general level of financial resources available to the firm	80
	• The quality of human resources available to the firm	80
	• The quality of existing technology and knowledge held by the firm	80
Processes	• The quality of partnership networks, especially in innovation, accessible to the firm	75
	• The ability to combine intangible resources (e.g. R&D, knowledge or other assets)	70
	• Processes and systems for building new knowledge	100
	• Processes dedicated to human resources, education & motivation	90
Outputs and performance	• The patent portfolio of the firm	60
	• Possession of strong brand names	50
	• The quality of final products or services	80
	• Possession of strong market share	70
	• Keeping down the cost of products and services	85
	• Barriers to entry or other protective barriers for your niche, sector or industry	95
	Average Performance Rating	80.0
	Average Index of competitiveness	0.8

3. From value indicators to intellectual capital value

On the basis of these value indicators, it now becomes possible to reconsider the problematic of intellectual capital measurement. As far as the value of a company is considered, different methods are available. The simplest one consists in considering the difference between market value[6] (MV) (for listed companies), or fair value[7] (FV) (for non listed ones) and book value[8] (BV). Therefore intellectual capital value becomes:

---

(3)

IC = MV (or FV) - BV

Other methods are also available (goodwill, Tobin's q, etc.). We can also consider the value of each intangible asset considered separately: brands, patents, software, specific knowledge, reputation, etc. This method has a major advantage: values for metrics are produced by those who are directly in charge of value creation, and not imposed by financial analysts or financial departments. It also presents the advantage of not creating perverse impacts such as those produced by purely financial metrics:[9] namely reduction in investment in order to satisfy the cost of capital requirements. Indeed, following this method, the organisation can estimate its expected revenues and cash flow generation for each of these assets, distinguishing those of separable or tradable nature (brands, softwares, patents), from those which are not separable (collective knowledge).

Whatever the method used, the most interesting idea to be developed here consists in weighting the IC value with the corporate overall value index. Indeed, it is important to consider these two ratios together. From a managerial perspective, this idea is stimulating. It has been previously presented by Edvinsson and Malone (1997: 179-188), when they calculated what they called a "coefficient of efficiency".

---

[6] The market value is calculated by referring to the value of a company on the financial market, by multiplying its share price - at one moment of time - by the number of shares.
[7] The fair value is suggested here for non-listed companies. It could be calculated by referring to recent transactions (mergers, acquisitions) in the market place, for similar businesses.
[8] The book value refers here to the accounting value of a company as calculated from its balance sheets.
[9] For a presentation of the main financial approaches for value creation see for instance: Fruhan (1981), Rappaport (1986), Stewart (1991).

The equation for IC performance becomes then:

> (4)
> **Dynamic Value for IC: cvi x IC**

If we reconsider the case of the previously considered SME, and by using one of the suggested methods (e.g. separable versus non-separable assets), we can then estimate the expected value for ten of its major assets (in order to simplify the exercise, the period considered here is that of the strategic plan). We will distinguish here items belonging to separable capital (and thus salleable in the market place), from those which are not separable, as follows (Table 2.5).

Table 2.5: Estimation of 10 major intangible assets for an SME

Intangible assets	Metric used	Internally estimated value
Separable assets		
• Patents	• Rent generation (licences)	10
• Brands	• Cost of replacement	10
• Standard software	• Cost of selling	5
• Structural capital (databases, clients, files, etc.)	• Cost of replacement	10
• Knowledge portfolio	• Cost of replacement	15
• Non-standard software, methodologies	• Cost of replacement	5
• Human capital: collective combining capacities	• Cost of acquisition in mature business	10
• New products and services	• Cash flow generation	20
• Market niches resulting from first mover advantage	• Cash flow generation	10
• Reputation	• Transaction costs reduction towards clients, human resources and general environment	5
• Total		100

We arrive then at a total anticipated value of 100 million euro for its major intangible assets. Therefore, its dynamic value is in fact 0.80 x 100, that is 80 million. This difference is in part explained by the fact that we are benchmarking each of the components of competitiveness against those best in class, and, as Edvinsson and Malone underlined, it is almost impossible for a company to be number one in all these components. However, can introduce a weighting procedure, with regards the key criteria of competitiveness, depending upon the nature of business, which may influence these results.

This simple equation provides in fact a very powerful indicator for managing corporate performance. Indeed, beyond the level of sophistication of calculation methods, what is important to consider here is the quality of managing interfaces within organisations, via the definition of simple parameters interrelated in a very consistent way and more importantly, that can be shared by most people within organisations. The "combining function" (*fonction combinatoire*), appears therefore as an important tool for managing intellectual capital in the knowledge economy.

From the technical point of view, this equation could be used at different functional policy levels within companies. For the human resources function, such an index could be used in determining performance rewarding systems over a long-term period. At the more global level, the analysis of the evolution of this equation should provide arguments for the measurement of goodwill over time. Finally, it could also help innovative companies in reducing the "market for lemons" effect, with outside partners (financial markets), while, at the same time, they could find new ways of rewarding collective efforts.

4. Alignment of practices with strategy: the role of managing intangibles

Processes are important levers in corporate competitiveness. But their implementation has to be inserted within an overall architecture, which integrates the most critical issues of intangibles within organisations (Figure 2.6): the organisation's project and identity, the quality of its knowledge creation and development, the organisation's image, its brands' impact and more importantly the singularity of its identity and strategy, the organisation's frontier and relational assets building, its capacity for mobilising human resources over a long-term period. By considering all these items, real competitive organisations are certainly among those that will develop a real 'total consistency' between all these items. Some of these thematics have been developed earlier. However, three of them merit specific comments.

Human capital mobilisation and durable performance

This is an important issue for managing organisations. Continuous changes in the scope of organisations' activities, developing outsourcing practices, and more generally the more and more short-term oriented nature of legal and (or) moral contracts concluded between organisations and their employees, create pressures on long-term performance. Hence the importance of investing in new "performance rewarding systems", as has already been underlined.

Signalling and singularity of organisations' strategy

Competitiveness is not solely an affair of quality and pricing for products and services. It is also a question of signalling at the internal level as well as at the external level. Externally, organisations are competing via different signals: brands, names, products and services, networks, tangible assets, employees, performances and more and more via the singularity of their project and strategy. Clients, financial markets, potential partners are naturally concerned by the content and consistency of these signals. At the internal level, competitiveness is ensured via the translation of the organisation's project into efficient processes dedicated to maximising stakeholders' value.

Figure 2.5: The architecture of management of intangible resources (MIR)

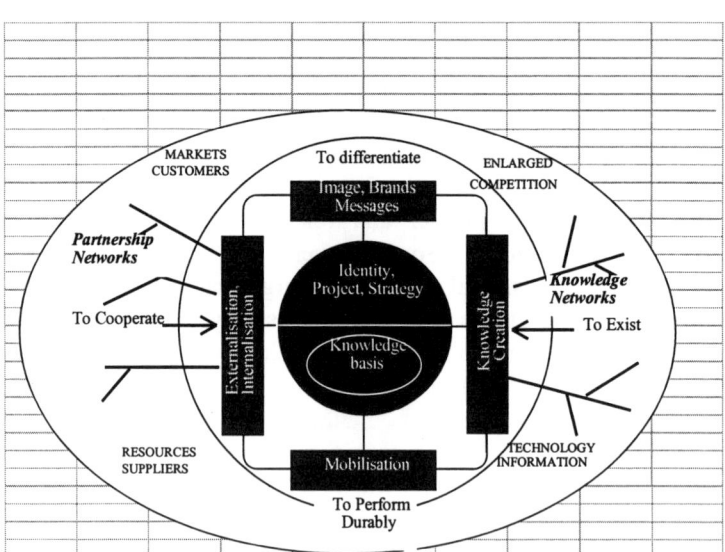

Attractiveness of organisations' identity

Defining organisations' identity should be the starting point for any reflection on corporate competitiveness. This topic is becoming a key issue in a context characterised by a continuous change in products, services, employees' involvement and organisations' boundaries.

These are important topics for managing organisations, especially in the European context, where a socio-economic model, based on knowledge creation and innovation, is still to be defined. Recent experimentations in reporting and managing intangibles, notably in Nordic countries (Denmark, Sweden, among others) have to be encouraged and cross-fertilised. Their aim is to develop an holistic vision of the organisation, based on its intangibles' resources and assets.

Conclusion

The objective of this chapter was to consider the problem of intangible assets building and management as a central issue for corporate competitiveness. When reviewing the literature, competitiveness appears as a complex notion that has to be assessed at different interrelated levels. In this framework, the work of Porter contributed to the definition and implementation of an interesting analytical framework for analysing competitiveness. However, Porter's approach has been strongly criticised during the last few years, particularly by the resource-based view of the firm. Indeed, during recent years, different approaches have been developed, which focused on the corporate intangible resources, competences and capabilities, as the main lever for creating competitive advantage. The heteroclitic nature of this theoretical framework, as well as the proliferation of practices around the concept of organisational processes and intellectual capital development, stimulate the need for comprehensive work.

In operational terms, more and more companies are now implementing an approach dedicated to the development of their intangible resources. This number is growing exponentially, if we consider the contiguous thematic of knowledge management.

The development of innovative practices dedicated to intangibles within and around organisations, as well as the multiplicity of concerned fields of research, requires the implementation of an integrated approach to intangibles: this is the subject of what we have called the *management of intangible resources* (MIR). Indeed, when considering the problematic of competitiveness, different thematics have to be considered: the organisation's project and identity, the quality of its knowledge creation and development, the organisation's image, its brands impact and more importantly the singularity of its identity and strategy, the organisation's frontier and relational assets building, and its capacity for mobilising human resources over a long-term period. By considering all these items, real competitive organisations are certainly among those that will develop a real *'total consistency'* between all these items. Taking into account recent practices in Intellectual capital management and valorisation, a dynamic approach to valuing intangibles was proposed - the IC-dVal approach -. Its main aim is to implement a consistent and dynamic view of intangibles' valorisation, within organisations.

References

Barney, J. (1991), 'Firms, Resources and Sustained Competitive Advantage', *Journal of Management*, vol. 17 (1), p. 99-120.

Bounfour, A. (1987), 'Vers l'industrialisation du conseil', *Revue Française de Gestion*, November-December.

Bounfour, A. (1995), 'Immatériel et stratégies compétitives, éléments de problématique', *AIMS Fourth Conférence*, Paris, 2-4 May.

Bounfour, A. (1998a), *Le management des ressources immatérielles, maîtriser les nouveaux leviers de l'avantage compétitif*, Dunod, Paris.

Bounfour, A. (1998b), 'Accounting for intangibles and value setting', *21st Congress of European Accounting Association*, 6—8 April.

Bounfour, A. (1998c), 'Outsourcing of intangibles and corporate performance: some strategic and accounting issues', *21st Congress of European Accounting Association*, Antwerp, 6-8 April.

Bounfour, A. (1999), 'Is outsourcing of intangibles a real source of competitive advantage', *International Journal of Applied Quality Management,* vol. 2 (2), p. 1-25.

Bounfour, A. (Forthcoming), *Managing of intangibles: the organisation's most valuable assets*, Routledge, London.

Brooking, A. (1996), *Intellectual Capital*, ITP, International Thomson Business Press.

Business Intelligence (1997), *Creating the knowledge-based business*, Business Intelligence Limited, London.

Clement, W., Hammerer, G., Schwarz, K. (1998*), Measuring Intangible Investment, Intangible Investment from an Evolutionary Perspective, OECD*.

Collis, D.J. (1991), 'A resource-based analysis of global competition: the case of the bearings industry', *Strategic Management Journal*, vol. 12, p. 49-68.
Danish Agency for Trade and Industry, (1999), *Developing Intellectual Capital Accounts, Experiences from 19 companies*, Ministry of Business and Industry, Copenhagen.
Dierickx, I., Cool, K. (1989). 'Asset stock accumulation and sustainability of competitive advantage', *Management Science*, pp. 1504-1513.
Dosi, G., Teece, D. (1993), *Organisational Competencies and the Boundaries of the Firm*. CCC working paper n. 93, University of California, Center for Research in Management, February.
Ducharme, L.M. (1998), *Measuring Intangible Investments, Introduction, Main Theories and Concepts*, OECD.
Edvinsson, L., Malone, M.S. (1997), *Intellectual Capital, Realizing your Company's True Value by Finding its Hidden Brainpower*, Harperbusiness, NY.
Fruhan, W.E. Jr (1981), 'Is your stock worth its market price? ', *Harvard Business Review*, vol. 59, n. 3.
Grant, R.M (1991), 'The resource-based theory of competitive advantage: implications for strategy formulation', *California Management Review*, Spring, p. 114-135.
Grant, R.M (1996), 'Toward a knowledge-based theory of the firm', *Strategic Management Journal*, vol. 17 (Winter Special Issue), 109-122.
Hall, R. (1993), 'A Framework Linking Intangible Resources and Capabilities to Sustainable Competitive Advantage', *Strategic Management Journal*, vol. 14, p. 607-618.
IFAC, International Federation of Accountants (1998), *The Measurement and Management of Intellectual Capital, an Induction*, NY.
Itami, H., Roehl, T.W. (1987), *Mobilizing Invisible Assets*, Harvard University Press.
Itami, H. (1989), 'Mobilising invisible assets: the key for successful corporate strategy', in E. Punset, and G. Sweeney (ed.). *Information Resources and Corporate Growth*, Pinter Publishers, pp. 36-55.
Johanson, U., Eklöv, G., Holmgren, M. and Mårtenson, M. (1998), *Human Resource Costing and Accounting versus the Balanced Scorecard, A Literature Survey of Experience with the Concepts*, A report to OECD.

Kaplan, R.S, Norton, D.P. (1992), 'The balanced scorecard-measures that drive performance', *Harvard Business Review,* January-February, pp. 71-79.
Kaplan, R.S, Norton, D.P. (1993), 'Putting the balanced scorecard to work', *Harvard Business Review,* September-October; pp. 134-147.
Kaplan, R.S, Norton, D.P. (1996a), 'Using the balanced scorecard as a strategic management system', *Harvard Business Review,* January-February, pp. 75-79.
Kaplan, R.S, Norton, D.P. (1996b), *The Balanced Scorecard,* Harvard Business School Press.
Lokken, S., Kindl, H., Steiner, H., Kramer, S. and Attermeyer, B. (1997), *COSMAS, A Survey of Corporate Knowledge Management, with a Focus on the Tehnology Enabler,* Siemens.
Machlup, F. (1980), *Knowledge: Its Creation, Distribution and Economic Significance,* vol. 1. Princeton University Press, Princeton, NJ.
Mouritsen, J. (1998), 'Driving growth: economic value added versus intellectual capital', *Management Accounting Research,* vol. 9, pp. 461-482.
Nelson, R.R., Winter, S.G. (1982). *An Evolutionary Theory of Economic Change,* Belknap Press and Harvard University Press.
Nonaka, I. (1994), 'A dynamic theory of organizational knowledge Creation', *Organization Science,* vol. 5, February.
Nonaka, I., Takeuchi, H. (1995), *The Knowledge-Creating Company,* Oxford University Press.
Penrose, E. (1959) *The Theory of the Growth of the Firm,* Wiley, NY.
Peteraf, M.A. (1993). 'The cornerstones of competitive advantage: a resource based view', *Strategic Management Journal,* 14 (3), pp. 179-192.
Pfeffer, J. (1991), *Power in Organizations,* Pitman Publishing, Massachussets.
Pfeffer, J. (1994), *Competitive Advantage through People, Unleashing the Power of the Workforce,* Harvard Business School, Boston.
PIMS Associates (1994), *Building Business for Europe, Evidence from Europe & North America on 'Intangible' Factors behind Growth, Competitiveness and Jobs.*
Prahalad, C.K., Hamel, G. (1990), 'The Core competence of the corporation', *Harvard Business Review,* May-June, pp. 79-81.
Porter, M. (1980), *Competitive Strategy,* Free Press, NY.
Porter, M. (1985), *Competitive Advantage,* Free Press; NY.
Porter, M. (1990), *Competitive Advantage of Nations,* Free Press, NY.

Porter, M. (1994), 'Towards a dynamic theory of strategy', in Rumlet et al. (eds.), *Fundamental Issues in Strategy*, Harvard Business School Press.
Quinn, J.B. (1992), *Intelligent Enterprise*, Free Press, NY.
Rappaport, A. (1986), *Creating Shareholder Value, the New Standard for Business Performance,* Free Press, NY.
RCS Conseil (1998), *Intangible Investments*, The Single Market Review Services, Office for Publications of the European Communities, Kogan Page.
Stewart, G.B. (1991), *The Quest for Value,* Harper Collins, NY.
Stewart, T.A. (1997), *Intellectual Capital, The New Wealth of Organizations*, Nicholas Brealy Publishing, London.
Sveiby, K.-E. (1997), *The New Organizational Wealth, Managing and Measuring Knowledge-based Assets,* Berrett-Koehler Publishers, San Francisco.
Teece, D.J., Pisano, G., Shuen, A. (1997), 'Dynamic capabilities and strategic management', *Strategic Management Journal*, vol. 18, pp. 509-533.
Wenerfelt, B. (1984), 'A resource-based view of the firm', *Strategic Management Journal*, vol. 5, pp. 171-180.
Wenerfelt, B. (1989), 'From critical resources to corporate strategy', *Journal of General Management,* Vol. 14 (3), pp. 4-12.
Winter, S., (1987), 'Knowledge and competence as strategic assets', in D. Teece (ed.), *The Competitive Challenge, Strategies for Industrial Innovation and Renewal*, Harper & Row Publishers, NY.
Womack, J.-P., Jones, D.T., Roos, D. (1990), *The Machine that Changed the World,* Macmillan, NY.

3. Making Intangibles Visible: The Value, the Efficiency and the Economic Consequences of Knowledge
Gunnar Eliasson

Abstract

Capital carries a confusing range of somewhat different meanings. It represents *wealth*, it is a *factor of production*, it serves as a benchmark for *internal* firm *control* purposes or it appears as information in the balance sheet of firms. Each purpose requires a somewhat different definition and method of measurement. For a long time measured hardware capital attracted all the attention of economists. It soon, however, became apparent that *intangible capital* was a source of industrial competitiveness of growing importance. We want to quantify this capital in this role on a generally understood format. This ambition is, however, frustrated by the multidimensionality of intangible knowledge capital which makes its value in all respects dependent on its allocation. Above all, a distinction has to be made between the truly *tacit* or entrepreneurial part of intangible capital and the part that can be *measured* by traditional methods.

The value of intangible knowledge capital as it appears in economic growth is found to be partly (1) a property rights issue, partly (2) a matter of the competence to understand the business by the valuators/stock market agents and partly (3) a matter of the abstract market context (the theory) in which the measurement technique is defined.

Two market contexts are discussed:
(a) the static general equilibrium (Walras-Arrow-Debreu, WAD) model in which prices are exogenous, actors price takers and structures permanent and

(b) the *Experimentally Organized Economy* (EOE), its direct opposite, in which experimental selection dominates, organizational structures change endogenously and prices and quantities are simultaneously determined as the result of an ongoing market process.

The dominant role of a multidimensional knowledge capital is found to be a key determinant of the properties of the EOE in which the value of knowledge is critically dependent on its own allocation. To understand the role of knowledge in resource allocation *competence bloc* analysis is used, notably to demonstrate how to link the measurement of knowledge capital to its purpose/use. This makes critical parts of the knowledge base of an economy embodied in people and teams of people and its allocation dependent on its tradability in decentralized markets and its property rights characteristics. This tacit part of intangible capital has to be distinguished from the rest like R&D and marketing capital which can be measured very much like machine capital.

The decentralized allocation of knowledge in the EOE through markets draws considerable resources. The organization of this allocation within competence blocs, hence, is also critical for the values of capital achieved in the economy. The information industry provides excellent case illustrations.

1. The valuation of capital

It took a long time for academe to recognize the importance of intangible knowledge capital in economic growth (Abramovitz 1988; Eliasson 1992a). One reason was that such capital is difficult to measure and if quantification is asked for you tend to get what you *can* measure. The rest tends to be ignored.

Intangible capital, or knowledge, however, has not always been ignored. Managers in industry certainly know that knowledge matters critically for their performance and the old economists were, indeed, aware of the importance of knowledge. Adam Smith (1776) understood very well that labor input was something more than labor hours, and John Stuart Mill (1848) regarded education as the important investment in society. Even before Smith the Swedish economist Johan Westerman (1768) visited England and the Netherlands to figure out why Swedish shipyards needed twice as large a labor input as the English and Dutch manufacturers. He found that the new machines from England, of course, were good to have, but they did not help much if workers did not know how to use them, and if managers did not know how to organize production around them. This importance of *receiver competence* (Eliasson 1986, 1990a), and notably organisational knowledge, was something the early users of robotics equipment and advanced computer installations certainly learned the hard and costly way.

The crux of the matter is that the problem orientation of economists has provided us with a theory that is not capable of dealing intellectually with a dynamic economy, rich in multidimensional human embodied competence capital. Yet, it provides a transparent but biased method of measurement. To interpret those biased measures, however, we need a richer and more general intellectual framework. This is not very different from the sound practice of business people (Eliasson 1976, 1996) to use the internal statistics of the firm in an ad hoc manner, as they find them reliable and useful. To that end a broader intellectual interpretation framework is introduced in the following logical order; the *Knowledge Based Information Economy* introduces knowledge as the dominant production capital and resource allocator, defining the vastness and non-transparency of the state space (or the *investment opportunity set*) of the *Experimentally Organized Economy* (EOE). In the EOE decentralized experimental selection of business projects occurs in dynamically competitive markets. *Competence bloc* theory, finally, defines the efficient organization of that selection in terms of a minimum number of actors with competence, institutions and incentives. Information technology (IT) provides useful illustrations. This presentational format unavoidably gets rather complex but simplifying the presentation, unfortunately, will eliminate the main message:

1. Capital in general, and intangible capital and tacit entrepreneurial capital in particular, are core factor inputs in production that are impossible to define uniquely, to quantify reliably and to price properly.[1] But the pricing or valuation of capital is critical for incentives and its effective allocation in markets. When it cannot be done analytically one has to substitute anonymous market competition, supported by the right institutions and incentives.
2. Secure property rights are critical for effective market functions, and property rights cannot easily be defined for tacit and intangible capital.
3. It follows that efficient valuation through markets is difficult and interferes negatively with the efficient allocation of the same capital under 1 above.

---

[1] Cf. Jonasson's (1999) analysis of the pricing of difficult to define telecom services.

To get the message right, let me rephrase it somewhat differently. In the WAD model no distinction is made between information, knowledge and competence. Standard neoclassical capital measurement principles apply to all three. In the EOE the three differ conceptually and have to be defined differently. It even becomes necessary to ask: what do we mean with information in the EOE?

Competence defines the *ability to use knowledge and information* for a particular purpose. To define competence capital the purpose has to be defined (see below). Information, in fact, is most appropriately defined as part of knowledge, namely that part that can be coded and communicated. The remaining part is what is increasingly being recognized as "tacit" and incommunicable knowledge (Eliasson 1986, p. 24). The problem is that tacit knowledge cannot exist (by definition) in the WAD model, and that other models that "accept it", like the EOE, have to deal with it as an unquantifiable entity (see below on competence bloc theory). Incommunicable information due to limited *receiver competence* (of the information) is sufficient to demonstrate the existence of "tacit knowledge" (Eliasson 1990a).

The value of a firm's intangible capital, hence, is the value of the competence capital embodied in that firm to the extent the value can be expropriated by the owners/holders of the same capital. Consequently, the concept of competence is related to the concept of *bounded rationality*, which defines the intellectual capacity of the individual or the firm to choose the right business strategy ("theory") to act upon, but also the ability to identify and correct business mistakes in the EOE (Eliasson 1986, p. 18,[2] 1992b, p. 261). It is easy to see that we have a conceptual dichotomy between operational measurements and theoretical concepts to deal with and that it is easy to slip, without noticing, into the easy terminology of WAF theory.

The information technology (IT) or computer and communications (C&C) industry provides perfect illustrations of this dilemma. C&C technology deals with the communication of coded information. Information is a key factor input in financial economics which has difficulties dealing with knowledge in any other meaning than stored information. But knowledge "beyond stored information" in embodied or tacit form necessarily exists when communication is limited by inadequate *receiver competence*. Hence, the limits of information technology to

---

[2] Note that the concepts of competence and business mistakes here are introduced in terms of the EOE.

make the world around us, and internal to us, fully transparent provide the best illustrations (Eliasson 1999a).

Section 2 (below) introduces the *Knowledge-Based Information Economy*, establishing the vastness of the state space (or the *opportunity set;* see Eliasson 1990a, 1990b) in which economic actors operate and explore the ways in which extremely differentiated knowledge embodied in human beings as competence and information can be (more) efficiently transmitted and allocated. Because information and knowledge are both related[3] concepts and critical factors in economic development, the new computer and communications (C&C) or information technology (IT) can be used as illustration. The vastness and heterogeneity of state space defines (Section 3) the *Experimentally Organized Economy* (EOE; Eliasson 1991a) in which actors figure as grossly uninformed with a fragmented and widely different knowledge about their local environments. This makes more or less serious business mistakes the normal outcome of all decisions. A key question is how economic choices are made in the EOE, notably how winners are not lost, and losers not kept in the budget for too long. *Competence bloc* theory (see Section 4 and Eliasson and Eliasson 1996) deals with that problem.

But what is the value of competence in production distributed over actors in the competence bloc? How do we define, value and measure knowledge used in production when experimental selection dominates behavior rather than fully informed decisions. The logical approach is to (in Section 5) carry out the standard measurements *as if* the selection problem does not exist. We then (Section 6) establish the new theoretical context needed to interpret the same data in terms of the experimentally organized economy. There decisions take place as more or less uninformed or misinformed business experiments.

2. The knowledge-based information economy

The knowledge-based information economy has been a topical issue in economic discussion during the last few years. The term has been partly used to mark a distinction from the earlier discussion of the information economy. The information economy, on the other hand, ties in nicely with the notion of tradable and transferable information which is the key knowledge concept in the mainstream economic model. In this chapter the two notions from economics are integrated, starting with the role of

---

[3] But not synonymous, as is implicitly assumed in financial economics. See below.

knowledge capital in computer and communications (C&C) industry. C&C technology represents the fifth generation of computing (after the fourth, the microprocessor and the PC) and the merging of computing and communications, or the distribution of computing over a network. This industry is also interesting in a European competitiveness perspective and the imminent Internet organization of the world economy (Eliasson 1999b). Europe has a strong presence in the telecommunications industry, notably its wireless part (Ericsson and Nokia) but hardly any presence in the computer industry. Since the two technologies are rapidly and dramatically merging, the only real European stronghold in high tech is being challenged at the core.[4] How should knowledge capital be measured under such dynamic and experimental circumstances?

Three questions

During the analysis three questions will be addressed:

1. How large a part of total resource use in an economy is accounted for by information and communications activities?
2. How large a part of those information and communications services are already, and will be in the future produced with the help of modern IT?
3. What is the nature of the knowledge or competence capital that will be involved in moving the information and communications part of the economy? How can it be represented or measured?

To begin with the purpose of measurements has to be established. Are we interested in capital as a wealth object, as a production factor or as an internal benchmarking or control variable in firms? The purpose decides what method of measurement to use.

Knowledge as property

Economic incentives influence the use of knowledge in society. This influence depends critically on who manages the knowledge capital, the extent to which the profits generated by the management of knowledge capital can be appropriated, and by whom and to what extent trade in knowledge assets can take place.

---

[4] Which will come most easy; for the US internet-based computer industry to acquire telephone technology, notably radio technology, or for the Europeans to acquire computer technology?

Some in the legal community (for instance Ross 1945; see also Strömholm 1970 and Petrusson 1999) only accepted tangible goods as property, a conservative attitude that is similar to the still prevalent aversion among accountants to accept intangibles in the balance sheet. But that is a narrow legislative view that is hardly interesting for economic analysis. Property should rather (Eliasson 1998a, 1998d) be defined as assets that can be managed, the returns of which can be accessed and traded freely. These are the attributes of property that define economic value (wealth) to you as an owner. Wealth is a capital item to the extent that this asset is capable of contributing to production and profits. According to this neoclassical view property is defined in terms of accessible wealth, and wealth is defined in terms of the present value of income believed to be accessible by some party, for instance a buyer of the same property. We can now define several stages of control or ownership of property:

1. Hands-on control (possession). You have the apple and nobody can prevent you from eating it.
2. Landed property that you own by possession and can defend by arms, or in court since it is registered in your name. Here the legal system enters.
3. Present value of future profits from commitments (an investment) today. This is a financial asset that is only supported by the legal system.
4. Intangibles (patents, copyrights, ideas, knowledge or competence embodied in human beings or teams of people).

The dependence on the legal system increases as you move down the list and your property becomes increasingly more abstract, intangible and embodied. The financial assets are under your physical control as long as you can manage the production capital that generates the income. Then, if legal protection becomes shaky you can at least prevent others from benefiting from the income by destroying the physical capital.

This is not possible with intangible property like a copyright or critical information. You cannot physically prevent somebody from using your information. Enforcement through the legal system, however, becomes increasingly shaky the more intangible and mobile the property becomes. Eventually only economic arrangements can protect your profit flow from outside intruders, for instance through internalizing the use of the knowledge in a business and/or by rapidly making innovations obsolete through rapid upgradings of the knowledge base.

As the values invested in, produced by and traded in the economy are being increasingly defined as intangibles, the importance of an efficient legal system to assert these values, to make them an effective support of investment incentives and to direct the resource allocation process, or in short, for economic performance, increases. These are typical features of the knowledge-based information economy, in which the efficiency of property rights definitions and enforcement influence capital values.

Embodiedness, tradability and the allocation of knowledge

Knowledge, as distinct from information, is typically embodied in human beings or teams of people and, hence, *tacit* in the sense that it cannot easily be communicated, except through reallocation of people or groups of people, in firms or markets.

Except for being intangible and tacit, knowledge differs from hardware capital only in degree. Its typical characteristic is extreme (1) *heterogeneity* and, hence, (2) *redundance* in each application. This means that (3) the value of knowledge or competence will be critically dependent on its *allocation*. Allocation of knowledge largely occurs in markets. Hence, tradability (property rights) matters significantly. Since knowledge capital is mostly tacit and embodied in human beings or teams of people ("firms") it is mostly traded in the labor market and the markets for mergers and acquisitions (M&A; see Eliasson 1991b, 1998a). Besides its intangible nature (it is difficult to define) this explains its particular property rights and tradability characteristics. Competence normally is not approachable by objective definition and analysis. Its efficient allocation, hence, can only be achieved through decentralized markets in which competent actors get involved at different stages. This is why you need competence bloc theory to represent allocation processes in the EOE. This sets the stage for the analysis. Now back to the three questions.

3. The experimentally organized economy[5]

Three circumstances force us to abandon the traditional mainstream model, as reference model for the valuation of capital:

---

[5] The prototype model for the EOE is the (Swedish) micro-to-macro model which has actually inspired the more general formulation of the theory of the EOE (Eliasson 1991a, 1992a).

1. In the (real) knowledge-based information economy, information processing and communication costs make up the bulk of resource use. This is in contrast to the negligible fraction that has to be assumed as a prior in static general equilibrium analysis.
2. With the bulk of resource use going into information processing and communication, prices and quantities are simultaneously determined as an ongoing process and static equilibrium becomes a non-existent entity. Productivity advance at the macroeconomic level, furthermore, becomes closely related to productivity advance in information processing and communication, which is in turn closely related to the rate of organizational change in the economy. Hence, the standard reference for the measurement of capital - its value in a full information equilibrium situation - can never be observed.
3. With a dominant multidimensional knowledge capital governing economic behavior, complexity becomes overwhelming and we have to deal analytically with concepts like tacit knowledge and enormous state spaces that are non-transparent from all places. Heterogeneous tacit knowledge embodied in human beings or teams of people can only be efficiently allocated and coordinated through *decentralized organization*, notably in labor markets or in the M&A markets (Eliasson 1991b). The value of knowledge capital in the economy becomes dependent on its own allocation (Eliasson 1992a). No such thing as an optimum (full information, equilibrium) situation can then be ascertained, even in theory.

Choice and selection dominate and move organizational structures and prices

In the mainstream economic model, a stochastic version of which dominates financial economics, actors are price takers (exogenous prices) that optimize their position over a smooth (convex and differentiable) very well-known and externally given production surface. Not so in the EOE.
The work specialization theory of Adam Smith naturally extends to the theory of the knowledge-based information economy. Reorganizing for further specialization is an act of *innovative organizational choice and selection*. The greater the specialization (decentralization), the higher the demands on *coordination* in space and time which occurs in hierarchies (*management*) and over markets (*competition*). Each such organizational choice involves a change in the composition of hierarchies and markets and, hence, in the structure of firms as more or less monolithically

controlled hierarchies. Once a new solution has been found, an entirely new price regime will be established temporarily and all actors in the market will observe and *learn* as best as they can. Table 3.1 lists the four information and communication activities that occur on top of actual physical production.

Table 3.1: The statistical accounts of the knowledge-based information economy

		The creation of new knowledge	*Actors*
1.	**Expanding business opportunities** (exploring state space)	- science - research & development - technical development	Customers Innovators
2.	**Choice and selection** (identifying business opportunities)	*Filtering* - entry - exit - mobility of people with competence	- Entrepreneurs - The competent venture capitalists - Exit markets
3.	**Coordination**	*Disciplining* - competition (in markets) - management (in hierarchies)	Industrialists
4.	**Learning**	*Knowledge transfer* - education - imitation - diffusion (mobility)	

Source: Eliasson, G. (1990), p. 73.

One activity, choice and selection (item 2), is principally different from the other three. Each choice determines the *new structure* within which the other three information and communication activities occur. It is, therefore, a dominant activity and has to be discussed separately from the other three. While the other three draw measurable resources, the resource use incurred from experimental selection in the market consists of the cost of business mistakes.

Resources for coordination and learning

Most reasonable statistical definitions of innovation, coordination and learning will show that these three activities together dominate over physical production as resource users (Eliasson 1990a, p. 281) in private service production, but also in modern manufacturing firms. This contrasts with the WAD model where information use is at best a marginal calculable activity.

For the EOE the dominance of knowledge-based information processing means *that productivity advance at the macro level is predominantly a matter of productivity advance in information processing and communication, which in turn - as we have defined it - occurs in a large measure through, or is accompanied by, organizational change at all levels of production.* Organizational change is the key part of the choice process. Each organizational regime is costly to achieve and associated with a new price system. This reorganizing process is evolutionary and should be modeled endogenously such that individual agents' quantity behavior influences prices and vice versa. Hence, the EOE involves simultaneous price and quantity determination at the micro level. Consequently, when structure (organization) is changing as part of ongoing market processes, theories such as the WAD model, based on stable exogenous structures and price taking "behavior", will lose their explanatory power and provide misleading advice.

Experimental choice in the EOE

In the EOE, information and communication activities are guided by a dominant and highly diversified knowledge capital embodied in human beings and teams of human beings in hierarchies and markets. The economic potential of this economy is only limited by the ability of the actors in the economy to comprehend this mass of heterogeneous competence. It is, thus, enormous in principle, but limited in practice. And the limits are set by the ability of actors to learn.

While the most valuable economic inputs originate in the entrepreneurial activity of identifying and selecting projects (account 2 in Table 3.1 and 9 in Table 3.3), the most directly measurable resource use occurs through the coordination and learning (knowledge transfer) accounts. These are, however, the least important information and communication activities in the experimentally organized economy. When state space is enormous, experimental choice and selection dominate, and business mistakes not allowed in the mainstream economic model occur constantly, and *should be regarded as a standard learning cost for economic development.*

Hence, entrepreneurial knowledge appears in the EOE as the most important and at the same time the most difficult capital item. The superimposition of human or organization embodied knowledge capital creates the almost infinite variety of allocational combinations that constitutes the knowledge-based economy, and an enormous, for all practical purposes, infinite, state space, or investment opportunity set. It becomes important to understand how the economy can be efficiently organized for selection and learning. Competence bloc theory explains this.

4. Competence bloc theory[6]

When state space is introduced into economics as an enormous investment opportunity set, we land in the knowledge-based information economy. Then and there economic behavior becomes experimental, and business mistakes a normal cost for economic development (in the EOE). Then it becomes important to ask the question: how are firms and the whole economy organized for efficient selection of projects in terms of minimizing the economic loss of two types of error; to keep losers on for too long (type I) and to lose the winners (type II). In the knowledge-based information economy this becomes almost synonymous with the allocation of knowledge or competence capital. This activates the selection item (2 in Table 3.1) and the kind of organizational change that impairs the reliability of the price system as an information signaling device. This in turn excludes the price taking assumption of the WAD model and removes the standard assumptions for neoclassical capital stock measurement. To understand the value of competence capital we have to understand the efficiency characteristics of the business choice and experimental selection process. For this we need the intellectual support of competence bloc theory.

Selection and business choice - competence bloc theory

The selection item in Table 3.1 is principally different from the other three items. Here entrepreneurial competence enters and the main resource use under this item is business mistakes. This resource use is difficult to measure since you lack a well-defined reference (benchmark) that is, what you would have achieved if you had not made a business mistake on selection account (i.e. under item 2 in Table 3.1).

---

[6] This theory was first formulated in Eliasson and Eliasson (1996). Even though the concept has certain features in common with the notions of technological systems (Carlsson 1975), development blocs (Dahmén 1950) or so-called new growth theory (Romer 1986, Lucas 1988), the concept is much closer to Marshall's (1890, 1919) theory of *industrial districts* and his attempts to come to grips, using a micro approach, with increasing returns in the Walrasian model. These shortcomings of the WAD model are still our problem of measurement today.

The entrepreneurial task under selection and business choice is to minimize the incidence of two types of business mistakes; to allow losing projects to go on for too long and to terminate the winners prematurely (Eliasson and Eliasson 1996). By far the largest cost incurred is when a winner is lost, but this cost can only be computed if you know the alternative, that is, what you would have gained had you captured the winner. To know that, you have to be able to compute not only the alternative production (quantity) structure with the winner in place but also the alternative prices that would then be established. This is not easy but at least we know that business mistakes should be counted as a normal cost for industrial development.

Business history abounds with spectacular business mistakes that are known because they almost failed or because somebody else turned them into a great business:

- The punch card machine producer IBM almost missed computers in the early 1950s.
- IBM misunderstood the commercial significance of the haloid copying technology it was offered, which became the foundation of Xerox.
- Xerox did not understand the commercial significance of the PC and the mouse, first developed in its own Palo Alto Research laboratory. Steve Jobs understood them and founded Apple.
- William Gates almost missed the Internet.
- Ericsson almost missed mobile telephony (Case 1 below).

And so on.

Some would argue that if one actor misses, the winner will soon turn up elsewhere. In the EOE (see discussion in Eliasson 1996) this is not generally the case. Under all circumstances the lost winner may turn up in a different economy or after such a long time that its capture then is of no concern to anybody today. The difference is so significant that another outcome of the choice process may leave a permanent imprint on economic history.

This critical importance of selection points towards another disturbing feature for the statisticians. Productivity advance in production is not only dominated by productivity advance in information processing and communication (transactions costs), but this productivity advance is in turn dominated by the organizational changes occasioned by the discrete choices under the selection item 2 in Table 3.1.

The competence bloc lists the minimum interacting agents with competence needed to initiate and develop an industry. It is end user (functionally), not input defined (Eliasson and Eliasson 1996). The efficiency of selection in terms of minimizing the two errors depends on the organization and completeness of the competence bloc. Completeness is critical for efficient incentives.

The actor that establishes himself in the competence bloc both benefits from and contributes to the competence bloc which thus abounds with industrial spillovers. To achieve that degree of attraction, critical mass has to be reached. But when critical mass has been achieved, competition is also ferocious and less than able actors (that do not contribute) are repelled.

Competence bloc analysis dealing with the efficiency of selection thus takes you outside the traditional production function approach and into the obscure domain of tacit and difficult to communicate knowledge. It has been used to analyze Swedish aircraft, health care and house building industries. A highly illuminating competence bloc analysis of fifteenth century art production in Florence, emphasizing the critical role for development of the competence contribution of customers has recently been published.

The minimum number of agents with competence who have to be present in an efficient choice process are listed in Table 3.2.

Table 3.2: Actors in the competence bloc

1. Competent and active customers
2. Innovators that integrate technologies in new ways
3. Entrepreneurs that identify profitable innovations
4. Competent venture capitalists that recognize and finance the entrepreneurs
5. Exit markets that facilitate ownership change
6. Industrialists that take successful innovations to industrial scale production.

Source: Eliasson and Eliasson, 1996.

Customer choice and marketing in the experimentally organized economy

The customer comes first and the customer of competence bloc theory is much more than a demand agent. The customer determines what price the producer will get for quality supply and thus sets the limit for product quality. A sophisticated industry requires a sophisticated customer base and in the long run the products will never get better than what customers are willing to pay for. If you are a sophisticated producer you don't adjust quality down to your current customer base. You may attempt to improve your customer, but since competent customers contribute to technology development by supplying product and user knowhow, the *marketing strategy* of an advanced firm must be to *actively look for competent customers to avoid getting locked into inferior technologies* (Eliasson 1998b). The contribution of sophisticated customers to technological development, and the active search by artists for competent customers that were both able to appreciate the art and willing and capable of paying for it are very manifest in the markets for art in Renaissance Italy (Eliasson and Eliasson 1997). The situation is very similar in aircraft production. But in the EOE there are more things to attend to for the producer. High quality products have to be developed and there are significant risks both technological and market. Above all, data from the past tell very little about the future demand for the new product. The satisfaction of the final customer can never be ascertained until the product has been developed, marketed, sold and used. When the competent customer actively enters development work these risks are often shared between producer and customer. But the main thing is that in the EOE marketing too becomes an experimental activity and efficient marketing method is not a matter of analysis but (a) actively identifying competent and technology contributing customers and (b) engaging them in product development work.

The innovator and the entrepreneur

The innovator integrates new and old technologies into new product technologies. The greater, easier and more varied the availability of technology supply, the more efficient the innovation process. The availability of a deep and varied technology supplying subcontracting industry is becoming increasingly important for future industrial development in the advanced industrial countries when outsourcing of both production and development work in the market is beginning to dominate both new and old industries.[7] In an advanced environment innovative technology development will be a risky activity and the supply

---

[7] The so-called "technology system" (Carlsson 1995, pp. 7, 23, 49) is defined from the technology input side and enters the competence bloc under the innovation item, since its "purpose" is to create and diffuse one generic technology for multiple applications in many industries.

of technological solutions for the same problems will be many. The role of the entrepreneur will be to contribute commercial competence to help select commercially viable technological solutions. The entrepreneur introduces the economic and industrial dimensions in the industrialization process.

Competent money

But the entrepreneur rarely has the financial resources to take innovations one step further. For that competent money (item 4 in Table 3.2) is needed, that is, venture capitalists sufficiently competent to understand what the entrepreneur is offering to be willing to contribute financial resources at reasonable terms (Eliasson and Eliasson 1996), that is, with a reasonable risk premium in his or her project evaluation. The terms of this risk valuation will also be influenced by the availability and competence of secondary exit markets (item 5 in Table 3.2).

The main and most important task of the (financial) resource provider - almost always forgotten in financing literature - is a sufficient understanding of the business idea of the entrepreneur to dare to use a sufficiently low risk premium in the project evaluation for the investment to take place. Such conditions are needed to keep competent innovators and entrepreneurs in business. Without such an understanding, the terms by which venture financing is supplied will be unreasonable to the innovator/entrepreneur. This competence or capacity to understand is extremely rare when it comes to the new entering industries and it is a complete mistake to believe that the banks, the large investment institutions or the large companies in mature industries have that competence. Much further down in importance comes the routine business knowhow in financial control, marketing, management etc. that the venture capitalists also supply or demand to be recruited from their network (Eliasson 1997, 1998c).

Upgrading to industrial scale

If a real winner has been identified and properly established, it remains to bring it up to industrial scale production and distribution. In many new industries this last step has to be taken fast to secure the potential cash flow needed for fast growth, before imitators or new and better technologies have hit the market.

Industrial skills learned in mature industries, however, rarely suffice as a competence base in radically new industries. Large-scale industrial management is increasingly concerned with organization in new industries like biotech and C&C production and increasingly with managing innovation and efficient manufacturing simultaneously. To get managers from large-scale engineering focused on operational efficiency in such firms normally spells failure. Hence, markets for differentiated management competence are becoming increasingly important for economic progress in the wealthy Western economies.

The necessity of a complete competence bloc for effective incentives (completeness)

There is a common saying among bankers that there is plenty of money, but no good projects. The problem may be the reverse; there are plenty of good projects, but the bankers don't understand them. It follows that the lack of entrepreneurship that we believe we have, for instance in Sweden, may rather reflect a lack of competence in the so-called venture industry. Without competent venture capitalists there will be few live entrepreneurs to observe. Completeness (of the competence bloc) is key and should be the prime concern of the policy maker (Eliasson 1998c). Without competent industrialists and venture capital, incentives for entrepreneurship will be lacking, and without competent entrepreneurs, incentives for innovators will be lacking. Very rarely will the situation be as good as in the market for new fine art in fifteenth century Florence - lacking financial markets almost altogether - so that the sophisticated customers fund the projects.

5. The measurement of competence input and the evaluation of competence capital

Experimental selection is what causes the analytical problems of this chapter. Efficient selection is the key function of the competence bloc organization. It dominates resource use and should dominate capital measurement. I will now go through the measurement of resource use for innovative, coordination and learning activities, and then (in the next section) turn to the entrepreneurial selection or choice of projects that constitutes the most competence demanding activities. They have to be treated separately since resource use for choice activities is almost unmeasurable even in principle. The bulk of it comes out in the form of business mistakes that are never recorded in the books. The most costly choice experience for a business is not keeping the losers on for too long, but to lose (reject) the winners. The minimization of those business errors is the main task, not only of top management in firms but of the configuration of actors with competence that filter the choices in markets, that is, the competence bloc.

The measurement method will be first to close your eyes to the experimental choice process and only look at the other three items in Table 3.1 (this section). You are then in WAD territory by assumption and "can" use static equilibrium methods. In the next section (6) we break out of the WAD confines to present an intellectual framework for interpreting the biased measures that have mostly, by necessity, been made under the assumptions of WAD theory (Eliasson 1998e).

Innovation, coordination and learning costs measured: manufacturing

The relative share of resources going into information processing and communication in manufacturing is first estimated. It is found (Eliasson 1990a) that resources going into innovative (R&D), coordination (marketing, administration, bureaucracy), learning,[8] supervision etc. account for significantly more than 50 percent of total resource use. Workers at machines account for no more than 20-25 percent of total resource use in the average Swedish manufacturing firm. That means that *transactions costs dominate resource use* and that productivity change at the firm level is dominated by productivity change in the internal firm use of information and communication. The investment flows into innovative, coordination and learning activities have been "activated as assets" in the balance sheets of firms and have been found significantly and positively to improve firm productivity and profitability, notably in a balanced combination with each other and with hardware capital (Eliasson and Braunerhjelm 1998).

Making intangibles visible

A large part of the costs incurred on innovative, coordinating and learning accounts are carried as invisible assets for many years, generating income (profits) and thus, due to their absence in the balance sheet, biasing rate of

---

[8] The learning item is probably grossly understated since it only includes costs for external teachers and for people participating in external courses etc. excluding their wages and salaries.

return records. If the true investment items could be separated from the cost accounts and reasonable life length estimates could be obtained, a revised "true" balance sheet could be constructed. For years attempts to do this have been criticized by the accountants' profession. Part of this criticism undoubtedly has been based in a desire of the profession to protect the value of their skills. In so far as such criticism has been formulated on the principal grounds that intangibles, as distinct from visible hardware capital, cannot be measured, the criticism has been dead wrong. As has been thoroughly analyzed and concluded, it can be argued that no capital measure independent of its expected profit flow can be determined at all. This goes for both hardware *and* intangibles. The difference (Eliasson 1992b, pp. 51 ff.) is only a matter of degree: the multidimensionality of intangibles, notably knowledge and competence. Any capital measure is a crude proxy for something fuzzy, unquantifiable called capital.[9] To read the accounts of firms, this has to be understood and factored into the analysis. Hence, only the business decision makers, not the accountants, are capable of understanding the accounts properly.[10] But the critical stand of the accountants' profession carries a point. Since any measure of capital that you design will be a crude, biased and unstable reflection of what you want to know, it is better to stick to simple conservative measures that you are familiar with than to attempt to be sophisticated. This view, however, is untenable today when intangibles not only dominate the true balance sheets of firms, but also dominate productivity development in hardware capital (see Eliasson 1992a and Eliasson and Braunerhjelm 1998).

Now look at Table 3.3. Take items A (1, 2) as they are in the accounts of a firm and recompute the hardware capital on a replacement valuation basis. Then under B do the same for software assets. There should be no principal difference or difficulty compared to items A if you have the input data.

---

[9] Only in static equilibrium does the known future profit flow exactly reflect the capital.
[10] Note that this is also our method. We measure as if WAD theory is OK (this section) and provide (in the next section) a more general framework for interpreting these biased results, i.e. the knowledge-based information economy, the EOE and competence bloc theory.

Table 3.3: The complete balance sheet of a firm (9 and 17 Swedish firms)

Items	9 largest manufacturing firms, global operations Percent 1985	1988	17 largest manufacturing firms, global operations, end of 1988 Percent
A *"Visible" capital*			
1. Machines, buildings, inventories (replacement valuation)	-	-	-
2. Financial assets, net	-	-	-
3. Total visible assets (replacement valuation) [(1)+(2)]	54	50	70
B *"Intangible" capital*			
4. Software	na	7	6
5. Technical knowledge	17	16	13
6. Marketing knowledge	20	19	6
7. "Educational" capital	10	8	5
8. *Sum*: Total tangible and intangible assets	100	100	100
9. Tacit entrepreneurial competence	?	?	?
10. Debt	65	66	77
11. Net worth (8-10) according to the revised books in percent of (8)	35	34	23
12. For comparison: market value of (11) in percent of (8)	30	37	51

Source: Eliasson (1992), p. 88.

The problems begin to show up with technical, marketing and education knowledge capital. Most firms have fairly detailed cost categories for these items and it is possible in principle to select those that should be labeled investments. That has been done in great detail for nine large Swedish firms (Eliasson 1990a, 1990b, 1992b). The experience from those cases has then been used to collect the same data for a larger sample of firms. Interviews with firms were used to determine depreciation data for the knowledge assets[11] and the rates were then conservatively applied. The results are shown in Table 3.3.[12]

---

[11] We did not follow the standard procedure of neoclassical theory of assuming knowledge to have eternal life, and that obsolescence of knowledge is a problem of using the correct price deflator. Cf. von Weizäcker (1986).

[12] One particular problem should be reported here. While hardware production is covered in extreme detail in the accounts of firms, other cost items are more aggregate, reflecting their lesser importance in the past and the conservatism of the accountants' profession. Thus,

So far all this can be handled under the assumptions of WAD theory. The table then gives the picture of a 50/50 division between visible hardware capital and intangibles now made visible.

The real problem arises when we want to account for the competence capital embodied in the firm hierarchy to make the top level selective business decisions (item 2 in Table 3.1), deciding *what* to do, *which market* to operate in, *what technology* to adopt, thus changing the operating structure of the firm and shifting out of the WAD model into the theory of the EOE.

The "item 2" problems are illustrated in Case 2 below. How should you have valued investment in R&D research on the stomach ulcer drug Losec (Astra) and mobile telephony (Ericsson) before the two companies understood they had winners on hand, when they were even close to closing down the projects, definitely in 1985 and almost in 1988? The two companies are among the nine in Table 3.3.

The softening economy

The general picture is that the hardware part of production is falling and the soft and intangible parts are increasing as a share of the total, making measurements increasingly difficult. The increasing digitalization of previously hardware products associated, among other things, with Internet trade are causing even more measurement trouble (Eliasson 1999b).

While the hardware manufacturing part of total production has been steadily declining, from 28 percent of GNP in 1950 to just above 20 percent in 1996, the soft part of related service production has expanded rapidly making the total "extended manufacturing industry" stay constant at about 50 percent of GNP from 1950, or even increasing in the last decade (Eliasson 1990b, p. 79; Sjöholm 1993; Johansson 1999).

Contrary to the gloom of the "deindustrialization" debate, this is a positive sign since it means that simple, low paying jobs in the industry have been cut while the quality content of manufacturing production, closely related to internal and external service production has increased. A large and growing manufacturing industry by the national accounts definition would have been a cause for serious concern. This, however, means that an increasing part of inputs as well as output is made up of

---

costs incurred for educational purposes only included time spent in external educational facilities and externally hired teachers, disregarding the large costs incurred increasingly internally for on-the-job learning and internal education.

quality intensive and difficult to measure activities. The paradoxical result is that we are becoming less and less informed about what is becoming more and more important (Eliasson 1990b, p. 16 f.).

All economy, GNP level

The same "figures" at the Swedish GNP level cause even more concern. A small industry for direct private consumption services of almost 13 percent should be compared with a larger sector for infrastructure provision (more than 15 percent), most of it consisting of public provisions of health care and education. Finally there is a sizable information design "industry" of some 8.5 percent including the church, political activity, unions and private lobbying. Altogether some 75-85 percent of GNP is accounted for by typical service production.

A rough calculation shows that about half of that share (almost 40 percent of GNP) consists of "pure" knowledge creation, transmission and application, economic coordination and learning in terms of Table 3.1. Wallis and North (1986) has come up with a similar figure of some 45 percent for transactions costs in the US economy. Wallis and North, however, did not have data on internal information and communications costs in manufacturing firms, a circumstance that supports our view that our estimates are cautious and on the low side. Again, a little more than half of the 40 percent of GNP share (or 23 percent) consists of innovation, coordination and learning activities that are potentially codable as information and constitute a potential market for modern C&C technology (Eliasson 1990b, pp. 49 ff.). This figure of 23 percent, that may be growing faster than GNP, compares with the small C&C industry share, estimated to be in the range 2-4 percent in the industrial world (Johansson 1999). We can perhaps talk about a large unexploited market for C&C technology that will move this industry into the future. But we also have to recognize that these figures may be grossly understated. Other estimates indicate that US C&C industry actually accounts for 10 percent of GNP (Johansson 1999).

6. The problem of measuring competence when choices and experimental selection matter

Measurement of competence under the prior assumptions of the WAD model was fairly straightforward. Knowledge input is pure information input and knowledge capital, can be computed by standard present value formulae. In the assumed static equilibrium firms have adjusted their quantities, including capital to the given prices and under the assumptions of the model, we may believe in the asset values computed. Not so when experimental choice and the decentralized use of knowledge in the competence bloc rule the markets. One seemingly academic but critical problem concerns the choice of one production organization rather than another, each being associated with a different price structure in the WAD model, making efficiency and welfare comparisons arbitrary. The same incomparability applies to capital, and for the same reason. This problem, of course, applies to both physical and intangible capital. Since the choice process is intimately associated with intangible capital it was perhaps excusable to neglect that capital problem in the period of intense hardware concern in the 1960s.

When entrepreneurial choice matters

The higher up in the decision hierarchy, the more important selective choices and the tacit entrepreneurial competence (item 9 in Table 3.3) that enters under item 2 in Table 3.1 become, and the more so the more pronounced the multidimensionality of the knowledge capital applied. All of a sudden objective measurement is no longer possible and each decision taken at that level means a reorganization of all other activities in the table. If the decision is right and a winner captured, enormous value suddenly emerges, first to be understood by the insiders, eventually to be understood by the market. We may talk about a new product or about a new organization of production. The problem is that to maximize the value of knowledge capital, it has to be both efficiently allocated and understood by the market agents (receiver competence, incentives). If not understood by the venture capital people (item 4 in the competence bloc, Table 3.2), the allocation won't be efficient. If not finally understood in the market, incentives to carry the new innovative idea to industrial scale production will not be sufficient.

One way to study the level of competence (NB not information) in the financial markets is to study the value placed on entrepreneurial capital (item 9 in Table 3.3) by the market "experts". The nine companies valued in 1985 and 1988 are the Swedish industrial flagships, including Ericsson and Astra. 1985 was a generally good cyclical year. 1988 was the year when Losec became the winner for Astra and when Ericsson was on the verge of becoming the winner in mobile telephony (see Case 1 below). None of this is reflected in the market evaluation of the nine flagships. The market value of visible and measurable intangible capital was only slightly larger than the revised book value of measurable capital in 1988.[13]

Let me illustrate the valuation problems by way of two examples/cases representing different dimensions of the use of knowledge and its measurement.

Cases

The first case (1) documents the near loss of two extreme winners in Swedish manufacturing industry. The second case (2) tells why Sweden, a European leader in the second (transistor based) computer generation, never developed a computer industry. The two cases are illustrations of the importance of intangible capital for firms' productivity and profit performance and above all of the critical significance of a complete competence bloc. They are all indicative of the problems of measuring the same intangible capital and the associated property rights problem.

Case 1: The near miss of two extreme winners in Swedish manufacturing industry

The nine firms analyzed in Case 1 included Astra and Ericsson, but the analyses were made a few years before (in 1985) and about the year (1988) their winning products (the ulcer substance Losec and mobile telephony) had finally been understood by insiders (top management), but not yet by the market agents. What is the situation in the early entrepreneurial phases when the agents (the venture capitalists and the insiders) have to understand the commercial value of something entirely new?

The Losec story began in the mid-1960s and the idea - completely new at the time - was positively reviewed by top management, even though not well understood. As usual the costs and efforts needed were grossly underestimated, and as one deadline after the other was passed without tangible results, reviewing was intensified and supplemented by external academic expert advice. Apparently this advice did not enhance internal understanding of the project but rather confused management and raised the risk of throwing out a winner. Thanks to a stubborn research leader at Astra/Hässle, a small contribution from the Swedish Technology Research Board (now NUTEK) that Astra simply had to match, and despite several

---

[13] Apparently the entrepreneurial capital was assessed by the market at a somewhat higher value for the larger group of 17 international firms.

blunders in the clinical testing - after a total of five near shut downs - the project was finally a winner that went on to become the world's best-selling prescription drug ever. Only then did the value of a winner begin to show in the stock valuation of Astra. And the stock market experts needed years to fully appreciate the new value of the company.

The story of Ericsson's mobile phone "venture" is similar. With the large cash flow from the winning new switching technology – the Axe system – Ericsson jumped on the premature bandwagon in business information systems. It acquired DataSaab in 1981 and announced its entry into the business information systems market on the basis of its PBX and telecommunications technology in 1982 when Ericsson Information Systems (EIS) was founded. Focus on this costly venture was intense and (Eliasson 1996 pp. 194 ff., 243 f.) Ericsson failed miserably together with all other 40 or so premature ventures into this market between the late 1970s and 1985. This focus was such that other activities were forced out of the Ericsson research budget, including radio-based telephony. Top level attempts were in fact enacted to close down such non-strategic research. Had it not been for secret research activity within Ericsson Radio Systems, funded through a military budget for which one stubborn man was responsible, Ericsson would not have been ready when the market suddenly took off in the late 1980s. Again the traders in the stock market were even slower to understand what had happened than the insiders in Ericsson, and little value was placed on the entrepreneurial capital value of Ericsson in 1988 (see Table 3.3).

Case 2: Why Sweden has no computer industry

Competence bloc theory demonstrates that the economic value of new technology has to be built by a whole "bloc" of supporting competencies. The market either runs off on the observation of a single new and path breaking technology, or understands nothing when a tidal wave is slowly built on the basis of a number of new and old technologies, each seemingly irrelevant, but that combine in a new and powerful way.

Sweden was the European technological leader in the early phases of the second generation of computing but failed to develop a sustainable computer industry. Saab was ready with a fully transistorized commercial computer (called Sank, later D2) in 1960,[14] just about a year behind Control Data (in 1958) and Philco, RCA, GE and IBM (in 1959). That was all, and Europe was well behind. A traditionally narrow evaluation would have given Saab a high probability of being at least the European

---

[14] Based on a fully transistorized control computer for a robot for the fighter plane Viggen.

leader. But this was not to be the case. Philco, RCA and GE left the computer market very soon. Control Data continued until recently. Saab struggled on, reorganized its computer activity into DataSaab, but eventually (in 1981) sold the DataSaab division to Ericsson, which messed up and almost went under with its information systems business. The latecomer, among the six world leaders, IBM made it, and killed almost all competition when it "prematurely" introduced the third generation of computers (based on integrated circuits) in 1965. IBM had, what the others did not have, namely an almost complete competence bloc (see Table 3.2) inhouse or in close context, notably an excellent market and customer knowhow and contact (item 1), competent internal venture capital (item 4) and industrial leadership expertise in the right markets (item 6). Such factors certainly mattered and eventually made their way into the valuation of IBM stock, but when they really mattered for getting IBM on the right track, these competence bloc intangible capital items were neither understood by outsiders nor shown in any accounts. Similarly, it took a long time for the market to realize that Ericsson, with its information systems venture, was on a catastrophe track, and also to realize that it had a winner with its mobile telephony. Furthermore, if IBM had not made it in computers there were other firms in the USA to carry on, maybe not with the same marketing competence and maybe not as fast. There were no other competent actors in Sweden, and in Europe policy makers were pushing firms in the wrong direction (Eliasson 1996).

7. Conclusions

The value of invisible knowledge capital is multidimensional and depends critically on its allocation. But its definition and value also depend on the purpose of the measurement. Should it be used to measure economic wealth, for internal control, for external information purposes or in economic studies of firm or macroeconomic performance. Each purpose requires a different definition and method of measurement, and each definition and measurement is influenced by its floating nature.

This paper has, however, demonstrated two things.

1. When the industry is not affected by radical technological and organizational change, standard asset accounting as advised by WAD theory tells an intelligible story. Otherwise not.
2. When experimental or entrepreneurial selection dominates the economic process, which is the case under radical technological and

organizational change, gross uncertainty and unpredictability prevail and the quantity outcome has to be valued in an entirely new price system. This makes the valuation of capital more or less arbitrary as reflected by standard accounting methods and the valuation in the stock market.

The arbitrary valuation by standard accounting methods depends on the context in which the valuation methods have been defined. The insiders of the firm have access to more data than anybody else and also, presumably, a better understanding of the firm than anybody else. In principle this understanding should make it possible for insiders to evaluate and intuitively "correct" the standard accounts. The parallel valuation in the stock market depends on similar, but less reliable and not as complete data and on a different competence or understanding of the firm. For an external observer to use the internally collected and composed data on intangible capital use in production on the basis of standard accounting (WAD based) methods, a more general dynamic model is needed for the proper interpretation of these data.

We have thus accepted that simple WAD measures of capital value, even though biased, carry an information value. A more general model is, however, needed to help interpret those data, to correct them for biases and to relate the results to a more real world. We have introduced that model in terms of the *Knowledge-Based Information Economy*, the *Experimentally Organized Economy* and *Competence Bloc theory*.

The overall conclusion, however, is that no unique definition of capital exists that serves all purposes. Even though firm executives need internal measures on the magnitude of intangible capital employed to be able to assess their required profit flows, they need a much broader theoretical understanding to be able to use these measures intelligently. This understanding will vary a lot between firms. The efficient allocation of all capital in production will, therefore, require that firms be experimentally organized business machines that are subjected to a broadbased and hardnosed exposure in the markets to optimize the use of competence in the overall allocation of capital in the economy. No one can claim to know better than anybody else, and they will all leave a trail of more or less failed business ventures. But this is the essence of the EOE. The competence bloc organization is there to minimize the trail of errors, notably the loss of winners, thus contributing to economic growth. The situation of the individual actor is well illustrated by the reaction of the director of the Swedish Meteorological survey (SMHI) to criticism for its bad forecasts during the exceptionally bad summer of 1998. In a press release he apologized for its bad weather forecasts last summer. It was due partly to exceptional and complex weather constellations. There were many possible interpretations, and the one offered by the SMHI was not necessarily the best one. With new and better computers, that SMHI was asking the Government to provide, SMHI would, however, be able to make much better forecasts in the future. In addition, the director added, this new computing capacity would make source data easily available so that anybody could make up his or her own mind about the weather.

References

Abramovitz, Moses (ed.), 1988. *Thinking about Growth*. New York: Cambridge University Press.
Carlsson, Bo (ed.), 1995. *Technological Systems and Economic Performance: The Case of Factory Automation*. Boston/Dordrecht/London: Kluwer Academic Publishers.
Dahmén, Erik, 1950. *Svensk industriell företagarverksamhet, band 1 och 2* (Entrepreneurial Activity in Swedish Industry 1919-1939). Part 1 and 2. Stockholm: IUI.
Eliasson, Gunnar, 1976. *Business Economic Planning – Theory, Practice and Comparison*. London/New York/Sidney/Toronto; John Wiley & Sons.
--------, 1986. Företaget som skapare och förvaltare av mänskligt kapital (The firm as a creator and manager of human capital); Chapter II in G. Eliasson, B. Carlsson, T. Pousette, E. Deiaco, T. Lindberg, 1986, *Kunskap, information och tjänster* (Knowledge, information processing and service production). Stockholm: IUI.
--------, 1990a. The Firm as a Competent Team, *Journal of Economic Behavior and Organization*, 13 (3), 275-298.
--------, 1990b. The Knowledge-based Information Economy; Chapter 1 in G. Eliasson, S. Fölster, T. Lindberg, T. Pousette, and E. Taymaz, 1990, *The Knowledge-Based Information Economy*. Stockholm: IUI.
--------, 1991a. Modeling the Experimentally Organized Economy, *Journal of Economic Behavior and Organization*, 16 (1-2), 153-182.
--------, 1991b. Financial Institutions in a European Market for Executive Competence; Chapter 7 in Wihlborg, C., Fratianni, M. and Willet, T.A. (eds.), 1991, *Financial Regulation and Monetary Arrangements after 1992*. Amsterdam: Elsevier Science Publishers B.V.

--------, 1992a. Business Competence, Organizational Learning, and Economic Growth: Establishing the Smith-Schumpeter-Wicksell (SSW) Connection; in F.M. Scherer and M. Perlman (eds.), 1992, *Entrepreneurship, Technological Innovation, and Economic Growth. Studies in the Schumpeterian Tradition*. Ann Arbor: The University of Michigan Press.

--------, 1992b. The MOSES Model, Database and Applications; in *MOSES Database*. Stockholm: IUI.

--------, 1996. *Firm Objectives, Controls and Organization – The Use of Information and the Transfer of Knowledge within the Firm*. Boston/Dordrecht/London: Kluwer Academic Publishers.

--------, 1997. The Venture Capitalist as a Competent Outsider; mimeo, KTH, INDEK, TRITA, IEO R 1997-06, Stockholm.

--------, 1998a. The Competence of Computing the Capital Value of Competence, *European Journal of Vocational Training*, No. 14.

--------, 1998b. The Nature of Economic Change and Management in the Knowledge-based Information Economy. KTH, TRITA, Stockholm.

--------, 1998c. Industrial Policy, Competence Blocs and the Role of Science in Economic Development, TRITA-IEO R 1998-08, KTH, Stockholm. To be published in *Journal of European Economics*, 10 (1-2), 2000.

--------, 1998d. From Plan to Market, *Journal of Economic Behavior and Organization*, 34 (1), 49-68.

--------, 1998e. Information Efficiency, Production Organization and Systems Productivity - Quantifying the Effects of EDI Investments; in Macdonald, S. and Madden, G. (eds.), 1998, *Telecommunications and Socio-Economic Development*. Amsterdam: North-Holland.

--------, 1999a. Communication, Information and Firm Performance; in Macdonald, S. and Nightinggale, J. (eds.), 1999.

--------, (ed.). 1999b. *Internet Economics and Internet Technology*, TRITA, KTH, Stockholm.

Eliasson, Gunnar and Pontus Braunerhjelm, 1998. Intangible, Intangible, Human Embodied Capital and Firm Performance; in G. Eliasson and C. Green, (eds.), 1998, *The Micro Foundations of Economic Growth*. Ann Arbor: University of Michigan Press.

Eliasson, Gunnar and Åsa Eliasson, 1996. The Biotechnological Competence Bloc, *Revue d'Economie Industrielle,* N°. 78, 4, Trimestre.

Eliasson, Gunnar and Ulla Eliasson, 1997. *Företagandets konst - om konstproduktionen i Renässansens Florense* (The art of

entrepreneurship - on art production in Renaissance Florence). Stockholm: City University Press.
Johansson, Dan, 1999. Den C&C-användande industrin, konsekvensanalys; in G. Eliasson and D. Johansson, 1999, *Dynamik och flexibilitet i svensk IT-industri*. Stockholm: City University Press.
Jonasson, Andreas, 1999. Trading in, and Pricing of Not Easily Defined Products and Services; in Eliasson (1999b).
Lucas, R.E. Jr., 1988. On the Mechanics of Economic Development, *Journal of Monetary Economics*, 22 (1), 3-41.
Marshall, Alfred, 1890. *Principles of Economics*. London.
Marshall, Alfred, 1919. *Industry and Trade*. London.
Mill, J.S., 1848. *Principles of Political Economy with Some of Their Applications to Social Philosophy*. London.
Petrusson, Ulf, 1999. *Patent och industriell omvandling – en studie av dynamiken mellan rättsliga och ekonomiska idésystem*. Stockholm: Norstedts Juridik AB.
Romer, P.M., 1986. Increasing Returns and Long-Run Growth, *Journal of Political Economy*, 94, (5), (Oct.), 1002-1037.
Ross, Alf, 1945. Ophovsrettens grundbegreber, *TfR*.
Sjöholm, K.R., 1993. Den reviderade industrisektorn, Supplement in *Den långa vägen* (The Long Road). Stockholm: IUI.
Smith, Adam, 1776. *An Inquiry into the Nature and Causes of the Wealth of Nations*. New York: Modern Library, 1937.
Strömholm, Stig, 1970. *Upphovsrättens verksbegrepp*. Stockholm: PA Norstedt & Söners Förlag.
Von Weizäcker and Carl Christian, 1986. Rights in Relation in Modern Economic Theory; in R. Day and G. Eliasson (eds.), 1986, *The Dynamics of Market Economies*. Amsterdam: North-Holland.
Wallis, J. and Douglass North, 1986. Measuring the Transaction Sector in the American Economy; in S. Eggerman and R. Gallman (eds.), 1986, *Long Term Factors in American Economic Growth*, University of Chicago Press, 95-148.
Westerman, Johan, 1768. *On Svenska Näringarnes Undervigt emot de Utländske, förmedelst en Trögare Arbets-drift* (On the inferiority of the Swedish compared to foreign manufacturers because of a slower work organization), Stockholm.

4. Accounting for Intangibles: Issues and Prospects
Graham Vickery

This chapter focuses on key issues surrounding business investment in and use of intangibles and intellectual capital.[1] Although it has long been recognised that intangibles are crucial elements for value creation and growth of firms, industries and countries, they have not been identified, measured and reported adequately at firm level and generally have not been well-identified statistically at aggregate sector or national level. Intangibles can be measured in terms of inputs, or investments and effort to add value to economic activities, or they can be measured in terms of the assets created by such investments and effort. All contribute to the value creation process.

On the investment and expenditure side, a particular set of intangibles that appear to give rise to the most useful set of assets have captured attention. They comprise investments in: R&D, innovation and technology development; training and education of workers; internal organisational structures and external supplier, customer and institutional networks; market exploration and development; and software and information technology. Of these, investment and asset-formation in R&D and innovation, software and information technology, and training and human resources have most often been the focus for business strategists, policy-makers and statisticians.

The chapter sets out to discuss some aspects of the literature on various aspects of intangibles, and to summarise selected measurement and reporting issues surrounding intangibles. The structure of the chapter is as follows. The importance and relative lack of information on

---

[1] The terms intangibles and intellectual capital are used to capture the same set of investment activities and outputs in this chapter. However, the terms often have separate definitions and are used differently, intangibles having a more accounting and balance sheet orientation and intellectual capital being more oriented towards human resources and human capital measurement. More important are the misleading distinctions between intangible assets and tangible assets, excluding most expenditures on intangible from being classified as investments. See e.g. Hill (1999).

intangibles and the knowledge economy is first sketched out, both at aggregate and enterprise level. This is followed by discussion of the need for improved information on intangibles. Then follows a review of some aspects of the measuring and accounting treatment of intangibles, and finally there is a brief presentation of some solutions which may help to improve information on intangibles for the purposes of firm decision making, resource allocation and improved public-policy making.

Aggregate information on intangibles

Intangible investment appears to be increasingly important as economies shift from being based on production using resource-intensive physical capital towards being more technology and knowledge-intensive. At aggregate level, this is reflected in many OECD countries in the increasing share of investment that goes to intangibles. Figure 4.1 summarises some of the broad trends which can be seen in available but limited aggregate data for a wide range of countries (OECD, 1999a).

These investment variables and data can be summarised as follows. Investment takes various forms, all of which are necessary for economic growth, productivity gains and increases in wealth. Investments in intangibles are the basis for the development and application of knowledge, for innovation and for the productive development and use of new technologies. Physical investment, which mainly covers expenditure for construction, machinery and equipment, allows the diffusion of new technology, especially in manufacturing industries. Investment in knowledge-related intangibles at aggregate level can be partly but imperfectly captured in expenditures on a limited set of intangibles comprising R&D, investment in software and public spending on education. Only including this limited set of intangibles amounts to 8% of OECD-wide GDP, a level similar to investment in equipment across all OECD countries.

Moreover, if intangibles investment data which are not generally available at country level, such as business expenditures on education, training, firm organisation and market development, were included in the measure of investment in knowledge-related intangibles, the total spend would be well over 10% of GDP across all OECD countries. If other intangibles were included the figure would be higher again. Furthermore, since the mid-1980s, investment in knowledge and intangibles has grown somewhat more rapidly than GDP in the OECD area, indicating the shift towards economies which are built on new kinds of investments and the exploitation of new kinds of assets to create value. For a longer

74 *Intangibles: A General Framework*

discussion of which intangibles can be identified, measured and compared at national and international level see Croes (1998).

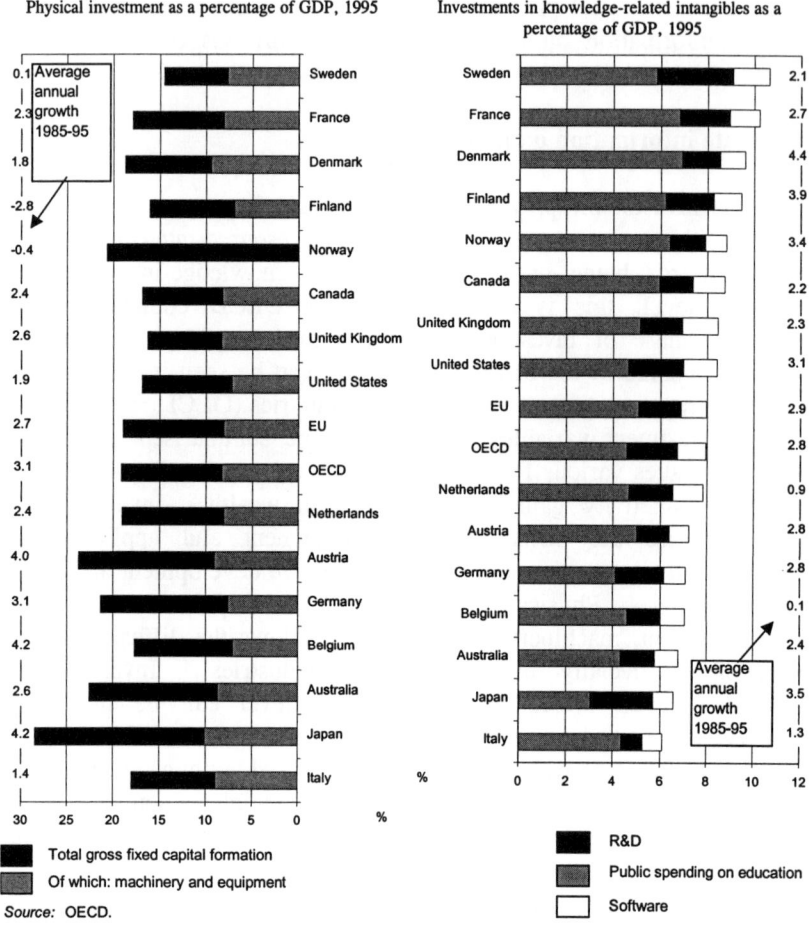

Figure 4.1: *Investment in tangibles and knowledge-related intangibles*

These trends from aggregate OECD data across a large number of countries are confirmed in some recent attempts for individual countries to measure the growth of intangibles by a variety of means. For example, a study in the United States using data similar to that described above shows that R&D and advertising expenditures have been a rising share of non-financial corporate gross domestic product particularly since the mid-1970s. If executive time, creativity costs and software were included, this share would be much higher (Nakamura, 1999). A recent study in

Australia using other approaches has shown that in the 50 years from 1947 to 1998, estimated intangible enterprise capital as a ratio of all enterprise capital has grown at an average annual rate of 1.3% (from balance sheet estimates of intangible capital). Furthermore, the proportion of the labour force engaged in direct production of enterprise intangible capital doubled from 1971 to reach some 22% in 1996 (Webster, 1999).

The growth of the knowledge economy

These developments are further captured in the shift towards knowledge-based industries. There are many definitions of knowledge-based industries and activities. The "knowledge economy" is an intuitively appealing concept, but one that is difficult to define in simple operational terms, and measure and explain in a convincing way.

The difficulty of defining the "knowledge economy" at the end of the twentieth century is akin to the task of describing the industrial revolution two centuries ago. It is difficult to define because there are no obvious physical frames of reference, and because knowledge is generated, stocked, diffused, used and depreciated differently from other production factors and it has quite different economic, often non-exclusive, characteristics from physical capital (for a discussion, see for example OECD, 1996).

"Knowledge" is nothing new however. It is what drives technical change and technological progress and it is the harnessing and application of knowledge, which drove the Industrial Revolution forward. Nor is the economic value of knowledge anything new; it is embodied in a more or less explicit or implicit way in everything from machinery, intellectual and industrial property rights, the way that firms are organised, and the way that markets are developed. However, the emergence and reinforcement of knowledge as a much more important factor in the economy has potentially enormous implications for what constitutes wealth, for who owns and controls it, and is bound to change the way that firms and industries are organised and function. It is in this climate that strategies aiming to increase the visibility of "intellectual capital" – one of the bases of value creation in a knowledge economy – have been described for example as "at best, useless. At worst, 'stakeholder' meddling" (Rutledge, 1998).

Nonetheless, there is increasing evidence of various kinds which points towards an emerging, large and growing "knowledge economy". Furthermore, enterprises, governments and society cannot ignore the business and policy implications of the emergence of this knowledge economy. For example:

> The production, diffusion and use of technology and information are key to economic activity and sustainable growth. This is of course not new, but the role of knowledge (as compared with natural resources, physical capital and low-skill labour) has taken on greater importance. Although the pace may differ, all OECD countries are moving towards a knowledge-based economy. Knowledge increases the value of equipment, workers, firms and public bodies.... (OECD, 1999a).

This observation is backed up by a variety of aggregate measures:

- The broadly defined group of sectors aggregated to form knowledge-based industries and services (sectors with high R&D activity, high ICT use and/or a significant proportion of highly skilled workers) accounted for more than 50% of OECD business value added in the mid-1990s, rising from around 45% in the mid-1980s. These industries include a considerable range of services which use advanced technology and that employ highly-skilled workers, including finance, insurance and business services, which account for the biggest share in all countries, as well as health and education in the business sector. See Figure 4.2 (OECD, 1999a).

Figure 4.2: Knowledge-based industry and services

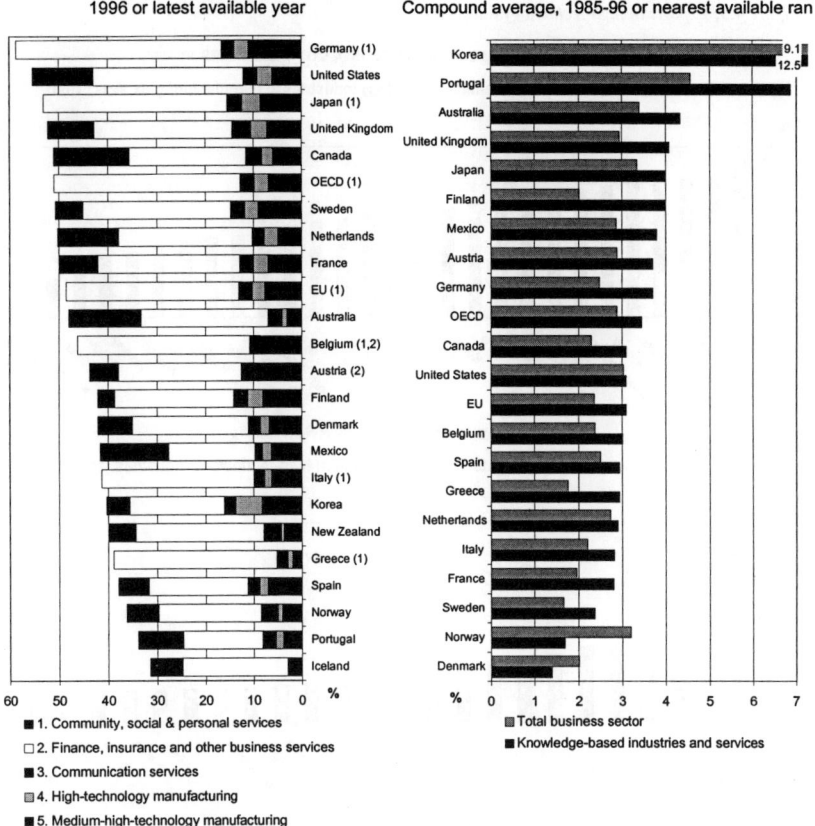

1. Community, social & personal services included in Finance, insurance and other business services.
2. High-technology manufacturing included in Medium-high-technology manufacturing.
Source: OECD.

- The value of high technology exports from OECD countries has grown considerably over the last decade or so, exceeding the growth rates in all other manufacturing areas. Between 1990 and 1996, exports by OECD countries of high-technology industries (aerospace, computers, electronics, pharmaceuticals) and medium-high-technology industries (such as cars or chemicals) grew by 7% a year, as compared with 5% for other types of goods. Furthermore, the share of high- and medium-high- technology industries in exports of manufactured goods is substantially higher than their share in production, reflecting a higher degree of internationalisation in their supply and demand patterns (Figure 4.3, OECD 1999a).

Figure 4.3: Exports in high-technology industries

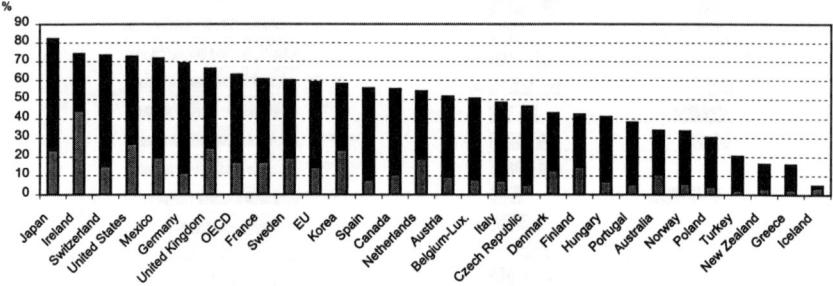

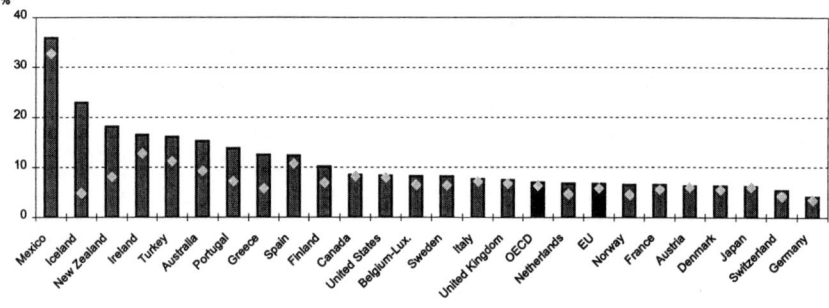

Source: OECD.

- Investment in information and communication technologies (IT hardware, software, services and telecommunications expenditure) by OECD countries on average was almost 7% of GDP (US$ 1.6 trillion in 1997), and these expenditures have grown steadily in the OECD region, by over 6% a year since 1992 with high recent growth. Telecommunications accounts for a large share of ICT expenditures. (Figure 4.4, OECD 1999a).

Figure 4.4: ICTs

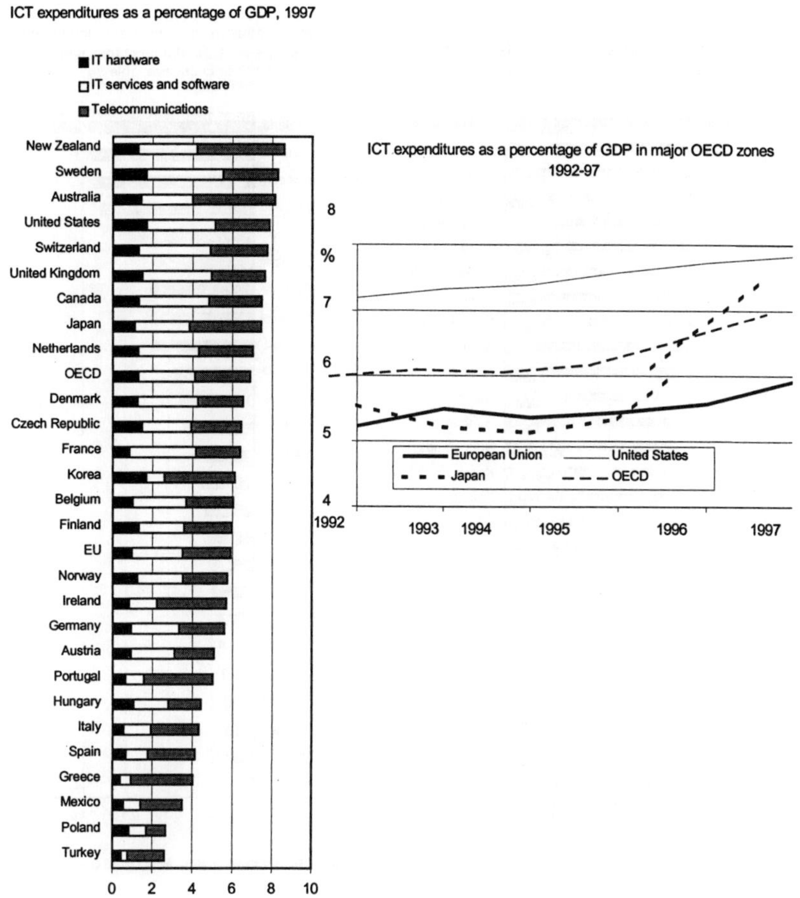

- Finally the composition of employment is shifting markedly towards white-collar occupations and higher levels of qualifications, and the quality of human resources is the major factor behind the invention and diffusion of technology. Measures of educational attainment are the most commonly used proxies for human capital, despite their imperfections, as they do not cover quality of schooling and formal or on-the-job training are missed. Despite considerable heterogeneity higher levels of qualifications are increasing (Figure 4.5, OECD 1999a).

Figure 4.5: Human resources

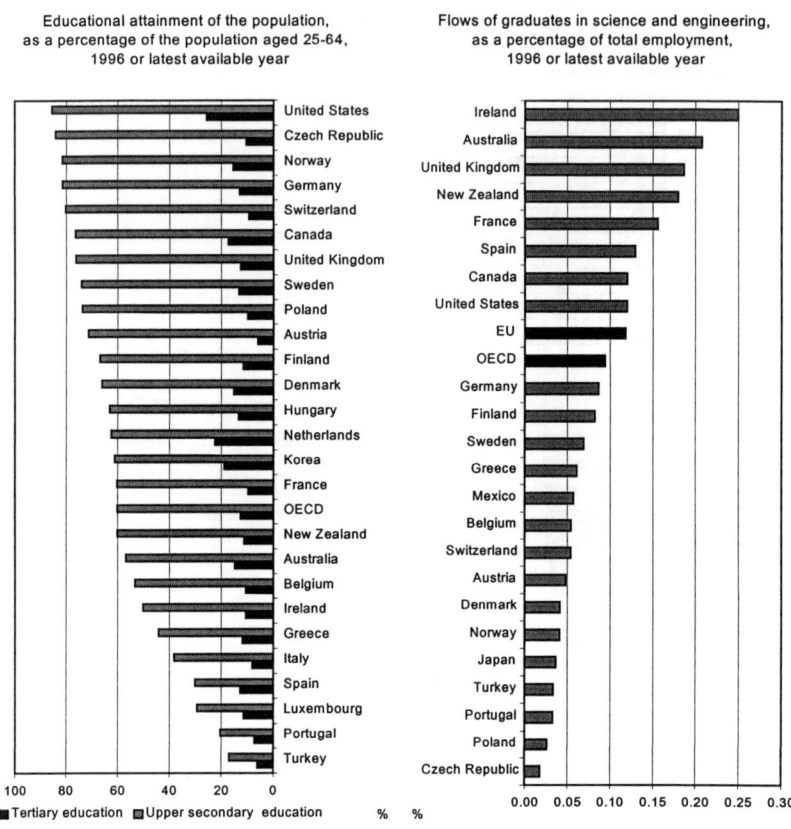

These measures, although partial, give some indications of the shift towards knowledge-based economies and the importance of knowledge and intangibles in driving these economies forward.

The knowledge economy at the level of the enterprise

These measures of the development of the knowledge economy at aggregate level are a reflection of changes in the process of value creation at firm level. Enterprises have changed business strategies, structure and behaviour and are placing an increasing premium on technology, skills, organisation, markets, and software, even if economic theory and government statistics have not adequately kept up with a great deal of the micro-economic reality of the emerging knowledge economy.

Surveys of micro-economic enterprise behaviour in a number of OECD countries have identified more clearly the changes in business strategy, corporate structure, work organisation and external relationships that enterprises are adopting. These surveys have in many cases been designed to evaluate the extent to which enterprises are creating "high performance workplaces" (which incorporate various elements of knowledge management), and reorganising themselves around new skill strategies, technology, IT and market development, and the impact of such innovations on enterprise performance. Two broad strategies have generally been identified: new forms of work organisation to better exploit technology; and more attention being given to investing in and managing intangible assets linked to technology and human resources. These strategies have been characterised as being "high skill, high trust" work practices and workplaces. In particular the strategies display several distinct features, which typify the knowledge economy and its greater accent on intangibles:

- marked specialisation of enterprises or business units (focus on "core activities");
- effective use of technology;
- employees are better trained and more responsive;
- multi-skilling and job rotation increase, blurring differences between traditional work activities;
- increasingly flattened hierarchies in which greater importance is accorded to horizontal communication and horizontal links, with less importance attached to vertical or hierarchical ones;
- information is gathered at more levels and channelled less hierarchically;
- authority to act is less dependent on hierarchical models of authority;
- small self-managing or autonomous work groups are common and take more responsibility;
- horizontal inter-firm links for subcontracting (purchase of components or services that are part of the final product) or outsourcing (purchasing supporting business services, transport, cleaning, cafeteria or other ancillary services) (OECD 1998a).

These work organisation innovations tend to be found in about a quarter of all enterprises or establishments surveyed. Such innovations are more likely to be found in larger firms, those in more competitive product markets, and those producing high technology and knowledge-intensive goods and services. It appears that there are considerable differences in the incidence and use of these practices from country to country nonetheless (OECD, 1999b). Moreover, though it is difficult to prove causal impacts, there are strong associations between the above average use of various strategies and tactics associated with better knowledge management and flexible organisation, and company performance measures such as output growth, sales, productivity, profitability and customer satisfaction. These practices are also linked with various incentive compensation schemes, such as profit sharing and pay linked with skills and flexibility in working time practices (see, for example, OECD 1997, 1999b, and Bassi and van Buren, 1998 and 1999).

To complement the deployment of intangible assets within firms, a wide range of strategic services industries have developed. These strategic services provide external inputs and complements to internally generated intangibles, and are essential for business processes, firm competitiveness and growth.

These business services comprise: computer software and information processing services, research and development and technical services, marketing services, business organisation services (management consultancy and labour recruitment services) and human resource development services. Business services, and strategic business services in particular, have shown rapid growth and strong employment generation in the recent past in the OECD countries. Strategic business services employed directly at least 11 million people in OECD countries in the mid-1990s and generated turnover in excess of US$ 1 100 billion. For comparison, this employment is well over twice as many as are employed in the entire motor vehicle producing industry in OECD countries.

These services have been growing at around 10% per year in current terms so that their combined turnover in 1999 is likely to be close to US$ 1 500 billion. In turnover terms, computer services are the most important, generating US$ 350 billion turnover in the mid-1990s. Of the 11 million employed in these activities, business organisation services represented the most important employer, employing 3.6 million in personnel recruitment services and 1.5 million in management consultancy (see OECD, 1999c).

The strong performance of strategic business services has been driven by a range of factors, including:

- the rise of the knowledge-based economy, which relies on more expertise and specialised service inputs;

- the need for greater flexibility within firms;
- specialisation and increased division of labour in many areas;
- outsourcing by established firms; and
- the growth of smaller production units and firms using external services to supplement internal resources.

All of these factors are associated with the shift towards an economic system where intellectual capital and intangible assets are the driving forces for value creation, economic growth and enhanced productivity.

But what of the knowledge base and knowledge management in individual firms?

Although the growth of expenditures on intangibles and intellectual capital and strategic business services are encouraging, how well do firms identify and measure their "new" assets and how well are they able to more systematically manage knowledge? The 1997 Knowledge Management Survey, an international survey sponsored by the Journal of Knowledge Management, in association with the Best Practice Club™ and the Benchmarking Exchange, collected results from a sample in which the vast majority of respondents (92%) reported to be working for "knowledge-intensive" organisations. The results of this survey showed that:

- Only 6% of respondents described their organisations as being "very effective" in using and multiplying knowledge to improve business performance.
- Only 12% of respondents reported their organisations as being extremely good or very good at facilitating knowledge growth through enterprise culture and incentives.
- Only 9% were extremely good or very good at embedding new knowledge in the organisation.
- Only 3% were extremely good or very good at measuring the value of knowledge assets.

Furthermore, it would seem that these relatively poor results are not due to a lack of concern with knowledge management. A survey of senior managers found that nearly two-fifths reported suffering costly mistakes due to employees lacking sufficient knowledge or expertise. A later survey of a broader cross-section of practitioners found nearly 90%

reporting costly mistakes for those reasons (Chase, 1997).

The lack of progress is not due to lack of top-level commitment. Another survey by the American Society for Training and Development found that more than three-fifths of top executives found intellectual capital to be an important issue. But one of the main conclusions was that managers are still a long way from being able to identify, measure and manage more effectively intellectual capital and knowledge. "Measurement is a critical issue for executives...What intellectual capital managers are searching for are measurable aspects of their work as well as new types of measurement that will be acceptable to the financial and investment community" (Bassi, 1997).

There is, moreover, substantial anecdotal evidence of companies adopting strategies that range from more systematic management of intellectual property rights (patents and copyrights); to assessment of skills and competencies of workers; to organisational changes and restructuring; to communication strategies to improve links and feedback across operating divisions and hierarchical boundaries. These are all aimed at identifying, measuring and managing various aspects of knowledge, intangibles and intellectual capital. A summary of examples can be found in Gallagher (1997); and for detailed case studies and models used in measuring and managing intellectual capital, see Skyrme, (1998).

More recently, considerable evidence has been gathered on the approaches of firms to improve measurement and management of intellectual capital. These include the balanced scorecard approach (see Johanson *et al.* 1999, Ernst & Young 1999); accounting approaches (Canibano *et al.*, 1999); and ad hoc measurements of what firms can actually do to identify and report their intellectual capital and intangibles coherently and consistently (Danish Trade and Industry Development Council, 1997). See also the collection of papers from the 1999 OECD Amsterdam Symposium (OECD, 1999d).

However, despite much activity, it has remained dispersed overall, with a diversity of competing approaches and rather little comparability in the way that intangibles and intellectual capital, and hence the knowledge base, is identified and measured. Slow progress in making knowledge management operational at the level of the enterprise translates into an uneven transition to the knowledge economy. The slow pace stems in substantial part from the substantive complexity of the ideas embodied in "knowledge management", unclear definitions and limitations on measurement. These in turn feed a confusing competition of ideas and philosophies about how far and in what ways knowledge can be defined, measured, reported and managed.

From the point of view of governments, important issues arise in the midst of all this. These include ideas about economic measures of investment and output. If aggregate expenditures on intangibles were treated in the same way as expenditures on tangible assets, this would raise measures of business investment and would also raise measured production of goods and services and GDP, and hence standards of living. Such changes would also affect aggregate measures of productivity and productivity growth, and hence their links to national competitiveness.

Need for information on intangible assets

From the preceding discussion, it is clear that intangibles and intellectual capital are increasingly important, despite being poorly identified and measured at both firm level and at more aggregate levels. Furthermore, there seems to be a clear community of interest to improve information on intangible assets.

Two main classes of users of information on intangibles can be identified: managers, employees and other users inside firms; and investors and lenders, financial analysts, statisticians and government policy-makers outside firms.

Use inside the firm

The increasing need for better information inside firms is demonstrated by attempts to provide metrics for various indicators of intangibles, and, more importantly, for improved ways of measuring the links between these intangibles and various measures of enterprise performance. This is also shown by the considerable consultant and advisory industry which has grown up, to provide firms with a myriad of approaches to improve management of technology, knowledge, organisation, markets, information, quality and the like. Many of these approaches are based on devising ways of identifying, measuring, reporting and using information on intangibles. But they have tended to be very different and at best national in focus if they are pursued by national administrations. Or, alternatively, they may be beset by individualised and partial approaches such as some of the "knowledge management" packages offered by consultants, who often wish to differentiate their products and hence their measurement and reporting strategies from each other, leading to fragmentation and lack of comparability and stability in reporting.

Some of the many attempts to improve information inside firms have been extensively reviewed very recently in a set of country studies and literature overviews focusing on firm-level identification and reporting of intangibles and intellectual capital prepared for the 1999 OECD Amsterdam Symposium on Measuring and Reporting Intellectual Capital (see OECD 1999d).

Various approaches to identifying indicators of intellectual capital or intangibles and measuring their value and links with firm performance are under experimentation. Research teams that participated in the work have used a variety of approaches to examine different aspects of firm-level management and reporting in Australia, Austria, Canada (two reports), Denmark, Finland, France, Germany, Ireland, Italy, Japan, Netherlands (four reports), Norway, Spain, Sweden, the United Kingdom (two reports) and the United States. They identified five broad categories of intangible investment where experiments in measurement and reporting are taking place at firm level, but in all of which improvements are needed: (1) technology (e.g. research and development, patents), (2) human resources (e.g. training), (3) organisational capital (e.g. management and business strategies and networks), (4) marketing and reputational capital (e.g. brands, marks) and (5) information technology (e.g. software).

The work employed three broad approaches to gathering information on measuring and reporting intellectual capital:

- case studies of a few particular firms;
- surveys of large numbers of firms, use of administrative data furnished by firms and/or annual reports and other forms of information disclosed by firms; and
- reviews of literature on theory from different disciplines with a bearing on the importance of intangibles and/or the role of information in improving decision making.

Different analytical approaches to evaluating the importance of intellectual capital included:

- seeking the views of different actors (managers, investors, financial analysts);
- correlations between measures of flows and stocks of intellectual capital and company performance; and
- multivariate techniques examining relationships between variables such as measures of flows and stocks, and reporting/ disclosure practices, on the one hand, and company performance, in terms of profitability and/or market capitalisation, on the other.

The overall results from the review of the available information and of the most comprehensive set of case studies available, is that, as yet, information on intellectual capital is neither adequately measured nor reported by companies, and is not transparent, reliable or comparable. Continuing experimentation in measurement and reporting is needed as it would aid in developing a framework for collecting information on intellectual capital as well as for understanding its role in value creation and firm performance.

Use outside the firm

Outside the firm there is increasing evidence of investor interest in getting a much better view of the current and future value of intangibles and their likely links to the performance of firms.

This is in part driven by the increasing divergence between market values and book asset values of firms (increasing value of Tobin's q) and the rising value of technology and knowledge-intensive firms, where it is just as misleading if intangibles are overvalued as if they are undervalued. Market-to-book ratios of public companies in the United States (and most other countries) have been tending upwards, with the yearly medians breaking 1.00 around 1980, then averaging around 1.6 from the mid-1980s through up until the early 1990s, and subsequently moving higher (Lev and Zarowin, 1998).

At the same time, there has been a continuous decrease over the last 20 years in the extent of association between stock prices and returns on one hand, and key financial statement variables, such as earnings and cash flow, as well as for book values (Lev, 1999). Multivariate analyses examining the relationship between earnings and variation in share value for US companies have shown that, over time, the relationship has weakened substantially. While reported earnings accounted for nearly a quarter of the variation in share price performance in the period 1954-60, they accounted for less than 8% during the period 1981-91. This has been accompanied by increasing volatility, as measured by the frequency and extent of firms changing size rankings, which also suggests that the informativeness of financial information has decreased.

Furthermore, the association between earnings and stock returns appears in the United States to have decreased most sharply for firms which have experienced large increases in R&D intensity (Lev, 1999). Though it has been argued on theoretical grounds that the efficiency of capital markets cannot be evaluated entirely on the basis of whether share prices are related in the short run to expected earnings and underpinning fundamentals, the empirical evidence that they are efficient is ambiguous (Tease, 1993). This further suggests that better information on intellectual capital and intangibles would at the very least reduce the deterioration in the usefulness of firm information as a key to guiding returns to investors.

To back this up, various surveys of investors have shown that their greatest unmet needs for information include information in the areas of intellectual capital and intangibles, and that these are also the areas which have the greatest opportunities for improvement. Examples of these surveys show conclusively that large institutional investors are increasingly looking for improved disclosure from major corporations in a variety of areas, but particularly in areas such as intellectual capital. But this is where reporting and disclosure is weakest under present accounting rules and with the present system of annual and corporate reports. For example one sample of large, mainly international, firms showed that only 8% of them disclosed information on intellectual capital, and yet this is an area where large investors are looking for more information (Taylor, 1998).

Similar reviews of information disclosed by the Fortune 500 companies in the United States shows equally little information on important variables such as human resources. For example annual reports for the year 1996 showed that for human resources, at best only one half of the total reports even gave useful information as to number of employees, and 15% gave no information at all. On training only 6% were informative and two-thirds gave no information at all, and disclosure for a range of other critical human resource issues (productivity, pay for performance, labour relations, safety, diversity, etc.) was even more sparse or non-existent (O'Connor, 1998).

A similar recent survey of major UK fund managers suggested that problems of ignorance and uncertainty in stock selection and in asset allocation decisions are exacerbated by an ever-larger intellectual capital and intangibles component to share prices. Fund managers have increasing incentives to directly contact senior management to discuss sources of value creation. Future orientated information on human capital, intellectual capital and intangibles was a significant part of the private information-gaining agenda of fund managers, providing inside knowledge advantages to fund managers, and raising significant questions regarding information asymmetries (Holland, 1999).

Furthermore, the role of major investors and financial analysts is increasing in a world where intellectual capital is increasingly important but poorly reported and disclosed in conventional accounts. An analysis of telephone conference calls among financial analysts and high-tech companies suggests that as traditional financial statements become less relevant, informal communications channels such as conference calls will become ever more important. This is particularly the case for technology companies, where information on new products (and related R&D and customer information) are the most common kind of information pursued, with attendant problems related to the quality of new kinds of restricted information, and inside information (Tasker, 1998).

There is also some research showing that financial analysts and other market agents having access to non-financial information sources beyond financial reports augment the information for investors, particularly for high-tech companies. But even here, there is evidence that over time there has been a decrease in the quality of information available to capital markets, increasing the cost of capital for firms and increasing problems of resource allocation (Lev, 1999).

Finally, non-financial elements which are either intangibles, or which have major intangibles-related attributes such as staff, products, new activities, clients, markets and brands, are the ones where information is most needed for mergers and acquisitions, alliances and similar strategies. Such strategies play a significant role in the rationalisation of productive activity and value creation of firms, but they are beset with lack of information in key areas.

Does financial accounting practice help?

Despite the clear need for improved information on intangibles and intellectual capital inside and outside enterprises, formal financial accounting and reporting practices are not particularly informative on intangibles.

In general, intangibles are not capitalised and therefore do not appear on the balance sheet. This applies to almost all intangibles in almost all countries. Reasons for this are due to recognition and measurement issues. Recognition may take a variety of forms, but essentially the principle is that intangibles should be separable, that is, the asset must be separable from other assets without compromising the activities of the firm, or, at the very least, it should be separately identifiable. Considering that intangibles are often "bundled" together to be useful, this causes considerable problems of recognition.

The situation regarding accounting treatment of intangibles in the early 1990s is summarised in Table 4.1. For a very similar listing and description in the mid-1990s, see European Commission (1996).

Accounting treatment is relatively stable and the picture has not changed a great deal in the 1990s. The table shows that intangible assets *could* broadly be recognised for capitalisation purposes, except for human resource training. However, in practice there are strict criteria to be met before the intangible item can be recognised as an intangible asset, and most intangible items are excluded as assets.

Intangible assets are recognised at cost in financial statements, if, and only if, strict definition criteria (e.g. advertising, training, start-up, research and development activities), and recognition criteria are passed. The following criteria are adapted from the International Accounting Standards Committee (IASC, 1998), but similar approaches are adopted across individual countries. Recognition criteria include: (a) the asset must be identifiable, controlled and clearly distinguishable from enterprise goodwill, (b) it is probable that future economic benefits attributable to the asset will flow to the enterprise, and (c) the cost of the asset can be measured reliably. These requirements apply whether the asset is acquired externally or generated internally. If the intangible item does not meet definitions and criteria then the expenditure must be recognised as an expense when it is incurred.

Application of the definitions and recognition criteria means that most intangibles, and in particular R&D, training, marketing and advertising, are recognised as expenses. For R&D some kinds of development costs can be capitalised in some countries (see Table 4.2). Some software development expenditure may result in the recognition of an intangible asset, for example internally developed computer software, following the same approach as for purchase of software. In the European Union, the Fourth European Directive (Articles 9, 10 and 37) allows companies to capitalise their costs of R&D as an intangible asset, or expense them immediately in their income statement. But, again, criteria are strict and in most cases firms do not capitalise. Italy is one of the few exceptions, allowing capitalisation of most intangibles (including R&D, training, marketing and advertising) and capitalisation is common in Italy for marketing and advertising (European Commission, 1996).

Where firms do have choices in intangibles accounting and reporting between capitalisation and expensing and between disclosure and non-disclosure, the overall choice is for non-disclosure, and often for expensing. Recent analysis in Belgium has highlighted this choice for firms active in R&D. Only 30% of the firms active in R&D in a sample of 321 firms disclosed the amount of R&D spend in their financial statements. Disclosure is determined by firm organisational characteristics such as formal R&D departments, high R&D intensity,

R&D co-operation and by poor financial performance. About 30% of firms disclosing choose not to capitalise, and those capitalising are more likely to be R&D intensive, and have losses, using capitalisation to avoid cutting R&D budgets. So overall, conventional financial accounting practice is not likely to provide large amounts of information across firms on such crucial inputs for growth as research and development. Furthermore, some firms will disclose information without capitalising expenditures, whereas many active R&D performers will not disclose expenditures, and firms use the capitalisation/expensing decision to avoid cutting R&D when making losses (Gaeremynck and Veugelers, 1999).

On the other hand purchased brands, copyrights, patents and licences and goodwill are generally capitalised. These are quite commonly capitalised in OECD countries and appear on the balance sheet in the financial statements, as they can be readily identified, controlled, distinguished, valued and traded, and future economic benefits attributable to these assets will flow to the enterprise.

National accounts and the international statistical framework follow similar practices. In the 1993 System of National Accounts (SNA) some core items of intangible investment are deemed to be economic assets. These are assets over which ownership rights are enforced by institutional units, individually and collectively; and from which economic benefits may be derived by their owners by holding them and using them over time. Capital items include software and rights, along with subscriptions to databases, patents and goodwill. Non-capital items are R&D, training and marketing, along with engineering and design, organisational development, innovation and other human resource development (OECD, 1998b).

Overall, apart from software, intangibles are not treated in a way that encourages their separate identification and measurement in national accounts. Nevertheless, proposals are made for some intangible items to be separately available in the SNA (notably R&D, but also other items), for example in functional classifications such as the "outlays of producers by purpose" or satellite accounts. The recent Central Product Classification adopts broadly the same approach as the SNA, with little distinction of almost all intangible items as intangible assets. The group of intangible assets only comprises financial assets and liabilities and non-financial intangible assets (patents, trademarks, copyrights, and other similar exclusive rights), although R&D, training and human resource development, organisational structure services, marketing and software activities and services are all well-identified (United Nations, 1998).

Tax rules and the ability to charge expenditures on intangibles against current revenues strongly influence accounting treatment. As described above, where intangibles are recognised as assets, this is mostly limited, for example for development (but not research) or software projects (once they are technically feasible). But there has been a general shift wherever possible, towards expensing rather than capitalising across assets and activities. There is considerable anecdotal evidence that firms will take advantage of accounting rules to expense, and write off intangibles wherever possible. For example in the United States (and other countries) when companies acquire other firms, they should enter the resulting "goodwill" - the excess of the purchase price over the cost of the tangible assets - on their balance sheets. This goodwill must then be amortised for lengthy periods (normally five years in many European countries and Japan, 20 years in Australia and the United Kingdom, and 40 years in Canada and the United States). However, large amounts of such expenditures can be written off as purchased intangibles - for example as purchased "in-process" R&D assets which can be immediately deducted - which reduces assets and makes returns on assets larger than they would otherwise be.

There are also measurement issues arising between cost-based approaches, which are usually conservative and backward-looking, based on opportunity costs of resources used, and valuations-based approaches drawing on likely future benefits to be derived from intangible and intellectual capital assets. Measurement raises fundamental questions regarding the purposes of company accounts, and particularly the balance sheet, in dynamic knowledge-based economies. This further suggests that the focus should perhaps not be on conventional financial reporting, and the balance sheet, but more on designing dynamic forward-looking frameworks which capture the essence of the process of value creation in knowledge economies.

Table 4.1: Nature of intangible assets recognised: early 1990s

	Research & development expenditure	Computer software	Formation expenses	Human resources training	Patents/ trade marks/ brands/licences/ publishing rights etc.	Purchased goodwill
AUSTRALIA	YES	ng	ng	NO	YES	YES
BELGIUM	YES	ng	YES	NO (R&D only)	YES	YES
CANADA	YES	ng	ng	ng	YES	YES
FRANCE	YES	YES	YES	NO (1)	YES	YES
GERMANY	NO	ng	YES	NO	YES	YES
ITALY	YES	YES	YES	YES	YES	YES
JAPAN	YES	YES	YES	NO	YES	YES
LUXEMBOURG	YES	ng	YES	NO	YES	YES
NETHERLANDS	YES	YES	YES	NO	YES	YES
PORTUGAL	YES	YES	YES	NO	YES	YES
SWEDEN	YES	YES	ng	NO	YES	YES
SWITZERLAND	YES	ng	YES	ng	ng	YES
TURKEY	ng	ng	YES	ng	YES	YES
UNITED KINGDOM	YES	YES	ng	NO (2)	YES	YES
UNITED STATES	NO	YES	ng	NO	YES	YES
EUROPEAN UNION	YES	ng	YES	NO	YES	YES
IASC	YES	YES	YES	YES	YES	YES

Notes: (1) Unless results in new items/increased value of items.
(2) Unless generating future revenues.
Ng = not given.
Source: OECD Summary of questionnaire responses: Roundtable on intangible assets: accounting and disclosure issues. 21-22/05/1991, Working document

Table 4.2: Measurement of research and development

	Asset with amortisation	Asset without amortisation	Immediate write-off against income
AUSTRALIA	YES	NO	YES
BELGIUM	YES	NO	YES
CANADA	YES - restricted to development costs	NO	YES
FRANCE	YES - restricted to development costs	NO	YES
GERMANY	NO	NO	YES
ITALY	YES	NO	YES
JAPAN	YES	NO	YES
NETHERLANDS	YES - restricted to development costs	NO	YES
PORTUGAL	YES	NO	YES
SWEDEN	YES	NO	YES
SWITZERLAND	YES - restricted to development costs	NO	YES
UNITED KINGDOM	YES - restricted to development costs	NO	YES
UNITED STATES	NO	NO	YES
EUROPEAN UNION	YES	NO	YES
IASC	YES - restricted to development costs	NO	YES - except development costs

Source: OECD Summary of questionnaire responses: Roundtable on intangible assets: accounting and disclosure issues. 21-22/05/1991, Working document.

Alternative ways forward

Despite these difficulties, a number of alternative ways forward are being tested which are likely to help to improve information on the intangible assets fundamental for growth, thereby enhancing market efficiency and resource allocation. These approaches are based on the premises that:

- there is a need for better information on intangibles and intellectual capital and their relation with value creation, focusing on areas that matter most for company performance;
- there is a need for structured experimentation, systematic monitoring and evaluation to improve information; and
- general principles or guidelines could prove useful for reporting key indicators of intangibles and information on value creation in the knowledge economy.

Alternative approaches being tested include:

- In financial reporting, recent proposals to clarify and somewhat extend financial reporting of intangibles, for example as reflected in the IASC International Accounting Standard 38 Intangible assets. However, despite the requirement to disclose R&D expenditures recognised as an expense (see below), due to the intrinsically conservative nature of financial accounting these proposals are likely to provide only limited extension of recognition, measurement and reporting of intangibles. Furthermore, complete international acceptance of IAS is not assured;
- In non-financial reporting, proposals by the International Organisation of Securities Commissions (IOSCO) regarding non-financial statement disclosure standards for cross-border offerings and listings by foreign issuers contain some elements which may be useful in extending the reporting of intangibles (IOSCO, 1998);
- At national level, requiring more detailed reporting of current expenditures in company income/profit and loss statements, for example reporting expenditures on R&D, acquired in-process technology, training expenditures, etc.
- Harmonising and improving comparability of management discussion and analysis reporting and similar reporting. Different countries already require a considerable amount of information in notes to the accounts and annual reports. This has been given considerable impetus by the recent spate of principles and guidelines for corporate

governance disclosure (see OECD, 1999e, Principles of Corporate Governance; CACG, 1999) and sustainability reporting (Global Reporting Initiative, 1999). Furthermore there have been considerable efforts to sketch out what new and forward-looking reporting of information on intangibles and value creation should look like (Institute of Chartered Accountants in England & Wales, 1998, Price Waterhouse, 1997);

- Using safe-harbour legislation to lessen the threat of litigation regarding forward-looking information, including information on intangibles;
- Encouraging structured experimentation at firm level to identify, measure and report intangibles for internal management of resources and for external users, to provide a broad base of good practice for the development of valid, comparable and verifiable indicators of intangible assets.

References

Bassi, Laurie (1997), "Leveraging intellectual capital", *HR Executive Review,* Vol. 5, Number 3, p. 9.

Bassi, Laurie and Van Buren, Mark E. (1998 and 1999), *The State of the Industry Report,* Alexandria, Virginia, American Society for Training & Development.

Canibano, Leandro, García-Ayuso Covarsí, Manuel, and Sánchez, Paloma (1999), "The value relevance and managerial implications of intangibles: A literature review", at www.oecd.org/dsti/sti/industry/indcomp/act/Ams-conf/symposium.htm

Chase, Rory (1997), "The knowledge-based organization: An international survey", *The Journal of Knowledge Management,* Vol. 1, No. 1, September, pp. 38-49.

Commonwealth Association for Corporate Governance (1999), *CACG Guidelines. Principles for Corporate Governance in the Commonwealth,* Marlborough, New Zealand.

Croes, Michel (1998), *Intangible Investments. Definition and Data Source for Technological, Marketing, IT and Organisational Activities and Rights,* Central Bureau voor de Statistiek, Voorburg, The Netherlands.

Danish Trade and Industry Development Council (1997), *Intellectual Capital Accounts: Reporting and Managing Intellectual Capital,* translated from the original Danish, at

www.oecd.org/dsti/sti/industry/indcomp/act/Ams-conf/symposium.htm
Ernst & Young Center for Business Innovation (1999), "Measuring business performance", *Perspectives on Business Innovation*, Issue 2, sections: "Innovation in action", and "A blueprint for change", pp. 26-65.
European Commission, DGIII (1996), *The Influence of Accounting and Tax Rules on Corporate Investment Behaviour*, August, Appendix 1.
Eustace, Clark and Mortensen, Jørgen (1998), *Report of the Intellectual Capital Roundtable*, Centre for European Policy Studies, Brussels.
Gaeremynck, Ann and Veugelers, Reinhilde (1999), "An empirical analysis of the disclosure and capitalisation of research and development spending: Some results for Flanders", May.
Gallagher, Anne L. (1997), *Intellectual Capital: A Summary of Corporate Initiatives*, Alexandria, Virginia, American Society for Training & Development.
Global Reporting Initiative (1999), *Sustainability Reporting Guidelines*, Boston.
Hill, Peter (1999), "Tangibles, intangibles and services: A new taxonomy for the classification of output", *Canadian Journal of Economics*, Vol. 32, No. 2.
Holland, John (1999), "Fund management, intellectual capital, intangibles and private disclosure", at www.oecd.org/dsti/sti/industry/indcomp/act/Ams-conf/symposium.htm
Institute of Chartered Accountants in England & Wales (1998), *The 21st Century Annual Report; Performance Measurement in the Digital Age; and Prototype plc*, London.
International Accounting Standards Committee (1998), *IAS 38: Intangible Assets*, at www.iasc.org.uk
International Organisation of Securities Commissions (IOSCO), (1998), "International Disclosure Standards for Cross-Border Offerings and Initial Listings by Foreign Issuers", at www.iosco.org/docs-public/1998-intnl_disclosure_standards.html.
Johanson, Ulf, Eklöv, Gunilla, Holmgren, Mikael, and Mårtensson, Maria (1999), "Human resource costing and accounting versus the balanced scorecard: A literature survey of experience with the concepts", at www.oecd.org/dsti/sti/industry/indcomp/act/Ams-conf/symposium.htm
Lev, Baruch (1999), "The inadequate public information on intellectual capital and its consequences", at
www.oecd.org/dsti/sti/industry/indcomp/act/Ams-conf/symposium.htm

Lev, Baruch and Zarowin, Paul (1998), "The boundaries of financial reporting and how to extend them", in *Measuring Intangible Investment*, at OECD intangibles web-site: www.oecd.org/dsti/sti/industry/indcomp/prod/intang.htm

Nakamura, Leonard (1999), "Intangibles: What put the *New* in the new economy?", *Business Review*, Federal Reserve Bank of Philadelphia, July/August.

O'Connor, Marleen (1998), "Rethinking corporate financial disclosure of human resource values in the knowledge economy", *Journal of Labor and Employment Law* (University of Pennsylvania), Vol. 1, Fall 1998, No. 2, pp. 527-613.

OECD (1991), Summary of questionnaire responses: Roundtable on intangible assets: accounting and disclosure issues. 21-22 May 1991, Working Document.

OECD (1996), *Technology, Productivity and Job Creation,* Vols. 1 and 2, Paris.

OECD (1997), *Lifelong Learning to Maintain Employability,* [OCDE/GD(97)162], Paris, OECD.

OECD (1998a), "High performance workplaces and intangible investment", Chapter 10 in *Technology, Productivity and Job Creation: Best Policy Practices,* Paris, p. 273.

OECD (1998b), "Treatment of the components of intangible investment in the 1993 system of national accounts", OECD Secretariat, Paper 6, at www.oecd.org/dsti/sti/industry/indcomp/prod/intang.htm

OECD (1999a), *The Knowledge-based Economy: A Set of Facts and Figures*, Paris, June.

OECD (1999b), *Employment Outlook*, Paris, Chapter 4.

OECD (1999c), *Strategic Business Services*, Paris. Countries covered in the publication are: Australia, Austria, Canada, Denmark, Finland, France, Germany, Ireland, Italy, Japan, Mexico, Netherlands, New Zealand, Norway, Portugal, Spain, Sweden, Switzerland, Turkey, the United Kingdom and the United States.

OECD (1999d), *International Symposium: Measuring and Reporting Intellectual Capital: Experience, Issues, and Prospects*, 9-11 June 1999, Amsterdam, www.oecd.org/dsti/sti/industry/indcomp/act/Ams-conf/symposium.htm

OECD (1999e), *OECD Principles of Corporate Governance*, Paris.

Price Waterhouse (1997), *Pursuing Value: The Emerging Art of Reporting on the Future*, USA.

Rutledge, John (1998), quoted in Skyrme, David, *Measuring the Value of*

Knowledge: Metrics for the Knowledge-based Business, London, Business Intelligence Ltd., p. 10.

Skyrme, David (1998), *Measuring the Value of Knowledge: Metrics for the Knowledge-based Business*, London, Business Intelligence Ltd.

Tasker, Sarah (1998), "Technology company conference calls: A small sample study", *The Journal of Financial Statement Analysis*, Fall, 1998.

Taylor, Shelley (1998), "Full disclosure 1998: New corporate governance for the global economy", Shelley Taylor & Associates, London.

Tease, Warren (1993), "The stock market and investment", in *OECD Economic Studies,* Paris, OECD, No. 20, Spring, pp. 41-63.

United Nations (1998), *Central Product Classification (CPC) Version 1.0*, New York.

Webster, Elisabeth (1999), "The growth of enterprise intangible investment", Melbourne Institute of Applied Economic and Social Research.

PART II

INTANGIBLES: IMPACT ON SECTORS AND ENTERPRISES

5. The Adaptive Capacity of the Firm as a Key to European Competitiveness
John Kay

Introduction

The world is, of course, changing. The deregulation of markets: the proliferation of computers in home and workplace: the emergence of global brands: constant shifts in the definition of industries and the boundaries of the firm. The competitive environment is changing and with it the structure of the firm.

The purpose of this chapter is to distinguish the essential from the evanescent. Some of what we see is, indeed, a fundamental change in the nature of the business environment. But we need to appreciate such changes without projecting every current trend into the indefinite future. A glance at the groaning shelves of the business section of the aircraft bookstall will confirm the difficulty.

There is one, overriding, theme in the arguments of this chapter. It is that the globalisation of business means that the structure of modern industry is based increasingly around competitive advantage, and that these competitive advantage, are more and more based on knowledge, intellectual capital and the management of information. These claims sound familiar. But their implications are not. Worked through carefully, they contradict most popular assertions about business trends.

The structure of this chapter is as follows.

Section 1 asks how changes in information technology change the nature of firm organisation and sources of competitive advantage. Section 2 describes some key aspects of the globalisation of product and capital markets, and the effect of this on the structure of firms. The section emphasises that the consequences of these trends arise directly from the ways in which the differentiation of firms, and social and cultural environments, relates to their competitive advantage.

Section 3 reviews more general changes in the nature and range of products available to consumers and asks how these influence firm organisation and sources of competitive advantage. Section 4 draws together the implications of sections 3 and 4 and describes how the origins of the differentiation have altered. Sections 5 and 6 develop some more specific consequences of these changes: widening inequalities of performance at industry, firm and individual level: opportunities for firms to focus on very limited portions of the value chain while yet deriving most of the competitive benefit associated with the process as a whole.

1. The information age

That we live in an information age is perhaps the most reiterated truism about modern society. It is particularly difficult here to penetrate the hype and understand the specific consequences for business organisation.

Economic growth increases the complexity of products and widens the range of products which is available with the result that consumers have a growing need for information. These effects on the demand for information are at least as important as the more widely emphasised supply factors which come from the much reduced costs of processing and transmitting information. The central point is that the information processing capacity of individuals, limited by the only slowly changing capacity of the human brain, does not expand in line with the quantity of information which is either necessary or potentially available.

Take retail financial services. There is justified concern among regulators that consumers have been poorly advised and insistence on fuller disclosure is seen as a remedy. The results of this are generally disappointing: not only is it difficult to package the information in comprehensible or comparable form but consumers take little interest in it when it is provided. This should not come as any great surprise, although it does. Consumers have neither the ability nor the inclination to process such information: that is why they sought the services of intermediaries in the first place.

The main mechanisms for processing information in this market – as in others – are supplier reputation and intermediary services. Few customers buy complex products, such as automobiles, on the basis of detailed specifications of model characteristics: they rely on manufacturer brand. The problem which has arisen in retail financial services is that supplier reputations proved not to be well founded, which is in the end acting to the detriment of the suppliers concerned.

Branding and reputation have grown in importance as consumers have found increasing need of signals of these kinds to enable them to navigate their way through product complexity. Initially of relevance mainly in business to consumer transactions, branding and reputation have gained significance in business to business transactions. It is worth emphasising that these factors operate not only between firms, but within firms themselves.

Intermediation as a response to problems of information management takes many forms. Retailers have always provided intermediary functions, narrowing the range of potential products and offering quality and suitability certification. Some industries have always been dominated by professional intermediaries – medicine or travel, for example. Publishers have sought out material of relevance to particular audiences and marketed it to them. We can now add electronic search engines to the list of forms of intermediation.

Thus the view sometimes expressed that changes in information technology will reduce the demand for intermediation by enabling consumers to access information directly is probably the reverse of the truth. It is likely that changing technology will displace older inefficient forms of intermediation – for example, organised search procedures on the internet may be more useful than poorly qualified clerks in travel agencies. But it is improbable that self-diagnosis based on electronic browsing will greatly erode the market share of doctors. The public has for long had access to medical textbooks, and rarely availed itself of the facility: in this market, above all, people seek trusted intermediaries.

The more likely development is a tiering of intermediation. Doctors for example already have access to far more information than they had before, and will increasingly themselves need help – both personal and electronic – in managing that information.

There are other issues at play here too. Discussion of the information age naturally focuses, given the extraordinary pace of change in information technology, on information which can be communicated by electronic means. Of equal significance to modern business, however, is tacit knowledge: knowledge how, rather than knowledge that, in Polanyi's famous distinction.

This is not "information" in the sense of physically readable, processable data. Indeed, the point here is that the role of innovation and information of this explicit kind is not necessarily the central factor in corporate success in the next century. The capacity of firms to replicate the innovations of their rivals is increased by the very fact of the greater availability of information. What is harder to replicate is the system which produces innovation in the first place and has the capacity to do so repeatedly. Such systems rely on tacit knowledge.

Tacit knowledge is commonly embedded in organisational routines, sustained by groups of employees and may be developed without any necessary understanding on the part of senior management, or even by those who themselves hold it, of its significance. Its relevance is greatest in knowledge based firms, as in professional services or some high tech industries: it often forms the basis of competitive advantage for the widely recognised clusters of small co-operating entities – from Silicon Valley to the tie manufacturers of Como and the shoemakers of Varese. It is a powerful source of competitive advantage because it not only is not written down, but cannot be, and therefore is particularly difficult to replicate. So part of the importance of information technology is the social context in which information is exchanged.

In summary, the effects of the information age on competitive advantage will be to

- increase the extent to which competitive advantage arises from branding and reputation;
- lead to rapid growth in intermediary services, concerned with the packaging, interpretation, selection and management of information;
- increasingly favour firms and groups of firms whose competitive advantage is centred on the exchange of tacit information.

2. From national to global organisation

In major manufacturing sectors, the key elements in the transition from national to global organisation have now been in place for some time, as a consequence of the trade liberalisation which took place in the thirty years following the Second World War. The balance of the forces at work here varies from industry to industry, but automobile production exemplifies the general situation. In 1960, the industry was organised largely on the basis of national production for national markets. Components purchased locally and trade mainly took the form of exports to countries too small to support indigenous manufacturers. Today, firms plan and operate on a global basis, sourcing both components and finished products internationally.

Contrary to common perception and belief, globalisation has not increased concentration in this industry: it has reduced it. The share of the largest firms in world automobile output has fallen steadily and substantially and there have been many new entrants to the industry.

Two conflicting forces have been at work. Globalisation has worked against the interests of weak local firms. That is why there are many fewer European car manufacturers than there were. But globalisation has favoured firms with limited domestic markets but strong competitive advantages: Proton could not have become a viable producer if obliged to rely on the Malaysian market; Toyota, the most important new entrant, has achieved world leadership even though its home market is smaller than that of General Motors. The size of the domestic market has become less important than competitive advantage, which is why US firms have lost their earlier dominance.

In other industries, the balance of these forces has been different. In the large commercial aircraft market, weaker local firms have failed, which is why there is now only one manufacturer in the United States and one in Europe. But the costs of entry are so high that no competition from (say) Japan or Korea, which might have been powerful, has emerged. Thus concentration in this sector has increased.

It will be seen that many of the loose generalisations about the effect of globalisation on industry structure and firm organisation which are widely circulated are unsustainable. Globalisation does not – necessarily – lead to increased concentration, or even require that firms operate globally, or impose either greater centralisation or greater decentralisation of operations. (Both these latter claims are commonly made.) All these things depend on industry-specific factors, particularly the nature of technology and the sources of competitive advantage.

There is, however, one absolutely clear generalisation. It is that the effect of internationalisation on all these industries – as with all cases of increased competition – is to substitute industry organisation based around competitive advantage for industry organisation based around history and geography. The US airline industry – which went through a twenty year transition from ossifying regulation to full competition – is widely regarded as a paradigm of the effect of increased competition on structure. During the transition, there was much new entry, little of it ultimately successful, and some established firms whose dominant position had once seemed impregnable – Pan American, Eastern – disappeared. The final outcome favoured some old firms which had competitive strengths, some new firms which were sufficiently successful to challenge these incumbents, and other newer smaller firms which established strong competitive advantages in particular niches. The overall outcome was probably as concentrated as the initial position, but differently concentrated. Similar developments have already ended in European aviation.

The key point, then, is that the main influence on firm structure and industry organisation in the changing competitive environment is the nature of firm- and industry-specific competitive advantage.

The globalisation of capital markets, and its implications, is such an important aspect of changing contemporary capitalism that it deserves specific attention in its own right. It is the result partly of changes in technology, which have facilitated the instantaneous transmission of money and data around the world, and of changes in policy which have liberalised financial markets. The two interact since technological changes have made separate national policies harder to maintain for those countries that have sought to do so.

These developments have had immediate consequences for the financial services industry itself. For the purposes of this chapter, however, the more important questions concern the impact of financial market globalisation on non-financial firms. The key issue is the following. In different national jurisdictions, different styles of firm organisation have emerged. These differences include differences in the relationship between investors and the firm, but extend to differences in the nature and expectations of relationships between firms and employees, and to the nature and extent of subcontracting relationships.

These different forms of capitalism generate distinctive capabilities and competitive advantages peculiar to their country of origin. The American model is well suited to the organisation of capital markets. And the globalisation of capital markets is spreading that model around the world. But it is a form of organisation which is not always appropriate in other sectors and countries. Neither is it desirable in any case for the world to enjoy one universal model of capitalist organisation.

The American model is located at one end of the spectrum of types of firm organisation. American firms have a relatively diffuse shareholder base, associated with extensive and liquid equity markets, and considerable managerial autonomy. This is nevertheless threatened, from time to time, in a rather public and confrontational way through hostile take-over and other external pressures. There is a hire and fire culture towards both senior managers and lower level employees. Firms tend to be vertically integrated: important sub-activities are generally under the ownership and control of the firm itself.

At the other end lies Japan, where equity shareholders are by contrast unimportant constituencies. Management is consensual, both within the firm and as between the firm and the wider community, and managerial accountability is to these local constituencies. Employment in large firms is long term, with flexibility provided by the different styles of management and operation of smaller firms. There is much less vertical integration and the boundaries of the firm and between firms are much less clear cut.

Europe lies somewhere in between, with different variants to be found within Europe itself. The United Kingdom is closest to the American end of the spectrum while German organisation has some affinities with Japan. France and Italy have distinctive features of their own: large companies are often closely associated with the state, smaller companies often function in collaborative networks.

These differences are increasingly frequently noted, and there is much debate about the merits and problems of different styles of capitalist organisation. While this debate is often illuminating, there is a sense in which the question at issue is fundamentally misconceived. These differences are the product of different patterns of historic and social evolution, and are closely bound up with other aspects of the cultures of which they are part. Not only is what is best for the United States not necessarily what is best for Japan, but the capacity of either to absorb transplanted practices from the other is quite limited.

And from a properly global perspective, these different models of firm organisation are associated with different kinds of competitive advantage for the businesses concerned. The record of US firms in pioneering innovation in almost all business sectors is enviable: but so is the dominance of German and Japanese firms in many fields of precision manufacture. And these differences are not fortuitous: they are the product of wider cultural differences which are embedded in firm structure. In line with the general economic principles of comparative advantage, the persistence of these differences works to the benefit of the world economy taken as a whole as well as to the advantage of the individual firms and countries concerned.

This perspective is substantially different from two conflicting, widely held positions. One is that forms of capitalism found outside the United States are essentially transitional and that development towards the US model is desirable and inevitable: the other that Europe has achieved a superior form of social and economic organisation which requires protection from alien neo-liberal values. Both views persist because there is an element of validity in both. The superiority of the Anglo-American *as a model of capital market organisation* means that the globalisation of capital markets spreads it round the world. However the performance of firms is the product of an interaction between capital, labour and product markets. In this broader context, homogenisation of markets through globalisation can work initially to the disadvantage of countries experiencing it and ultimately to the detriment of all. Competitive advantage is based on differentiation, and firm organisation is one important source of differentiation.

To the extent that capital market liberalisation diminishes this source of differentiation, it reduces competitive advantages at the level of both firm and nation.

3. The changing nature of products and value added

At the beginning of the twentieth century, the largest industrial companies in the world were US Steel (now USX), Exxon (then Standard Oil of New Jersey), J & P Coats (a textile manufacturer), and Pullman, which made railcars. Other leading manufacturing companies included Singer, International Harvester, and Armstrong-Whitworth. The equivalent list today includes Merck, the pharmaceutical company, Coca-Cola, Intel, Philip Morris and Microsoft.

This simple comparison exemplifies important and continuing changes in the nature of contemporary capitalism. At a very elementary level, the products of Merck, Coca-Cola, Intel, Philip Morris and Microsoft are all things you can carry around with you: US Steel, International Harvester and Pullman made products you could climb inside. The proportion of the value of output which is accounted for by raw materials has fallen dramatically. So has the proportion of that value accounted for by the value of physical labour. The major part of the value added by Merck, Coca-Cola, Intel, Philip Morris and Microsoft is established by design, research and development, intricacy of manufacture (whether controlled by robotics or human agency) and from branding.

Notice that this is true within the manufacturing sector itself. The shift in the structure of output from manufacturing to services is often noted with concern, both in aggregate and in individual countries, but it merely parallels a similar change in the nature of manufacturing. While Merck, Intel, Coca-Cola and Philip Morris are all classified as manufacturing businesses, few workers in these companies go home in the evenings exhausted by physical labour: in contrast to the former employees of US Steel, Pullman or International Harvester. There is surplus capacity of undifferentiated manufacture of commodities, such as steel and mass-market automobiles: production of these goods is migrating to the developing world, and there are few profitable companies in these sectors.

Earlier I noted that the effect of liberalization in many industries was to allow firms based on genuine competitive advantage to outpace those based on advantages inherited by history. At the same time, the nature of those competitive advantages is changing too.

Changing patterns of output feed into the growth of, and changes in, competitive advantage. The leading manufacturing firms of a century ago produced largely undifferentiated products and were distinguished from their competitors mainly by their size. In so far as they held competitive advantages at all, they came mainly from scale economies and the market power that went with them.

The strength of firms like Merck, Intel, Coca-Cola, Microsoft and Philip Morris rests only incidentally in their size. In each case, it is clear that their size is the product of their competitive advantage, not the cause of it. And these competitive advantages rest in brands (Coca-Cola and Philip Morris), innovation and patent protection (Merck and Intel), control of standards (Microsoft). None of these knowledge based factors were of material significance for the market leaders at the beginning of the century.

4. The changing nature of competitive advantage

In general, competitive advantages are the product of distinctive capabilities – characteristics of firms which are hard to replicate even when competitors realise the benefit which they confer on those who possess them. In the main, factors such as size of market position do not form the basis of sustainable competitive advantage because they are replicable by firms which do not yet have the same size, or have not yet occupied the same market position, but which do have competitive advantages which are relevant to these markets.

The brands of Coca-Cola and Philip Morris, the innovations of Merck and Intel, and the exclusive rights which Microsoft holds to the MS-DOS operating system and the graphical user interface based on it are distinctive capabilities held by these firms. There are non-replicable sources of competitive advantage. Historically, for many of the firms discussed above, competitive advantages were based on strategic assets –

market power based on monopoly, with competitors excluded through the dominance of incumbents or statutory protection, or through trade restriction of a formal and informal kind, or from exclusive access to scarce factors. Competitive advantages of these kinds are much diminished, and, as globalisation increases, will continue to diminish.

While innovation was traditionally a source of competitive advantage, and remains so, it is increasingly the case that innovation has a short life cycle, is readily transmitted, and is easily replicable. The main exceptions to this are where intellectual property rules give strong protection to innovation, as in pharmaceuticals, although even here it may be that changes in the nature of the industry – with several firms developing products on the basis of a common body of fundamental research – will diminish this. Few product innovations can be protected from replication for long, and innovations in the financial services sector are generally immediately replicable. Often what appear as competitive advantages based on innovation are in fact competitive advantages which allow more effective exploitation of innovation, such as brands and reputation.

More commonly, competitive advantage now rests on aspects of the structure of relationships within and around the firm. Typically, the specific benefits of these relationships come from flexibility and co-operative behaviour, information sharing, and the creation of organisational knowledge. Such relationships may be with customers, sometimes through impersonal relationships such as brands and reputation, and sometimes through personal involvement: with the firm itself typically through organisational routines and the accessing of firm-specific knowledge; sometimes between firm and suppliers, as with sustained trust-based component provision or through the development of a labour market reputation which makes a firm attractive to certain types of employee; or among networks of firms which effectively share a common regionally based body of skills and knowledge.

5. Rents grow

The increasing rewards to be gained in the global market from certain competitive advantages at an individual and corporate level have consequences for degrees of inequality within societies.

Rents are the returns to competitive advantage. They are the difference between the earnings of a firm, or an individual, and what that firm or individual could obtain in their best alternatives. As competitive advantages became more significant, rents grow. As the market in which these competitive advantages can be deployed expands, rents grow further. In this way, globalisation and competitive advantage interact to widen the differentials between individuals and between firms.

The growth of international trade among developed countries has led to widening income differentials and to higher levels of unemployment everywhere. The broadening market generates greater demand for individuals whose abilities are hard to replicate – for example computer programmers, opera singers and biotechnologists. So the rewards these individuals can earn from their talents are bid up. Unskilled individuals are correspondingly becoming more easily replaceable because they have no unreplicable skills to offer. They can succeed in the labour market only by competing on price alone and accepting lower rewards for their labour. Although the connections between trade liberalisation and growing inequality and rising unemployment are controversial, the pressures described here are difficult to dispute.

What is true for individuals is true at the corporate level too. Firms with abilities which are hard to replicate – Microsoft with its proprietary standards, Italian fashion houses – find their rents bid up. Meanwhile, governments have absorbed low-skilled workers into the public sector in the vain attempt to arrest the decline of firms and even of whole industries, for example steel, automobiles and airlines, which have no competitive advantages.

This shift reinforces the value of competitive advantages at the corporate level. And as competitive advantages depend less on size, engineering and strategic assets, and more on organisational structures and on knowledge, competitive advantage becomes relevant in industries where firms had not previously thought in these terms. The recent mergers of the accountancy majors are instructive here. Audit is an easily imitated, undifferentiated, locally produced product which corporations buy because they are obliged to. Where firms are operating in unfamiliar environments, an accountant's brand name empowers it to add value relative to its other local competitors by taking advantage of the caution of these hesitant cross-border clients. Thus branding becomes dominant in an industry where producers traditionally regarded advertising as unethical.

The privatisation of public utilities has created a host of brands in areas where people have historically been uncomfortable with them. There will be opportunities in the next century to pioneer global brands in activities such as education. Many existing markets then present opportunities to companies whose distinctive ability lies in their ability to deliver a consistent product, to meet changing consumer needs and earn a reputation for this which is tied to a global brand.

6. Towards hollow corporations

This creates the potential for a radical shift in the relationship between manufacturing processes and the organisation of firms. If the rents associated with an activity derive from a competitive advantage based on brand or reputation or patent or standard or knowledge, it is only necessary for the firm to manage a small part of the process to earn the whole of that rent. Thus its share of the value added in the process may be completely disproportionate to their share of the process judged in terms of employment or other direct measure of the scale of the activity. This is the phenomenon of the hollow corporation.

The profits of corporations like US Steel came from the sheer size of their operations. Today the position of firms focused on competitive advantages is very different. The largest corporations of the earlier years of the century thrived on low unit costs generated from long mass-production runs. General Motors' dominance was based on economies of scale and its centralised management. But nowadays many successful firms do not necessarily build the products sold under their names, though they still extract the rents from manufacturing processes that they do not control.

Coca-Cola has control only of the syrup used in Coke, Nintendo owns the right to the standard in games consoles. Glaxo's share of the value of Zantac, the anti-ulcerant, lay in its patent. Microsoft's strength is not in its manufacturing capacity, but its proprietary standards in MS-DOS and Windows software, through which it adds value to the manufacturing capacity of others. Benetton adds value by its co-ordinating of the manufacturing process. And so the hollow corporation thrives: none of these firms needs to employ many people to make substantial profits.

The lesson here is not just that you do not make money without adding value. It is also that there are many more opportunities to add value, but through control, rather than ownership, of the value chain. In a fully competitive market, manufacturers, distributors, retailers and middlemen have the opportunity to earn in equal proportion to the cost and value of the services they provide. Vertical integration thus adds to profits only to the extent that it offers access to a new source of rents.

And since there are few opportunities for scale economies in the production of undifferentiated goods, there are going to be fewer rather than more industries in which control of the manufacturing chain is a source of added value. The largest companies of the next century will more resemble Microsoft, and add value to the manufacturing processes of others, than General Motors. Companies can concentrate solely on those activities in which have competitive advantage – they can float other activities away to other companies enjoying competitive advantages they lack.

Conclusions

To return to the central task of this paper, which of the changes under way in contemporary capitalism are permanent? Which are ephemeral?
We can consider the changes under way in terms of three categories.

The evolving significance of national boundaries

- National boundaries do not become irrelevant. Their significance erodes as markets become more global and firm operations more dispersed. But the most persistent impact of nationality is on the cultural identity of corporations, which is often to an important degree bound up with the sources of competitive advantage. This will erode only slowly, and it may not be particularly desirable that it should erode.
- Technological advances in information processing do not necessarily mean that geographical concentration of firms will become less prevalent. Informal structures of relationships between firms allow that sharing of tacit knowledge with trust acquaintances through face to face meetings is a source of competitive advantage of growing importance.
- Liberalisation will have an effect only slowly in many industries where an advantage belongs to incumbents, but firms with genuine competitive advantages will increasingly be able to seek greater rents from their abilities in widening markets.
- Ultimately, competitive advantage replaces history and geography as organising principles of industry structure.

Scale – myth and reality

- It is not generally true that liberalisation, globalisation and the

explosion of information makes industries either more concentrated or more fragmented. The effects of liberalisation on a particular industry depend upon the specifics of technology and the nature of supply and demand in that sector. The only generalisation is that competitive advantage replaces commercial advantages inherited from history.
- Whilst it has become more important for firms to possess competitive advantages, many historic competitive advantages, in particular economies from scale, have diminished in importance because of the growing differentiation of products and the degree to which knowledge is embedded in products or important in distinguishing them.
- Firms can exit from activities in which they lack competitive advantage, whilst still adding value to a small part of, or even controlling, the manufacturing process.
- That firms do not employ many people to engage in arduous labour is not, in itself, a worry. A growing source of added value is tacit knowledge – both in terms of turning technical expertise into commercial success, and in terms of organisation techniques. However this increasing focus of firms on their particular competitive advantages rather than on the whole process may reduce employment opportunities in advanced economies.

The information revolution

- People lack the mental capacity to process the growing mass of information available to them. The growing complexity of the marketplace has put a premium on the signalling devices of brands and reputation. It also will generate more intermediary services to process information about products.
- As the information economy progresses the knowledge content of products increases relative to their physical content. The increased complexity of such products, and their widening range, increases the need to provide product information to customers. Both these factors influence the structure of competitive advantage of firms.

6. Intangible Assets and the Competitiveness of European Industries
Michael Peneder

Introduction

Our understanding of the competitive process will remain fundamentally incomplete until we acquire at least some basic knowledge regarding the empirical relationships between the economy and its intangible factors of production. Because intangibles are, by nature, difficult to measure and to value, the lack of reliable, comprehensive and internationally comparable data is a major barrier to empirical analysis. The specific purpose of this research is to make at least some of the "intangibles" a bit more "tangible" in quantitative analysis. Complementing the contribution by Mahony et al. (1999), based on data from company accounts, this paper follows a deliberately structuralist approach, focusing on an international comparison at the industry level.

The analysis is built upon the application of a new empirical tool presented in Peneder (1999), which by means of statistical cluster techniques, created two new taxonomies of manufacturing industries. The first focuses on the distinction between sources of exogenous, location - dependent comparative cost advantages, such as relative endowments with capital and labour, and endogenously raised firm - specific advantages created by intangible investments in marketing or innovation. The second taxonomy discriminates between industries according to their typical requirements for skilled labour. Besides establishing the basic analytic tools for the investigations carried out in this chapter, the analysis also confirmed the existence of pronounced differences and rather robust sectoral patterns with regard to the relative importance of intangible investments and skill profiles.

The general argument is organised as follows: to begin with, this chapter addresses the ways in which structural characteristics at the sectoral level are linked with typical patterns of competitive strategy at the firm level. The empirical results of this first section strongly support the claim that the structural differences with regard to *intangible assets significantly affect the set of strategic choices* available to firms. In contrast, the second part of the argument sets out to test whether the structural differences between industries actually matter, as far as their contributions to overall economic performance and specifically the creation of income are concerned. Again, it can be shown that *intangibles do matter* - this time with regard to the vertical differentiability of products, labour productivity and affordable wages. Having established the basic empirical facts – first, that structural differences do exist and secondly, that they do indeed matter – the analysis finally turns to the international comparison of specialisation patterns, intended to reveal information about the underlying competitive strengths and weaknesses of European industry. For the specific purpose of this volume, special emphasis will be placed on the careful mapping of relevant information on the individual member states of the European Union.

The new WIFO (Austrian Institute of Economic Research) taxonomy of manufacturing industries

The creation of two new taxonomies has enabled the circumvention of major limitations in international comparisons, which otherwise result from a lack of comprehensive data on intangible activities. These two new taxonomies group individual industries according to their typical combinations of factor inputs and various requirements for skilled labour. The first classification ("taxonomy I") distinguishes between (i) exogenously given competitive advantages based on *factor endowments*, such as physical capital and labour, and (ii) endogenously created advantages based on purposeful *investment in intangible assets*, such as marketing and innovation. In contrast, the second classification ("taxonomy II") clusters industries according to their respective skill requirements, which are both intangible and largely location bound. This provides important information on a complementary dimension which is of particular relevance to the comparative analysis of competitive performance. Both classifications correspond to EUROSTAT's revised NACE system at the three-digit level.

The clustering process for taxonomy I is based on data for wages and salaries, investments in physical capital, advertising outlays, and expenditures on research and development. It is assumed that the data span four orthogonal dimensions of how to spend available units of productive inputs to the generation of revenues. Ratios to total value added have been calculated for wages and physical capital. Expenditures on advertising and R&D are expressed in their ratios to total sales. The latter are directly derived from balance sheet data. Because of the lack of appropriate EU data for all of the four dimensions and in order to maintain overall consistency only US data have been used. Although for examaple the ranking of individual three-digit industries with regard to particular factor intensities would certainly be sensitive to this choice, the final allocation into one of the five broad industry types can reasonably be expected to be much less affected. Data sources are DEBA (labour and capital inputs) and COMPUSTAT (advertising and R&D). Taxonomy II reflects the human resources perspective and is based upon occupational data from the OECD, distinguishing between white- and blue-collar workers and between high- and low-skilled labour.

Compared to earlier classifications, the new WIFO taxonomy is distinguished by its application of cluster analysis, which provides a powerful statistical technique specifically designed for classifying observations on behalf of their relative similarities with respect to a multidimensional array of variables. The basic idea is one of dividing a specific data profile into segments by creating maximum homogeneity within and maximum distance between groups.

In the end, 100 NACE three-digit manufacturing industries were completely categorised. Taxonomy I comprises five mutually exclusive groupings, namely *mainstream manufacturing* (MM), *labour intensive* (LI), *capital intensive* (CI), *marketing driven* (MDI) and *technology driven* industries (TDI). In contrast, taxonomy II distinguishes between typically *low-skilled, medium-skilled blue-collar, medium-skilled white-collar* and particularly *high-skilled* industries. Like any broad classification, this one must be interpreted with care, as industries within the categories are still highly heterogeneous and countries may, to large extents, differ in their actual factor combinations.

Corporate strategy

This opening section puts forward the hypothesis that a fundamental structural dimension to the competitive behaviour of firms does exist. Or in other words: observable and systematic differences across industries significantly shape the nature of competitive opportunities and the corresponding strategic choices of individual companies. As will be shown, intangible aspects of firm-level activities as well as the human resources linked to the firm's dynamic capabilities are highly involved in these structural differences.

The *Panorama of European Industry*, jointly published by EUROSTAT and the European Commission DGIII, provides extensive monographs on most of the individual NACE three-digit manufacturing industries. These monographs are authored by international consultants and European business associations representing the respective industries. Although the monographs differ much in style and language, they usually follow a common structure, which in most cases also encompasses a section on corporate strategy. This qualitative information is the basis of a content analysis (Kaniovski and Peneder, 1999), which compares the patterns of strategic choices across industry types and tests for the statistical significance of observable differences.

The research was carried out in four steps: first of all, for each available three-digit group all of the general strategic options relevant to the firms in each particular industry were collected and recorded under general headings. In a second step, this diverse qualitative information was consolidated, so that a cross-tabulation of industries times the general categories of competitive strategy could be established. This consolidation resulted in 10 types of strategic choices, which were further aggregated under the broad categories of (i) cost based strategies, (ii) product differentiation and (iii) matters of market organisation.

Cost Based Strategies:
Rationalisation of production, modernisation and process innovation
Relocation of production due to cost advantages

Product Differentiation:
Specific customer services, user-supplier links
Research and technology development
Introduction of new product varieties
Advertising and brand-marketing

Market Organisation:
Specialisation, focus on core activities
Joint ventures
Vertical integration
Horizontal integration

Thirdly, "1" was entered in the cross-tabulation for each three-digit industry, in which the particular type of strategy was said to have been of relevance, while "0" was entered for each case, in which relevance was not explicitly mentioned. Finally, these entries were aggregated according to each of the two industry taxonomies (described in the technical box), the first one focusing on the distinction between tangible and intangible factor inputs and the second one directed more closely towards the dimension of human resources. Based on these aggregates, binomial test statistics on the significance of the differences between the mean entry of a particular industry type and the mean entry of all the other types taken together were calculated.

To begin with primarily cost based strategies, the *rationalisation, mechanisation and modernisation of production* (including investments in new machinery and equipment, partly organisational reform within the company, as well as own process innovations) proves to be the most basic requirement for maintaining competitiveness, which is almost uniformly distributed across all industry types (Figure 6.1). As a consequence, no significant differences can be reported with regard to typical factor combinations, although the mean entries for both marketing and technology driven industries turn out to be lower than in the other categories. Discriminating industries along the human resources dimension, the rationalisation of production is of significantly higher importance in medium-skilled blue-collar industries, where this kind of cost based strategy was reported in 95% of the cases. In contrast, the *relocation of production* (which businesses often say is done to reduce labour costs) is typically most important in medium-skilled white-collar industries. Further discrimination according to types of intangible investments additionally shows that this is primarily related to significantly higher entries for marketing driven industries, whereas the relocation of production due to cost advantages is of hardly any importance within the strategic portfolio of technology driven industries.

Turning to competitive strategies involving product differentiation and related services, the key hypothesis states that intangible investments and higher labour skills increase the opportunities to differentiate output. A systematic analysis of the content of individual industry monographs indeed reveals sharp contrasts according to industry classifications. Reporting only the most significant differences, *customer services and specific user-supplier links* are most important in mainstream (that is, the category which, for example, includes most of the machinery sector) and high-skilled manufacturing, and least important in low-skilled industries. Differentiation through innovation, based on a substantial amount of research and development, is most pronounced in high-skilled and technology driven industries, as well as in mainstream manufacturing. It matters significantly less in medium-skilled blue-collar, as well as labour intensive and marketing driven industries. In contrast, product differentiation through the introduction of *new varieties* matters most in marketing driven and medium-skilled white-collar industries, but hardly matters in labour intensive industries. In the monographs of mainstream manufacturing and low-skilled industries, competitive advantage achieved through the introduction of new varieties was never mentioned at all. A similar picture appears as we consider the *creation of new brands* - here we see that marketing driven and medium-skilled white-collar industries rank far ahead of the other groups.

Although matters of market organisation play an important role across the entire range of industry types, a number of interesting differentiations do appear: *vertical integration* appears to be most important in the marketing driven consumer industries as a means of improving market access and bypassing bottlenecks in distribution services, which are often highly concentrated. In contrast, mainstream manufacturing and low-skilled industries show the highest entries for *horizontal integration*.

Figure 6.1: Intangible assets and competitive strategy: deviation of mean number of entries in %

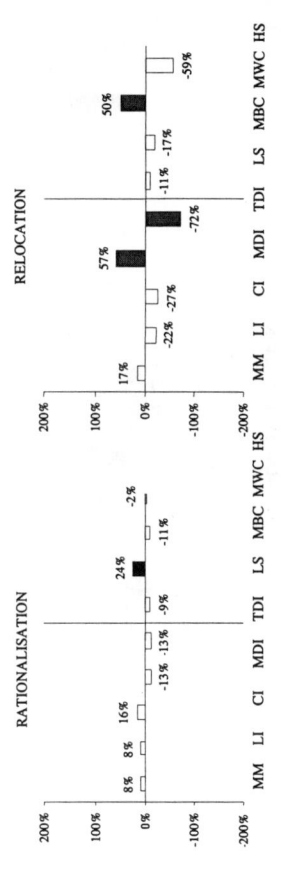
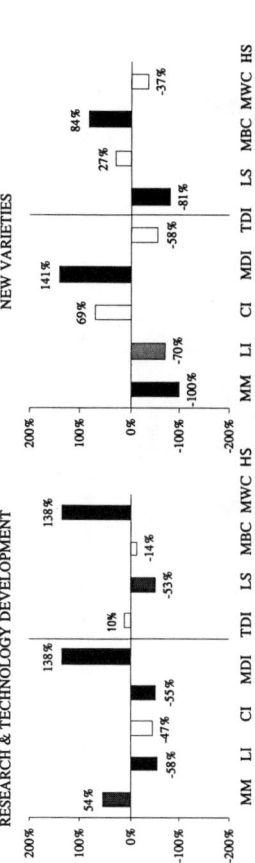

Figure 6.1: Intangible assets and competitive strategy (continued)

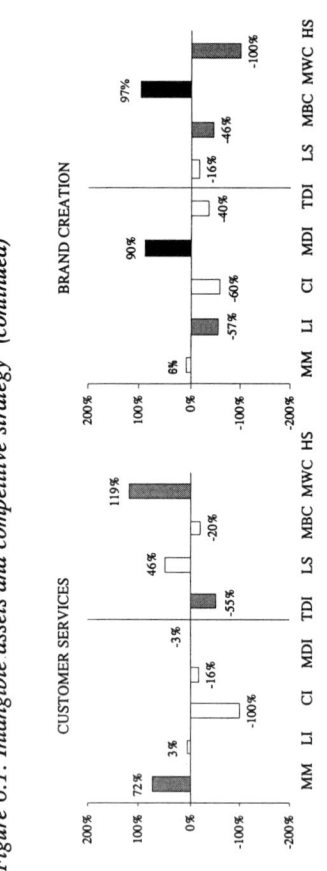
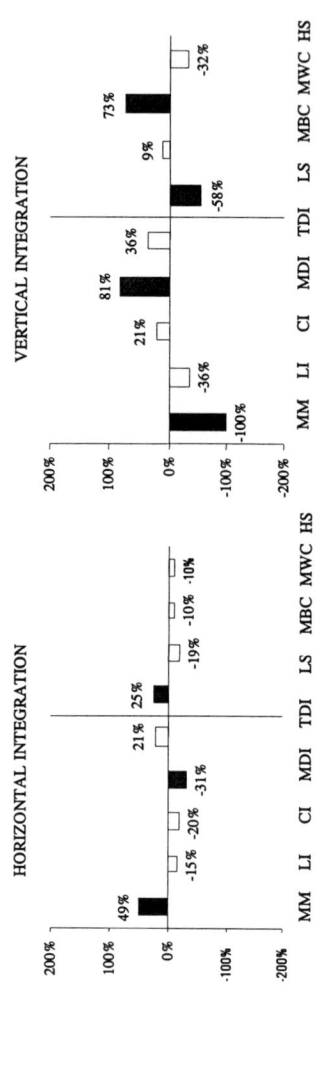

NB: MM - mainstream manufacturing, LI - labour intensive, CI - capital intensive, MDI - marketing driven, TDI - technology driven; LS - low-skilled, MBC - medium-skilled blue-collar, MWC - medium-skilled white-collar, HS - high-skilled industries.

Figure 6.1: Intangible assets and competitive strategy (continued)

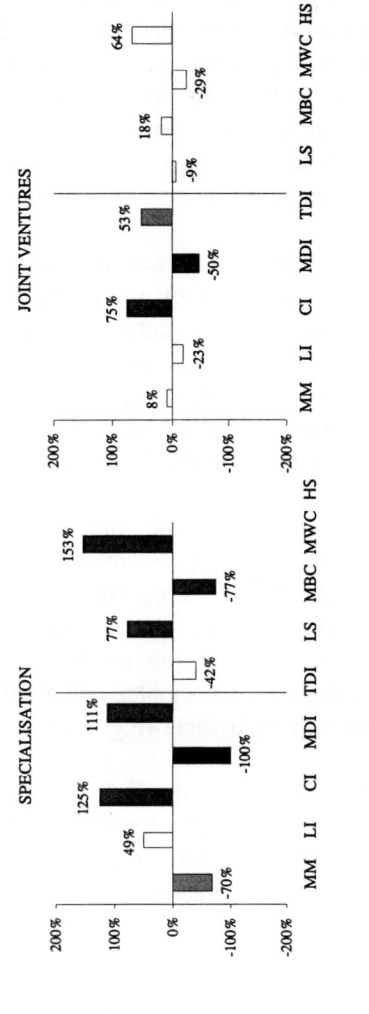

NB: MM - mainstream manufacturing, LI - labour intensive, CI - capital intensive, MDI - marketing driven, TDI - technology driven; LS - low-skilled, MBC - medium-skilled blue-collar, MWC - medium-skilled white-collar, HS - high-skilled industries.

Regarding the pair of opposing concepts – diversification versus increasing specialisation in core activities – the first was hardly mentioned explicitly. But *specialisation* was often referred to in capital intensive and technology driven, as well as high-skilled and medium-skilled blue-collar industries. Appropriate to the larger emphasis on the introduction of new product varieties, specialisation was never mentioned in any of the marketing driven industries. Finally, co-operation via joint ventures is most frequent in capital intensive, technology driven and high-skilled manufacturing, but lowest in marketing driven industries.

In summary, differentiations across industry types reveal a number of pronounced relationships between intangible assets and competitive strategy at the firm level.

Labour intensive industries show by far the lowest average number of entries for any kind of strategy (0.28), followed by marketing driven (0.34) and capital intensive industries (0.36). In contrast, mainstream manufacturing (0.37) and technology driven industries (0.41) rank highest. Similarly, the average number of entries increased with the corresponding levels of human resources: from low-skilled (0.30) to medium-skilled blue- (0.35) as well as white-collar (0.37) and high-skilled industries (0.41).

In all types of industries, cost savings through the continuous rationalisation and modernisation of production is the most basic and indispensable ingredient of any corporate strategy mix. Medium-skilled blue-collar industries appear to be most affected, ceteris paribus also implying a stronger downward pressure on their job numbers. This observation is consistent with the reported decline of blue-collar relative to white-collar jobs within manufacturing employment (e.g. in Colecchia and Papaconstantinou, 1996).

While marketing driven industries differentiate themselves primarily through the creation of new product varieties and brand affiliations, technology driven industries make a considerably more substantial investment in research and development. This finding is also consistent with the data on the vertical differentiability of products, presented in the next section. Both calculations independently suggest that compared to technology driven industries, typical marketing industries depend much more on horizontal rather than vertical product differentiation.

Whereas the relocation of production is an important option for marketing driven industries because it can, for example, help to cut the costs of labour, transport or the supply of raw materials[1], this choice appears to be of much less importance in technology driven industries. Considering their high and positive correlation with the demand for high-skilled labour, technology driven industries appear to be primarily bound in their locational choices by the respective pool of available human resources. This empirical observation is consistent for example with the theoretical setting on cluster formation by pooled labour markets in Peneder (1998).

While in technology driven industries joint ventures and co-operation between firms are common ways of achieving an efficient pooling of specific knowledge based resources, marketing driven industries are least willing to participate in such activities. Similarly, typical marketing industries are also least inclined to participate in horizontal mergers, but most often long for vertical integration. This suggests fewer knowledge based or efficiency oriented motives for mergers and acquisitions, and a greater strategic need to secure control over distribution systems.

In conclusion, the following stylised facts appear to be of particular importance to the remaining analysis:

Stylised Fact 1 – the portfolio of disposable strategies: Structural differences with regard to intangible assets significantly affect the choice of competitive strategies. In general, skill intensive and technology driven industries appear to have the largest portfolio of disposable strategies.

Stylised Fact 2 – structural differences in competitive strategy: The continuous rationalisation and modernisation of production constitutes the most basic cost-based strategy and is rather evenly distributed across all industry types. Compared to the other categories, the relocation of production is significantly more important in marketing driven and less so in technology driven industries. Marketing driven industries also rely much more on advertising and brand creation, whereas the latter are most involved in substantial research and technology development. The promotion of specific customer relationships is most pronounced in mainstream manufacturing.

---

[1] Unfortunately, the scope of multinational investments intended to improve market access could not be separately identified from the qualitative information in the monographs.

Economic performance

Dynamic capabilities to sustain the generation of income are invariably linked to the human resources dimension and the accumulation of intangible assets, such as superior technological knowledge or the emotional affinity to certain variations in product characteristics. Continuing in pursuit of the deliberately structuralist approach, the new WIFO taxonomy provides a powerful empirical tool for testing whether the sectoral characteristics make a significant difference with regard to the variables, which are regularly applied in the structural analysis of economic performance.

Quality differentiation and the "intangible component"

Similar to nominal productivity numbers, unit values reflect the valuation of goods and services by consumers and are therefore directly linked to the potential for quality competition and vertical differentiation. Their calculation is based upon the ratio of nominal *values* to physical *volumes* and in this sense reflects the most literal measure of the relative importance of non-material components. But as a consequence, unit values also tend to rise relative to their position in the vertical organisation of production. As the non-material values of a product accumulate along its specific "value-chain", downstream industries require more prior processing stages and therefore tend to exhibit a higher economic value relative to the pure volume of initial material inputs. Based upon such common considerations, the following hypothesis can be formulated:

H1a: $\dfrac{UV_{i=TDI}}{UV_{i \neq TDI}} > 1$; H1b: $\dfrac{UV_{i=MDI}}{UV_{i \neq MDI, TDI}} > 1$; H1c: $\dfrac{UV_{i=CI}}{UV_{i \neq CI}} < 1$

UV: Unit values; TDI: technology driven; MDI: marketing driven; CI: capital intensive industries

The hypotheses simply state that industries characterised by typically high intangible investments and highly skilled labour also tend to exhibit the highest unit values. These are assumed to increase the value of non-material inputs in the final product. In the knowledge that a large part of marketing driven industries, for example the food sector, generally involve fewer vertical stages of production, it is additionally anticipated that the unit values for MDIs might be lower than those for TDIs (H1a and H1b). Based on the same argument, products from capital intensive industries, which mainly supply basic goods and primary inputs to other industries, are expected to show the lowest unit values (H1c). Similar tentative predictions can be derived with regard to the typical skill patterns of industries. Hypotheses H1d and H1e formulate the expectation that labour skills strongly correspond to the size of the "intangible component" and thus unit values will be highest in typically high-skilled industries, followed by medium- and low-skilled production:

H1d: $\dfrac{UV_{i=HS}}{UV_{i \neq HS}} > 1$ H1e: $\dfrac{UV_{i=LS}}{UV_{i \neq LS}} < 1$

HS: high-skilled; LS: low-skilled industries

If we first look at the aggregate values for the different industry types, the overall picture corresponds nicely to the prior expectations (Figure 6.2). Considering data on trade between the EU15 and the outside world, *technology driven* industries show by far the highest unit values, presumably because of their ample opportunities for vertical differentiation. *Mainstream manufacturing* with its high share in the skill dependent and development oriented *machinery* sector comes second, followed by *labour intensive, marketing driven* and finally *capital intensive* industries. Nevertheless, the particularly low unit values for marketing driven industries are a surprise, especially since the latter has a reputation for creating largely intangible competitive assets, such as specific brand affiliations.

Figure 6.2: Unit values in EU trade: 1997 in ECU per kg

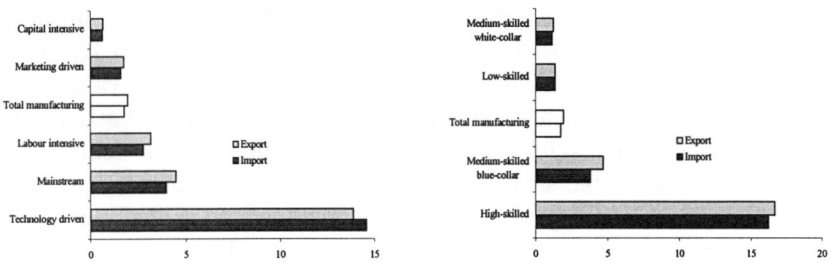

Looking at the typical skill patterns in relation to the "intangible component", high-skilled industries outperform all the other types by a wide margin, but low-skilled industries are just as good as for example medium-skilled white-collar industries. A first glance at the aggregate numbers could not fully confirm H1e.

This last observation, however, is only based on a comparison of the mean values weighted by the relative size of individual industries. In order to confirm or reject our hypotheses more consistently, the statistical significance of differences in unit values across industry types has to be tested. Because the groupings vary in size and lack homogeneous variances (heteroscedasticity), we applied the following four non-parametric tests, which were designed for unrelated samples and non-categorical data: The *Median test* reveals whether the differences in the median of two or more samples are significant. Similarly based on the Chi-square statistics, the *Kruskal-Wallis H* statistic is used to test for the significance of differences across all five industry types, by comparing the number of times a score from one industry grouping is ranked higher than a score from another. The *Mann-Whitney U* test statistic is also based on the mean ranks of different samples, whereas the *Kolmogorov-Smirnov Z* statistic compares the distribution of values in each pair of industry types. While the Kruskal-Wallis H statistic and the Median test reveal whether the typology as such discriminates significantly according to the particular variables, both the Mann-Whitney U test and the Kolmogorov-Smirnov Z statistic are additionally applied in the comparison of individual pairs of industry types.

As can easily be seen in light of the Median- and the Kruskal-Wallis tests, both taxonomies discriminate significantly with regard to the "intangible component", as revealed by the measurement of unit values. Looking at the pairwise comparisons of the Mann-Whitney and the Kolmogorov-Smirnov test statistics, technology driven industries show by far the highest unit values, significantly outperforming any other group, whereas the unit values in capital intensive industries are by far the lowest (Table 6.1). As a consequence, hypotheses H1a and H1c are confirmed, but hypothesis H1b must be rejected. Turning to the human resources dimension, low-skilled industries have significantly lower unit values than any of the others, which is consistent with our earlier hypothesis (Table 6.2). Similarly, high-skilled industries show the highest mean ranks of all groups, but due to the smaller number of observations, this difference is only significant with regard to low-skilled and medium-skilled blue-collar industries. Besides this minor restriction, H1d and H1e can generally be confirmed.

Stylised Fact 3 - Unit values and the scope of the "intangible component": Industries differ significantly with regard to the relative scope of the "intangible component" embedded in traded goods. Technology driven and high-skilled industries exhibit significantly higher, but capital intensive and low-skilled industries significantly smaller unit values relative to all the other groups.

In order to measure the degree of vertical product differentiation more directly, it is of additional interest to compare the standard deviations of unit values in European trade. Another two hypotheses emerge:

H1f: $\dfrac{STD(UV_{i=TDI})}{STD(UV_{i\neq TDI})} > 1$; H1g: $\dfrac{STD(UV_{i=HS})}{STD(UV_{i\neq HS})} > 1$

STD: standard deviation

Taking into account the suspected horizontal nature of product differentiation by advertising and brand creation, H1f simply states that technology driven industries are expected to exhibit higher degrees of vertical differentiation than any other industry type. Similarly, H1g predicts that vertical differentiability is positively related to the employment of high-skilled labour. Both predictions are broadly consistent with the general comparison of the mean standard deviations of the individual 3-digit industries within each category (Figure 6.3).

Figure 6.3:   Standard deviation of unit values in the EU 1996

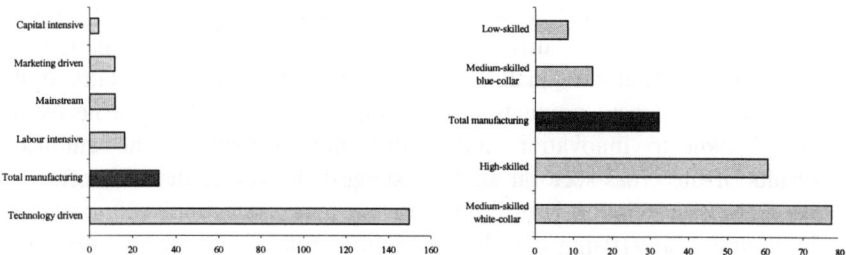

Hypothesis H1f corresponds precisely to the corresponding test statistics (Table 6.1), showing that technology driven industries are the only sub-group which consistently exhibits the highest degrees of vertical differentiability. The grouping of particularly marketing driven industries, for example, does not appear to be any more vertically differentiated than mainstream manufacturing, labour- or capital intensive industries are. In contrast, H1g is not entirely confirmed, since high-skilled industries cannot be discriminated significantly from medium-skilled white-collar industries (Table 6.2). Summing up our observations, we can now establish the following stylised fact:

Stylised Fact 4 - vertical differentiability: Technology driven as well as high-skilled and medium-skilled white-collar industries are characterised by significantly higher degrees of vertical product differentiation than any other industry type.

Since advertising has entered the analysis precisely because of its presumed ability to raise perceived quality, rejection of hypothesis H1b may be disappointing at first glance. Maintaining the nevertheless reasonable assumption that advertising is undertaken in order to differentiate one's own goods and services from competing products, the stylised empirical facts strongly (albeit indirectly) support our prior suspicion that those industries which have been singled out as particularly marketing driven mostly engage in horizontal rather than vertical differentiation.

More generally, at least three plausible arguments may explain the absence of distinctly higher unit values in marketing driven industries: First of all, the *lack depth in the value added chain* and the correspondingly high importance of initial material inputs in most industries included within this group may lower unit values analogously to the case of capital intensive industries. The most typical example of this explanation may be provided by the many industries within the food sector. Secondly, the nature of product differentiation within advertising industries may be more *horizontal* than initially anticipated. The hypothesis was founded on the common assumption that advertising serves to increase vertical differentiability through its dissemination of information about the quality of products, supporting for example the introduction of new products into the market and thus being a necessary complement to innovation and quality improvement. The empirical results of the cross-sectoral analysis suggest, however, that this effect of vertical differentiation is of comparatively minor quantitative importance. In contrast, advertising may better be interpreted as primarily serving to increase the consumer's *perception* of quality and his loyalty to particular brands. The important difference is that although individual consumers may still experience differentiation as vertical, the same does not necessarily apply to aggregate markets. Since consumers may have distinct opinions on a product's differentiated attributes, perceived quality is a somewhat "softer" criterion, which is not strictly comparable on a single vertical scale. Last, but not less important, average unit values might be considerably dampened by the often dualistic nature of marketing driven industries, where high quality brands regularly coexist with low priced unbranded products.

Table 6.1: Non-parametric tests for significant differences in unit values 1997: factor inputs

Shares in total employment	Number of Industries	Mean rank	Industry type	Mann-Whitney U test / Kolmogorov-Smirnov Z test				
				MM	LI	CI	MDI	RDI
Export Unit Values: EU15								
Median Test: ***	24	48	MM	-	-	***	-	***
Kruskal-Wallis H test: ***	22	44	LI	-	-	*	-	**
	11	21	CI	***	**	-	*	***
	22	43	MDI	-	-	**	-	***
	13	75	RDI	***	***	***	***	-
Import Unit Values: EU15				MM	LI	CI	MDI	RDI
Median Test: ***	24	48	MM	-	-	***	-	***
Kruskal-Wallis H test: ***	22	43	LI	-	-	-	-	**
	11	22	CI	***	**	-	*	***
	22	43	MDI	-	-	**	-	***
	13	76	RDI	***	***	***	***	-
Standard deviation (X-UV):				MM	LI	CI	MDI	RDI
EU15, 1996	24	41	MM	-	-	-	-	***
Median Test: *	22	36	LI	-	-	-	-	***
Kruskal-Wallis H test: ***	10	24	CI	-	-	-	-	***
	23	33	MDI	-	-	-	-	***
	13	68	RDI	***	**	***	***	-

*** significant at the 1% level; ** 5% level; * .. 10% level

Table 6.2: Non-parametric tests for significant differences in unit values 1997: skill types

	Number of Industries	Mean rank	Industry type	Mann-Whitney U test / Kolmogorov-Smirnov Z test			
				low skill	Med/bc	med/wc	high skill
Export Unit Values: EU15	36	37	low skill	-	***	**	***
Median Test: ***	23	45	med/bc	-	-	-	***
Kruskal-Wallis H test: ***	24	53	med/wc	**	-	*	*
	9	70	high skill	***	***	*	-
Import Unit Values: EU15	36	36	low skill	-	**	**	***
Median Test: ***	23	45	med/bc	-	-	-	**
Kruskal-Wallis H test:***	24	55	med/wc	***	-	-	-
	9	69	high skill	***	***	-	-
Standard deviation (X-UV):	36	36	low skill	-	-	***	***
EU15, 1996	23	40	med/bc	-	-	*	**
Median Test: ***	24	61	med/wc	***	***	-	-
Kruskal-Wallis H test: ***	9	67	high skill	***	***	-	-

*** significant at the 1% level; ** 5% level; * 10% level

The productivity of labour

The measurement of unit values is centred on *products* and reveals information about vertical differentiability, product quality and the "intangible component" of traded goods, irrespective of the actual economic value added by the particular kind of economic activity under investigation. In contrast, labour productivity is an *activity* based measure, indicating success in generating income, thus relating more directly to what is generally considered the ultimate goal of economic undertakings. The productivity of any single input factor depends on how efficiently it is used and on the amount of complementary inputs used for the production of economic value. Consequently, high amounts of physical capital, installed to support pure labour in production, should imply higher value added per employee. But the same rationale extends to other more intangible inputs as well. Following these considerations, the most plausible prediction is that labour productivity will be higher in industries where pure labour is complemented by other inputs such as physical capital, research, advertising or skills.

As shown in Peneder (1999a) the category of particularly labour intensive industries is most strongly characterised by a lack of pronounced dependence on any additional input factor other than labour. Consequently, we must expect labour productivity to be lowest in industries of this type (H2a). Assuming that wages generally correspond to labour productivity, the same prediction applies to wage levels (H2b). Similarly, labour skills can be interpreted as additional input, merely complementing the tangible amount of labour in terms of persons employed. Therefore skill levels are expected to be positively related to productivity and wages (H2c and H2d):

H2a: $\dfrac{(Y/E)_{i=LI}}{(Y/E)_{i \neq LI}} < 1$;   H2b: $\dfrac{(W/E)_{i=LI}}{(W/E)_{i \neq LI}} < 1$

H2c: $\dfrac{(Y/E)_{i=HS}}{(Y/E)_{i \neq HS}} > 1$; H2d: $\dfrac{(W/E)_{i=HS}}{(W/E)_{i \neq HS}} > 1$

$\dfrac{(Y/E)_{i=LS}}{(Y/E)_{i \neq LS}} < 1$ $\dfrac{(W/E)_{i=LS}}{(W/E)_{i \neq LS}} < 1$

* Y: value added; E: employment; W: wages and salaries.

Comparing the aggregate values for the industry types and ranking triad totals according to the level of labour productivity places *capital intensive* and *technology driven* industries first, followed by *marketing driven* industries (Figure 6.4). In all of these cases, the value of pure labour is augmented by complementary inputs such as physical capital, research or advertising. Partly reflecting the higher skill level of trained workers, labour productivity in *mainstream* manufacturing is still above that in *labour intensive* industries. With regard to human resources, medium-skilled white-collar industries show the highest levels of labour productivity, followed closely by high-skilled industries, whereas low-skilled as well as medium-skilled blue-collar industries perform considerably less well. Interestingly, in labour productivity, there seems to be greater divergence between blue- and white-collar labour than in the more obvious distinction between low- and high-skilled industries. This observation suggests that blue-collar workers are typically employed in industries with less potential use for productive inputs complementing purely manual (albeit skilled) work.

Figure 6.4: Aggregate labour productivity: EU-Japan-USA 1997 in 1000 ECU

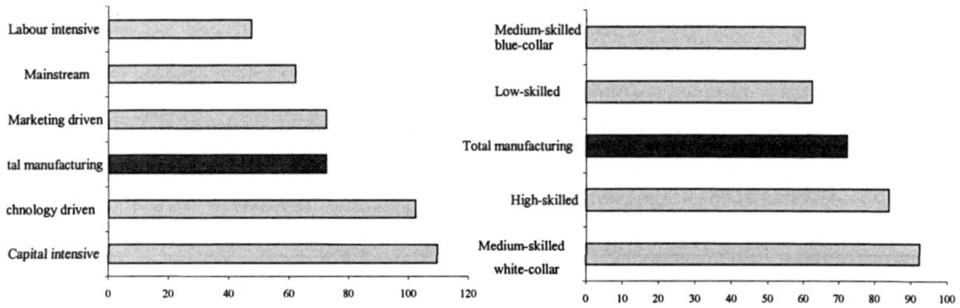

Turning to non-parametric tests of variance, the hypotheses H2a and H2b can generally be confirmed, except for the paired comparison of labour intensive and marketing driven industries (Table 6.3). Although the former show consistently lower mean ranks and mean values (both weighted and unweighted) than the latter with regard to both productivity and wage levels, this difference generally does not appear to be statistically significant. The paired tests additionally reveal that capital intensive and technology driven industries significantly outperform all the other categories. The former reflects the particularly high quantities of complementary capital inputs, which allow real production per employee to be increased. The latter may be reasonably explained by the vertical nature of product differentiation through technology driven innovations observed in the earlier investigations.

Table 6.3: Non-parametric tests for significant differences in labour productivity and wages 1997: factor inputs

Shares in total employment	Number of Industries	Mean rank	Industry type	Mann-Whitney U test / Kolmogorov-Smirnov Z test				
				MM	LI	CI	MDI	RDI
Labour productivity: EU15								
Median Test: ***								
Kruskal-Wallis H test: ***								
	25	49	MM	-	***	***	-	***
	25	25	LI	***	-	***	*	***
	11	78	CI	***	***	-	**	-
	24	49	MDI	-	***	**	-	***
	14	76	RDI	***	***	-	***	-
Labour productivity: EU+Japan+USA								
Median Test: ***								
Kruskal-Wallis H test: ***								
	25	49	MM	-	***	***	-	***
	25	24	LI	***	-	***	***	***
	11	72	CI	***	***	-	*	-
	24	52	MDI	-	***	*	-	**
	14	78	RDI	***	***	-	**	-
Wage level: EU15								
Median Test: ***								
Kruskal-Wallis H test: ***								
	25	50	MM	-	***	***	-	***
	25	29	LI	***	-	***	-	***
	11	73	CI	***	***	-	**	-
	24	42	MDI	-	*	***	-	***
	14	83	RDI	***	***	-	***	-
Wage level: EU+Japan+USA								
Median Test: ***								
Kruskal-Wallis H test: ***								
	25	48	MM	-	***	***	-	***
	25	33	LI	**	-	***	-	***
	11	77	CI	***	***	-	***	-
	24	39	MDI	-	*	***	-	***
	14	82	RDI	***	***	-	***	-

*** significant at the 1% level; ** 5% level; * 10% level

Table 6.4: Non-parametric tests for significant differences in labour productivity and wages: skill types

	Number of Industries	Mean rank	Industry type	Mann-Whitney U test / Kolmogorov-Smirnov Z test			
				low skill	Med/bc	med/wc	high skill
Labour productivity: EU15							
Median Test: ***	38	45	Low skill	-	-	***	-
	25	34	Med/bc	-	-	***	***
Kruskal-Wallis H test: ***	27	68	Med/wc	***	-	-	-
	9	64	High skill	-	***	-	-
Labour productivity: EU+Japan+USA							
Median Test: ***	38	42	Low skill	-	-	***	**
	25	36	Med/bc	-	-	***	***
Kruskal-Wallis H test: ***	27	69	Med/wc	***	***	-	-
	9	67	High skill	**	***	-	-
Wage level: EU15							
Median Test: ***	38	37	Low skill	-	-	***	***
	25	38	Med/bc	-	-	***	***
Kruskal-Wallis H test: ***	27	70	Med/wc	***	***	-	-
	9	77	High skill	***	***	-	-
Wage level: EU+Japan+USA							
Median Test: ***	38	36	Low skill	-	-	***	***
	25	42	Med/bc	-	-	***	***
Kruskal-Wallis H test: ***	27	67	Med/wc	***	***	-	-
	9	77	High skill	***	***	-	-

*** significant at the 1% level; ** 5% level; * 10% level

With regard to the typical patterns of occupations, the distinction between high and low skills in hypotheses H2c and H2d proved to be too simplistic and failed to work. Although skill levels obviously are positively related to productivity, the distinction between blue- and white-collar occupations must additionally be taken into account (Table 6.4). The most plausible general explanation for the significantly higher levels of productivity and wages in typically white-collar industries lies in the presumably more complementary nature of the relationship between white-collar skills and other productivity enhancing inputs, such as research and development (see also Peneder, 1999a).

Stylised Fact 5 - contribution to income creation: Testing for significant differences, labour productivity and wages are highest in technology driven and capital intensive industries, but lowest in merely labour intensive industries. Labour skills are positively related to productivity, but persons in typically white-collar occupations appear to benefit more from productivity enhancing complementary inputs than blue-collar workers.

The pronounced, but nevertheless complex relationships revealed so far, naturally raised the interest in testing a more explicitly specified econometric model on the presumed causal relationships, by means of regression analysis. In particular, we might want to know more about the relative magnitudes of the respective impacts which the individual factors of production have on labour productivity. Or, in other words, we can ask what types of factor input combinations are the most rewarding in terms of labour productivity?

In principle, the cross-section regression could be specified in terms of the general Cobb-Douglas framework, extending the usual approach by introducing skills, as well as research and advertising outlays, as additional inputs to the generation of revenues. Taking revenues as a function of both physical output Q and the price of products p, we can assume that the former is determined exclusively by the inputs of capital C and pure labour L, whereas prices are determined by the consumer's willingness to pay. In the current setting, this depends on the perceived quality of products, which can be raised by expenditures on research R and brand creation B. Related differences concerning market structure and the bargaining power of firms are not considered explicitly, but can be thought of as corresponding to the case of monopolistic competition with a large number of firms. For the sake of simplicity, it is also assumed that labour skills S enter the function via their impact on quality and prices, although alternatively they may be considered as contributing to the technical efficiency of production and the corresponding amount of physical output. Total revenues are thus defined by Y = Q(L,C)p(R,B,S).

In the present context, the specification of the model takes the respective factor intensities Fij/Yi of inputs j in industry i as independent variables, intended to explain the variation in the productivity of labour Yi/Li. This factor intensity version bears similarity to Griliches (1979) or more recently Fors (1997) and can be considered a kind of linear approximation to the common Cobb-Douglas framework. However, the approximation is not exact and therefore the resulting coefficients cannot be strictly interpreted as elasticities. It seems best to read them as the percentage change of labour productivity due to an increase in the respective variables of one percentage point.

Substituting the factor intensities and employment shares of the explanatory variables with lower case letters, the following equation was first estimated by simple OLS:

(1) $\quad \text{Log}(Y_i/L_i) = a + \beta c_i + \gamma b_i + \delta r_i + \varphi s_i + \varepsilon_i.$

As can easily be seen, the specification in equation (1) poses a serious problem with respect to the endogeneity between factor inputs and labour skills. In particular, investments in R&D and shares of skilled labour are strongly correlated. A single regression, which takes both variables into account, turns out to produce a significant coefficient only for the skill variable. As a consequence, a second equation was simultaneously set up, in order to estimate the presumed causal relationship between factor inputs and the demand for white-collar high-skilled labour:

(2) $\quad s_i = \mu c_i + \nu b_i + \phi r_i + \varepsilon_i$

The joint results of the two estimations are illustrated in a path analysis (Figure 6.5). Arrows indicate the presumed causal link underlying the specifications in equations (1) and (2). All the given numbers represent coefficients, which are at least significant at the 5% level. Numbers in brackets correspond to the total effect on labour productivity, calculated by multiplying the standardised coefficients of both regressions. Arrows in dotted lines signal that only an indirect effect via the demand for skilled labour could be detected, due to econometric problems of multicollinearity. Bowed lines indicate correlations between variables without any causal presumption.

All variables except research intensity exert a significant and positive direct effect on the productivity of labour - white-collar high-skilled labour has the greatest impact, followed by capital investment (+0.402) and advertising outlays. The impact of research expenditures is shed by its high correlation with labour skills. However, if we take equation (2) into account, the demand for high-skilled labour itself largely depends on research activities (+0.672) and to a lesser extent on capital investment (+0.201), but not on advertising. Thus, the multiplication of standardised coefficients reveals an indirect effect of research and development on labour productivity, which is still of considerable size. Taking into account all indirect effects via the demand for white-collar skilled labour, the latter continues to have the largest single impact on labour productivity, followed by capital investments (+0.511), the indirect effects only of R&D expenditures (+0.365) and advertising outlays (+0.198). In both equations, the coefficients of variation ($R^2=0.447$ and 0.509, respectively) are quite high, compared to typical outcomes in cross-section analysis.

Figure 6.5: Intangibles and labour productivity: factor intensities, shares of skilled labour

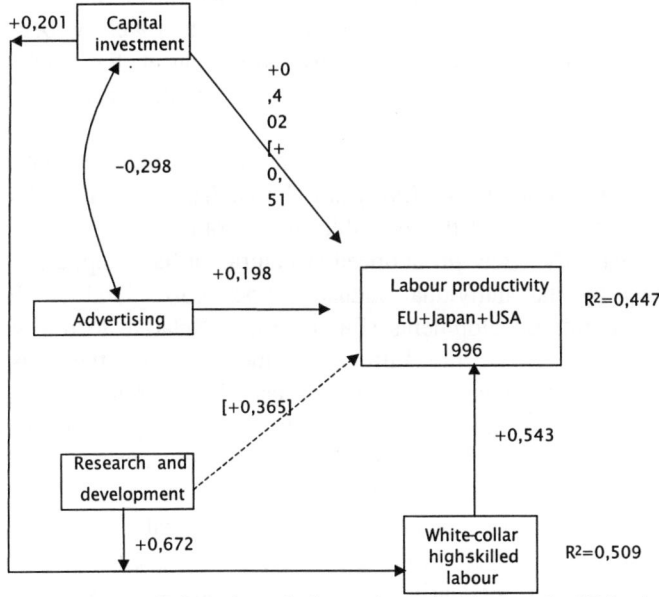

Note: All the coefficients shown in the graph are significant at the 5% level.

Stylised Fact 6 – relative magnitudes of impact on labour productivity: Tangible investment in physical capital has a major influence on labour productivity, but as the empirical evidence underlines, it only constitutes one among several contributing factors. Taking direct as well as indirect effects into account, the share of white-collar high-skilled labour has the strongest positive impact, followed by capital investment, research expenditures and advertising outlays. At the industry level, all of these factors significantly increase the productivity of labour.

International comparison

Although intangible investments such as advertising and R&D offer firm specific choices for the enhancement of a companys competitive position in the market place, we must naturally expect that more general economic, political and other institutional factors, which could differ considerably between distinct economic areas and business locations, have an impact on the actual realisation of the underlying competitive opportunities. Consequently, we must also expect that some significant differences will appear in the international patterns of specialisation in production. This final section sets out to close the overall argument by investigating whether and to what extent such differences do appear among the member states of the European Union as well as between the EU15, Japan and the USA. As promised at the outset, the results will be illustrated in a highly condensed format through the careful mapping of the respective country profiles.

To begin with, the aggregate shares of different industry types in the total joint value added of the European Union, Japan and the USA will be compared. Inspection of the available figures ranging from 1985 to 1997 confirms that only a few pronounced structural shifts do appear and most movements by the individual industry types correspond to the more general economic developments (Figure 6.6). Relative to the two other major economic areas, the European Union enjoyed the most stable development of shares in value added measured at current exchange rates. In contrast, Japan seemed to pursue a solid path of expansion for most of the period, only to see its shares slide dramatically during recent years. Precisely the opposite development can be observed for the USA, where manufacturing industries recently achieved a dramatic increase in their value added shares, after suffering a rather steady decline relative to the others for most of the earlier years. Comparing 1985 to 1997, the dramatic reversal of value added shares in favour of the USA, now documented for the years from 1995 to 1997, appears to have just offset the effects of the earlier upturn in Japanese manufacturing from 1986 onwards.

Figure 6.6: The dynamics of value added shares in the EU15, Japan and the USA

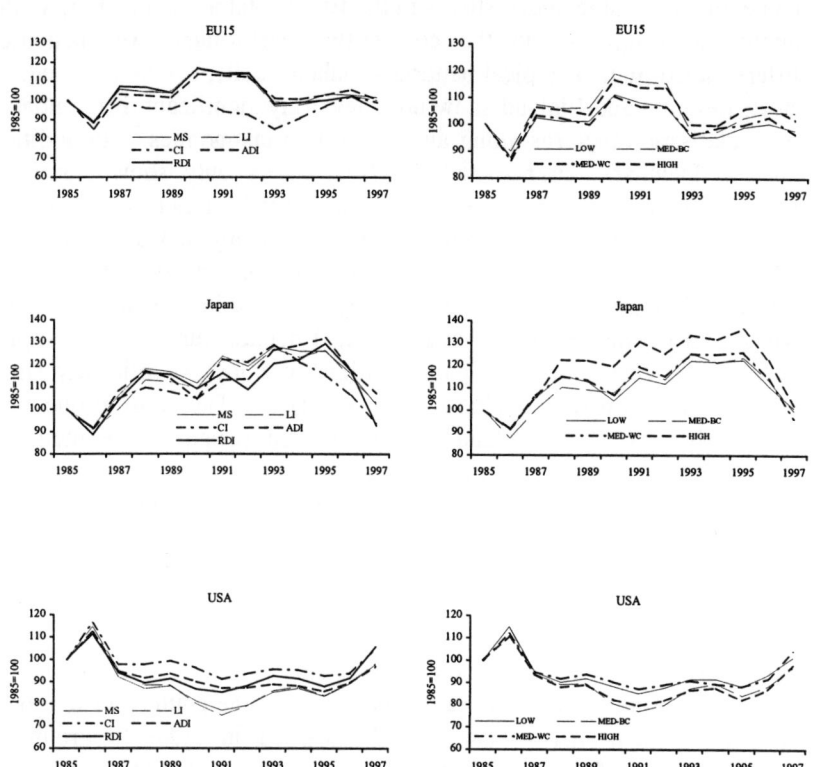

Turning again to industry structures, even these broad patterns bring to the surface the major difficulties European capital intensive industries have experienced during most of this period, nevertheless showing remarkable signs of recovery during more recent years. This recovery might be partially obscured by the fact that capital intensive industries were the first to be caught by the overall economic downturn in Japan. Finally, the charts most remarkably illustrate the great extent to which in the USA technology driven industries have indeed acted as powerful engines of growth, being the one type of industry which achieved the sharpest rise in value added shares from 1995 onwards.

Human resources

To begin with, value added shares in the EU15 total are compared, so that significant differences in the competitive performance of industries, differentiated by their typical patterns of labour skills, can be detected. In short, Belgium and Finland show no noteworthy significant differentiation in specialisation patterns along any of the two taxonomies.[2] In addition, Austria, Denmark, France and the Netherlands only show significant patterns with regard to factor inputs, but not in industries discriminated by labour skills. For the remaining countries, Germany and Sweden clearly exhibit by far the smallest shares of the EU15 value added in the group of low-skilled industries. In contrast, Portugal has the lowest shares in high-skilled and the highest shares in low-skilled manufacturing. This applies equally to Greece, whereas Spain additionally enjoys significantly larger shares in medium-skilled blue-collar industries. The most pronounced characteristics of both Ireland and the United Kingdom are their low shares in the grouping of medium-skilled blue-collar industries. And finally, in Italy, the overall pattern slightly favours the two opposing poles of low-skilled labour on the one hand and high-skilled industries on the other. Looking at value added shares within the triad, Japan exhibits an even distribution, whereas the USA enjoys significantly higher shares in both high-skilled and medium-skilled white-collar industries. For the European Union as a whole, the opposite holds true.

Using the relative shares of value added within the country (Table 6.5), statistical cluster analysis can next be applied in order to group the individual countries according to the relative similarity of their specialisation patterns in the skill-type industry classification.

Table 6.5: Value added shares in total manufacturing 1997 (%): skill types

Country/ type of industry	Low skilled	Medium skilled/ blue collar	Medium skilled/ White collar	High skilled
Germany	23.65	27.32	30.69	18.35
France	29.15	21.37	32.92	16.56
Italy	35.87	19.19	26.89	18.05
Netherlands	33.55	14.70	39.88	11.87
United Kingdom	32.07	17.90	32.77	17.26
Ireland	28.38	6.17	39.08	26.37
Denmark	34.96	19.48	23.51	22.05
Greece	51.09	15.32	26.33	7.26

---

[2] Detailed tables on the relevant test statistics are presented in Miles et al. (1999).

Spain	40.31	25.51	24.35	9.82
Portugal	52.52	19.02	22.68	5.79
Austria	33.01	22.84	31.83	12.32
Sweden	19.07	24.58	38.02	18.33
Finland	23.40	15.25	46.30	15.05
Japan	29.15	21.71	33.67	15.46
USA	25.50	17.44	38.88	18.19
Belgium	36.42	20.68	31.19	11.71
Greece	50.81	12.73	29.66	6.80

The result is visualised in a so-called dendrogram (Figure 6.7), where countries are interpreted as being more similar in specialisation patterns, the closer to the origin their respective branches join the same trunk. Thus, the figure reveals that in Austria, Belgium, France, the United Kingdom and Japan the relative patterns of specialisation according to labour skills are very similar and relatively close to Germany and Sweden, which are both characterised by much higher shares of high-skilled industries. This is also the most robust pattern in the data, which has never been altered by any of the many variations of the distance measures, which can in principle be applied. In addition, close similarities between Italy and Denmark on the one hand, Finland and the Netherlands (often joined by the USA) on the other, as well as between Greece, Portugal and Spain did repeatedly appear. In all the different settings, Ireland was treated as a highly specific and outlying observation.

In the final mapping of the European Union's member states by their relative specialisation in value added shares, according to the discrimination of industries by labour skills (Figure 6.8), Germany and Sweden are most distinguished by their large shares in high-skilled, as well as both types of medium-skilled industries. In contrast, Italy and Denmark have equal shares in high-skilled industries, but perform less well in the medium-skilled categories. Finland, Ireland and the Netherlands constitute a heterogeneous group, which is difficult to classify. However, their most pronounced common characteristic is that they have particularly small shares of medium-skilled blue-collar as opposed to particularly high shares of medium-skilled white-collar industries. Following the prior cluster analysis, Austria, Belgium, France and the United Kingdom more or less represent the average pattern, whereas Spain, Portugal and Greece constitute the set of countries which are most specialised in low-skilled industries.

146   *Impact on Sectors and Enterprises*

Figure 6.7: Relative similarity in value added shares across industries 1997: labour skills

HIERARCHICAL CLUSTER ANALYSIS

Dendrogram: Average Linkage Between Groups; Squared Euclidean Distances

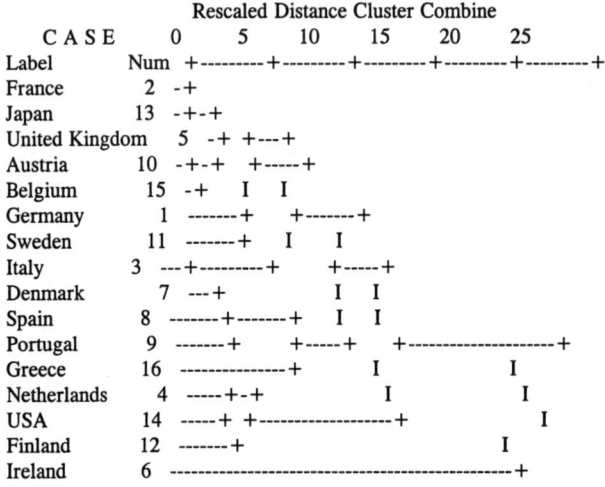

Figure 6.8: Mapping European specialisation (I): value added shares by skill types 1997

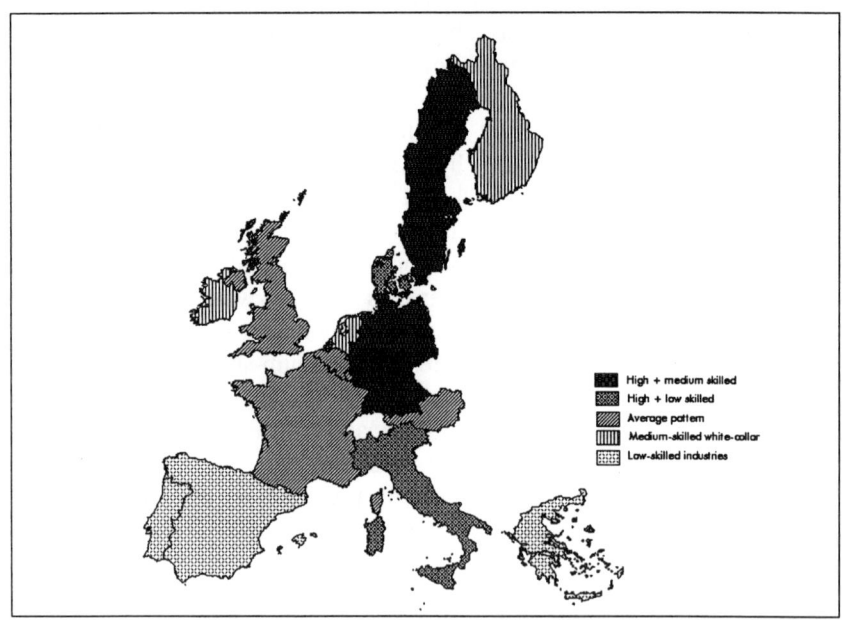

Tangible versus intangible inputs

Following the same steps, the analysis can be analogously applied to taxonomy I, discriminating between tangible and intangible factor inputs. First screening the appearance of statistically significant differences between a country's share in EU15 manufacturing, the following particularly pronounced patterns appear (Table 6.6). Beginning with Austria, the value added shares of technology driven industries are significantly smaller than in any other grouping. This pattern is shared with Greece, Portugal and Spain, whereby the latter is additionally characterised by much higher shares of labour intensive industries. Italy performs significantly less well in both marketing and technology driven industries, compared to the groupings of mainstream manufacturing, labour- and capital intensive industries.

At the opposite end of the spectrum, Ireland does best in precisely those industries which characteristically are particularly marketing or technology driven. France also shows the most pronounced specialisation in technology driven and the Netherlands in marketing driven industries. Denmark is unique in its particularly small shares of capital intensive industries. In the United Kingdom, the same applies to labour intensive industries. In both Germany and Sweden, the shares in EU15 value added are rather evenly distributed across industry types. The only significant differences reveal a larger share for mainstream manufacturing as opposed to typical marketing industries in Germany and compared to labour intensive industries for Sweden. As was already the case with regard to labour skills, the test statistics reveal no noteworthy significant differentiations for Belgium and Finland.

Table 6.6: Value added shares in total manufacturing 1997 (%): factor inputs

Country/ type of industry	Mainstream manufacturing	Labour intensive	Capital intensive	Marketing	Technology driven
Austria	26.39	18.83	16.29	24.61	13.88
Belgium	22.12	15.63	22.24	21.08	18.93
Denmark	29.50	14.68	12.08	28.60	15.13
Finland	22.82	14.98	28.59	17.54	16.07
France	21.94	13.57	14.69	22.10	27.69
Germany	28.06	14.13	15.46	16.22	26.13
Greece	19.61	17.71	19.26	35.36	8.06
Ireland	12.06	6.25	12.56	31.48	37.66

Table 6.6 continued:

Italy	28.88	19.84	15.90	17.65	17.73
Japan	24.86	16.00	16.01	21.00	22.13
Netherlands	21.50	11.75	19.23	31.20	16.32
Portugal	21.92	23.65	13.94	29.77	10.72
Spain	21.17	20.78	16.47	26.73	14.84
Sweden	21.95	12.07	21.25	16.16	28.57
United Kingdom	22.85	13.21	14.33	25.52	24.08
USA	21.26	12.22	13.51	23.17	29.84

Again examining the relative similarity in specialisation patterns by means of a cluster chart (Figure 6.9), the most robust relationship is the close similarity between France, the United Kingdom and the USA, as the only countries with particularly high shares in both marketing and technology driven industries.[3] On an equal basis with the first group in terms of specialisation in technology driven manufacturing, Germany, Sweden and Japan are commonly distinguished by their smaller shares in marketing driven industries, compensated either by higher shares in mainstream manufacturing or capital intensive industries. In all the technical variations applied during the testing of the robustness of the results, these six countries clustered together closely.

The same, however, cannot be said about the other country clusters. Finland, Belgium and Italy are often but not always grouped together, seemingly sharing an intermediate position in most variables. The same applies to the repeatedly common grouping of the Netherlands, Denmark and Greece on the one hand; or Austria, Portugal and Spain on the other. While the countries in the first grouping all have high shares in typical marketing industries, the second grouping is mostly based upon small shares in technology driven industries, compensated to different degrees by higher shares of labour intensive industries or mainstream manufacturing in the case of Austria.

The two latter cases also illustrate the intricate dangers of overinterpreting results, which are necessarily based on rather broad classifications. The industries comprised therein can still be highly heterogeneous and countries may, to large extents, differ in their actual

---

[3] The only exception is Ireland, whose outlying position in the cluster chart once more underlines its well-known status as a very special case in structural analysis.

factor combinations. Among the so-called marketing driven industries, food processing in Greece, for example, can still be expected to follow quite different rules of market organisation and competitive strategy than for example in Denmark. And the truth of this observation is even more evident when we compare the situation in Greece to the marketing driven consumer electronics or household supplies industries in the Netherlands.

Figure 6.9: Relative similarity in value added shares across industry types: factor inputs

HIERARCHICAL CLUSTER ANALYSIS

Dendrogram: Average Linkage Between Groups; Squared Euclidean Distances

```
Rescaled Distance Cluster Combine
C A S E         0     5    10    15    20    25
Label          Num  +---------+---------+---------+---------+---------+
France          2   -+
USA            14   -+---+
United Kingdom  5   -+   +-+
Germany         1   ---+-+ +-------+
Japan          13   ---+ I      I
Sweden         11   -------+    +---------+
Finland        12   -----+---+  I         I
Belgium        15   -----+   +-----+      I
Italy           3   ---------+     +----------------------+
Spain           8   -+-+           I                      I
Austria        10   -+ +-----+     I                      I
Portugal        9   ---+     +-+   I                      I
Netherlands     4   -----+---+ +--------------+           I
Denmark         7   -----+   I                I           I
Greece         16   -----------+               I
Ireland         6   --------------------------------------------+
```

The same argument applies when we look at the pattern of Austrian specialisation compared to Portugal and Spain. The fact that in 1997, the labour productivity of total manufacturing in Austria was nevertheless 46% above that of Spain and 69% above that of Portugal illustrates that similar patterns of specialisation can still comprise very different kinds of activities. Given the otherwise strong econometric relationship between structural characteristics and labour productivity, Austria appears to be a somewhat paradoxical case, maybe best regarded as an outlying observation placed somewhere at the opposite end from Ireland.

In short, the above results revealed similar patterns of specialisation between the mostly larger economies such as France, the United Kingdom and the USA on the one hand, as well as Germany, Sweden and Japan on the other. Their similarity can be considered a robust empirical observation. However, the same does not hold true for all the other relationships made evident by the cluster analysis. The results therefore do not support any neat classification of countries as they did for examplewith regard to industries, since this might induce a severe overinterpretation of otherwise revealing empirical regularities. The purpose of a comprehensive international comparison was therefore thought to be best served by the subtle and differentiated mapping as attempted below (Figure 6.10).

Figure 6.10:   Value added shares by skill types and factor inputs 1997

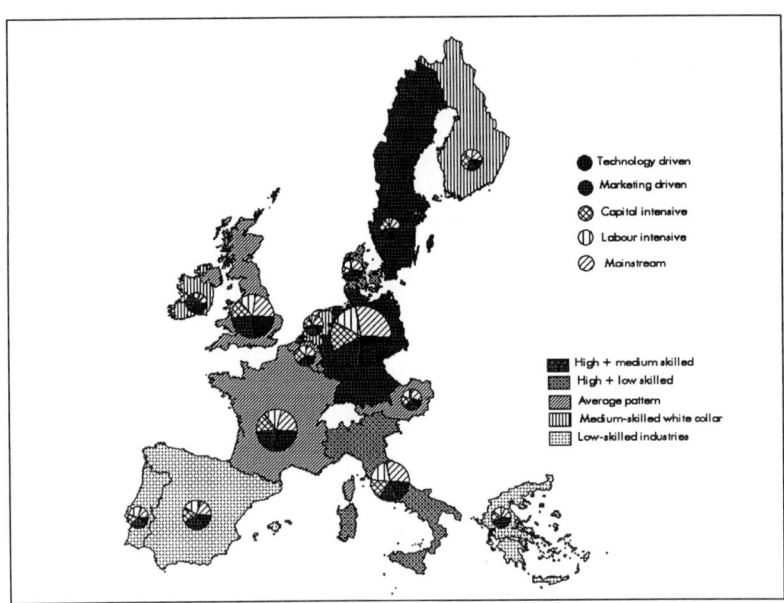

Summary

Complementing the firm level analysis of Mahony and Vecchi (1999), this contribution explored a deliberately structuralist approach, in an effort to make the increasingly important issue of "intangible assets" more "tangible" to empirical analysis and to link it to international comparisons on competitive performance. Based on recent work by Peneder (1999a), which established that between industries there exist pronounced and systematic differences concerning typical skill requirements and intangible inputs to production, this chapter further developed the overall argument in three consecutive analytic steps.

First, the structural analysis was linked to corporate strategy by an examination of the systematic differences in the strategic choices available to firms. The examination included a content analysis of about 100 industry monographs. The results confirmed that statistically significant differences do indeed exist. In addition to other conclusions, the results also showed that industries characterised by a greater amount of intangible inputs to production, on average have a larger set of competitive strategies at their disposal. Furthermore, a number of strong statistical relationships were established, showing for example that typical mainstream manufacturing industries (such as the machinery sector) rely most on the establishment of strong user-supplier links and complementary customer services, whereas typical marketing driven industries try to implement more horizontal differentiation through the introduction of new product varieties. In contrast, technology driven industries are more often characterised by vertical differentiation.

The second step demonstrated that the structural distinctions by industry type also make a difference with regard to economic performance. The case of labour productivity was explored in most detail, showing that investment in physical capital still has a major influence on labour productivity, but nevertheless constitutes only one of several contributing factors. The shares of white-collar high-skilled labour were found to exert the strongest influence, followed by capital investment, research expenditures (although they were highly correlated with labour skills) and advertising outlays.

Finally, the structural patterns identified in step one of the analysis were applied in mapping the differences in the international division of labour both within the European Union as well as in comparison to Japan and the USA. The results suggest that for the European Union taken as a single economic entity, the triad's shares in total value added are significantly lower for technology driven industries than for all other categories. The contrary holds true for the USA, whereas the Japanese patterns of specialisation exhibit no remarkable differentiations in terms of value added shares within the triad. The results also show that lower aggregate shares in technology driven industries are mostly due to significant differences within the European Union, since the patterns of specialisation for example for France, the United Kingdom and also for Germany and Sweden correspond well to the USA.

Acknowledgements

The research presented has been undertaken on behalf of and funded by the European Commission, General Directorate III. I am deeply indebted to Dagmar Guttmann and Traude Novak for their ever reliable support in the preparation of data and to Sonja Patsios for showing much patience in responding to the ambitious demands for visualisation. Special thanks also go to Serguei Kaniovski, who carried out the laborious job of extracting quantifiable data from industry monographs for the content analysis presented in the first section.

BIBLIOGRAPHY

Colecchia, A., Papaconstantinou, G., The evolution of skills in OECD countries and the role of technology, in: *STI Working Papers*, 1996/8, OECD, Paris, 1996.

European Communities, The Competitiveness of European Industry: 1998 report, Luxembourg, 1998.

EUROSTAT - European Communities, *Panorama of EU Industry 97*, Luxembourg, 1997.

Fors, G., Utilization of R&D results in the home and foreign plants of multinationals, in: *Journal of Industrial Economics*; 45(3), September 1997, pp. 341-58.

Griliches, Z., Issues in assessing the contribution of research and development to productivity growth, in: *Bell Journal of Economics*, 10, 1979, pp. 92-116.

Kaniovski, S., Peneder, M., Intangible investment and competitive strategy, mimeo, 1999.

Mahony, M., Vecchi, M., More R&D or more advertising? Tangible and intangible investments and economic performance: evidence from company accounts, paper presented at the symposium on "Intangible assets and the Competitiveness of the European Economy", Louvain-la-Neuve, 28-30 April, 1999.

Miles, I., Peneder, M., Tomlinson, M., *Intangible Investments, Industrial Sectors and Competitiveness. International Comparison*, Report to the European Commission (DGIII-A5), June, 1999.

OECD, OECD data on skills: employment by industry and occupation, *STI Working Papers*, 1998/4, Paris.

Peneder, M., Cluster techniques as a method to analyse industrial competitiveness, in: *IAER-International Advances in Economic Research*, 1, 3, August 1995, pp. 295-303.

Peneder, M., Industrial location and sectoral specialisation. An extension to Krugman's model of cluster formation by pooled labour markets, paper presented at 25th annual EARIE conference, Copenhagen, 1998.

Peneder, M., Intangible investment and human resources. The new WIFO taxonomy of manufacturing industry, *WIFO Working Papers*, No. 114, May, 1999a.

Peneder, M., Creating a coherent design for cluster analysis and related policies, in: OECD, *Boosting Innovation. The Cluster Approach*, OECD proceedings, Paris, 1999b, pp. 339-59.

7. Intangible Assets and Service Sectors: The Challenges of Service Industries
Ian Miles and Mark Tomlinson

Introduction

The service sectors deal primarily with intangibles; their main products are largely "immaterial". They transform the state of goods, people, environments, or symbolic resources, rather than manufacture material products. Intangible investment presumably plays a role in the structure and performance of these sectors even more critical than elsewhere in the economy. But demonstrating how, to what extent, and why this is the case is not easy. In addition to the general problems in assessing intangible investment discussed elsewhere in this book, services tend to be particularly neglected in statistical appraisals, including analyses of innovation and competitiveness. Though considerable effort in defining and generating appropriate indicators is now under way, from Eurostat, OECD, and others, we still lack much systematic information. It is difficult to characterise subsectors of services in detail, which is particularly unfortunate because service sectors are extremely heterogeneous. At present we cannot approach the sort of taxonomic exercise that is undertaken in respect of the role of intangibles in manufacturing sectors elsewhere in this book.

Nevertheless, this chapter is able to present a preliminary examination of a number of data sources that throw light on different elements of services' own use of intangibles. The data refer to different countries and points in time, and cannot be systematically matched as of now. However, some comparison of the results of the different approaches in general terms is possible, and the material is indicative of what might be achieved as a result of considerably more detailed study.

The types of data that are available to work with include:

- Services' R&D activities, as recorded by the OECD and national statistical agencies (though we shall note reservations as to the scope of these statistics).
- Services' innovative activities and expenditures more generally, as assessed through CIS (Community Innovation Survey) and similar firm-level surveys. (These also provide some limited material on another intangible - intellectual property - though again there are reasons for caution with respect of such data.)
- Services' use of producer services, including IT services and other knowledge-intensive services (often aggregated together rather unhelpfully), as represented in input-output tables.
- Skill structures of employment in service sectors, as depicted in national surveys of employment (and as made comparable in recent OECD work on high and low skilled work cross-sectorally and cross-nationally). Some countries' data permits examination of very specific labour flows between sectors, and allow a first glimpse into issues of lifelong learning at work.

The chapter reviews such data sources and considers some of the results that may be extracted from them. It suggests a characterisation of service subsectors that is a step toward the sort of typology developed and implemented for manufacturing industry. Finally, it relates this characterisation to recent evidence on the economic performance of European service industries. The provisional conclusion is that the sectors with most technology-related intangible investment are particularly dynamic ones; but their trade performance, while impressive, is coming under challenge.

The Services Challenge

The limited scope of service sector statistics is well known. Efforts have begun in recent years to improve the situation, but these are only slowly bearing fruit. Analysis of intangible investment is always problematic, but for this reason it is even more problematic for services. A few "stylised facts" about services indicate how the study presented here has to be seen as only a very preliminary scouting-out of the field. We will merely mention:
- The *high level of aggregation* of many service sector statistics. Most

service sectors contain very diverse subsectors within them, and these are typically bundled together to provide very broad categories. Thus we find extremely advanced and very traditional branches coexisting within categories like "inland transport" and "financial intermediation". Even a "modern" sector like software will range from firms producing cutting-edge products, through those simply customising standard products to fit vertical niche markets, through to activities which are much more like retail.

- This *heterogeneity* of services has another important element. Most service sectors are extremely skewed in their size distributions, with a few international firms coexisting with a large tail of SMEs (small and medium-sized enterprises) and microbusinesses. The technology, management, organisation, and intangible investments of a hypermarket are very different from those of a corner shop, those of a global management consultancy company from those of one of the many one-person consultancies. Sectoral comparisons run the risk of overlooking the crucial nature of such size variations.

- There is an argument that the evolution of services varies considerably across countries, in consequence of several factors. Public sector services very much depend upon political decisions concerning the rise and decline of the welfare state. And business services have a great deal to do with national industrial organisation, which affects the decision as to whether to outsource or obtain services in-house. Furthermore, many services are or have been heavily regulated sectors and sheltered from strong international competition either because of this or because of the (historically) low tradability of their products. All of these factors are shifting under the influence of globalisation, but presumably their legacies are strong ones. (We shall not in the main examine government and public sector services in the following analysis, though these are important sectors for national competitiveness, if not in the main competitive in their own right.)

- Many *received indicators* have been forged with manufacturing industry in mind, and have less applicability or relevance to services than would be desirable. As with sectoral disaggregation, so many occupational categories used to describe service workers simply provide a recursive classification amounting to little more than "employees of this particular service sector", which allows for limited comparative work, of course. Other measures are poorly recognised by service firms – thus there is continuing evidence that even when service firms are systematically sampled in R&D surveys, they may fail to recognise that their technology development activities actually do fall within the Frascati definition of R&D. Equally, it may also be that services do invest more in other forms of technology development than conventional R&D.

- A similar point applies to *intellectual property regimes*, and thus to the data sets that can be formed from, say, patent statistics. Though some service firms do patent, this strategy for protection of IP is markedly less prevalent in services. In some service subsectors copyright plays an important role,[1] but there are no comparable indicator sets here, and copyright protects artistic expression as well as technical innovation. And some services protect their IP through other means like trademarks, design rights, and more importantly by contracts with business partners, employee regulations, and the like.[2]

This is a very partial list, which could be extended at great length. But despite these problems and issues, it is obvious that a scouting-out of the field is vital. Services are important parts of the economy, in their own right – they typically dominate Western economies – and in terms of their contributions to other sectors.[3] And, being largely involved in the production of intangible products, these are sectors where we would anticipate intangible investment to have particular significance.[4] Thus the first analyses presented below will hopefully be an encouragement to much more work at developing and interpreting relevant data in years to come.

Classification of Services

It is widely recognised that services are such a heterogeneous category that it is necessary to work with a more meaningful categorisation of different types of activity. One of the best—known approaches moved away from ISIC groups to provide a classification that mixes function with

---

[1] As it actually does in manufacturing. Analysis of the CBI Innovation Survey data for the UK actually shows the manufacturing firms replying to have greater propensities to make, and numbers of accumulated, copyrights, trademarks, etc.
[2] For small-scale survey data here see I. Miles et al., Services Processes and Property, *International Journal of Technology Management*, 1999.
[3] Considerable evidence is accumulating on the contribution of intermediate service inputs to the performance of user firms and sectors. See Tomlinson's chapter in I. Miles and M. Boden, 1999, *Knowledge, Innovation and Services*.
[4] Peter Hill, 1999, *Tangibles, Intangibles and Services: A New Taxonomy for the Classification of Output*.

market type.

Originally proposed by Singelmann (1979),[5] this classification has been used by many researchers seeking to chart the development of services in the national and international economies. The functional and market roles of the different groups of services address how far their operations are designed to support private consumers or businesses, to distribute goods and information or to provide social services.

The four groups in this approach are thus:

- Producer services (e.g. finance, business services);
- Distributive services (e.g. trade, transport, communication);
- Personal services (e.g. entertainment, hotels and catering, domestic service);
- Social services (e.g. medicine, health, government).

This classification has been useful, but has its problems. For example, postal services are placed in the "social services" category (why are they not treated as a distributive service? On the other hand, does it make sense to include telecommunications along with physical transport in distributive services?). The producer services category includes many services that support consumers as well as businesses, for example banks and insurance companies; at fairly high levels of aggregation many services are "mixed" in terms of the markets they serve.

Another approach differentiates three different types of service, in terms of their core processes.[6] These are services whose main functions are:

- effecting *physical transformations*,
- those directly concerned with changing the (biological or psychological)

---

[5] J. Singelmann, *From Agriculture to Services*.
[6] Set out e.g., in I. Miles, 1993, Services in the New Industrial Economy. All services – indeed all economic activities – are ultimately concerned with affecting the state of human beings, of course. This classification distinguishes those services which do this directly, where the service provider's medical or interpersonal interaction with the client is central, from those where what is being centrally acted upon is a physical product like a hotel room or a meal, or an information product like a bank statement or TV programme. There are many ambiguities and boundary issues, however. Some information services, for example, come close to education in helping individuals acquire knowledge highly tailored to their own requirements - some even provide routes to self-knowledge similar to counselling and even medical services. We classify financial services in general as an information service because the bulk of the activities here are essentially about transforming signs - processing information about property rights, interest rates, holdings of currency and stocks, etc.

state of *human beings*,
- and those whose main activities involve *information*.

Figure 7.1 presents an indicative guide to different services' location on these two dimensions – it is necessarily a rough guide, because within most branches of the service sector there are different niches, varying in the extent to which services are customised to client requirements.[7] The classification can be interpreted in both sectoral and product terms, though it should be remembered that some service products are not produced by service sector firms (e.g. computer hardware firms produce computer software and maintenance services), and some service firms produce products that are categorisable as manufactures (e.g. published reports from consultancies, packaged software sold on magnetic or optical discs through retail channels).

The threefold distinction of services in terms of their core transformative processes usefully differentiates both past patterns of technological development, and current patterns of IT development in services. We cite it here because it proves to have some relevance to the analysis of intangibles data presented later in this paper. The issue of client intensity and customisation is also extremely relevant, though is harder to get a handle on. Some recent innovation surveys do provide evidence as to the extent to which different service branches are providing standardised or specialised services – showing both cross-sectoral variations, and considerable variety within sectors.

Classification of Manufacturing Sectors in the Intangible Investment Perspective

As presented elsewhere in this volume, Peneder has used US data and cluster analysis of 100 NACE three-digit manufacturing industries, to identify five, mutually exclusive groupings:

- *Mainstream manufacturing* where input combinations did not show a pronounced reliance on any of the four particular input factors that characterise the subsequent clusters;

---

[7] A German survey of innovation in service industries allows for some examination of this. See B. Tether et al., 1999, "Standardisation and Specialisation in Services; Evidence from Germany". While sectors do vary in terms of average focus on standardised or specialised products, all sectors display great diversity.

- *Labour intensive industries*:
- *Capital intensive industries*;
- *Advertising intensive industries;*
- *Research intensive industries*.

On the basis of OECD data on skill composition of industrial sectors, a threefold classification is produced:

- *low-skilled industries* with particular low shares in white-collar high skills and mean to low shares in blue-collar high skills;
- *medium-skilled industries* (sometimes differentiated between blue- and white-collar industries);
- *high-skilled industries*.

The data for services industries is too aggregated, and too limited, to allow for such a detailed statistical analysis. However, this approach does suggest some lines that we can take further, which will allow for some broad and tentative conclusions to be reached in respect of services.

In what follows, we shall draw upon several sets of data. For examining human resources issues, we shall mainly use the same OECD data set[8] as does Peneder in his contribution to this volume. However, we shall use country-level data for only a few countries, rather than combining results from all of the different countries. (This enables us to see some rather puzzling variations across countries.) In examining investment patterns across services industries we shall use UK input-output (IO) data for 1990 in particular, which presents a relatively high disaggregation of services outputs and inputs. And in examining technology development efforts we shall be using results of the UK data set from the Second Community Innovation Survey (CIS2).[9]

---

[8] OECD, 1998, *Data on Skills: Employment by Industry and Occupation*. Thanks to OECD for making these data available on the Web!

[9] Data released to us by the UK Department of Trade and Industry, to whom thanks. In due course we hope to report data for other EU countries participating in CIS2, but it is taking much longer to obtain these data than anticipated. All of the analyses discussed here could be valuably extended to other countries, though it takes time to gain requisite familiarity with the data.

Figure 7.1: A classification and impressionistic mapping of services

Level of client intensity/ customisation:	Main Class of Transformation:		
	Physical services	**Human services**	**Information services**
High	Hotels	Surgery	Bespoke software
	Domestic service	Counselling, help and advice services	Management consultancy
		Hairdressers	Legal services
	Traditional restaurants	Mass education	Insurance
Moderate	Laundry	Welfare services	Accountancy
	Airlines		Real estate
	Retail and Wholesale Trade		Banking
			Telematic services
			Telephone services
	Fast food Restaurants		Package software
	Mass public Transport		Broadcast radio/TV
Low	Postal services		
	Freight transport		

Human resources

The OECD data set allows for cross-national and intertemporal comparison of employees in terms of white- and blue-collar workers, and high and low-skills. Underlying the occupational categories used in the OECD data set's classification are different levels of educational attainment. Occupations are aggregated into four groups:

- White-collar high-skill (WCHS): legislators, senior officials, and managers (Group 1), professionals (Group 2), technicians and associate professionals (Group 3).
- White-collar low-skill (WCLS): clerks, service workers (Group 4), shop and sales workers (Group 5).

- Blue-collar high-skill (BCHS): skilled agricultural and fishery workers (Group 6), craft and related trade workers (Group 7).
- Blue-collar low-skill (BCLS): plant and machine operators and assemblers (Group 8), elementary occupations (Group 9).

While many differences emerge across countries, as we would expect in manufacturing, the largest employment shares are accounted for by BCLS and BCHS, while in services the largest shares are accounted for by WCLS and WCHS. The skill profile of total employment showed similar patterns in three groups of countries: the United States and Canada; Australia and New Zealand; and the European countries. In the analyses below we concentrate on European data, finding interesting cross-national variations here too. Future work might well extend this to more countries and groups of countries.[10]

To begin with, Table 7.1 presents the OECD data for all UK service sectors represented in the study. Services are on average strikingly more white-collar-based than other sectors; overall they have a slightly lower level of high skills, but the level of white-collar high-skilled workers is higher. However, the interesting variations appear within services. Ordering the subsectors according to the share of high-skilled white-collar workers in their overall employment (Table 7.2), three groups emerge.

---

[10] Before presenting some results, we should sound a warning note: the OECD study authors concluded that, on the basis on analysis of within- and between-industry influences on changes in occupational levels, their measures of skill seem more comparable for manufacturing than for non-manufacturing.

Table 7.1: Occupations in UK services, 1991, OECD dataset

Sector	Shares of Total Employment				
	White-collar	Blue-collar	HSWC	High-skilled	Low-skilled
Wholesale / retail trade, hotels, restaurants	*86%*	*14%*	*30%*	*36%*	*64%*
Wholesale trade	66%	34%	33%	42%	58%
Retail trade	88%	12%	31%	37%	63%
Hotels and restaurants	97%	3%	25%	27%	73%
Transport, storage and communications	*54%*	*46%*	*21%*	*33%*	*67%*
Transport and storage	43%	57%	22%	30%	70%
Communications	77%	23%	21%	40%	60%
Finance, insurance, real estate, business services	*95%*	*5%*	*53%*	*56%*	*44%*
Finance	98%	2%	49%	49%	51%
Insurance	99%	1%	49%	50%	50%
Real estate and business services	93%	7%	56%	60%	40%
Community, social and personal services	*90%*	*10%*	*48%*	*54%*	*46%*
Public administration and defence	92%	8%	45%	49%	51%
Sanitary and similar services	81%	19%	16%	19%	81%
Social and related community services	96%	4%	60%	61%	39%
Recreational and cultural services	83%	17%	47%	59%	41%
Personal and Household services	67%	33%	18%	41%	59%
International services	93%	7%	64%	67%	33%
Total services	*87%*	*13%*	*41%*	*47%*	*53%*
Total economy by Occupation	*71%*	*29%*	*36%*	*52%*	*48%*

Source: Derived from OECD, *Data on Skills: Employment by Industry and Occupation*, STI Working Papers, 1998/4.

- *Very Low Skills.* The first group consists of services involved with personal and domestic services and sanitation. Many of these are physical services cleaning up after household and to some extent industrial activity (though there are also activities like hairdressing here). They have low shares of HSWC, though personal services do have a good share of HS workers more generally (still lower than the services average).
- *Low/Moderate Skills.* The second group consists largely of services which are involved in moving and storing artefacts – trade, horeca, communications, transport – and their share of HSWC also falls below

the average for the economy, though it is higher than for the first group. (Again, we note that within this group there are exceptional subclasses that do not fit the description above – communications is a case in point.)
- *Very High Skills.* The third group, in contrast, has extremely high levels of HSWC, and comprises symbol-processing services such as FIRE (finance, insurance, and real estate), and social, community, and cultural services, which combine symbol-processing with interpersonal and human operations. This group would appear to have outstanding volumes of intangible investment in terms of "knowledge workers".

Table 7.2: Services in UK ranked by HSWC intensity

	Shares of Total Employment
Sector	**High-skilled white collars**
Sanitary and similar services	16%
Personal and household services	18%
Communications	21%
Transport and storage	22%
Hotels and restaurants	25%
Retail trade	31%
Wholesale trade	33%
Public administration and defence	45%
Recreational and cultural services	47%
Finance	49%
Insurance	49%
Real estate & business services	56%
Social and related community services	60%
International services	64%

Source: OECD, 1998.

This classification differs from Peneder's – largely because of the low presence of blue-collar workers in these sectors.[11] However, it does show similarities, in terms of a grouping on a continuum of skill-intensity – which seems to correspond well to other ideas as to how service sectors might be classified.

Do these figures correspond to data for other EU countries? A preliminary comparison with data for France and Germany, from the same OECD source, reveals general similarities, but also some marked differences. These latter imply that caution needs to be taken in generalising from these data. Notably, the "sanitary services" group appears to have many more HSWC workers in France and Germany. The

---

[11] Neither has it been obtained by statistical manipulation, rather by visual inspection.

same is true for German personal/household services. Practically all members of the second group discerned in the UK data have similar characteristics in France, but these report fewer HS and HSWC workers in Germany. As for the third group, UK social and community services emerge as higher skilled than in the other countries, whereas German FIRE sectors are generally extremely high in HSWC shares.

Table 7.3: Three countries' data on the share of high-skilled employees in the workforce of service sectors

		UK 1991		France 1990		Germany 1990	
SIC	Industry	HSWC	HS	HSWC	HS	HSWC	HS
9200	Sanitary and similar services	15.74%	19.48%	49.57%	51.59%	73.47%	77.89%
9500	Personal and household services	18.23%	41.47%	11.25%	38.25%	32.35%	48.21%
7200	Communications	20.94%	40.40%	39.91%	45.40%	3.32%	19.00%
7100	Transport and storage	21.63%	30.27%	20.51%	30.27%	5.53%	13.96%
6300	Hotels and restaurants	25.48%	26.89%	34.19%	35.77%	6.17%	34.92%
6200	Retail trade	30.61%	36.93%	38.98%	48.64%	12.96%	25.86%
6100	Wholesale trade	32.82%	41.97%	43.66%	50.37%	17.15%	26.50%
9100	Public administration and defence	45.05%	48.84%	52.66%	59.72%	27.72%	40.33%
9400	Recreational and Cultural services	46.69%	58.58%	63.55%	72.29%	68.83%	73.27%
8100	Finance	48.63%	49.49%	43.59%	44.10%	81.96%	82.66%
8200	Insurance	49.25%	50.11%	52.86%	53.61%	76.12%	77.28%
8300	Real estate and Business services	55.58%	59.91%	53.93%	59.48%	56.43%	61.15%
9300	Social and related Community services	59.53%	61.41%	28.54%	33.86%	38.44%	41.18%
9600	International services	64.44%	67.37%	52.00%	54.14%	47.24%	57.85%
TOTS	Total services	41.47%	47.37%	42.43%	49.95%	34.05%	45.26%
TOT	Total economy by Occupation	35.68%	51.86%	33.73%	53.98%	26.69%	52.25%

Source: OECD, 1998.

Interpreting these variations is not easy. There may well be substantial differences in industry structure and occupational composition across the three countries – a possibility which raises intriguing questions. But it may simply be classification issues (on one or other axis) which are generating these variations, despite all the effort in achieving comparable NACE and ISCO classifications.[12]

---

[12] The sectoral classification derives from ISIC rev. 2, in fact, and may be more problematic than the ISCO88 occupational classification. But note the tendency for Germany to record

In the later parts of this chapter we shall again be largely reliant on UK data, so we shall use this as the benchmark here. However, these cross-national variations do suggest that we need to be cautious in assuming that the conclusions as to clusters and other features of services are universally applicable. This corresponds to the observations of many commentators that there are marked differences in the structure of service industries in different countries, even within Europe (and even more pronounced differences with the United States and Japan).

Recent work being undertaken using UK data on individual careers allows us to gain a first impression, too, of the accumulation of human resources through on-the-job training, technology use, and lifelong learning, within various sectors. It shows flows of professionally skilled staff out of manufacturing into Knowledge-Intensive Business Services, and a particularly strong concentration of learning in these sectors.[13]

The knowledge intensive business service (KIBS) sectors emerged as the most dynamic with respect to the learning economy framework. Exploring the evolution of the economy in terms of the shifts in the sectors and occupations of knowledge workers shows that many knowledge workers in UK manufacturing shifted into services during the 1980s. However, knowledge workers in services themselves have been highly stable with regard to occupation and sectoral position throughout this period. Thus, the embodied knowledge generated within the service sector has tended to remain within it. (Though these sectors contribute their knowledge to their clients.) As for other groups of worker, those from skilled manual as well as lesser skilled non-technical occupations had very little opportunity to move into the more dynamic KIBS sectors during the restructuring of the 1980s. This reflects and reinforces the more general polarisation that is evident between skilled and unskilled workers in the OECD studies. The learning economies transform the needs of the economy for skills, but workers with skills that are no longer required can find it very difficult to acquire new ones.

The sectoral disaggregation that was possible in the study described above is limited by the sample size. It may well be possible to undertake more detailed analysis using the sorts of labour force and career data available in several Nordic countries. This would seem to be another line

---

fewer HSWC shares, though more HS in general. This corresponds to a common view of German industry as being less inclined to deskill BC workers in favour of management than countries like the UK.

[13] See Mark Tomlinson and Ian Miles, 1999.

of work well worth advancing further.[14]

Input-output evidence on expenditures and investment

Internationally comparable IO tables are very heavily aggregated, so this section will be based heavily upon analysis of the UK data for 1990 only, which allowed for an analysis of a reasonable number of services sectors. In earlier studies we have shown services to be particularly IT intensive, in terms of their capital intensity (especially FIRE and business services).[15] The focus of this chapter on intangible investments means that it is "current consumption" data that are of more interest. Thus, we can examine the expenditure on various intermediate services. First, let us note that the consumption of KIBS is very much an activity of services themselves in the UK. Thus, the top 20 users of business services (excluding communication services) in the economy as a whole in 1990 were:

- Insurance
- Owning and dealing in real estate
- Other business services
- Computing services
- Renting of movables
- Personal services
- Estate agents
- Other professional services
- Legal services
- Banking and finance
- Air transport
- Ownership of dwellings
- Auxiliary financial services
- Advertising
- Printing and publishing
- Accountancy services
- Sea transport
- Oils and fats
- Electronic consumer goods, records and tapes

---

[14] Studies carried out by DRUID in Denmark, STEP in Norway, and NUTEK in Sweden, among others, usefully develop analyses in these directions.
[15] OECD, 1993 and I. Miles et al. 1990.

- Distribution and repair of vehicles, filling stations and other goods

Table 7.4: *Services' use of intermediate services and labour, UK 1990*

	As percentage of output				
	Advertising	R&D	Communications	Computer	Labour
Wholesale distribution	1.30	0.10	1.10	1.30	31.60
Retail distribution	1.30	0.10	0.50	0.90	45.60
Distribution and repair of vehicles	2.00	0.10	1.20	1.90	35.00
Hotels, catering, public houses	1.10	0.10	1.20	1.20	39.30
Railways	2.70	1.70	1.20	3.50	62.10
Road and other inland Transport	1.00	0.20	0.80	1.80	34.60
Sea transport	1.20	0.60	1.20	2.50	15.60
Air transport	2.20	0.00	1.00	5.50	24.60
Transport services	0.70	0.30	1.30	2.30	28.90
Postal services	0.70	0.20	1.00	1.70	57.40
Telecommunications	1.10	0.20	4.80	2.30	28.80
Banking and finance	1.70	0.20	2.60	2.70	30.00
Insurance	3.60	0.30	5.80	3.20	19.60
Auxiliary financial services	0.40	0.00	5.20	2.10	46.10
Estate agents	2.50	0.20	3.90	2.40	39.40
Legal services	1.30	0.20	2.40	1.10	38.80
Accountancy services	0.80	0.20	1.50	1.70	50.90
Other professional services	2.40	0.40	0.90	2.90	41.90
Advertising	2.90	0.70	1.50	1.00	37.30
Computing services	4.00	1.20	1.50	3.30	33.20
Other business services	1.80	0.80	1.50	2.30	38.30
Renting of movables	3.30	0.10	0.50	0.60	26.30
Owning and dealing In real estate	1.30	0.20	1.90	1.40	23.70
Sanitary services	0.40	3.40	0.30	1.00	71.40
Education	0.20	0.90	0.40	1.70	76.70
Research and development	0.20	3.90	0.40	0.70	52.50
Health services	0.10	5.90	0.80	1.10	33.20
Recreational and welfare services	1.60	0.30	0.70	1.30	41.60
Personal services	1.80	0.00	1.60	2.70	32.20

Source: UK IO tables.
Note: Public administration, domestic services, and ownership of dwellings are omitted due to data anomalies.

Most of these are actually services themselves. The service sector is in fact heavily dependent and interconnected with itself, and makes a great deal of use of these intangibles (at least in the UK). There are some notable additions from manufacturing, namely printing and publishing, oils and fats, and electronic consumer goods.

Examining the service inputs in more detail, we focus on the very interesting cases of telecommunications, computer services, advertising, and R&D services. The data are presented in Table 7.4. Several striking features are apparent. Thus, the following services appear to have particularly high labour shares in their output:

- Education
- Sanitary services
- Railways
- Postal services
- Research and development
- Accountancy services
- Auxiliary financial services
- Retail distribution
- Other professional services
- Recreational and welfare services.

Considering these in light of our earlier discussion and the OECD human resources information, it is apparent that there are two different types of service featured here: those dependent on highly skilled symbol-processing work, and those highly dependent on more physical work (whether blue-collar or not) distributing goods and servicing infrastructures.

In terms of *outsourced R&D* intensity (as a share of output), three services are outstanding:

- R&D itself,
- sanitary services,
- and health services.

The first two of these are among the most labour-intensive sectors, the third is moderately labour-intensive. *Thus it appears that, when we are seeking to classify sectors in terms of their intangible investments, the contrast between labour-intensive and R&D-intensive clusters may not hold up for services.* But recall that these data deal with outsourced R&D; and while at a firm level our analysis of innovation survey data indicates a high correlation between propensity to conduct in-house R&D and to purchase it from external sources, we also find considerable sectoral variations. In-house R&D is much more extensive than outsourced R&D,

despite the growth of this service in recent years.[16]

Advertising expenditure also cuts across the labour-intensity indicator, however, suggesting again that the taxonomy Peneder develops for manufacturing may not be readily transferable to services. If we consider the most intensive users of advertising services, these are:

- Computing services
- Insurance
- Renting of movables
- Advertising
- Railways
- Estate agents
- Other professional services
- Air transport
- Distribution and repair of vehicles, filling stations and other goods

And several of the most labour-intensive services come just below these.

What is more, some of the same sectors emerge as among the most *computer-service*-intensive sectors, which comprise:

- Air transport
- Railways
- Computing services
- Insurance
- Other professional services
- Personal services
- Banking and finance
- Sea transport
- Estate agents
- Telecommunications
- Transport services
- Other business services
- Auxiliary financial services

Clearly these data deserve a good deal more exploration, and extending the analysis to similar tables for different countries and periods will be

---

[16] Two rare and valuable studies of outsourced R&D are the more qualitative study by Jeremy Howells, 1997 and the very interesting "input-output" survey of sectors performing and using outsourced R&D by Antoine Rose, 1997.

worthwhile. While the result may not be a neat clustering in terms of intensity of use of one or other intangible asset, there may be useful empirical taxonomies of services developed. For instance, Tomlinson[17] has previously conducted some clustering of services from the 1990 UK IO tables, examining how far they have similar patterns of inputs and outputs represented in the data set.

Thus, using a standard principal components analysis with varimax rotation on the domestic flows matrix (for services only) gives a seven factor solution. Based upon the factor loadings, we derive the clusters in Table 7.5, graphically depicted in Figure 7.2 below. Note, however, that some services (such as insurance) have a high factor loading on more than one factor, which suggests that there is a considerable overlap between them. The clusters seem quite sensible in the sense that the sectors within them have intuitively common themes such as financial services, communications, etc. It has therefore been possible to show, in terms of the distribution profile of services, that certain commonalities are present in the input-output data and that it makes a good deal of sense to look at it in this way. Again, it would be valuable to replicate and extend this analysis with other years and countries' data.

Table 7.5: 'Clusters' of services from factor analysis 1990

Cluster	Sectors
Finance	Banking and finance; Auxiliary financial services; Estate agents; Legal services; Accounting; Other prof services; Advertising; Computer services; Other business services; Renting movables; Personal services
Public	Sanitation; Education; R&D; Health
Inland transport	Distribution and repair of vehicles; Railways; Road/inland transport
Transport services	Sea transport; Air transport; Transport services
Communications	Postal services; Telecommunications; Insurance
Distribution	Wholesale distribution; Retail distribution.; Hotel catering
Other	Recreation and welfare

---

[17] M. Tomlinson, 1997, Knowledge and technology flows in the service sector and manufacturing: Preliminary analysis using UK input-output tables, CRIC Working Paper, University of Manchester.

Figure 7.2: Service 'clusters' from UK IO data: overlapping clusters in services

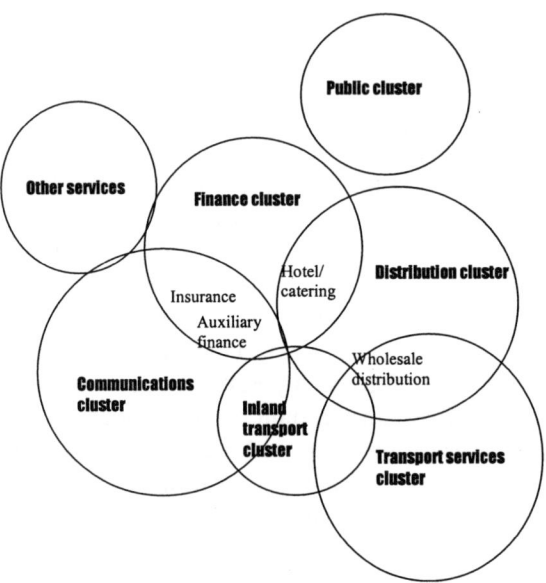

R&D and innovation survey data

For a long time it was widely claimed that services do not undertake R&D, despite the contradictory cases of telecommunications, software, and railways (for example). More recently, as services have begun to be included in R&D surveys, it is apparent that some of them do engage in considerable R&D activity. (Table 7.6 presents OECD data on intramural R&D in services). The figure is as high as 40% of BERD (Business Enterprise Sector) in some countries, and at around 25% of this figure in more current UK and US data. We suspect that it remains understated, both because of sample coverage (innovation surveys typically suggest higher levels of R&D expenditure than the standard R&D surveys), and because the R&D indicator has formulation and response biases which privilege manufacturing. (This is probably behind the negligible R&D recorded for UK financial services, and perhaps also retail, which case study work has shown to engage in considerable volumes of software and telematics development effort.)

Interpretation of the OECD data is made difficult by two issues in particular:

- Data coverage is very unevenly developed across countries. Only eight of the set of 24 countries covered all eleven of the service sectors in question; seven covered only five or fewer (Japan only covered one – financial services – thoroughly). Table 7.6 selectively presents data where coverage is more complete for services believed to have higher R&D propensities, but even here we see several recurrent omissions.
- The indicators deal with absolute expenditures of the sampled firms, and are not weighted by firm or sectoral expenditures in general. Thus they are not intensity measures, and comparison across countries is rendered problematic because of differences in industrial structure. The only intensity measures presented in this source deal with the services sector as a whole, comparing its share in BERD to its share in value-added.

The data are thus most useful for giving an indication of the role of services' production of technical knowledge in national innovation systems, more than for telling us about commonalities or differences in the share of services' intangible investments. Business services, computer services, and R&D services are important contributors to BERD in many countries (the latter are 10% of BERD in current UK data, for example)

Alison Young, in her commentary on the OECD data, noted that, first, "services R&D is no longer negligible". Second, "high service R&D spenders" consist of (1) those where R&D spending is also a relatively high percentage of value added (over 0.4%) i.e. Norway, United States, Denmark, United Kingdom, Canada and Australia plus Finland and (2) those where it is a low percentage (under 0.2%) i.e. New Zealand, Greece, Spain, Iceland, and Portugal. Norway and Denmark have higher than expected services R&D intensities. A larger group – Austria, Belgium, the Netherlands, France, Germany, Japan, and Sweden – have low apparent R&D intensities for the service industries and SMEs compared to manufacturing R&D efforts, probably due to the lower coverage of services industries included in their R&D surveys.

Table 7.6: OECD data on services' share of business R&D expenditures, c 1993

Industry	Norway	New Zealand 1991	Greece	Denmark
Service Sector	41.7	35.2	32.7	32.5
Wholesale and retail trade	0.6	..	0.7	5.3
Hotels and restaurants	0	..	..	..
Transport and storage	0.3	..a	0.9	..a
Communications	2.4	1.4	0.2	3.7
Post	0	..	..	..
Telecommunications	2.4	..	0.2	..
Financial intermediation	1.2	..	0.9	..
Real state, renting and bus activities	37.2	31.2	29.8	23.6
Computer and related	9.9	..	22.7	6.7
Software consultancy	5.8	..	22.7	..
Other computer services	4	..	0	..
R & D	23.7	7.5	4.5	1.8
Other business activities	3.7	..	2.6	15
Services not elsewhere classified	0	..	0.2	..

Industry	Australia	Canada	United States	Portugal 1992
Service Sector	31.7	30.6	26.1	21.2
Wholesale and retail trade	7.3	4.7	..	..
Hotels and restaurants	..	..	..	..
Transport and storage	..	0.3	..	0.5
Communications	..	2.8	4.6	12.1
Post	0.3	..	..	..
Telecommunications	..	..	..	..
Financial intermediation	3.7	6.7	..	..
Real state, renting and bus activities	17.2	16.1	..	8.6
Computer and related	7.3	4.9	8.5	..
Software consultancy	6.9	..	..	..
Other computer services	0.4	..	..	..
R & D	2.7	8.8	1.8	4.8
Other business activities	7.1	2.4	..	3.8
Services not elsewhere classified	0.4	..	..	0

Industry	United Kingdom	Iceland 1992	Spain	Finland 1994
Service Sector	18.2	17.3	15.9	13
Wholesale and retail trade	0.1	..	0.1	0.3
Hotels and restaurants	..	..	0	..
Transport and storage	0.1	1	0.3	0.4
Communications	3	..	2.6	2.5
Post	..	..	0	1.9
Telecommunications	..	..	2.6	0.6
Financial intermediation	..	..	0	..
Real state, renting and bus activities	14.9	16.3	12.7	9.6
Computer and related	5.3	..	3.1	4.8
Software consultancy	..	..	2.6	..
Other computer services	..	..	0.6	..

R & D	9.5	16.3	3.2	1.7
Other business activities	0.2	..	6.3	3.1
Services not elsewhere classified	0.1	..	0.4	0.2

Industry	Ireland	Italy 1991	Mexico	Turkey
Service Sector	11.4	10.7	7.8	7.3
Wholesale and retail trade	1.1	0.1	1.5	0
Hotels and restaurants	0	..	0	0
Transport and storage	0.3	0.1	0	0.6
Communications	*4.8*	*1.8*	*0*	*1.9*
Post	0.8	..	0	0
Telecommunications	4	..	0	1.9
Financial intermediation	0.5	..	0	..
Real state, renting and bus activities	4.7	8.5	4.7	4.9
Computer and related	*0*	*2.5*	*0*	*4.9*
Software consultancy	0	..	0	4.8
Other computer services	0	..	0	0
R & D	4.7	6	4.7	..
Other business activities	0	..	0	..
Services not elsewhere classified	1.6	0.2	1.6	..

Source: OECD, DIRDE database, January 1996 plus additional national sources, cited by Alison Young, *Measuring R&D in the Services*, OCDE/GD(96)132 STI Working Papers 1996/7, with notes on missing sectoral coverage added for this chapter.

Another source of data is innovation surveys, and the current round of CIS2 surveys (mostly in the field in 1997) provides coverage of services for a large majority of EU countries for the first time. To date we have only been able to examine the UK data set, and some preliminary results from this may be cited. Table 7.7 presents information on the expenditure of service sectors[18] (weighted up from the sample to correspond to the size structure of the sectors in question) on a number of technology related activities. Analysis of the data set indicates that *services, compared to manufacturing, put proportionally more effort into technology development activities other than R&D*. Nevertheless, several service sectors have very high R&D intensities, and are in many respects similar to the hi-tech manufacturing sectors in this and some other ways. Most notable here are: R&D services; computer services; and business activities. All of these are among the top sectors for total technology spend (the total spend vector consistently comes to more than the sum of the preceding parameters, and while this may in part be a result of weighting and rounding, we are still dubious about its accuracy, especially in the case of renting of machinery, where the result is so anomalous that we are

---

[18] Utilities and recycling have also been included, for their service-like features.

postponing analysis of this sector – based on a small sample of firms, but so are some of the others – until further clarification is obtained.)

They also have unusually high training expenditures, machinery, and (with the exception of business activities) expenditure on market introduction of innovations. Financial and other information-processing services (including business services) emerge as major consumers of "other external technology", presumably largely a matter of software and related systems. This corresponds with their high IT use. The distinctive distributions of total technology spend among these different categories are displayed in Figure 7.3. Despite fairly high correlations between these activities at firm level, there are marked sectoral differences.

There is clearly much to explore in such data, which allow us to look at collaborations and in some cases further labour force details. This promises to be a powerful line of analysis in the future. Perhaps indicative of the potential here is a recent study by Evangelista and Savona[19] who use data from a somewhat earlier Italian innovation survey. They apply factor and cluster analysis to establish a taxonomy of service sectors in terms of orientations to innovation. This has resemblances to the classifications developed for manufacturing industry by Pavitt, and extended to services by Soete and Miozzo.[20] Their classification suggests that two major dimensions differentiate innovative stance. The first distinguishes between sectors with much in-house technical effort, including R&D and design, and those which are more reliant on external technology acquired through investment. The second relates to the extent to which they are linked to manufacturing suppliers as opposed to being heavily linked to their clients. While there may be some doubt about the robustness of these classificatory dimensions, they do yield an intuitively appealing group of clusters, as represented in Figure 7.4.

---

[19] R. Evangelista and M. Savona, 1998.
[20] K. Pavitt, 1984; L. Soete and M. Miozzo, 1989. These are actually firm-level taxonomies, one consequence of which is that differentiation can be drawn between the very innovative large firms in say, retail and finance, and the long tail that exists in these sectors.

Table 7.7: UK services technology activities, CIS2 data (1997) - Percentage of turnover ordered by final column

Sector	R&D:		Acquisition of: (linked to innovations)		Training	Market introduction of innovations	Total technological innovation spend
	Intra-mural	Extra-mural	Machinery and equipment	Other external technology			
73 Research and Development	24.60	3.24	6.87	0.81	0.65	7.08	46.86
67 Auxiliary Financial Intermediaries	0.10	0.03	4.01	14.85	0.10	0.03	25.48
71 *Renting of Machinery*	*0.01*	*0.00*	*1.32*	*1.39*	*0.01*	*0.00*	*16.95*
74 Business Activities	2.37	0.00	4.15	2.62	0.46	0.04	12.25
72 Computer and Related Activities	6.40	0.25	1.56	0.66	0.57	0.54	12.19
37 Recycling	0.63	0.08	1.96	0.01	0.01	0.00	5.83
51 Wholesale	0.08	0.00	0.12	0.91	0.63	0.81	4.94
65 Financial Intermediaries	0.14	0.00	0.12	1.38	0.36	0.00	4.46
66 Insurance and Pensions	0.00	0.00	0.16	2.51	0.04	0.02	3.85
64 Post and Telecommunications	0.32	0.00	0.84	1.38	0.21	0.50	3.71
60 Land Transport	0.00	0.00	1.29	0.13	0.06	0.02	3.00
61 Water Transport	0.00	0.00	0.04	0.15	0.05	0.00	2.99
55 Hotels and Restaurants	0.02	0.00	0.01	0.01	0.02	0.00	2.01

Table 7.7 cont'd

70 **Real Estate**	0.17	0.02	0.29	0.23	0.05	0.04	1.80
45 **Construction**	0.05	0.01	0.07	0.01	0.02	0.00	1.35
52 **Retail**	0.00	0.00	0.02	0.01	0.00	0.02	1.08
40 **Electricity, Gas and Water**	0.04	0.01	0.37	0.08	0.00	0.00	0.85
62 **Air Transport**	0.03	0.00	0.02	0.03	0.01	0.10	0.67
50 **Sale of Motor Vehicles etc**	0.04	0.00	0.00	0.25	0.01	0.00	0.57
41 **Collection, Purification**	0.07	0.05	0.10	0.05	0.01	0.00	0.47
Entire Population, Including manufacturing	*0.73*	*0.05*	*1.25*	*0.58*	*0.15*	*0.30*	*6.75*

Figure 7.3: Selected services' technology related expenditures

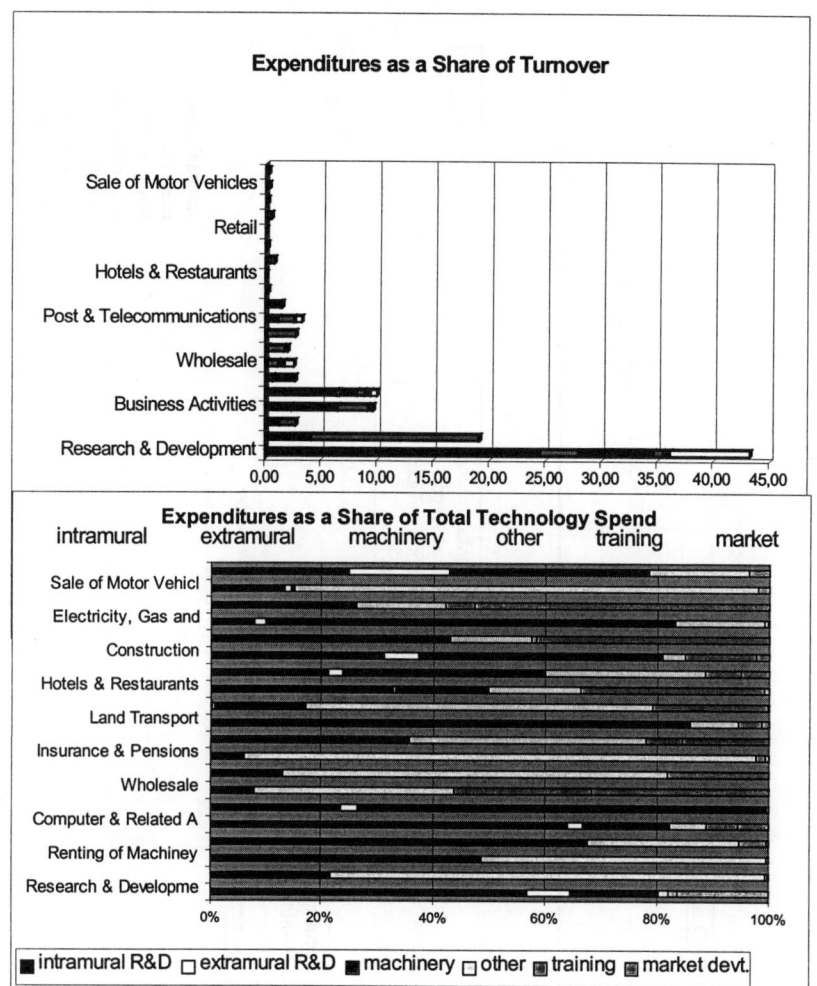

Figure 7.4: Classification of innovation stances of Italian services from innovation survey data

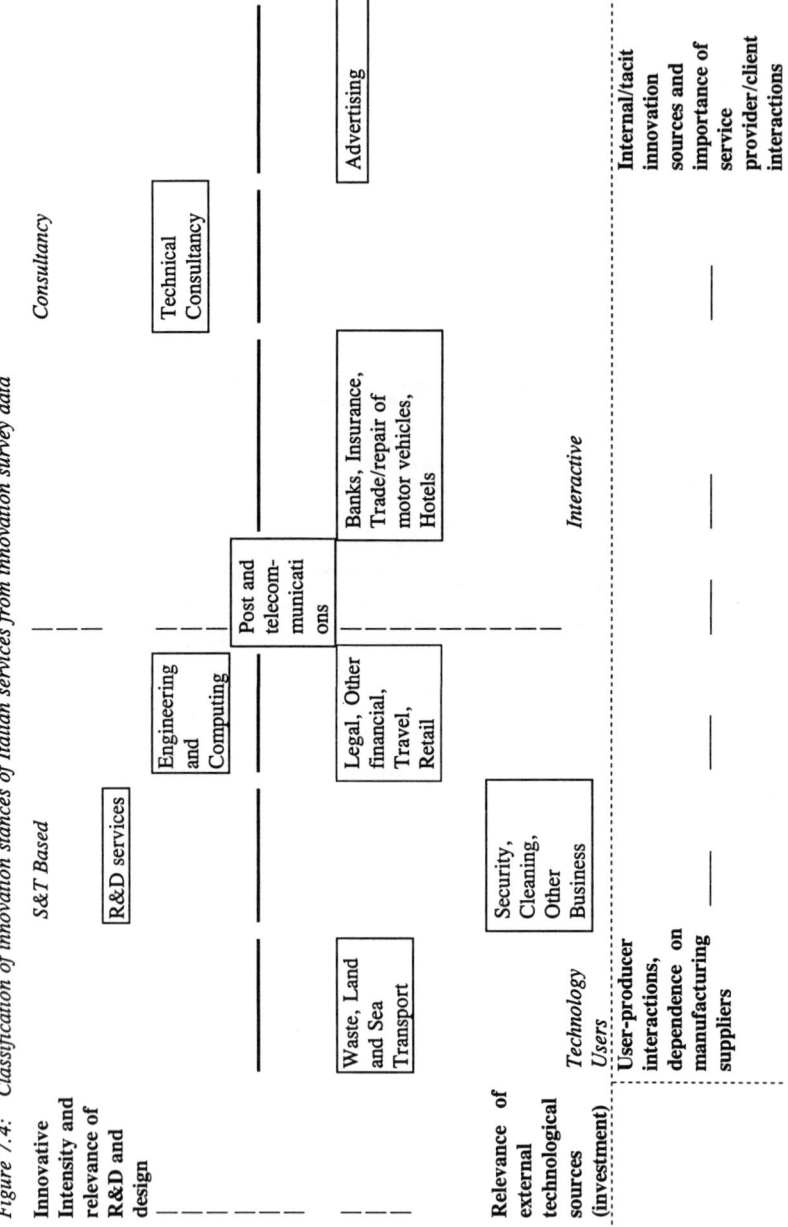

This classification again suggests the distinctiveness of a number of what are here termed "S&T based services" – the group of R&D, computer and software services, engineering services and some hard-to-classify business services.

Services categories and services performance

The study so far suggests that:

- a differentiation of service sectors in terms of patterns of intermediate inputs could be a useful approach to take further, with relevance to studies of innovation and competitiveness;
- approaches to clustering developed for manufacturing are unlikely to be reproduced for services;
- the identification of "neat" clusters for services sectors may well be made more difficult by the considerable heterogeneity of these sectors by sub-branches and by scale. Clustering needs to be sensitive to the acute diversity of service firms, especially large versus small firms.

Several useful measures for distinguishing between services do appear to emerge, however, especially those relating to the knowledge-intensity of their activities, as indicated by such variables as skill composition and investment in development of technological knowledge, and use of IT and IT services. Other parameters of intangible investment, such as advertising spend, do not appear to form the basis for distinct clusters. There may be historical reasons for this (e.g. bank and telecommunications deregulation prompting a great deal of advertising in these sectors at particular moments in time). But it is likely that in large part the different patterns reflect the distinctive articulation of service sectors into business and consumer markets.

Future work should further consolidate the classifications hinted at above, and systematically relate these to data on trade, value-added, productivity trends, and the like. Despite the ever-present data problems, there is considerable scope for exploring such approaches further.

Not only is there scope, there is need. As Eurostat and OECD data confirm, services as a whole have grown more rapidly than manufacturing, and business services[21] have grown more rapidly than

---

[21] Eurostat notes that: "the EU has some two million business services enterprises. In most Member States the number has doubled in a decade".

services in general. Business services achieved 5.5% in employment and 5.4% in value-added over 1980-94, as compared to 0.4% and 1.5% for manufacturing and services combined in the EU, and for the 1984-93 period the growth rate of exports and imports were 8.7% and 10.2% respectively, as compared to 5.1% and 5.2%.[22]

A more recent OECD source similarly comments, for a large sample of OECD countries, and discussing "strategic business services" - computer software and information processing services;[23] research and development and technical services; marketing services; business organisation services; and human resource development services - that:

> the growth of these business services, by whatever measurement, has been robust in general and spectacular ... in the recent years, including those years when overall economic growth was slow or absent. For example, in Finland, official data report that value added for the broad business services group grew by 9 per cent annually during the period 1985-95. Similarly, in the United Kingdom, official estimates for a somewhat broader group of business services, state that these are some of the fastest growing activities in the UK economy, with real growth rates in output being double those of the entire economy in the past decade. Value added in France for the strategic business services expanded by 19 per cent between 1993-95 and 20 per cent in 1995-96. Other measures, such as turnover, illustrate the expanding role of such services in other economies. For example, in the United States, growth in turnover for these activities totalled 50 per cent between 1990 and 1995 including much higher growth for individual activities while in Japan turnover increased by 31 per cent between 1989 and 1994.[24]

However, EU trade performance is surprisingly mixed, as is implied by the 1984-93 data cited above. Paraphrasing a recent Eurostat study[25] of trade, total EU services transactions (including trade between Member States) doubled over the decade to 1995 (reaching 821.4 bn ECU in 1995); but this growth was import led. The services' balance of trade worsened - from some 30 bn ECU in 1986 to nearly 2.2 bn in 1995 (this was a big drop from 1994's figure of 11.8 bn). The biggest falls were not

---

[22] European Commission, 1998.
[23] The largest of these, followed by business organisation services.
[24] G. Vickery and M. Murphy, 1998.
[25] Eurostat, 1998.

only in transport, but also in miscellaneous business, professional and technical services. Both of these declined dramatically between 1994 and 1995. Most of this decline involved trade with the United States, declining from a balance of 6.3 bn in 1994 to 4 bn.

Other Eurostat data indicates a growing and in some branches strong overseas presence in EU services. This is particularly marked in Knowledge-Intensive Business Services (KIBS) (Table 7.8), with the technology-based services and more social and organisational ones appearing side by side.

This may just be another indicator of the process of globalisation that is occurring in many dynamic sectors. There are evident opportunities from learning from overseas KIBS, which should be welcomed - cautiously, given evidence that in some cases in the past there has been some import of inappropriate organisational models derived from US specificities, and the possibility that KIBS might preferentially recommend other suppliers from their home countries.

But the data may also relate to the negative balance of trade trends in KIBS. These are sectors which are evidently of growing importance in the emerging knowledge economy. They are sectors which, our preliminary analysis suggests, are in many cases among the leading performers in terms of intangible investment. International trade and foreign presence should be welcome spurs to innovation and improved competitiveness. But the trends seem to suggest a declining EU position. This is despite the common view that these are areas of particular strength for Europe (or at least for some EU countries).

Thus the further analysis of relevant data is not merely a matter of academic interest – charting and, hopefully, understanding these developments is a highly policy-relevant task. The difficulties of service sector data must not be allowed to stand in the way.

Table 7.8: Employment by non-national enterprises in EU services (%)

Sector	Countries covered	%
Legal and accounting activities, tax consultancy, market research, management consultancy	DK, NL, S, FIN, UK	20.6
Labour recruitment activities	NL, FIN, UK	19.7
Computer and related activities	DK, E, NL, FIN, S, UK	18.1
Renting	DK, NL, S, UK	17.1
Wholesale trade	DK, FIN, F, IRE, I, NL, S, UK	15.8
Advertising	DK, NL, FIN, S, UK	15.0
Research and development	S, UK	12.5
Auxiliary transport activities, travel agencies	NL, FIN, S, UK	11.9
Security services and industrial cleaning	NL, S, UK	11.1
Architectural activities and technical testing	DK, NL, S, UK	9.4
Water transport	DK, NL, S	8.7
Retail and motor trade	E, F, IRE, I, NL, S, UK	6.1
Road freight transport	NL, S, UK	5.4
Hotels and restaurants	DK, E, NL, S, UK	5.1
Miscellaneous business activities	DK, NL, S, UK	3.8

Source: Eurostat, ***International Ownership in Trade in Service Activities, First Findings of a Study on Foreign Affiliates*** which notes that, due to different reference years, country groupings, etc., these statistics should be taken only as a rough indication.
Note: Foreign or non-resident enterprises are those where ownership or control is outside the country where the enterprise's activity takes place.

Conclusions

While data are limited and in some cases only just becoming available, it is possible to examine services' intangible investment in systematic ways. The chapter's preliminary study, utilising some of these data, allows us to reach some substantive – if tentative – conclusions. However, the conclusions as to the need and opportunity for further research are not at all tentative. There are both policy and intellectual reasons for seeking to advance such lines of enquiry rapidly, and there are promising directions and data sources for further analysis. The study of services needs to be rapidly brought up to a par with that of manufacturing, in the field of intangible investment as elsewhere.

References

European Commission (1998), Annexe 2 of *The Contribution of Business Services to Economic Performance: towards a common policy framework*, Brussels, European Commission, COM 1998 534 final.

Eurostat (1998), *Statistics in focus, economy and finance*, n₀.2/98, "Dynamism of Trade in Services: The Growth of International Trade in Services", Luxembourg.

Evangelista, R. and Savona, M. (1998), *Patterns of innovations in services: the results of the Italian innovation survey*, presented at RESER Conference, Berlin, Oct 8-10 1998.

Hill, P. (1999), "Tangibles, Intangibles and Services: A New Taxonomy for the Classification of Output", paper presented at CSLS Conference on *Service Sector Productivity and the Productivity Paradox*, Ottawa, Canada, April 11-12, 1999.

Howells, J. (1997), "Research and Technology Outsourcing", *Technology Analysis and Strategic Management*, vol 11,1, pp 17-29.

Miles, I. (1993), "Services in the New Industrial Economy", *Futures*, 25/6, July/August, pp. 653-672.

Miles, I., Andersen, B., Boden, M. and Howells, J. (forthcoming), "Services Processes and Property", *International Journal of Technology Management*.

Miles, I. and Boden, M. (forthcoming), *Knowledge, Innovation and Services*, London: Continuum.

Miles, I. et al 1990, *Mapping and Measuring the Information Economy*, Boston Spa, Wetherby: British Library, (LIR Report 77).

OECD (1993), "Usage Indicators - A New Foundation for Information Technology Policies", Paris: OECD, Information Computer Communications Policy ICCP 31.

OECD (1998), "Data on Skills: Employment by Industry and Occupation", *STI Working Papers*, 1998/4, OECD, Paris.

Pavitt, K. (1984), "Sectoral Patterns of Technical Change: Towards a Taxonomy and a Theory", *Research Policy*, 13 (6) pp. 343-373.

Rose, A. (1997), "Transfer of Funds for Research and Development in Canadian Industry 1993", Ottawa, *Statistics Canada Working Paper*, ST-97-05

Singelmann, J. (1979), *From Agriculture to Services*, Sage, Beverly Hills.

Soete, L. and Miozzo, M. (1989), "Trade and Development in Services: A Technological Perspective", *Working Paper*, 89-031, MERIT, Maastricht.

Tether, B., Hipp, C. and Miles, I. (1999), "Standardisation and Specialisation in Services: Evidence from Germany", University of Manchester, *CRIC Working Paper*.

Tomlinson, M. (1997), "Knowledge and Technology Flows in the Service Sector and Manufacturing: Preliminary Analysis Using UK Input-

Output Tables", *CRIC Working Paper*, University of Manchester

Tomlinson, M. and Miles, I. (1999), "The Career Trajectories of Knowledge Workers" paper presented at the "OECD Workshop on S&T Labour Markets", Paris, 17th May.

Vickery, G. and Murphy, M; (1998), "An International Study Of Selected Business Services", OECD, Paris.

8. Discussion
Lionel Fontagné

Chapters 6 and 7 point out the growing importance of intangible assets in world competition. Such an outcome can be viewed as the result of changing engines of growth in developed economies: there is a consensus over the dematerialization of growth. This is a well-known problem for the accounting of growth; this is also a puzzling issue for the design of economic policies. As far as international comparative studies are concerned, this renewed framework raises however three specific concerns:

- Firstly, what is the theoretical link between competitiveness, intangible investment and growth?
- Secondly, how does one handle activity data, occupational data and international trade data in order to tackle such issues?
- Lastly, is it possible to infer from the observed data any reliable relationship between intangibles, productivity and microeconomic performances?

Before addressing these three issues, it is worthwhile summarising the core of the convincing demonstration provided by these chapters. These papers provide an outstanding overview of competitiveness-related issues, using valuable data, original methodologies and reaching interesting results. They provide a valuable demonstration of *why* (if not how) *public policies are concerned by intangible investment in the manufacturing and service sectors*. The demonstration can be summarised as follows: structural differences do exist between countries, between activities and between firms; such differences matter for their competitiveness; hence, specialisation within the triad is increasingly driven by such differences. However, there is no way to classify activities according to their investment in intangibles along the same principles for the manufacturing and the service sectors.

Structural differences are revealed by data. At the macroeconomic level, countries are characterised by location dependent comparative advantages. Such advantages are based on the endowment in human capital and on R&D expenditures. These advantages are to be distinguished from the microeconomic specific advantages of firms, which are based on intangible investments in marketing and in innovation. Peneder stresses the former type of advantages, and identifies indirectly the latter, using micro-data, as the result of firms' strategies. Miles and Tomlinson use various sets of data and highlight the strong specificity of the service sector – which is not limited to the lack of data.

Industries characterised by large intangible investments highlight better competitive performances, as shown by Peneder, a result qualified by Miles and Tomlinson who stress the poor European trade performance in services transaction, especially as far as relationships with the United States are concerned. Notwithstanding the latter result, at the sectoral level "intangibles matter". Peneder, using the Panorama of European Industry, provides a clear-cut characterisation of corporate strategies: cost based strategies, product differentiation and market organisation strategies differ strongly between clusters of activities. If the rationalisation of production appears to spread all over the productive system, relocation strategies are concentrated in "medium-skilled white collar industries"; etc.

However, given that intangibles matter, it must not be the ultimate difference between firms belonging to a given sector – a dimension which cannot be identified on the basis on the related qualitative survey. A benchmark would provide more detailed information on the relationship between conduct and performances; a relationship that cannot be tackled properly here. To put it differently, it matters whether you produce potato chips or electronic chips, but if you produce electronic chips, do differences in intangible investment with your competitors (that must be weak anyway) provide a statistical significant explanation of differences in performances?[1] At this stage we would encourage the reader to compare

---

[1] Concerning the relationship between productivity and intangible assets, the central estimate in Peneder's paper is an OLS explaining the value added per employee using four factors intensities: capital, R&D expenditures, brand expenditures, skills. One gets a positive relationship between all these intensities and labour productivity. It is however difficult to interpret the impact of capital intensity, or that of skills. What one simply identifies is the fact that qualified labour is paid a high wage; and that the substitution of capital to labour enhances the apparent productivity of the latter. Hence, it would be more convincing to consider total factor productivity. In addition, what is interesting is the dynamics of the phenomenon, not the cross-sectional dimension. Hence, a panel of industries over a period

the results obtained so far at the sectoral level with the ones obtained by Mahony, also in this book, using data for individual firms.

In the same way, the causality could be reversal as suggested by the problems of interpretation raised by the bulk of IO empirical studies based on the Structure Conduct Performance Paradigm.[2] Here it is difficult to asses whether firms are performing because they invest in intangibles, or invest in intangibles in order to raise barriers to entry to potential competitors threatening their high profitability. Specifically, this question is a corner stone for the cluster "market driven industries" identified in Peneder's clustering.

In total, at the sectoral level, specialisation of countries within the Triad is driven by such differences. Since (manufacturing or service) *activities strongly differ in their propensity to undertake intangible investments in advertising or in R&D, it must* be the very source of comparative advantages for countries. The resulting international division of labour can be characterised as follows:

- *Labour intensive activities* that produce tradable goods are highly exposed to foreign competition, noticeably to price competition. The prospects for growth in production are limited. Relocation strategies will largely affect such activities.
- *Capital intensive activities* that pay high wages due to high productivity are also exposed to job losses and stagnating demand. Not surprisingly, capital as a tangible asset is no longer the source of comparative advantages for countries.
- *Advertising intensive activities* are characterised by high growth. Here, the horizontal differentiation of products (brand, variety etc.) is the very source of advantages. As a result, intangible assets such as marketing are the condition of job creation.
- *Research intensive industries* are powerful engines of growth. However, they do not create many jobs in Europe as a whole, for reasons that have to be investigated further. Noticeably, the frontier between these activities and new services activities is weak: knowledge intensive business services share common characteristics with high-tech industries (qualified workers, large amounts of incorporated R&D, outstanding volumes of intangible investments) and provide much job opportunities, even in Europe.

---

of at least ten years would certainly be more convincing. And this panel would have to control for fixed effect associated with the position of industries within the clustering.

[2] See Jacquemin, A., (1987), *The New Industrial Organization*, MIT Press.

- Within the growing immaterial economy, the quite mythical *KIBS* (knowledge intensive business services) emerge as the most dynamic and the most creative of value added.

The core of the argument having been briefly summarised, let us turn to the two concerns raised by this demonstration. Firstly, both papers being based on a tentative clustering of activities raise the concern of how to classify them properly using a unique ordering scheme for various countries. Secondly, and maybe more fundamentally, the ongoing theoretical developments of the growth and international trade theories suggest the consideration in more depth of the issue of quality ladders, qualification and innovation.

I now turn to the first part of my comments, addressing **the clustering methodology** used in various ways in both chapters. The latter can be briefly summarised as follows.

Peneder's idea is to depart from the clustering methodologies used in the literature, that are based on simple cut-off procedures, or on input-output related methods combined with expertise at the product level. Faced with multidimensional data, it is worthwhile, according to Peneder, using advanced statistical methods to cluster activities within sectors. This is done here at the three-digit level of the NACE. The variables used for the clustering are labour intensity, capital intensity, the advertising/sales ratio and lastly the R&D sales ratio. Appropriate tests highlight that these dimensions are roughly orthogonal. Due to lack of data, this must be done introducing a hazardous assumption: US input combinations are representative for all other economic areas. Hence, using US data, an optimisation clustering technique allowing for the minimisation of within group dispersion is implemented. This classifies 100 industries into homogeneous clusters. The first partition leads to 32 clusters. A hierarchical clustering implemented in a second step leads to the four clusters referred to above (R&D intensive, advertising intensive, capital intensive and labour intensive) plus a residual category "mainstream manufacturing".

An alternative clustering based on OECD data distinguishes between four categories of employees, namely low-skilled, medium-skilled blue-collar, medium-skilled white-collar and high-skilled.

Miles and Tomlinson spend much time in the search for such clustering in the service sector, without success: "the data for services industries is too aggregated, and too limited, to allow for such detailed statistical analysis". Moreover, they record "marked differences" between countries and "caution needs to be taken in generalising from these data".

Lastly, the clustering identified for industries may not be used for services: "when we are seeking to classify sectors in terms of their intangible investments, the contrast between labour-intensive and R&D intensive clusters may not hold up".

Accordingly, such methodology raises a major concern, even if Peneder notices that "like any broad classification, this one must be interpreted with care, as industries within the categories are still highly heterogeneous and countries may, to large extents, differ in their actual factor combinations". The differences in factor intensities are indeed very important between countries, especially for the intangible intensive activities. The question remains, for three-digit industries on the edge of a cluster, whether the differences between countries is larger or smaller than between industries, for a given variable. A good example is once again provided by the high tech sector. For this cluster, OECD has done input-output calculations authorising the classification of industries according to their direct and indirect content in R&D – a methodology providing sizeable differences between countries.

Table 8.1: *Average technological intensity for major industrialised countries (%), 1990-93*

Technology	Intensity in R&D (direct and indirect)		
	High	Average	Low
United States	11.1	3.6	1.1
France	10.4	3.6	0.9
Canada	10.2	1.4	0.5
United Kingdom	9.0	2.7	0.7
Germany	7.7	3.9	1.0
Japan	7.4	3.8	1.5
Italy	5.8	2.1	0.4

Note: R&D expenditures by unit of output or value added.
Source: OECD, *Technology and Industrial Performance* (1996).

The clustering based on US industries can hardly be considered as representative of the European case according to the results listed in the table. In addition, the European industry itself is far from being homogeneous. Differences are larger between France and Italy than between the United States and France.

In addition, one has to be aware that, within clusters, *differences between products* are very important. Consider once again the technological sector. The high tech cluster entails industries (at the NACE three-digit level) producing high tech but also low tech products. Computers for example (NACE 300, "research intensive" cluster) accounts for 4.6% of EU15 total trade (1996). But only 1.5% of the corresponding trade flows consists of high tech products. Hence, only one third of the NACE position is high tech, whereas the whole position is to be considered as high tech according to Peneder's taxonomy. This is an extreme case. For aircraft and spacecraft, the bias is lower, as it is for instruments for measuring or radio transmitters. But pharmaceuticals are also an industry that raises this issue.

Table 8.2: *Share of high tech products (OECD-Eurostat list) in EU15 trade by NACE three-digit position, 1996*

NACE	High tech	Other	Total
353 Aircraft and spacecraft	2.1	0.5	2.6
300 Office machinery and computers	1.5	3.1	4.6
332 Instruments and appliances for measuring	1.0	0.3	1.3
322 Television and radio transmitters	0.9	0.4	1.3
244 Pharmaceuticals	0.8	1.8	2.6
321 Electronic valves and tubes	0.7	1.4	2.1
323 TV and radio receivers, sound or video recording	0.4	1.2	1.5
294 Machine-tools	0.4	0.8	1.1
241 Basic chemicals	0.3	5.6	5.9
242 Pesticides and other agro-chemical products	0.3	0.0	0.3
291 Machinery for production and use of mechanical power	0.2	2.3	2.5
233 Processing of nuclear fuel	0.2	0.0	0.2
316 Other electrical equipment n.e.c.	0.2	0.8	1.0
331 Medical and surgical equipment	0.1	0.8	0.9
312 Electricity distribution and control apparatus	0.1	0.9	1.1
334 Optical instruments and photographic equipment	0.1	0.4	0.5
313 Insulated wire and cable	0.0	0.4	0.4
366 Other manufacturing n.e.c.	0.0	0.4	0.4
296 Weapons and ammunition	0.0	0.0	0.0
283 Steam generators	0.0	0.0	0.1
295 Other special purpose machinery	0.0	3.0	3.0
Other NACE positions	0.0	90.6	90.6
Total trade	**9.4**	**90.6**	**100.0**

Note: Sum of exports and imports.
Source: Fontagné et al. (1999b), op. cit.

Lastly, *differences between qualities of products, for a given range of products* are to be considered thoroughly, since they say something about the innovation and growth story. This is precisely the basis of our second concern.

The theoretical *link between competitiveness, intangible investments and growth has to be investigated in depth,* as a starting point for empirical studies. One avenue of research stresses the dynamics of comparative advantages. In contrast to the conclusions of the classical theory of international trade, the specialisation of countries is not neutral. And more specifically, the specialisation in the cluster of innovative activities may have a cumulative impact on growth.

The textbook version of the effects of international trade, based on the static comparative advantages, misses a key issue: the dynamics of specialisation do matter. Activities do not have the same technological content, leading to an allocation effect that can be beneficial or detrimental to countries: advances or lags in technological industries may be cumulative. And precisely because they are intensive in intangible investments, high technology activities are subject to particularly high barriers to entry, and authorise rents to be extracted at the international level. Therefore, differences in specialisation of countries in technological sectors may distort the distribution of world income (the latter result can be obtained even in a static framework of imperfect competition)[3].

New theories of *growth* aiming at endogenously determining a long-term positive *per capita* rate of growth interpret technology as the result of a market process where innovation is a profit seeking activity. Since the innovator cannot capture all the benefits of this activity, social benefits are larger than private ones, as a result of positive externalities. *As far as trade in intangible intensive products is concerned*, the key issue is that firms compete in advertising and R&D, increasing the variety or the quality of products available within the integrated market. An outstanding illustration of the above distinction is provided by Peneder's Figure 6.1. Consider two strategic options: research and technology development and new varieties. These options can roughly characterise two ways of tackling competitive pressures, namely the vertical and horizontal differentiation of products. The "variety option" is largely adopted in the market driven cluster, and not in the technology driven cluster. And conversely for R&D development.

While variety versus quality is a rather classical distinction where trade patterns are concerned, in the dynamic perspective we are considering, Grossman and Helpman[4] highlight that variety and quality of products become two complementary engines of growth. Various conclusions can be drawn on this renewed basis. First, *history matters*, since an initial

---

[3] See Helpman, E. and Krugman, P. (1989) *Trade Policy and Market Structure*, MIT Press, Cambridge, Massachusetts.
[4] Grossman, G. and Helpman, E. (1991), *Innovation and Growth in the Global Economy*, Cambridge, Massachusetts.

lead in one activity subject to technological spillovers and cumulative know-how may open access to a worldwide market for the initial innovator. This initial lead may be associated with a large domestic market, opening access to economies of scale, to a large endowment of human capital to a favourable industrial policy. Here, we come back to public policies, especially in the European context. The size of the economy is a matter of regional integration policies: the achievement of the single market will provide a sizeable "domestic" market to European innovators. Going beyond integration of markets, *European horizontal policies are concerned*: education, R&D subsidies etc.

Such mechanisms being identified, it must however be kept in mind that openness disseminates technology,[5] domestic productivity being positively related to foreign R&D. Open economies benefit not only from international technological spillovers, gaining access to a wide basket of knowledge. Hence, as far as a study is concerned by the specialisation in knowledge intensive activities, it is important not to adopt a "Colbertist" view of international trade. Even large deficits in high tech products benefit the whole economy of the importer. Fontagné et al.[6] highlight that the bulk of traded high tech products are intermediate or capital goods, re-entering production processes and spreading technological progress all over the economy. Moreover, the OECD recently pointed out[7] that the largest user of embodied technology is the service sector.

In total, specialisation matters for European countries, notwithstanding the importance of intra-industry trade in their total trade. As the Commission pointed out in the exercise of assessment of the single market, *comparative advantages continuously matter because products differ by their quality*.[8] And quality is the result either of perceived quality as determined by investments in advertising, or the result of differing positions on an objective quality ladder associated with ongoing innovation. Concentrating on the latter determinant, one comes back to the dynamic perspective we are concerned with here. Helpman and Grossman[9] highlight that variety and quality of products are two

---

[5] See Coe, D. and Helpman, E. (1993), "International R&D spillovers", *NBER Working Paper*, 4444.

[6] Fontagné, L., Freudenberg, M. and Ünal-Kesenci, D. (1999), "Trade in Technology, and Quality Ladders: Where do EU Countries Stand?", *Journal of Development Planning Literature*, 14 (4), 527-548.

[7] OECD, *Technology and Industrial Performance* (1996).

[8] European Commission (1996), "Economic Evaluation of The Internal Market", *European Economy*, 4.

[9] Grossman, G.M. and Helpman E. (1991), *Innovation and Growth in the Global Economy*, MIT Press, Cambridge, Massachusetts.

complementary engines of growth associated alternatively with an increase in the variety of inputs leads or to a permanent upward move on quality ladders for each of a given number of varieties. Under the latter assumption, profit seeking private agents engage in R&D in order to introduce new products of rising quality.[10]

Since *growth* is *interpreted as a permanent upward move on the quality ladders*, the position of countries on these ladders for different activities provided valuable information on their position in international competition. If one takes differences in unit values as a good proxy of differences in quality, and differences in quality in the intangible-assets-intensive sector as a proxy for the position on the quality ladder, one can assess an objective ranking of countries.

Figures 6.3 and 6.4 of Peneder's chapter are highly stimulating from this point of view. Figure 6.3 plots unit values in EU trade for five clusters of activity (a clustering to be discussed below) in EU trade, in 1996. Figure 6.4 plots the standard deviation of unit values in the EU for these clusters in 1996 (a coefficient of variation could have however be preferred, since it has no dimension).

It can be observed that *EU unit values for exports are systematically higher than for imports, in all clusters, with the exception of research intensive activities*. Secondly, the dispersion in unit values is by far the most significant for the same cluster. Hence there is "something special" to be looked at in this cluster, given the type of question we are interested in. However, the statistical hypothesis testing performed so far in Peneder's chapter misses this issue: just consider "H1a" to illustrate this. Is it worthwhile testing if products belonging to the technology driven sector have on average a higher unit value than other products? Is there any chance for a ton of standard steel to be more expensive than a ton of electronic chips? There is more to investigate since unit values are concerned, and more to say concerning the difference between market driven and technology driven activities.

Before addressing such a puzzle, let us interpret the ranking suggested by these figures. Firstly, capital intensive activities highlight a very low unit value, tabulated in ECU per kg. This means that bulky products, symbolising the material nature of growth in the past, belong to this cluster. At the opposite extreme, the new, immaterial nature of products is in research intensive activities. Turning to the spread in unit values, capital intensive activities clearly lead to homogeneous products, having

---

[10] Aghion, P. and Howitt, P. (1990), "A Model of Growth Through Creative Destruction", *NBER Working Paper*, 3223.

similar prices. This contrasts with advertising intensive activities and labour intensive activities, and moreover with research intensive ones. In advertising intensive industries such differences are the result of investments in intangible assets such as brands. In research intensive activities it is the result of investments in innovation, new products being sold at a higher price. It can also be in this case the outcome of an aggregation of very different products, as advocated below. Lastly, in labour intensive activities, the observed pattern, namely price discrepancies and lower unit values of imports, may be the result of traditional comparative advantages.

Tackling simultaneously the clustering of industries and the position on the quality ladder for each industry belonging to the clusters corresponding to activities intensive in intangible assets would better match the policy issue with ongoing developments in the theoretical field. Consider in the table below a simple example of such a strategy.

Table 8.3: Revealed comparative advantage by technological level and by position on the quality ladder, Germany and United Kingdom, 1996

NACE3 Quality	Low	Medium	High	Total
GERMANY				
Cluster High Technology	0.6	2.2	-0.4	2.4
of which > 1/°°				
322 Television and radio transmitters	1.1	0.6	1.8	3.5
332 Instruments and appliances for measuring	0.4	0.5	1.3	2.2
241 Basic chemicals	0.1	0.3	1.4	1.7
294 Machine-tools	-0.2	0.3	1.5	1.6
242 Pesticides and other agro-chemical products	0.2	0.2	0.7	1.1
Other clusters	-43.2	-52.9	93.7	-2.4
Total	-42.6	-50.7	93.3	0.0
UNITED KINGDOM				
Cluster High Technology	-1.7	-4.3	14.8	8.8
of which > 1/°°				
353 Aircraft and spacecraft	-1.1	-0.2	4.1	2.9
332 Instruments and appliances for measuring	0.7	0.4	1.5	2.5
244 Pharmaceuticals	0.3	0.5	1.3	2.1
242 Pesticides & other agro-chemical products	0.3	0.3	1.0	1.7
Other clusters	-29.2	9.6	10.9	-8.8
Total	-30.9	5.3	25.7	0.0

Note: Comparative advantage measured by the contribution to the trade balance, per thousands of GDP.
Source: Fontagné, L., Freudenberg, M. and Ünal-Kesenci, D. (1999b) "Haute technologie et échelles de qualité: de fortes asymétries en Europe", *Document de travail CEPII*, 99-08.

Namely the comparative advantages of Germany and the UK in the technology intensive sector (as defined by OECD-Eurostat, a slightly more restrictive definition than Peneder's), by level of quality. Germany has an outstanding advantage in top quality products (+93.3), but these products do not belong to the high-tech cluster (-0.4). The explanation of the high quality of non-technological German products is threefold:

- Eurostat and the OECD do not classify cars as technological products;
- Non-technological German products embody other intangible assets raising their value (brands, etc.);
- Non-technological products (e.g. cars) have a large content in costly technological components raising their value.

Only five industries (at the three-digit level of the NACE) do not follow this scheme: radio transmitters, measurement instruments, basic chemicals, machine tools and pesticides.

In contrast, the UK appears to have a more balanced position. It is specialised in high tech products having a high unit value (14.8), and hence being on the top of the corresponding quality ladders, especially in aircraft. It is also specialised in top quality non-technological products, but to a much lower extent than Germany.

That being said, can one re-examine the diagnosis referred to above, stressing the lower value of EU exports than imports in Peneder's technology intensive sector? Using the methodology illustrated by the German and British cases, EU15 can be considered as an integrated economy trading with the world, notwithstanding the fact that only a small number of member states contribute positively to the result obtained. One gets a positive value (1.7) for the high tech sector, to be interpreted as a (weak) advantage for the EU of such activities. In addition, EU15 is specialised in products located on the top of quality ladders, and has a structural disadvantage in those located at the bottom.

Price-Quality EU15, 1996	Low	Medium	High	Total
Total High Technology	-2.7	1.2	3.1	1.7

To put it differently, EU15 is specialised in new products of higher price and imports older products, at the end of the product cycle. Such a diagnosis contrasts with the comparison of unit values referred to in Peneder's Figure 6.3. The explanation for such difference lies in the clustering methodology. This is our second concern.

Having stressed these methodological concerns associated with the studies presented here, I would like to conclude by emphasising once again the originality and the outstanding technicality of the corresponding papers. Without doubt, they pave the way to a new area of research that has been until now too often neglected.

9. Tangible and Intangible Investment and Economic Performance: Evidence from Company Accounts
Mary O'Mahony and Michela Vecchi

Introduction

The primary purpose of this chapter is to examine the impact of capital, both tangible and intangible, on company performance. Tangible capital is defined as investment in machinery, equipment, vehicles and structures. In this chapter we include two forms of intangible capital, research and development expenditures and other intangible investment which includes advertising, marketing etc. Company performance is evaluated using two measures, labour productivity, real sales per employee, and profitability, the ratio of net income to sales (net of depreciation and taxes).

This chapter has a number of features that are different from previous research in this area employing company accounts data. First it takes an international perspective. Thus the paper uses company account data to evaluate the relationship between different types of capital and productivity in five OECD countries: the United States, the United Kingdom, France, Germany and Italy. Existing studies have mainly focused on the United States and France (Griliches 1979, 1986; Griliches and Mairesse 1983, 1984; Griliches and Lichtenberg 1984; Mairesse and Hall 1996). Thus we aim to provide evidence for a larger set of countries, using company account data, provided by *Worldscope*. To our knowledge, this data set has not been used for this type of analysis. Therefore it will provide further evidence and a valuable ground for comparison.

A second unique feature of this work is that we take account not only of R&D investment, as is the case in most related papers, but also extend the analysis to the impact on company performance of investment in advertising, as proxied by the variable "other intangible assets". This variable is defined in the database as "other assets not having a physical existence" whose value "lies in their expected future returns". These investments generally add to the 'goodwill' of the firm and include capitalised advertising costs, among other items.[1] We therefore include three types of capital in our analysis and we will be concerned to see to what extent each impacts differentially on company performance.

Thirdly both manufacturing and non-manufacturing firms are included in the analysis and the effect of R&D and intangible investments will be evaluated in the two groups. Most work in this area tends to concentrate exclusively on manufacturing since R&D activity occurs primarily in that sector. But the company accounts database does include a significant proportion of non-manufacturing firms which engage in R&D. These tend to be largely concentrated in the distributive trades and business services and our selection of non-manufacturing firms is guided by this.

The interest in both types of intangible assets is justified by the different patterns that characterise these two variables in different countries. Figure 9.1 shows the R&D expenditure/GDP ratio and the advertising expenditure/GDP ratio in the five countries, using data for the whole economy. The figure shows a very different pattern in R&D and advertising expenditure among the five countries. France, Germany and the United States have devoted more resources to R&D than to advertising, compared to Italy and the UK. In Europe, with the exception of Germany, investments in R&D are lower compared to the United States. This conclusion can be found in related studies (Davies and Lyons 1996). Italy appears to be the country where investments in R&D as a proportion of GDP are particularly low. On the other hand, more resources are devoted to advertising. The steady increase in advertising expenditure matches the development of private TV channels that took place in the 1980s (the "Berlusconi effect"). In most countries we can observe a downward trend in R&D throughout the 1990s, a trend which is most pronounced in the UK. This macroeconomic picture provides a background to our empirical analysis.

---

[1] Other intangible assets include: goodwill/cost in excess of net assets purchased, patents, copyrights, trademarks, formulae, franchises of no specific duration, capitalised software development costs, organisational costs, customer lists, licences of no specific duration, capitalised advertising costs, mastheads (newspapers), capitalised servicing rights, purchased servicing rights.

Figure 9.1: Advertising expenditure and R&D expenditure as a proportion of GDP in the five countries

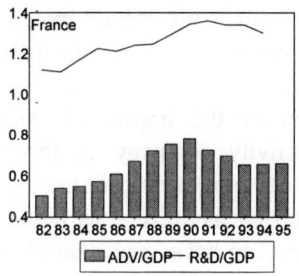
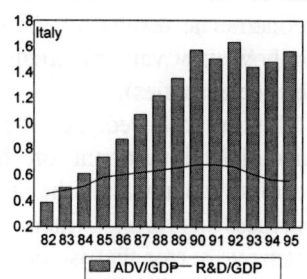
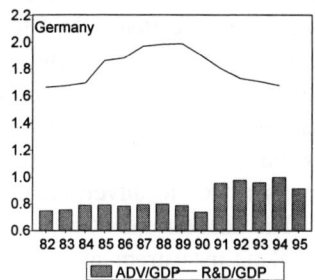
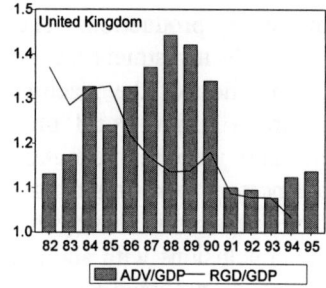
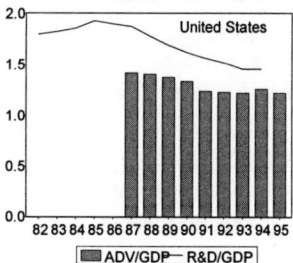

Sources: *European Advertising & Media Yearbook*, various years; *Advertising Statistics Yearbook*, several years. *Research and Development Expenditures in Industry, 1974-1995*, OECD, Paris.

We begin with a brief review of recent studies on R&D and productivity. We then discuss features of the data set, including the sample selection criteria, the size distribution of firms and mean productivity and profitability. We then turn to econometric issues. We first describe the theoretical framework that will guide our investigation. We then present econometric results for the entire sample of firms, which includes results on how they vary by country and by broad sector (manufacturing versus service activities).

This is followed by a consideration of the impact of tangible and intangible investment on firm productivity company in three specific sectors: chemicals, the production of non-electrical machinery and business services. Chemicals was chosen as it is a particularly R&D intensive sector that is commonly believed to have important effects in the whole economy, due to relevant externalities (Pavitt 1984). Machinery production is divided into computing and office equipment, generally considered to be a 'high technology' sector and more traditional machinery production. The latter does spend relatively low resources on intangible investment but, as shown below, this is not negligible. In our examination of the machinery sector we extend the analysis to include Japan, a major world producer, as well as other EU member states. Business services also covers a wide range of activities across the technology spectrum from computing services to advertising services to firms engaged in leasing equipment. The chapter ends with a summary of the conclusions with additional material on measurement and econometric estimation provided in an Appendix.

Previous studies linking intangible investment and economic performance

The relationship between R&D and productivity

Since Solow's (1957) decomposition of economic growth, much research by economists has focused on the factors which underlie the productivity residual, one of the major factors of productivity growth. This concern has led to the development of models of endogenous growth and to the inclusion, both in theoretical and empirical analysis, of other factors that could explain this residual. Investment in R&D has been one of these factors and the analysis of the relationship between R&D and productivity has played a major role in the economic growth literature (Griliches 1979, 1988; Grossman and Helpman 1991; Coe and Helpman 1995; Lichtenberg and Van Pottelsberghe de la Potterie 1996).

Both governments and private firms have devoted an increasing amount of resources to R&D. One of the main objectives of economic analysis is to evaluate whether the returns to this investment justify the initial expenditure. The analysis of the relationship between productivity and R&D is however particularly difficult for a number of reasons, frequently due to the poor data available for empirical investigation. In many sectors where R&D investments play a major role, such as health, the military sector or the computer industry, either output is particularly difficult to measure or its measure has not been adequately updated in order to account for the fast changes in technology. Griliches (1994) provides an example of the latter case, in relation to the late introduction of a computer price index and the consequent indeterminacy of the relationship between productivity and R&D in this sector.

Another issue concerns the measurement of R&D capital (similar remarks apply to other forms of intangible investment). As Griliches (1979) points out, there are three major problems to consider:

1. the effect of R&D on output growth can only be visible after a certain period of time;
2. R&D depreciates over time and an evaluation of this depreciation process is needed;
3. there are important spillover effects within R&D activities.

The first two issues have been addressed by constructing a series for R&D capital stock using a perpetual inventory model with declining balance depreciation (Griliches and Mairesse 1983; Mairesse and Hall 1996). This method is also used in this paper (see the Appendix for details).

As for the third point, attempts have been made to evaluate spillover effects both at the aggregate and at the industry level (Mairesse and Sassenou 1991; Griliches 1992; Coe and Helpman 1995; Lichtenberg and Van Pottelsberghe de la Potterie 1996). Even when spillover effects are not the direct object of the analysis, as is the case in this chapter, they do impact on comparisons between firms who engage in R&D and those who do not.

The analysis of the relationship between R&D and productivity also has to deal with econometric problems. Most empirical studies are based on the production function framework, which is extended in order to include R&D capital as a right hand side variable. Its contribution to production growth is assumed to be independent of the contribution of the other inputs. This is a very strong assumption but it is not specific to the introduction of R&D capital. Multicollinearity always characterises the estimation of production functions. More serious is the simultaneity problem. Future output depends on past investments in R&D and, at the same time, R&D depends on past and expected output (Griliches 1979). This problem also affects physical capital, as shown in Mairesse and Hall (1996). One of the methods used to address this problem is instrumental variable estimation. However, this technique does not always attain satisfactory results because of the difficulty in finding adequate instruments (Arellano and Bond 1991; Blundell and Bond 1998). The issue of simultaneity is discussed more fully below.

Firm-level studies

Despite the various data and econometric problems in dealing with the precise relationship between R&D and productivity, a large number of studies have attempted to evaluate this relationship. The analysis has been undertaken at different levels of aggregation: from the analysis of a particular sector (like agriculture – see Griliches 1956), to the whole economy (Coe and Helpman 1995), from the industry level (Griliches 1984), to the firm level (Griliches 1979, 1984; Mairesse and Hall 1996). In the present work our interest is in studies at the firm level.

Using firm-level data has the advantage of avoiding the problem of aggregation (Griliches 1994). However this type of data is not easily available. This explains why most studies have focused on very few countries, mostly France and the United States, where R&D expenditure at the firm level has been available for over twenty years. The various studies in this area do point to an important role for R&D in determining productivity, despite the different data sets used across different time periods. R&D is invariably found to have a significant and positive effect on output growth, after taking account of the influence of other inputs. But the range of estimates of the elasticity of output with respect to R&D does vary by study. For example, Griliches, in two successive studies, finds that, in the United States, the elasticity of output to R&D is around 0.07 on average, ranging between 0.1 for the research intensive sector and 0.04 for the rest of the manufacturing industries (Griliches 1979, 1984). In Shankerman (1981) and Griliches and Mairesse (1984), estimates of the output elasticity to R&D rise to about 0.18. In France the elasticities are higher than in the United States, ranging between 0.11 and 0.21 (Cuneo and Mairesse 1984). This difference can be explained by the availability of better data for France. In fact, the French data allow a distinction between capital and employment used in research departments from their use in other productive activities. This allows the research to deal with the problem of double counting, which imparts a downward bias in the estimates of the output elasticity of R&D (Shankerman 1981; see also the discussion of econometric methodology below).

The results mentioned above are mainly for the 1970s. A more recent study by Mairesse and Hall (1996), based on a panel of US and French firms, reveals that the contribution of R&D to productivity during the 1980s has slowed down in both countries, although this may have changed again in the 1990s (Hall 1999). Mairesse and Hall refine the econometric techniques used in this type of analysis, implementing Generalised Method of Moments (GMM) estimation, in order to find a solution to the simultaneity problem. The results are not very robust to various specifications and various sets of orthogonality conditions. This suggests that more work is needed on the econometric side in order to attain more clearcut answers on the relationship between R&D and productivity.

Thus the studies to date have not yielded any firm conclusions on the R&D elasticities, but suggest that they vary by time period, sector and country. In this chapter we cannot pretend that our estimates are more precisely estimated than in previous studies. But our results do confirm that there are important differences across countries and sectors in the magnitude of the R&D elasticities and also emphasise the differing impacts of various forms of tangible and intangible investment.

The company account data set

The company accounts database employed in the analysis, Worldscope, includes consolidated company accounts information for approximately 16,000 companies world-wide for ten years from 1988 to 1997. From this we have extracted information for the United States and the largest four European economies, Germany, France, Italy and the United Kingdom. Companies are sampled from a wide range of industrial sectors, both manufacturing and service sectors, which cover a broad range of factor intensities and exclude regulated industries and financial services. Also companies which were considered as outliers, for example, if they showed abnormally large sales or employment growth, were excluded from the analysis. Details of the sampling procedure is provided in O'Mahony and Vecchi (1999).

The resulting sample was just over 2,000 companies, about 70% in manufacturing and 30% in non-manufacturing. About 40% of firms report R&D expenditure of which about 85% are in manufacturing. The greatest proportion of companies was in the United States, followed closely by the United Kingdom, with lower coverage for the other European countries. The sample covers the entire range of company sizes, from those employing more than 100,000 workers to less than 200.

Output is defined in this chapter as sales deflated by price indices, where the latter are sector specific. Both tangible and other intangible capital appear in the firms' assets statements but at historic costs. These were converted to a replacement cost basis and then deflated by price indices to convert to real magnitudes. Total industry investment deflators for industry in each country were used for tangible assets whereas country specific retail price indices were used for intangibles (including R&D). R&D expenditures appear as a flow rather than a stock item in the company accounts and so were converted to R&D stocks using the perpetual inventory method, assuming a 15% depreciation rate and growth in the period before data were available of 5% per annum. Further details of methodology used to construct the variables are given in the Appendix.

This sample of firms was then analysed to see if there were obvious differences in performance between firms engaging in R&D and those which did not pursue this activity. The mean and distribution of productivity growth rates and profitability ratios showed very little difference by type of firm for the total sample and for most countries. But German R&D companies were more likely to have higher productivity growth than non-R&D firms. Also there were differences across broad sector with R&D firms in manufacturing outperforming those in service sectors in terms of both productivity growth and profitability.

The fact that the company sample did not pick up any significant difference in performance between R&D and other firms is probably due to spillovers from R&D producing firms to R&D using firms which imply that productivity improvements permeate the entire economy. Hence innovative activity may be very important in improving our well-being but cannot be picked up by examining innovators versus non-innovators. We now turn to the estimation of the impact of private gains on intangible investment by considering to what extent productivity and profitability are affected by these investments in the sample of firms where they are carried out.

Econometric estimates of intangibles: results for the whole sample

Theoretical framework

The theory that underlies most studies on R&D and productivity is based on a standard Cobb-Douglas function,[2] extended to include R&D capital (Mairesse and Hall 1996). In the present chapter, "other intangible assets" also appear among the left hand side variables in the production function, given by:

(1) $$Y_{it} = A_i K_{it}^{\alpha} L_{it}^{\beta} R_{it}^{\gamma} G_{it}^{\phi} e^{\varepsilon_{it}}$$

where Y is output, K is tangible capital, L is labour, R is R&D capital and G is other intangible capital, ε is a multiplicative disturbance, i denotes firms and t denotes years.

By using lower case letters to denote the logarithms of variables, we can re-write (1) as follows:

(2) $$y_{it} = a_i + \alpha k_{it} + \beta l_{it} + \gamma r_{it} + \phi g_{it} + \varepsilon_{it}$$

Our measure of output is "net sales or revenue", tangible capital is "net property plant and equipment", employment is "average number of employees", R&D capital is "research and development expense", and other intangibles is "other intangible assets".

In addition to a production function, we also estimate the following profitability equation:

(3) $$pratio_{it} = a_i + \alpha k_{it} + \beta l_{it} + \gamma r_{it} + \phi g_{it} + \varepsilon_{it}$$

where *pratio* is the log of the ratio of net income to sales. This part of the analysis will aim at evaluating the impact of the four inputs on profits.

Empirical methodology

We present two econometric specifications, OLS results for the pooled sample for equations (2) and (3) including country intercepts and time

---

[2] It would be possible to estimate with a more general functional form, such as the Translog, but this is generally not done in the literature. Presumably this reflects the fact that it is difficult enough to get results even with the Cobb-Douglas without further complicating the estimation by using alternative specifications of the production function.

dummies. In addition we present results for these equations in first difference form; the extreme heterogeneity found in the statistical analysis above suggests that the latter is the more appropriate model since it is equivalent to including firm specific fixed effects (Baltagi 1995). The panel runs from 1993 to 1997 and is unbalanced although only marginally so.[3]

There are three important econometric problems related to the estimation of equations such as (2), namely simultaneity, selectivity and double counting. The simultaneity problem is related to the endogeneity of R&D expenditure. In order to get consistent estimates in this situation, a number of techniques exist such as the GMM estimator (Arellano and Bond 1991; Mairesse and Hall 1996) or the asymptotic least squares method (Crepon et al. 1998). But, as is obvious from the discussion in Griliches and Mairesse (1995), the results are often very sensitive to the estimation method employed and attempts to correct for simultaneity can introduce more problems than they solve. We experimented with some of these estimation techniques but the results were not deemed to be satisfactory. Also we were then restricted to the balanced sample which made it more difficult to pick up country specific effects. Nevertheless, the results of this estimation, together with a discussion of the techniques used, are presented in the Appendix.

Another problem is related to the selectivity bias (Heckman 1979). Included in the estimation are those companies which perform and record the three types of investments (tangible, R&D and other intangible investments). Companies that either do not perform any of these investments or do not record them are not in the sample. While previous studies seem to suggest that the selectivity problem is not particularly serious (Mairesse and Hall 1996), some care is needed in the interpretation of the results. Conclusions concerning the returns to R&D and to other intangible investments will not have a generic scope, but they will only apply to firms that do perform those types of investment.[4]

Finally, another econometric issue relates to the problem of double-counting (Schankerman 1981). This measurement problem arises because research labour and tangible capital are double counted. To solve this problem we need to know how much physical capital and how many

---

[3] Experimentation using the entire sample period from 1988 (1989 for the first difference equation) led to some odd results – very few firms have observations for the entire period.

[4] The nature of R&D investment can however alleviate the selectivity bias problem given the recognised externality effect related to this type of investment. Although such effects are difficult to quantify empirically, it is generally recognised that firms investing in R&D positively affect other firms in the economic system.

workers are employed in the 'research and development department'. These should then be allocated to R&D and taken from these other inputs. Unfortunately such information is rarely available and, as a consequence, our estimates of the R&D elasticities in levels equations will be downward biased. Mairesse and Hall (1996) suggest that estimating the equation in first difference can lessen the bias. This problem will only have a significant impact on the first difference equation if the share of labour costs or capital in R&D is changing over time.

Econometric Results
A. Country Results

The econometric estimation was carried out on a sub-sample of 783 firms which comprises those who report both R&D and 'other intangible' investment. We estimated both levels and first difference equations using OLS. Estimates employing more sophisticated econometric techniques, in particular to take account of simultaneity, are discussed in the Appendix. These required the use of a balanced sample of firms with data for all years from 1993 to 1997, further restricting the sample to 404 firms. The results from alternative techniques were generally poor and so were not employed in the main body of the chapter.

Data for all countries were pooled together and dummy variables introduced in order to account for country specific effects. Table 9.1 presents two sets of results based on both log levels and first difference specifications. Columns 1 and 2 show the pooled regression results, where country differences have been introduced only in the form of intercept dummies, while equal coefficients have been imposed on the other parameters. In columns 3 and 4 the latter restriction has been relaxed. In the latter, the United States represents the reference category so that coefficients on the other countries measure the extent to which they differ from those in the United States. This is useful as it allows us to test the significance of these differences. Year dummies have been included in all regressions.

Columns 1 and 2 show that the coefficients on the three types of assets are positive and generally significant with the only exception being the lack of significance of intangible capital in the first difference specification (column 2). The R&D elasticity is higher than that for other intangibles and is particularly high in the first difference model. This is consistent with Mairesse and Hall's suggestion that the equation in levels underestimates the returns to R&D (Mairesse and Hall 1996) due to the impact of double counting. Thus moving to the first difference equation raises the coefficient on R&D while lowering the impacts of both employment and physical capital. Given this observation, and the fact that the sample is very heterogeneous suggesting the desirability of adjusting for firm specific effects in levels, we suggest that the first difference results are most likely preferable to those based on log levels of the variables.

More insights can be obtained by looking at columns 3 and 4 of Table 9.1, where coefficient differences across countries are taken into account. Again, for all countries, the coefficients on R&D are much greater and those on physical capital and employment are lower, in the first difference equation relative to the levels equations. In the United States (first four rows of columns 3 and 4), positive returns to tangible and R&D capital are observed but the coefficient on other intangibles is negative and significant in the first difference specification. The results for the levels equation shows little cross-country variation with the exception of all coefficients for France and the R&D coefficient for Italy. In the first difference specification there is much more variation across countries with all three continental European countries having significantly higher R&D elasticities than in the United States. In contrast the R&D coefficient for the United Kingdom is not significantly different from that in the United States. France, Italy and the United Kingdom all have significantly higher, and positive, coefficients on other intangibles. Only Italy has a significantly higher coefficient on tangible capital.

The coefficient for the United States implies an elasticity of output with respect to R&D of about 10%, comparable to results found in other studies for that country. But the R&D elasticities are very high for the continental European countries, particularly France. These suggest much higher returns on the relatively lower R&D stocks in these countries relative to the United States, consistent with diminishing returns to R&D assets. But the UK result does not fall into this general framework. Other possible explanations are differences in the mix of industries across countries, which we can only partially allow for in our sampling approach, and the more competitive environment in the United States and the United Kingdom which could imply more duplication of research effort. These considerations are worthy of further study. What is clear from the above results is that the impact of intangible investments on productivity does vary across country.

Table 9.1: Pooled regressions with interactive dummies (base category: United States)

	Level	Log first difference	Level	Log first difference
Employment	0.588*	0.465*	0.612*	0.556*
	(0.013)	(0.028)	(0.017)	(0.027)
Physical capital	0.318*	0.185*	0.290*	0.179*
	(0.011)	(0.019)	(0.013)	(0.022)
R&D	0.050*	0.250*	0.056*	0.098*
	(0.006)	(0.022)	(0.009)	(0.031)
Intangibles	0.029*	0.002	0.018*	-0.018*
	(0.005)	(0.005)	(0.008)	(0.007)
France				
Employment			-0.295*	-0.289*
			(0.038)	(0.064)
Physical capital			0.127*	-0.060
			(0.030)	(0.061)
R&D			0.084*	0.436*
			(0.019)	(0.057)
Intangibles			0.045*	0.043*
			(0.014)	(0.015)
Germany				
Employment			-0.024	-0.123
			(0.044)	(0.070)
Physical capital			0.041	-0.014
			(0.037)	(0.056)
R&D			0.037	0.169*
			(0.021)	(0.061)
Intangibles			-0.011	0.021
			(0.015)	(0.013)
Italy				
Employment			0.185*	-0.335*
			(-0.068)	(0.124)
Physical capital			-0.110	0.314*
			(0.059)	(0.128)
R&D			-0.083*	0.294*
			(0.015)	
				(0.120)
Intangibles			0.037	0.083*
			(0.033)	
				(0.127)
United Kingdom				
Employment			0.025	-0.130
			(0.044)	(0.075)
Physical capital			-0.039	0.089
			(0.039)	(0.057)
R&D			0.039	0.137
			(0.023)	(0.087)
Intangibles			0.008	0.053*
			(0.013)	(0.018)
	0.96	0.50	0.96	0.53

Note: Standard errors in parentheses
 * denotes variable significant at 95% level.

B. Broad Sector Results

We now turn to an examination of to what extent the capital elasticities vary across sector. Here we just consider the difference between manufacturing and non-manufacturing. In the sixth section, in addition, we consider three specific industries in more detail. In this section, the same sample of 783 companies is used to test whether there are any significant differences in the capital coefficients in the manufacturing and the non-manufacturing sector. To perform this test, a dummy variable is introduced in the specification of equation (2), that takes value 1 for manufacturing firms and zero otherwise. Hence results for the manufacturing sector are evaluated with reference to the non-manufacturing sector. Both intercept and interactive dummies are used for the two sectors. The specification also allows for country and year specific fixed effect.

Table 9.2: Pooled regressions with manufacturing and non-manufacturing dummies (base category: non-manufacturing)

	Levels	First difference
Employment	0.469*	0.477*
	(0.022)	(0.035)
Physical capital	0.363*	0.243*
	(0.019)	(0.028)
R&D	0.098*	0.042
	(0.013)	(0.042)
Intangibles	0.012*	-0.006
	(0.009)	(0.009)
Manufacturing employment	0.174*	-0.011
	(0.028)	(0.045)
Manufacturing physical capital	-0.061*	-0.091*
	(0.023)	(0.036)
Manufacturing R&D	-0.071*	0.286*
	(0.014)	(0.050)
Manufacturing intangibles	0.021*	-0.011
	(0.011)	(0.011)
Adjusted R^2	0.96	0.51

Note: Standard errors in parentheses.
* denotes variable significant at 95% level.

The most important result in this section concerns the R&D capital coefficient. Compared to non-manufacturing firms, the R&D elasticity in manufacturing is much higher in the first difference specification. This result confirms the finding of the preliminary statistical analysis for the entire sample, that is, non-manufacturing R&D firms appear to have lower productivity than manufacturing firms engaging in R&D. This appears to be an important finding of the present chapter. The focus given, in previous related papers, to the manufacturing sector has completely neglected the importance of R&D investments in non-manufacturing firms. Our sample of non-manufacturing companies is not homogeneous across countries and it is too small to draw firmer conclusions. But this result is supported also in the sector analysis discussed below. Hence this result deserves further attention and research.

C. *Profitability and tangible/intangible assets*
This section presents results from the estimation of equation (3), the profitability equation. Results are presented in Tables 9.3 and 9.4. Table 9.3 presents results for country differences while Table 9.4 is based on the distinction between the manufacturing and non-manufacturing sectors.[5] The first thing to note in these results is the very low value for the adjusted R^2 which is not surprising given the large variability in profit rates referred to above. For the entire sample the levels equation shows that R&D has a significantly positive impact on profitability but this disappears in the first difference equation. In contrast other intangible capital has a positive impact on profitability in both specifications. The country slope dummies are generally not significant in the first difference specification. The R&D coefficient is positive and significant in manufacturing but R&D appears to have no impact in non-manufacturing. Thus intangible investments such as advertising and marketing do appear to raise the profitability of firms whereas they have little impact on productivity. This appears to be a plausible result given the nature of these investments which are designed more to raise the profile of products and possibly reap some monopoly returns rather than serving to increase output for given inputs. In fact the issue of market structure is not covered in this analysis, given our data limitations, but this is likely to be an important determinant of firm profitability. Hence this equation probably suffers from omitted variable bias so the results should be treated with some caution.

---

[5] The dependent variable is the log of the profit ratio so that firms with negative profits are excluded from the analysis. This is not very satisfactory but experiments with linear specifications gave very poor results.

Table 9.3: Profitability rate regression (base category: United States)

	Level	Difference	Level	Difference
Employment	-0.335*	-0.430*	-0.431*	-0.540*
	(0.033)	(0.074)	(0.044)	(0.101)
Physical capital	0.147*	0.238*	0.176*	0.211*
	(0.026)	(0.059)	(0.033)	(0.083)
R&D	0.057*	0.011	0.118*	0.095
	(0.014)	(0.038)	(0.022)	(0.053)
Intangibles	0.057*	0.067*	0.076*	0.108*
	(0.013)	(0.027)	(0.021)	(0.039)
France				
Employment			0.326*	0.323
			(0.094)	(0.223)
Physical capital			-0.148	0.159
			(0.077)	(0.184)
R&D			-0.156*	-0.199
			(0.049)	(0.137)
Intangibles			0.261*	0.426*
			(0.106)	(0.209)
Germany				
Employment			-0.001	-0.163*
			(0.036)	(0.073)
Physical capital			-0.177	-0.193
			(0.089)	(0.167)
R&D			0.571*	-0.035
			(0.173)	(0.290)
Intangibles			-0.069	-0.093
			(0.052)	(0.114)
Italy				
Employment			-0.020	-0.026
			(0.037)	(0.076)
Physical capital			-0.269*	-0.370
			(0.116)	(0.287)
R&D			-0.633*	0.000
			(0.148)	(0.248)
Intangibles			-0.113*	-0.167
			(0.036)	(0.103)
United Kingdom				
Employment			-0.050	-0.087
			(0.081)	(0.135)
Physical capital			0.291*	0.188
			(0.100)	(0.177)
R&D			-0.014	-.001
			(0.060)	(0.169)
Intangibles			-0.011	.061
			(0.033)	(0.098)
	0.19	0.13	0.24	0.15

Note: Standard errors in parentheses. * denotes variable significant at 95% level.

Table 9.4: Profitability ratio in the manufacturing and non-manufacturing sector

	Levels	First difference
Employment	-0.310*	-0.743*
	(0.058)	(0.125)
Capital	0.202*	0.409*
	(0.049)	(0.111)
R&D	-0.002	-0.015
	(0.034)	(0.071)
Intangibles	-0.025	0.131*
	(0.024)	(0.048)
Manufacturing Employment	-0.339*	-0.319*
	(0.041)	(0.083)
Manufacturing Capital	-0.067	0.122*
	(0.059)	(0.067)
Manufacturing R&D	0.063	0.112*
	(0.038)	(0.040)
Manufacturing Intangibles	0.102*	0.043
	(0.027)	(0.029)
Adjusted R^2	0.20	0.23

Note: Standard errors in parentheses
* denotes variable significant at 95% level.

One further result worth noting in the profitability equation is that the coefficients on employment and tangible capital have opposite signs with increases in employment, implying reductions in firm profits and increases in tangible capital, implying profitability increases. This result is strongest in Germany and in manufacturing relative to service activities. It suggests that the substitution of capital for labour has a positive impact on firm profitability which in turn may reflect high unit labour costs. This is considered to be a particular problem in the European Union with its relatively high unemployment rates.

Intangible assets and company accounts: results by sector

This section considers the impact of intangible investment on productivity for three specific industries, chemicals, machinery and business services. These sectors were chosen as they represent a broad spectrum of intensities of the three forms of capital. We present the econometric estimation of the productivity equation for each sector. Following the discussion on econometric methods above, only results from the first difference specification are shown. In O'Mahony and Vecchi (1999) general features of the company accounts for these sectors are highlighted together with some general features of the industries involved. In particular, as in the total sample, there appears to be little difference between productivity growth in firms who spend resources on R&D and those who do not, in these more detailed sectors.

The importance of Japan as an international player in the machinery sector suggested we include that country in the analysis of the sector. In machinery and business services, in order to increase the sample size, we included as many firms as were available for all fifteen EU countries. The mean and distribution of employment size varied by sector with the largest mean size in chemicals and office machinery (over 10,000 employees) and considerably smaller in traditional machinery and business services (about 5,000 employees). The mean R&D to sales ratios in the samples vary considerably across the manufacturing sectors, being equal to about 8% in chemicals and in computing equipment manufacturing, 3% in traditional machinery production and a surprisingly large 13% in business services.

Table 9.5 shows results of the econometric estimation of the productivity relationship in the chemicals sector. Country and time intercept dummies were included. Country interaction dummies were not found to be significant in this sector and so are not shown. The elasticity of sales with respect to R&D is somewhat greater than that for the entire sample of manufacturing firms. The coefficients on tangible capital also tend to be slightly larger in chemicals than in manufacturing. The coefficient on other intangible capital is small and insignificant so no firm conclusions can be made regarding the impact of this variable in chemicals.

Table 9.5: The chemical sector

Variable	Pooled regression
Employment	0.286*
	(0.048)
Physical capital	0.191*
	(0.039)
R&D	0.354*
	(0.067)
Intangibles	0.016
	(0.011)
No. obs	470
Adjusted R^2	0.39

Note: Standard errors in parentheses
* denotes variable significant at 95% level.

We next consider econometric results for machinery production, shown in Table 9.6. The first column shows the pooled first difference equation, estimated from 1993 to 1997. The coefficients on all four variables are significant but the coefficient on employment is small relative to that for all manufacturing firms. The coefficient on physical capital is somewhat larger than that for total manufacturing (0.15) and on R&D somewhat smaller than for all manufacturing firms (0.328). The coefficient on other intangibles is significant but very small. Note that we cannot statistically test for differences in the machinery sector against the general manufacturing sample since the latter contains only a sample of machinery producing firms included in the former.

In terms of country dummies, the sample size dictated that we could only consider Japan and all European countries combined relative to the United States. Here the results were somewhat surprising in that the coefficients on R&D were significantly lower for Japan and Europe than in the United States. This may be affected by the much greater proportion of computing equipment firms in the United States. Also the employment coefficient for Japan is significantly smaller whereas that for Europe is significantly larger than in the United States. Finally the coefficient on other intangibles for Japan is significantly greater than in the United States, implying that advertising and marketing activities may be more important in driving productivity growth in Japan than in either the United States or Europe.

We then examined the possibility that the coefficients differ between computer manufacturers and other machinery manufacturers. The results in the third column show coefficients on R&D and other intangibles significantly greater in the former group. In fact the elasticity of output with respect to R&D in computer manufacturing, at about 0.45, is the largest of the sectors considered in this chapter. The coefficient on other intangibles is also significant in the computer producing sector. Finally inclusion of area dummies in the traditional machinery sample gives similar conclusions on R&D as that for the total sample, that is, significantly smaller elasticities in Japan and Europe. This suggests that the returns to R&D in the United States machinery sector is larger than in its major competitors. In fact the mean R&D to sales ratio in the US, at over 4%, is nearly twice that in the large European producers and Japan. This could reflect a greater US presence in highly innovating niches of the machinery sector. Our data is incapable of ascertaining whether this is the case but it is obviously worthy of further research.

Table 9.6: Econometric results: machinery sector

Variable	All firms	Base US		Base US (other machinery)	All firms, except computers	Base US, except computers
Employment	0.272* (0.027)	0.435*	(0.047)	.305* (.042)	0.298* (0.037)	0.256* (0.06)
Physical capital	0.255* (0.023)	0.199*	(0.032)	.260* (.030)	0.258* (0.027)	0.321* (0.041)
R&D	0.191* (0.038)	0.297*	(0.056)	.119* (.042)	0.137* (0.037)	0.265* (0.036)
Intangibles	0.022* (0.006)	0.003	(0.009)	.006 (.009)	0.007 (0.007)	0.001 (0.012)
Employment (Japan)	-	-0.036*	(0.059)	-	-	-0.170 (0.088)
Physical capital (Japan)	-	-0.049	(0.051)	-	-	-0.182* (0.057)
R&D (Japan)	-	-0.190*	(0.083)	-	-	-0.201* (0.088)
Intangibles (Japan)	-	0.032*	(0.013)	-	-	0.028 (0.016)
Employment (Europe)	-	0.299	(0.112)*	-	-	0.272* (0.121)
Physical capital (Europe)	-	-0.126	(0.090)	-	-	-0.175 (0.099)
R&D (Europe)	-	-0.228*	(0.083)	-	-	-0.199* (0.085)
Intangibles (Europe)	-	0.021	(0.020)	-	-	-0.023 (0.022)
Employment (Computers)	-	-		-.066 (.054)	-	-
Physical capital (Computers)	-	-		-.030 (.047)	-	-
R&D (Computers)	-	-		.328* (.084)	-	-
Intangibles (Computers)	-	-		.034* (.013)	-	-
No. OBS	1042	1042		1042	790	790
adjusted R^2	0.42	0.47		0.43	0.44	0.47

Note: Standard errors in parentheses. * denotes variable significant at 95% level.

Table 9.7 shows the econometric results for the business services sector. When we exclude all firms who do not report both R&D and other intangibles the sample size becomes very small (160 firms). We therefore do not include country dummies. The first column shows an R&D elasticity equal to about 17% which is smaller than in other sectors but still significant. The coefficient on employment is somewhat higher than in previous estimates whereas that on tangible capital is lower than that for the complete non-manufacturing sample. Surprisingly the coefficient on other intangibles is small and insignificant. However in this sector there are a large number of firms who report other intangibles but not R&D; excluding these halves the sample size. Therefore we also ran a regression excluding R&D as a variable. The results do now show a sizeable impact from other intangibles for this much larger sample of firms. Therefore we can tentatively conclude that activities such as advertising, marketing etc. are likely to have an impact on productivity in the business services sector.

Table 9.7: Econometric results: business services

Variable	All firms	All firms**
Employment	0.535 *	0.211*
	(0.051)	(0.19)
Physical capital	0.159*	0.306*
	(0.037)	(0.020)
R&D	0.168*	-
	(0.051)	
Intangibles	0.027	0.051*
	(0.014)	(0.011)
No. obsS	480	913
Adjusted R^2	0.51	0.47

Note: Standard errors in parentheses.
* denotes variable significant at 95% level.
** excluding R&D.

Conclusions

The purpose of this chapter was to employ company accounts data to evaluate the importance of intangible investment on company performance. We also were concerned to see if its impact varied by sector and country and if any conclusions emerge regarding the importance of intangible investment relative to other forms of investment. Taking productivity as the performance indicators the analysis shows little difference between firms engaging in R&D versus those not pursuing this activity. But this conclusion does not suggest R&D is unimportant as there are likely to be important spillover effects which are not distinguishable in the data. R&D tends to be concentrated in particular industries or sectors but often the beneficiaries of this innovative activity are users in other sectors.

Examination of those firms which engage in R&D, which also report other forms of intangible investment such as advertising etc., invariably shows significant elasticities of output with respect to R&D. But these elasticities vary by country, with much greater impacts in France, Germany and Italy than in the United Kingdom or United States. They also were found to vary by broad sector, with higher values in manufacturing versus non-manufacturing and by detailed sector, with higher values in computing equipment manufacture and chemicals than in more traditional machinery producers or business services. Other intangible capital has a much smaller impact on productivity and varies in significance across countries and sectors.

The econometric results do not point to any significant differences in the R&D versus tangible capital elasticities. But there is a sense in which the former outperforms the latter. In competitive markets the elasticities should equal the shares of each input in total output; these are the input weights employed in traditional growth accounting calculations. The estimated coefficients on tangible capital are generally close to growth accounting values but those for R&D are much greater than the typical values of about 0.5 found in these calculations. Hence R&D does tend to produce more per unit of output expended. Finally other intangible investment such as advertising marketing etc. does appear to be more important than R&D in determining profitability, but the econometric results were not very satisfactory in the profitability equations and so this result should be treated with some caution.

References

Arellano, M., Bond, S. (1991), "Some tests of specification for panel data: Monte Carlo evidence and an application to employment equations", *Review of Economic Studies*, 58, 277-97.

Baltagi, B.H. (1995), *Econometric Analysis of Panel Data*. John Wiley & Sons Ltd., West Sussex.

Blundell, R., Bond, S. (1998), "Initial conditions and moment restrictions in dynamic panel data models", *Journal of Econometrics,* 87, 115-43.

Coe, D.T., Helpman, E. (1995), "International R&D spillovers", *European Economic Review,* 39, 859-87.

Crepon, B., Duguet, E., Mairesse, J. (1998), "Research, innovation and productivity: an econometric analysis at the firm level", *NBER Working Paper Series,* No. 6696.

Cuneo, P. and Mairesse, J. (1984), "Productivity and R&D at the Firm Level in Manufacturing Industry", *R&D, Patents and Productivity*, ed. Zvi Griliches, pp.375--92. Chicago: University of Chicago Press.

David, R., Mackinnon, J.G. (1993), *Estimation and Inference in Econometrics*, Oxford University Press, New York.

Davies, S., Lyons, B. (1996), *Industrial Organisation in the European Union*, Claredon Press, Oxford.

Geroski, P., Machin, S., Reenen, J.V. (1993), "The profitability of innovation firms", *Rand Journal of Economics*, 24, 198-211.

Griliches, Z. (1956), Hybrid corn: an exploration in the economics of technological change, *Econometrica*, 25, 501-22.

Griliches, Z. (1979) "Issues in assessing the contribution of research and development to productivity growth", *Bell Journal of Economics*, 10, 92-116.

Griliches, Z. (1984), "R&D and productivity growth at the firm level". In *R&D, Patents and Productivity*, Z. Griliches (ed.), 339-74. Chicago: University of Chicago Press.

Griliches, Z. (1986), "Productivity, R&D and basic research at the firm level in the 1970s", *American Economic Review*, 76, 141-54.

Griliches, Z. (1988), "Productivity puzzles and R&D: another nonexplanation", *Journal of Economic Perspective*, 2, 9-21.

Griliches, Z. (1992), "The search for R&D spillovers", *Scandinavian Journal of Economics*, 94, S29-S47.

Griliches, Z. (1994), "Productivity, R&D and data constraint", *American Economic Review*, 84, 1-23.

Griliches Z., Lichtenberg, F. (1984), "R&D and productivity growth at the industry level: is there still a relationship?". In *R&D, Patents and Productivity*, Z. Griliches (ed.), 465-96. Chicago: University of Chicago Press.

Griliches, Z., Mariesse, J. (1983), "Comparing Productivity Growth: an exploration of French and U.S. industrial firm data", *European Economic Review*, 21, 89-119.

Griliches, Z., Mairesse, J. (1984). "Productivity and R&D at the Firm Level. in R&D, Patents and Productivity", Z. Griliches. Chicago: University of Chicago Press: 339-74.

Griliches, Z., Mairesse, J. (1995), "Production functions: the search for identification", *NBER Working Paper Series*, No. 5067.

Grossman, G.M., Helpman, E. (1991), *Innovation and Growth in the Global Economy*, Cambridge MA, MIT Press.

Hall, B. (1999), "Innovation and market value". In R. Barrell, G. Mason and M. O'Mahony, eds., *Productivity, Innovation and Economic Performance*, Forthcoming, Cambridge University Press.

Hamilton, J.D. (1994), *Time Series Analysis*, Princeton University Press, Princeton.

Hansen, L.P. (1982), "Large sample properties of generalised method of moments estimators", *Econometrica*, 50, 1029-54.

Heckman, J.J. (1979), "Sample selection bias as a specification error", *Econometrica*, 47, 153-61.

Lichtenberg, F., Van Pottelsberghe de la Potterie, B. (1996), "International R&D spillovers: a re-examination", *NBER Working Paper Series* N°. 5668.

Mairesse, J., Hall B.H. (1996), "Estimating the productivity of research and development: an exploration of GMM methods using data on French and United States manufacturing firms", *NBER Working Paper Series*, N°. 5501.

Mairesse, J., Sassenou, M. (1991), "R&D and productivity: a survey of econometric studies at the firm level", *STI Review* (OECD Paris), 8, 9-43.

OECD (1998), "The OECD STAN database for industrial analysis, 1976-1995", OECD, Paris.

OECD (1999), "Research and development in industry", OECD, Paris.

O'Mahony, M. (1998), "The comparative competitiveness of the EU chemicals and rubber and plastics industries", Report to the European Commission, DGIII, July.

O'Mahony, M. (1999), *Britain's Productivity Performance: 1950-1996: An International Perspective*, National Institute of Economic and Social Research, London.

O'Mahony, M., Vecchi, M. (1999), "Intangible investment, companies and competitiveness: an international comparison", Report to the European Commission, July.

Pavitt, K. (1984), "Sectoral patterns of technical change: towards a taxonomy and a theory", *Research Policy*.

Peneder, M. (1999), "Intangible assets and the competitiveness of european industries", paper presented to a symposium on intangible assets, Louvain, April.

Schankerman, M. (1981), "The effect of double-counting and expensing on the measured returns to R&D", *The Review of Economics and Statistics*, 63, 453-58.

Solow, R.M. (1957), "Technical change and the aggregate production function", *The Review of Economics and Statistics*, 39, 312-20.

APPENDIX

Data measurement

The capital data extracted from the database have to be transformed before being used in the estimation. Following Arellano and Bond (1991), capital stock at historic (HCK) cost is converted into capital at replacement costs (RCK), using the following formula:

$$RCK(t) = HCK(t) \cdot (P(t))/(P(t-A))$$

where P represents deflators and A is the average asset life. This estimate of gross capital at replacement cost then needs to be deflated by the appropriate price indices to derive a series at constant prices. For tangible assets we assume $A = 10$ and for intangibles (other assets) $A = 5$.

To obtain a measure of the stock of R&D capital, we adopt the method used in Mairesse and Hall (1996) based on a perpetual inventory method. The stock of R&D capital in year 1 (k_1) is given by:

$$k_1 = \frac{R_1}{g+\delta}$$

where R_1 us R&D expenditure, g is the pre-sample growth rate of real R&D, and δ is the depreciation rate. Again, we follow Mairesse and Hall in assuming $g=5\%$ and $\delta=15\%$.

Nominal sales were converted into real sales by deflating by two-digit industry deflators for each country.

Empirical methodology

The empirical analysis is conducted in two stages. In the first stage, we pool the data for all countries together and we compare results from different estimation techniques. This restricted the sample size considerably by only including firms with complete observations for the years 1993 to 1997. These results are discussed below. The techniques used are OLS, in level and in first difference, fixed effect and random effect and Generalised Method of Moments (GMM). The latter is an instrumental variable estimator and it is used in order to address the problem of simultaneity. In the second stage we returned to the larger unbalanced sample and estimated using OLS, in levels and first differences.

Simultaneity is related to the endogeneity of R&D expenditure (and other capital expenditure). In order to get consistent estimates in this situation, a number of techniques exist such as the GMM estimator (Arellano and Bond 1991; Mairesse and Hall 1996) or the asymptotic least squares method (Crepon et al. 1998). The GMM estimator is particularly popular in this type of study as it corrects for simultaneity and measurement error problems and it also provide standard errors which are robust to serial correlation and heteroschedasticity. However, the weak power of the instruments can result in a reduced efficiency and it can increase estimate bias. This problem has led authors to suggest different specifications of the orthogonality conditions (Blundell and Bond 1998). In the following section we investigate this issue and attempt to evaluate the contributions of the alternative specifications.

Econometric results

The following tables show the results of using various techniques on the balanced sample of 404 firms with 5 observations per firm. Equation (2) is first estimated by pooling all the data together and using different estimation techniques. Table 9.A.1 presents results for the estimation using OLS, fixed effect and a random effect model. The OLS in first difference, together with the fixed effect and the random effect model, allow for individual industry effect. The extreme heterogeneity discussed in the statistical analysis in O'Mahony and Vecchi (1999, section 3), suggests that the latter is the more appropriate model since it is equivalent to including firm specific fixed effects.[6]

---

[6] The use of panel data estimation techniques can be particularly problematic when there is simultaneity between the dependent variable and regressors. Simultaneity invalidates estimates based on data where firm means have been removed, even if instrumental variables are used (Mairesse and Hall 1996).

Table 9.A.1: Econometric results: panel methods

	OLS LEVEL	OLS FIRST DIFF.	FIXED EFFECT	RANDOM EFFECT
Employment	0.580* (0.014)	0.477* (0.027)	0.658* (0.026)	0.632* (0.020)
Physical capital	0.321* (0.012)	0.214* (0.022)	0.164* (0.021)	0.246* (0.016)
R&D	0.054* (0.006)	0.246* (0.029)	0.209* (0.022)	0.104* (0.011)
Intangibles	0.038* (0.005)	0.007 (0.006)	0.007 (0.006)	0.014* (0.005)

The results in Table 9.A.1 are consistent with our expectations, with the only exception being the fixed effect model, where the capital coefficient is significantly lower than the coefficients in the other equations. The coefficients on the three capital expenditures are positive and, apart from intangible investments, they are all significant. The results from the first difference model show lower employment and capital coefficients compared to the OLS level regression, while the elasticity of R&D is significantly higher. This result captures the double counting effect, mentioned above.

The first difference and random effect model take into account differences across companies and hence they are preferred to the level specification. The random effect model allows for a fixed effect together with a random effect across companies, under the assumption that the individual effect is not correlated with the other regressors. If this assumption is violated, the random effect estimator will not be consistent. The results from a Hausman specification test, comparing the fixed and the random effect, rejects the hypothesis of the lack of correlation between regressors and individual effect,[7] hence no further investigation will be conducted using the random effect model.

Table 9.A.2 presents the results of the GMM estimation. The reason for using GMM in this type of framework is the presence of a simultaneity bias. In order to correct for this bias, instrumental variables are

---

[7] The test is distributed as a χ^2_k, where k is the number of estimated coefficients. In our example, $\chi^2_{(4)} = 64.96$, with a probability value = 0.000, hence we reject the hypothesis that the fixed effect and the random effect coefficients are the same. Under the hypothesis of a correctly specified model, the test tell us that the assumption of zero correlation between the individual effect and the regressors is violated.

introduced in the estimation process. The most common way of introducing instruments in this context is by estimating the model in first difference and using levels of the regressors lagged (t-2) as instruments (Arellano and Bond 1991; Mairesse and Hall 1996). Column 2 in Table 9.A.2 uses this specification. This method has been subject to criticism because of the weak power of the instrumental variables used (Arellano and Bond 1991; Blundell and Bond 1998). In order to further investigate the issue, we also run a GMM estimator with regressors in levels, using lagged levels as instruments (column 1, Table 9.A.1), as well as a system GMM (Blundell and Bond 1998) that combined (t-2) equations in first difference and (t-2) equations in levels, using lagged levels and lagged differences as instruments (see above for more details). Results are shown in column 3 of Table 9.A.1. The GMM results are not very robust. We can see, for example, that the employment parameter ranges from 0.266 to 0.729 in the three different specifications, while the capital coefficient becomes insignificant in the GMM model in first difference. The instability of the results is probably caused by the weakness of the instrumental variables used. A test of overidentifying restrictions, reported at the bottom of Table 9.A.2 (IV test), suggests that, in most cases, the instruments used are not valid. In this case, the instrumental variable estimator can create more serious problems than the simultaneity problem it is trying to correct. For these reasons, in addition to increasing the sample size, we did not employ instrumental variables techniques in the main body of the chapter.

Table 9.A.2   Econometric results: GMM estimation

	GMM Level	GMM First difference	GMM System
Employment	0.266*	0.510*	0.729*
	(0.075)	(0.250)	(0.098)
Physical capital	0.446*	0.018	0.283*
	(0.076)	(0.150)	(0.081)
R&D	0.439*	0.790*	0.251*
	(0.097)	(0.172)	(0.066)
Intangibles	0.061*	0.092	0.099*
	(0.021)	(0.065)	(0.031)
IV test	$\chi^2_{(12)} = 28.8$	$\chi^2_{(8)} = 13.73$	$\chi^2_{(32)} = 54.16$
	$pvalue = 0.004$	$pvalue = 0.09$	$pvalue = 0.01$

10. Research and Development, Innovation and Corporate Performance in the Chemical Industry: A Case Study

Alfonso Gambardella, Walter García-Fontes and Gérald Petit[1]

1. Introduction

The estimation of the economic returns of innovative activities has been of central interest to both governments and firms for many years. Indeed, from the pioneering work of economists like Griliches (e.g. Griliches, 1957, 1958, 1979, and 1986) or Mansfield (e.g. Mansfield et al., 1977; Mansfield, 1980), this topic has been analyzed systematically by the economic literature. Many studies have tried to empirically estimate the effects of R&D, innovation and patents on economic performance. (See Mairesse and Mohnen, 1995, for a survey.) This literature has also been comprehensive in terms of type of data used. Not only are there studies using aggregate country-level data, but many of them have used meso- or micro-level data at the level of industries and firms.

Even in the latter cases, however, the goal has typically been to assess the general determinants of productivity growth or performance of an economy. In other words, even when industry or firm data were used, the focus has most often been on the aggregate effects of the explanatory variables, and little attention has been paid to distinguish these

---

[1] The views presented here are exclusively the opinions of the authors and do not necessarily correspond to the views of the European Commission. The authors are very grateful for the comments of Pierre Buigues (Head of the Chemical, Plastics and Rubber unit at the Directorate-General for industry) throughout the preparation of this paper. In addition, Alfonso Gambardella and Walter García-Fontes acknowledge the financial help of the European Commission through the TSER program, contract SOE1-CT97-1059.

determinants for specific industries. Studies of individual industries are most important. If anything, different or peculiar effects that are relevant for specific sectors are netted out by cross-industry estimations which typically focus on the invariants across them. In turn, the peculiar features of individual industries can be important both to select adequate industry-specific policies, and for evaluating a range of policy measures, or managerial implications, that may be suited for certain industries and not, or less so, for others.

This chapter estimates the returns to R&D and innovation in the chemical industry. Our focus on the chemical sector is justified for many reasons. First, the chemical industry is one the largest manufacturing industries in the world. In 1995, the sales of the US chemical industry amounted to $372 billion, while those of Western Europe taken together added up to $495 billion, against sales of $252 billion for the Japanese chemical industry. In value added terms, the industry accounts for between 1.5 and 1.9% of US GDP, more than any other manufacturing sector (CMA, 1997), and second only to the food and drink sector in Europe. Clearly, this also implies that the chemical sector can have significant direct and indirect impacts on employment.

Second, not only is the chemical industry very large, but it is also a very old and complex industry. Many of the products are new, the results of product innovation, but many older products survive. There are sectors in the industry, such as dyes, that are mature but remain R&D intensive, while others are experiencing rapid technological change. (See Arora and Gambardella, 1998.) Average R&D intensity in the chemical industry – measured as the ratio of R&D expenditure to output – was over 11% in the US, EU and Japan in 1994 (with a maximum of 17% in the UK), against less than 9% for manufacturing as a whole.

Relatedly, innovation is of critical importance for the competitiveness of chemical firms. In this respect, EU chemical companies are facing particular challenges as witnessed by the large-scale restructuring that started at the beginning of the 1990s. This has been accompanied by fluctuations in market shares for existing products; product quality improvements; challenges from new, R&D intensive specialty productions, in the context of increasingly globalised chemical markets. Restructuring resulted in a reduction in employment by firms operating in Western Europe. (See Figure 10.1). However, most of the firm strategies for improving performance have impinged on innovation, whether related to products or processes, as will be highlighted by this case study. (See also Albach *et al.*, 1996.)

Figure 10.1: Chemical industry indicators, EU

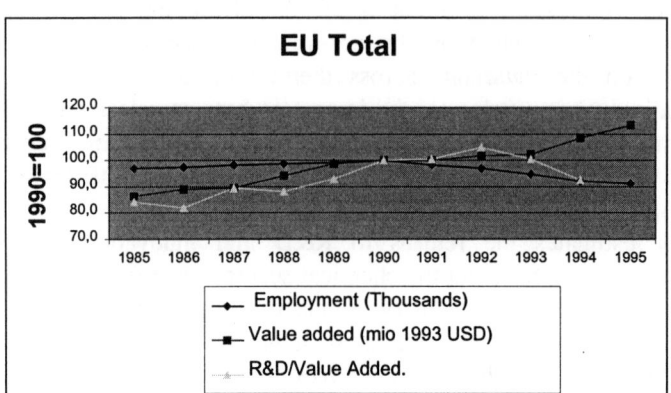

Source: O'Mahony, M. "The Comparative Competitiveness of EU, US and Japanese Chemical Industries", Report for the European Commission (1998).

Last, but not least, the European chemical industry has been internationally very competitive for many years. But recently, there have been several accounts of a gradual loss of competitiveness of the European chemical industry compared to the US. On many occasions, the lower ability of the European chemical companies to invest in R&D and innovate, is suggested as being one of the major causes of this trend. It is therefore important to understand how much this industry really depends on innovation and R&D and whether this is connected with a reduced competitiveness of the European chemical firms in the 1990s. These are clearly important issues both for European managers of chemical companies and policy-makers.

The estimations presented in this study are based on a balanced sample of 47 Fortune 500 chemical companies. These are all the Fortune 500 chemical firms for which we could obtain a complete set of economic and financial variables during 1990-96. By any standard these are leading chemical producers worldwide. Twenty-seven companies in our sample are Europeans, 16 are North Americans, and 4 are Japanese companies. By type of activity, 10 firms are engaged in the production of several types of chemicals (SIC code 280), 3 in industrial inorganic chemicals (SIC 281), 6 in plastics and rubber (SIC 282), 17 in pharmaceuticals (SIC 283), 4 in soaps and detergents (SIC 284), 2 in paints and varnishes (SIC 285), 2 in agricultural chemicals (SIC 286) and 3 in miscellaneous chemicals (SIC 289).

We estimate the determinants of the economic performance of these firms by using two different methodologies. The first one is based on regressing the financial market value of the firm's assets on different measures of the tangible and intangible stocks of the firm. The underlying assumptions here are that the market value of a firm measures its expected future profitability, and that rational financial markets equalize the market value of a firm to the sum of its main assets, weighted by their shadow values. The latter are then estimated from regressions of market value on the assets of the firms. We complemented this analysis with a more "classical" analysis of the determinants of economic performance and productivity growth. Thus, apart from a market value equation of the firms in our sample, we estimate a total factor productivity (TFP) equation, and an equation of the determinants of net profits and sales. In so doing, we can the check the robustness of our results under different specifications.

The chapter begins by providing a brief survey of the literature on the effects of innovation on market value and other measures of economic performance (section 2). Section 3 presents descriptive statistics of our chemical companies. Section 4 presents our estimation results. We first present our market value estimation, and we then check our results using a TFP and net profit over sales equations. In discussing these results, we try to identify in particular possible patterns of behavior that could have policy implications, especially at the European Union level. Section 5 concludes.

2. The literature on market value, innovation and economic performance

Recent work in the economic literature has attempted to use the financial market evaluation of firms to measure the impact of tangible and intangible assets, particularly patents, innovation and R&D, on economic performance. The theoretical background of this empirical literature is that, in equilibrium, the market value of a company is equal to the book value of its capital assets. Higher or lower market value denotes higher or lower returns to the asset. This is Tobin's classical q, whereby the ratio of market value to book value of an asset provides an indication of the marginal value of further investments in that asset.

This idea was extended by Wildasin (1984) to the case in which firms can accumulate multiple assets. Wildasin shows that, under certain conditions (particularly price-taking firms and constant returns to scale), the market value of the firm is equal to the sum of its assets weighted by their shadow values. This has given rise to an empirical literature, which has used this basic equation to estimate the shadow values of various assets that the firms may accumulate. Particularly, apart from physical capital, the literature has attempted to estimate the effects of intangible or knowledge assets of the firm. The problem with these estimations is how to measure the knowledge asset. Following pioneering work by Pakes (1985) and Cockburn and Griliches (1988), most studies in this area have used the stock of R&D or patents of the firm. The most recent studies (i.e. Hall, Jaffe and Trajtenberg, 1998) also used measures such as the citations to patents. All in all, these studies find that, using a Compustat-based sample of a very large number of US firms during the 1980s and the early 1990s, the knowledge asset has a positive and significant impact on market value, beyond that of physical capital. (See Hall, 1999, for a survey.)

Apart from market value, there are clearly several studies that have attempted to estimate the economic returns to R&D using TFP-type equations or other measures of performance. As noted in the introductory section, these studies arose from Griliches' early work on the returns to innovation in the agricultural sector (Griliches, 1957, 1958). Griliches finds that innovations have high social and private returns, and this is confirmed by similar studies conducted by Mansfield (e.g. 1980). In short, what these studies show is that R&D, patents, or R&D (patent) stocks have a positive elasticity with respect to output, even after controlling for other factor inputs like labor and physical capital. (See Mairesse and Mohnen, 1995, for a survey.) Further development of this literature has attempted to assess various other aspects of the effects of R&D or patents, like the extent of the spillovers that investments in knowledge assets can generate. Broadly speaking, these studies also document the importance of such spillovers (e.g. Griliches, 1979; Jaffe, 1986).

Interestingly enough, one study we know that attempted to estimate the returns to innovation in specific industries is Albach *et al.* (1996), which focused on the chemical sector. Albach *et al.* present a comprehensive study of the determinants of innovation in this industry, based on quantitative data (and particularly the recent Community Innovation Survey, CIS), as well as qualitative case studies of individual sub-sectors of the chemical industry and chemical firms. They also estimated the returns to innovation by regressing new product sales on R&D expenditures, and found evidence of decreasing returns to R&D in chemicals, even though these returns tend to be different across countries.

Particularly, they find evidence of increasing returns to R&D for Germany.

In a recent paper (O'Mahony and Vecchi 1999), returns to innovation using firm-level micro-data (Worldscope) are also estimated for the whole economy, distinguishing several countries and also, manufacturing versus services. Tangible and several forms of intangible capital (R&D, advertising etc.) are used. A few case studies of TFP estimates by industry are also presented, including chemicals (see sub-section 4.2 below for a brief comparison with our results).

3. The sample: company performance, assets and strategies

3.1 Construction of the sample

The sample of 47 firms used in the present analysis was obtained as follows:

1. We first selected chemical or pharmaceutical firms, excluding firms primarily engaged in oil extraction or refinery, or perfumes and cosmetics (those deemed to have entirely different innovation patterns) with a 1996 turnover greater than US$ 2 billion (90 firms). The selection was made from the Compustat database on the basis of sales data and SIC codes. Pharmaceuticals is a profitable segment in which several large chemical firms tend to specialise over time (e.g. Hoechst) - hence pharmaceutical firms were retained.
2. Then we extracted those firms for which full information on sales and R&D for 1990-96 was available (we were left with only 47 firms). The result of this process highlights the difficulty of obtaining full information for firm samples (see above).

The available annual information for each firm includes market value, annual sales, net profit, employment, R&D expenditure data (Compustat), patents granted (own or joint patenting, EPO - European Patent Office - database), plant location (Chemintell database), and detailed counts of firm co-operation items: alliances, joint ventures, mergers and acquisitions (SDCA database, provided by Securities Data Company).

All databases have been linked at University Pompeu Fabra (Barcelona), in the framework of the TSER project "From Science to Products".

3.2 Brief description of performance measures

Market values

The 6 biggest firms hold over 50% of the total 1996 market value of the sample (table 10.1). These are all pharmaceutical firms (except Procter and Gamble) and all US-based firms. The 10 biggest firms in terms of market values (70% of the total in the sample) are also US-based. The only non-pharmaceutical firms in these 10 are in addition to Procter and Gamble (soaps, detergents) and E.I. Dupont de Nemours (plastic materials).

Table 10.1: Firms with highest 1996 market values

Name of Firm	Market Value 1996 (US$ billion)	SIC3 Code	Nationality
Merck & Co. Inc.	153,9	283	US
The Procter & Gamble Co.	114,7	284	US
Pfizer Inc.	114,2	283	US
Johnson & Johnson	100,4	283	US
Bristol-Myers Squibb Co.	100,3	283	US
Eli Lilly & Co.	72,8	283	US
E.I. Du Pont de Nemours & Co.	69,1	282	US
American Home Products Corp.	60,0	283	US
Abbott Laboratories (Inc.)	57,9	283	US
Schering-Plough Corp.	55,6	283	US

See Introduction for the definitions of SIC codes

Sales

A quick analysis of firm category (by annual sales size) over time (1990-96) shows the effects of restructuring, a bigger proportion of firms becoming "very large" (annual sales greater then US$ 5 billion) after 1994. Sales history also shows the effects of the mid-90s crisis which particularly affected EU-based firms. Average annual sales growth 1990-96 is contrasted along industry segments, pharmaceuticals again ranking first (Table 10.2).

Table 10.2: Average annual growth rate of sales 1990-96 (%), by sector

SIC3	Nb of firms in sample	Average annual growth rate
280	10	1,29
281	3	4,10
282	6	0,24
283	17	9,09
284	4	5,05
285	2	5,38
286	2	-0,63
289	3	1,19
All	47	4,17

See Introduction for the definitions of SIC codes

Profitability

Table 10.3 below shows that both pharmaceutical and US firms had, on average, higher profitabilities in 1996, which is in line with the above findings.

Table 10.3: Average profitability 1996 (%), by sector and origin of firm

Average of net profit margin 96 (%)	Origin of Firm			
SIC3	EU	US	JP	All
280	4,76	6,05	3,25	5,13
281	6,27	9,26	NA	7,26
282	7,06	9,36	2,37	6,65
283	10,38	17,32	14,05	15,08
284	6,62	9,68	NA	8,15
285	NA	7,93	NA	7,93
286	NA	9,26	NA	9,26
289	NA	12,02	NA	12,02
All	7,24	12,21	5,51	10,05

See Introduction for the definitions of SIC codes

3.3 Fixed assets and patent stocks

Fixed assets 1996 averaged US$ 3.8 billion in the sample (Table 10.4). They are highest in plastics and rubber (SIC 282), where the average number of patents by firm is also highest. This may reflect the fact that plastics is a very diverse segment of industry, where much process innovation occurs in mass-produced plastics and coexists with the development of new specialised plastics (see e.g. Albach *et al.* 1996).

Plant location (Chemintell database) shows a slightly higher proportion of US-based companies holding their plants in North America (65.5%) than the corresponding proportion of plants of EU-based companies holding them in Western Europe (51.9%). This would seem to indicate that EU-based companies in our sample are more "globalised" than their US counterparts.

A summary analysis of the patent stock 1990-96 first shows that the propensity to patent at the European Patent Office (EPO) seems to vary largely by origin of firm: overall, the average stock of patent was 289 for all firms, 539 for EU firms, 176 for US firms and 147 for Japanese-based firms. This may reflect the fragility of patent collection, but also the fact that patenting strategies may depend on industry segments: in more local markets (e.g. detergents), firms may be satisfied with local protection, at least in the short run.

The average stock of patents by firm, for each industry segment is summarised in Table 10.4. Pharmaceutical patenting is lower than the average, which beyond differing propensities to patent by origin of firm, may also indicate that "numbers" do not show everything: an indicator of "patent" quality would usefully complement patent counting for performance analyses (see e.g. Hall 1999 for an indicator using patent citation).

Table 10.4: Average stock of patent by firm, by sector

SIC3	Average fixed assets 1996 (USD bln)	Stock of Patents, 1990-96
280	4,4	537,7
281	4,5	150,3
282	6,1	356,3
283	3,4	225,2
284	3,8	292,5
285	1,7	90,0
286	3,0	147,5
289	0,9	52,7
All	3,8	289,3

See Introduction for the definitions of SIC codes

3.4 Firm strategies

R&D intensity

A brief analysis of R&D intensity (R&D nominal expenditure over sales) shows that R&D intensity is highest in pharmaceuticals, followed by rubber and plastics and firms engaged in "general" activities (Table 10.5). The dispersion around averages is relatively smaller by industry segment than by origin of firm, which would seem to indicate that firms tend to compete on the basis of product specialisation (global effect). Data by industry segment where the number of selected firms is small should be interpreted with caution.

Table 10.5: Average R&D intensities (1990-96), by sector

SIC3	Average R&D intensity	Standard Deviation of R&D intensity
280	4,54	2,06
281	3,29	0,93
282	4,59	1,18
283	11,82	3,93
284	2,38	0,91
285	2,06	1,46
286	2,47	0,42
289	2,71	0,30
All	6,61	4,79

See Introduction for the definitions of SIC codes

Joint ventures (JVs), alliances, mergers and acquisitions

Chemical companies are increasingly entering into strategic alliances in the areas of production and R&D (see section 4 below). Table 10.6 below summarises the number of joint ventures, alliances, mergers and acquisitions (the latter being divided into acquisitions where the firm is the acquirer and acquisitions where the firm, or part of it, was acquired), by industry segment (average numbers by firm). As observed in the sample, these movements mainly concern the largest firms. Alliances have been predominant, particularly in plastics and rubber and pharmaceuticals. Joint ventures follow (also important for plastics). The number of mergers has been relatively smaller compared to other types of growth strategies, and has increased after 1993 - illustrating the globalisation effect.

Table 10.6: *External growth strategies (average numbers by firm, 1990-96), by sector*

SIC3	Joint Ventures	Alliances	Mergers	Acquisitions (where firm is acquirer)	Acquisitions (where firm is target)
280	30,6	30,2	2,6	21,2	24,2
281	16,0	19,3	1,0	19,0	11,3
282	52,3	63,8	0,8	24,2	23,5
283	12,9	52,4	3,2	16,8	10,2
284	14,8	13,0	1,5	24,3	18,8
285	10,5	6,0	3,0	16,0	5,0
286	36,0	23,5	1,0	23,5	31,5
289	10,0	9,0	0,7	7,7	9,0
All	22,8	37,7	2,2	19,1	16,3

See Introduction for the definitions of SIC codes

4. Relating assets and strategies to performance: estimation results

4.1 Analysis of market values

Analyses of the determinants of the market value of a firm typically assume that market value is a function of the different assets that a firm has:

$$V(A_1, A_s, ...) = f(A_1, A_2, ...),$$

where f is an unknown value function associated with the dynamic maximization problem that the firm faces in combining its assets. As noted in section 2, for a single asset and constants return to scale the market value of the firm is simply equal to the book value of the single asset multiplied by Tobin's q, which can be interpreted as the shadow price for the asset. When multiple assets are assumed, then, under constant returns to scale, it can be shown that the market evaluation of the firm is equal to the sum of the assets weighted by their shadow values (Wildasin, 1984).

Different functional forms for f have been used in the literature. The most common one is the Cobb-Douglas or log-linear model:

$$V_{it}(A, K) = q_t A_{it}^{\sigma_t - \alpha_t} K_{it}^{\alpha_t},$$

where A denotes the physical capital, K denotes knowledge or intangible capital, and q can be interpreted as Tobin's q. Taking logarithms, one obtains the following expression:

$$\log V_{it} = \log q_t + \sigma_t \log A_{it} + \alpha_t \log \frac{K_{it}}{A_{it}}$$

Table 10.7: Definition of variables used in the regressions

Dependent variables:
Log of Market Value = 1990-1996 market value of the company (from Compustat Global) deflated by the GDP deflator of the country of origin of the company.
Output growth = 1991-1996 real sales growth of the company (from Compustat Global). Sales deflated by the GDP deflator above
Net profits over sales = 1990-1996 net profits over sales (from Compustat Global).

Explanatory variables:
LFA = Log of fixed assets (from Compustat Global). Fixed assets deflated by the GDP deflator above.
LKRDFA = Log of the ratio of R&D stock to fixed assets. R&D investments from Compustat Global. R&D stock was obtained from the recursive formula $K_t = I_t + (1-d)K_{t-1}$, where I_t is real R&D investments (nominal deflated by GDP deflator above), K_{t-1} is the R&D stock in the previous period, and d is a knowledge depreciation rate set equal to 0.15. The initial value of the R&D stock was obtained by dividing the 1990 real investments in R&D by the depreciation rate of 0.15. (See Hall, 1999, for further discussion about this method of computing the R&D stock.)
GFA = 1991-1996 log of ratio between fixed assets (in real terms) at time t and (t-1).
GKRD = 1991-1996 log of ratio between R&D stock at t and (t-1).
GEMP = 1991-1996 log of ratio between employees at t and (t-1).
YEAR90-YEAR96: Year dummies, 1990 omitted.
LHERF = Log of Herfindahl index for the distribution of plants in different regions of the world (Africa, North America, Asia, Western Europe, Eastern Europe, Middle-East, Central and Latin America). Lower LHERF denotes more "globalized" firms. Plant counts in different regions from Chemintell (1998).
INCH, PLRU, CHEM, DRUG, DETG, PNTS, IOCH, SPEC = Dummies for main activity (sector) of the company – INCH = inorganic chemicals (SIC 281); CHEM = generic chemicals (SIC 280); PLRU = plastics and rubber (SIC 282); DRUG = pharmaceuticals (SIC 283); DETG = soap and detergents (SIC 284); PNTS = paints and varnishes (SIC 285); IOCH = industrial organic chemicals (SIC 286); SPEC = speciality chemicals (SIC 289). INCH is omitted.
DEUR: Dummy for European firms
DJV = Dummy equal to 1 if the firm performs more joint venture than the average in the sample (joint-ventures from SDC, 1998).
DMERGE: Dummy equal to 1 if the firm performs more mergers than the average in the sample (SDC, 1998).
DALLIAN: Dummy equal to 1 if the firm performs more alliances than the average in the sample (SDC, 1998).
DACQAS: Dummy equal to 1 if the firm performs more acquisitions than the average in the sample (SDC, 1998).

We estimated this basic log-linear specification for our sample of 47 chemical companies during 1990-1996. Our dependent variable is the log of market value of the firm. As explanatory variables, we used the log of the fixed assets of the firm, the log of the ratio between the R&D stock and the fixed assets of the firm, along with time dummies, dummies for chemical sub-sectors, and other variables that may affect the market value of the firm. Table 10.7 defines all the variables used in the OLS regressions presented in this and the next section, along with their sources.

Among the other explanatory variables in our market value equation, we employed a dummy for European firms. The purpose of this dummy is twofold. First, we wanted to account for the possibility that European firms may be more or less responsive to market value because of differences in the extent to which the financial market evaluates them vis-à-vis the American firms.[2] Second, we wanted to assess whether, given all our other controls, there were still unexplained effects that influenced the performance of the European firms in our sample. In fact, the latter effect is likely to be more important than the former in our analysis. Most of the firms in our sample are leading multinationals worldwide, and this is true for the European firms as well. As a result, it is unlikely that they face severe differences compared to the US firms in terms of how they are assessed by the financial market.

As reported in Table 10.7, we used other controls as well. Most of them are variables that account for various characteristics of the strategies of our companies. Thus, we computed the Herfindahl index for the "spread" of the plants of our companies in different regions of the world (Africa, Asia, North America, Western Europe, Eastern Europe, Middle East, Central and Latin America). A high value of the Herfindahl index denotes firms that concentrate their plants in fewer regions. By contrast, a low value of this index denotes firms that spread their plants in many areas of the world. Put simply, a low value of the Herfindahl of plants denotes chemical firms that are more "globalised".

Finally, we used various measures of the external growth strategies of our companies. It is well known that today alliances, acquisitions, joint ventures and the like play a central role in the strategies of many companies, and especially of the largest companies. (See for instance Mowery, 1988.) Moreover, alliances, acquisitions and joint ventures

---

[2] In principle, we should have included a dummy for the Japanese firms as well. However, there are only 4 Japanese firms in our sample, and therefore, in our analysis, the significance of this dummy would be very limited.

have played an important role in the chemical industry in recent years, both as a way to cope with the needs for restructuring, and as a means for developing innovations or pursuing other growth opportunities (e.g. internationalisation of marketing and production). (See Arora and Gambardella, 1998.) We therefore used several dummies that account for the propensity of our companies to undertake external growth operations.

We estimated our market value equation by Ordinary Least Squares. The results are in Table 10.8. Table 10.8 presents three sets of regressions where we gradually introduce our various controls. The table shows that the R&D stock of the chemical companies has a positive and significant effect on the market evaluation of these firms. To the extent that market value measures the expected future profitability of a company, this result suggests that R&D investments play an important role in affecting the expected future performance of the chemical manufacturers. Note also that the shadow price of the R&D stock drops from about 0.9 to about 0.35 when moving from the first column of Table 10.8 to the other two columns. This is because the two right-most columns of Table 10.8 include sector dummies. It therefore appears that the result in the first column includes both effects of the R&D stock that depend on company investments, and the sector in which the company operates. Put differently, the higher value of the first column hides the fact that sectors with higher R&D intensity are also more profitable. Nonetheless, the fact that the shadow value of the R&D stock is sizable and significant even after introducing sector dummies suggests that, even within the same sector, companies with a higher R&D stock are valued more by the financial market. In short, there are advantages in terms of expected future profitability that would depend both on moving into R&D intensive segments of the chemical industry, and on the R&D investments that companies undertake within each sector.

Table 10.8: Market value in chemicals, 1990-1996 – OLS

Dependent Variable = Log of Market Value	Estimates	Estimates	Estimates
Constant	6.622 (10.344)	3.733 (6.951)	6.814 (10.082)
LFA	0.797 (18.306)	0.895 (28.066)	0.659 (14.095)
LKRDFA	0.885 (15.337)	0.333 (4.062)	0.349 (4.484)
LHERF	--	--	-0.634 (-6.548)
YEAR91	-0.488 (-2.969)	-0.212 (-1.803)	-0.223 (-2.086)
YEAR92	-0.832 (-4.941)	-0.391 (-3.038)	-0.410 (-3.465)
YEAR93	-1.033 (-5.994)	-0.471 (-3.396)	-0.470 (-3.682)
YEAR94	-1.184 (-6.794)	-0.583 (-4.075)	-0.556 (-4.227)
YEAR95	-1.311 (-7.410)	-0.649 (-4.343)	-0.611 (-4.430)
YEAR96	-1.352 (-7.544)	-0.640 (-4.133)	-0.573 (-3.880)
PLRU	--	-0.432 (-2.623)	-0.385 (-2.531)
CHEM	--	-0.277 (-1.809)	-0.440 (-3.109)
DRUG	--	1.233 (6.093)	1.019 (5.437)
DETG	--	1.086 (6.689)	0.964 (6.474)
PNTS	--	0.638 (3.269)	0.766 (4.291)
IOCH	--	-0.359 (-1.889)	-0.212 (-1.150)
SPEC	--	0.198 (1.085)	-0.239 (-1.337)
DEUR	-0.656 (-6.995)	-0.568 (-8.001)	-0.578 (-7.975)
DJV	--	--	-0.238 (-3.102)
DMERGE	--	--	-0.079 (-1.100)
DALLIAN	--	--	0.300 (3.796)
DACQAS	--	--	0.171 (2.205)
N. Observations	329	329	329
R-squared	0.625	0.830	0.863

t-statistics in parenthesis

To further assess our estimated effect of intangible assets, and its importance relative to tangible assets, one can compute the ratio of the marginal shadow values of K relative to A:

$$\frac{\partial V / \partial K}{\partial V / \partial A} = \frac{\alpha_t A_{it}}{(\sigma_t - \alpha_t) K_{it}}$$

Using our estimated values of α and σ, we found that the average value of this ratio for our sample is 4.15. This means that intangible assets are valued much more than tangible assets. A one dollar increase in the R&D stock would produce a return on the value of the company that is 4.15 higher than a one dollar increase in its physical assets.

The other variables we used in our regression provide further evidence about the different factors that affect the market evaluation of chemical companies. Specifically, LHERF has a negative coefficient, which suggests that globalisation positively affects the expected performance of our firms. As far as our external growth operations are concerned, we find that alliances and acquisitions have a positive effect on market value, while joint ventures and mergers have a negative effect.

The dummies introduced into the model affect only the intercept, which theoretically can be interpreted as Tobin's q. It is just a multiplier for the bundle of tangible and intangible assets. DEUR is a dummy for European firms, and has a negative coefficient. European firms are less capable of capitalising the value of their assets than North American and Japanese firms. This is an interesting result, as it suggests that factors other than tangible or intangible investments negatively affect the expected performance of the European companies. Most other dummies, for products and years, are also significant.

4.2 Total factor productivity and net profits over sales

In this section we further check our results by conducting a more classical analysis of the performance of our firms. Specifically, we examine the factors that influence output growth (and total factor productivity – TFP) and the ratio between net profits and sales for the firms in our sample.

Analysis of TFP is typically based on the assumption that the output of a company depends on a production function of the form

$$Q = f(T, K_1, K_2, \ldots)$$

where Q is output, the K's are the various inputs to the production process, and T is any other factor that influences the productivity of the company. In this analysis, we assume that chemical production depends on three key inputs: the stock of fixed assets (in real terms) at time t, the R&D stock at time t, and the number of employees of the firm at time t. We then used the same controls that we used for our market value equation to assess other factors that may affect the TFP of the chemical companies.

Using a simple Cobb-Douglas specification, it is customary to estimate this equation in its analog TFP counter-part. By taking the time differentials on all the variables on the left and right hand side of this expression, one obtains

$$\frac{\dot{Q}}{Q} = \alpha_1 \frac{\dot{K_1}}{K_1} + \alpha_2 \frac{\dot{K_2}}{K_2} + \alpha_3 \frac{\dot{K_3}}{K_3} + \theta$$

where the left hand side is now the growth rate of output, and the right hand side expression is the sum of the growth rates of the factor inputs weighted by their elasticities with respect to Q, plus another set of variables θ. The latter measure any other factor that affects the TFP of the company.

Our estimates of the output growth equation above are shown in Table 10.9. Like in Table 10.8, we show the results of three sets of OLS regressions, where we gradually add new explanatory variables on the right hand side. Clearly, as we have to use a one-year lag to compute growth rates, our panel now covers only 1991-96.

Table 10.9 shows that the R&D stock has the highest elasticity with respect to output (about 0.46). This confirms the importance of intangible assets in chemical production, as found earlier for market value. Note also that our elasticity estimates are very robust to different specifications of our regressions. They do not change once we introduce new regressors. Most interestingly, no other variables, apart from the growth rates of the three inputs, affect output growth. In other words, TFP seems to be fully explained by our measured factors of production. These results are in line with O'Mahony and Vecchi's (1999), but with a smaller return to R&D (0.36). They also found that intangible capital other than R&D was not significant in estimating their TFP equation.

Table 10.9: TFP in chemicals, 1991-1996 – OLS

Dependent Variable = Output growth	Estimates	Estimates	Estimates
Constant	-0.236 (-5.591)	-0.267 (-5.145)	-0.266 (-4.742)
GFA	0.244 (5.010)	0.251 (5.017)	0.245 (4.858)
GKRD	0.426 (5.701)	0.467 (5.207)	0.474 (5.034)
GEMP	0.397 (7.016)	0.386 (6.571)	0.380 (6.400)
LHERF	--	--	-0.001 (-0.053)
YEAR92	0.133 (6.030)	0.142 (5.758)	0.145 (5.676)
YEAR93	0.131 (4.560)	0.145 (4.350)	0.147 (4.234)
YEAR94	0.232 (7.001)	0.248 (6.447)	0.249 (6.212)
YEAR95	0.286 (8.489)	0.302 (7.709)	0.302 (7.422)
YEAR96	0.186 (5.208)	0.204 (4.876)	0.203 (4.678)
PLRU	--	0.010 (0.471)	0.006 (0.266)
CHEM	--	0.011 (0.574)	0.012 (0.593)
DRUG	--	0.004 (0.194)	0.012 (0.601)
DETG	--	0.012 (0.517)	0.011 (0.455)
PNTS	--	0.034 (1.210)	0.027 (0.938)
IOCH	--	0.019 (0.679)	0.006 (0.190)
SPEC	--	-0.000 (-0.007)	-0.006 (-0.248)
DEUR	-0.013 (-1.382)	-0.011 (-1.072)	-0.019 (-1.631)
DJV	--	--	0.017 (1.392)
DMERGE	--	--	0.003 (0.229).
DALLIAN	--	--	-0.022 (-1.690)
DACQAS	--	--	0.001 (0.053)
N. Observations	282	282	282
R-squared	0.697	0.700	0.705

t-statistics in parenthesis

Finally, we performed a similar set of regressions for the net profits over sales of our companies. Accounting profits are typically affected by many accounting decisions of the companies, which may not in turn reflect real performance factors or other opportunities (e.g. companies often "measure" strategically their depreciation rates to purposely manipulate profits). This is why we prefer our earlier market value estimation as a measure of the potential profitability of the companies. At any rate, a net profit over sales equation is useful to check whether the results obtained earlier are robust to this different specification.

The results of this OLS estimation are shown in Table 10.10. As right hand side variables, we used the growth rates of the factor inputs that we employed in our TFP regression. All the other explanatory variables are the same variables used in our market value and TFP equations. As one moves towards the right hand columns of Table 10.10 we gradually add new regressors as we did in our previous estimations.

Table 10.10 confirms most of the results that we obtained earlier. Both the growth of tangible assets and the growth of the R&D stock affect the current profitability of the firms. The impact of the R&D stock is substantially higher than that of physical assets. As with our market value estimation in Table 10.8, the impact of the R&D stock reduces once we introduce sector dummies. This confirms that profitability is partly related to sector-specific characteristics of the chemical industry, with the more R&D-intensive segments of the industry being also the more profitable ones. However, since the impact of the R&D stock persists even after introducing sector dummies, it appears that the company-specific propensity to invest in R&D and innovation can produce differences in their profitabilities even within the same sector. Table 10.10 also shows that the growth of employment does not affect current profits in the chemical industry. This was only to be expected, as the chemical industry is typically capital and R&D-intensive, and little effect is produced by variations in the labor input.

As far as our other variables are concerned, Table 10.10 confirms two important results of the previous market value equation. First, the impact of our globalisation, Herfindahl index, is negative and statistically significant. Profitability in the chemical sector appears to be strongly associated with the degree of globalisation of the companies. Second, other things being equal, the DEUR dummy is negative, and significantly so. The European chemical firms appear to be less profitable than their American competitors, even after controlling for a number of other factors. Finally, the results about the effects of our external growth strategies are more confused than those that we obtained in our market value equation. This is likely to reflect the high correlation among these variables. In short, the reduced form estimations that we performed in this chapter do not really enable us to draw clear conclusions about the effects of these strategies.

Table 10.10: Net profits over sales in chemicals, 1991-1996 – OLS

Dependent Variable = Net profits/Sales	Estimates	Estimates	Estimates
Constant	-15.351 (-4.990)	-3.642 (-1-108)	-8.849 (-2.633)
GFA	7.375 (2.077)	7.344 (2.322)	7.697 (2.553)
GKRD	43.185 (7.917)	18.391 (3.241)	23.618 (4.196)
GEMP	-1.931 (-0.468)	-1.714 (-0.461)	-2.358 (-0.664)
LHERF	--	--	-4.181 (-5.198)
YEAR92	9.735 (6.048)	4.296 (2.749)	5.351 (3.512)
YEAR93	14.595 (6.975)	6.225 (2.958)	7.972 (3.847)
YEAR94	18.103 (7.498)	8.359 (3.439)	10.513 (4.377)
YEAR95	20.134 (8.197)	10.117 (4.075)	12.668 (5.197)
YEAR96	21.676 (8.318)	10.834 (4.092)	13.577 (5.240)
PLRU	--	-2.253 (-1.655)	-0.596 (-0.440)
CHEM	--	-1.751 (-1.409)	-1.078 (-0.904)
DRUG	--	5.325 (4.314)	5.788 (4.737)
DETG	--	0.865 (0.601)	1.992 (1.442)
PNTS	--	2.999 (1.692)	5.634 (3.232)
IOCH	--	0.201 (0.114)	2.484 (1.397)
SPEC	--	2.763 (1.745)	1.713 (1.111)
DEUR	-3.411 (-5.121)	-2.852 (-4.473)	-2.850 (-4.170)
DJV	--	--	-0.699 (-0.950)
DMERGE	--	--	-1.862 (-2.074)

DALLIAN	--	--	0.048 (0.063)
DACQAS	--	--	-1.403 (-2.031)
N. Observations	282	282	282
R-squared	0.392	0.546	0.601

5. Conclusions

The objective of this chapter was to empirically explore the determinants of economic performance and the returns to R&D in the chemical industry during the 1990s. To perform our analysis, we employed a sample composed of 47 Fortune 500 chemical firms for which we could obtain complete data for 1990-96 from various sources. By any measure, these are the leading chemical manufacturers worldwide. Our 47 companies include 16 North American firms, 27 European firms and 4 Japanese firms.

We performed our analysis using different measures of performance. Specifically, we used the market value of these firms during the sample period, and their net profits over sales, as measures of their future and current profitability. In addition, we estimated a TFP equation linking the output growth of these companies to the growth of their tangible assets, R&D stock and employment, along with other factors.

Our main result is that R&D and innovation affect in a significant way the performance of the large chemical companies. We estimated that the returns to R&D in chemicals are about 4.15 times higher than the returns to physical capital. This is confirmed by our TFP regression which shows that R&D has the highest elasticity with respect to output, compared to physical capital and labor. The effect of R&D on current or future profitability in our estimations reduces when we introduce sector dummies for the main three-digit SIC segments of the chemical industry. This suggests that the effects of R&D on profitability in chemicals are partly due to sector differences, with the more high-tech segments of the industry also showing higher profitability. However, the effect of R&D on performance does not disappear after one introduces the sector dummies. This suggests that there are differences in the performance of our firms even within the same sector, and these differences are explained by differences in the extent to which they invest in R&D. This clearly has implications for company strategy. Companies are more likely to improve profitability if they move into more innovative sectors of the industry, and within these sectors if they invest more resources in R&D.

We also obtained some other notable results. First, we found that more "globalised" companies exhibit higher performance. Globalisation then appears to be another important strategy in the chemical business. Our reduced form analysis prevents us from indicating the direction of the causation. Nonetheless, the correlation is worth mentioning, as it is consistent for instance with the increased attention paid by many chemical companies towards foreign investments in emerging countries.

Second, we found that, other things being equal, the European chemical companies are less profitable than the American ones. Our analysis was not sophisticated enough to find out which are the factors that account for this observed lower performance of the European firms. This topic is left to further research. Nonetheless, we thought that this result should sound as a warning for the European chemical managers and policy-makers, as it confirms a widespread perception about the reduced competitiveness of an industry wherein Europe has had significant international performance for many years.

Finally, we also tried to assess the effects on performance of various types of external growth operations and strategies by the chemical companies (strategic alliances, joint ventures, mergers and acquisitions). Our results were not definitive on this issue. We found that some of these variables had positive effects on performance, while others had a negative effect, and yet others – or even the same variables in other regressions – had no significant effect. This is another topic that requires further and more specific investigations.

References

Albach, H., Audretsch, D.B., Fleisher, M., Greb, R., Höfs, E., Röller, L.H. and Schulz, I. (1996), "Innovation in the European Chemical Industry", Discussion Paper FS IV 96-26, WZB, Berlin.

Arora, A. and Gambardella, A. (1998), "Evolution of Industry Structure in the Chemical Industry", in Arora, A., Landau, R., and Rosenberg, N. (eds.), *Chemicals and Long Term Growth*, John Wiley and Sons, New York.

CMA, 1997, "Statistical Yearbook", Chemical Manufacturer's Association, Washington DC.

Cockburn, I. and Griliches, Z. (1988), "Industry Effects and Appropriability Measures in the Stock Market's Valuation of R&D and Patents", *American Economic Review*, Vol.78 (2), 419-423.

Griliches, Z. (1957), "Hybrid Corn: An Exploration in the Economics of Technological Change", *Econometrica*, Vol.25 (4), 501-522.

Griliches, Z. (1958), "Research Cost and Social Returns: Hybrid Corn and Related Innovations", *Journal of Political Economy*, Vol.66 (4), 419-431.

Griliches, Z. (1979), "Issues in Assessing the Contribution of Research and Development to Productivity Growth", *Bell Journal of Economics*, Vol.10 (1), 92-116.

Griliches, Z. (1986), "Productivity, R&D, and Basic Research at the Firm Level in the 1970s", *American Economic Review*, Vol.76 (1), 141-154.

Hall, B. (1999), "Innovation and Market Value", Discussion Paper No. 1999-W3, Nuffield College, Oxford.

Hall, B., Jaffe, A., and Trajtenberg, M. (1998), "Market Value and Patent Citations: A First Look", mimeo, NBER, Cambridge MA.

Jaffe, A. (1986), "Technological Opportunity and Spillovers of R&D: Evidence from Firms' Patents, Profits and Market Value", *American Economic Review*, Vol.76 (5), 984-1001.

Mairesse, J. and Mohnen, P. (1995), "R&D and Productivity Growth: What Have We Learned from Econometric Studies", paper presented at the EUNETICS Conference on Evolutionary Economics of Technological Change: Assessment of Results and New Frontiers, Strasbourg, France, 6-8 October.

Mansfield, E. (1980), "Basic Research and Productivity Increase in Manufacturing", *American Economic Review*, Vol.70 (5), 863-873.

Mansfield, E., Rapoport, J., Romeo, A., Villani, E., Wagner, S. and Husic, F. (1977), *The Production and Application of New Industrial Technologies*, Norton, New York.

Mowery, D. (ed.) (1988), *International Collaborative Joint Ventures in US Manufacturing*, Ballinger, Cambridge MA.

O'Mahony, M. and Vecchi, M. (1999), "Intangible Investment, Companies and Competitiveness: An International Comparison", report to the European Commission (July).

Pakes, A. (1985), "On Patents, R&D, and the Stock Market Rate of Return", *Journal of Political Economy*, Vol.93 (21), 390-409.

Wildasin, D. (1984), "The q Theory of Investment with Many Capital Goods", *American Economic Review*, Vol.74 (1), 203-210.

11. Discussion
Christian Huveneers

The chapter "Tangible and Intangible Investment and Economic Performance: Evidence from Company Accounts" by M. O'Mahony and M. Vecchi is very rigorous and has many merits. The database is not the least one: it is interesting and original, and enables the authors to do original empirical work.

First, there is the distinction between the two types of intangible assets, R&D and advertising. Specifically, the inclusion of advertising, as of other intangible assets like patents, copyrights, trademarks etc, is most valuable.

Second, the database includes non-US and non-manufacturing firms.

Following the literature, the discussion of O'Mahony and Vecchi's empirical study of R&D and advertising should address the question of identification and interpretation. This is clear from the work of Stephen Davies *et al.* (1996) and also from the WIFO typology. For the pioneers of "Structure - Conduct - Performance", R&D and advertising were key indicators of industry conduct, and they had important roles to play as "barriers to entry".

In the modern theory of the multinational firm, specific assets are the dominant theme and they are proxied by spending on R&D and advertising. Similarly in trade theory, one emphasizes intra-industry trade and product differentiation, and this is identified by large flows of R&D and advertising. And in the work of John Sutton, one central issue is the distinction between industries in which sunk costs are endogenous and those where they are exogenous. And the empirical distinction between them is made by observing advertising and R&D expenditures: those intangible investments are typical endogenous sunk costs.

This shows that R&D and advertising can mean different things and this makes new empirical studies, like this one by O'Mahony and Vecchi, so difficult to interpret but also very interesting to industrial economists.

In this instance, O'Mahony and Vecchi estimate the impact of R&D and advertising on two measures of corporate performance, net sales per employee, that is, productivity and profitability. Some of the empirical results are worth emphasizing: for example, non-manufacturing firms with R&D are both more profitable and productive than their counterparts in manufacturing.

Depending on the theoretical underpinning, interpretations of a positive impact of intangibles may be different: they could mean that those activities are effective ways of securing monopoly profits; or they can show that multinational firms are more efficient, or they can be evidence that endogenous sunk costs expand with the size of the market.

So, future research along those lines is deserved, in order to distinguish between those different interpretations and to answer for example the following questions: how do intangible expenditures affect the product market? Does the mix between trade and multinationality matter? Are some firms strategically interdependent? And how are intangible assets themselves determined?

Interestingly, O'Mahony and Vecchi devote special attention to the chemical sector, which is also the subject of the empirical research by Gambardella, García-Fontes and Petit.

Gambardella *et al.* estimate the determinants of the economic performance of 47 chemical firms by using two different methodologies.

The first methodology is a classical one: it is based on the analysis of the determinants of economic performance (net profits and sales) and productivity growth.

The other methodology is based on regressing the financial market value of the firm's assets on variables measuring tangible and intangible stocks of the firm. The underlying assumption is that rational financial markets equalize the market value of the firm to the sum of its main assets weighted by their shadow values.

The authors use this basic equation to estimate the shadow values of the various assets that the firm uses. Specifically, according to this literature, the knowledge asset has a positive and significant impact on market value. And this confirms the results obtained by several studies using Total Factor Productivity type equations or other measures of performances.

The empirical study by Gambardella *et al.* confirms that R&D and innovation affect in a significant way the performance of the large chemical companies. And their results also show that there are differences in the performance of firms within the chemical sector, and that these differences are explained by the differences in the extent to which they invest in R&D.

It is interesting to stress that this confirms results obtained by other work, for example empirical work on the existence of strategic groups - as pioneered by Caves and Porter - within the chemical industry confirms that the main criterion to delimitate strategic groups according to competitiveness in the chemical and pharmaceutical industry is the importance of R&D expenditures.

At this point, we may already draw the conclusion that intangibles have a positive impact on competitiveness, through their effect on productivity and profitability.

In our own empirical research to assess the impact of intangibles on competitiveness, we took the same starting point as Meeusen and Rayp: non-price competition, that is, factors other than price considerations must be important in explaining international competitiveness, as measured by market shares.

Whereas Meeusen and Rayp stress the importance of a hysteresis hypothesis, we have taken a model of market share inspired directly by Industrial Economics: expenditures in intangibles like R&D may exert an effect on market share through their strategic use in the competition among firms, in models à la Brander and Spencer (1983).

Specifically, R&D is a strategic investment in a first period, which influences positively the produced quantities in the second period: it is a Cournot model. As far as quantities of the domestic producers may be expressed as a market share vis-à-vis the quantities produced by foreign competitors, the model can be used to estimate the impact of R&D on competitiveness, as was done by Yamawaki and Audretsch (1988) for Japanese manufacturing vis-à-vis the US producers.

We have tested this approach for Belgium with a cross-section on industries: the market shares of Belgian firms, at industry level, and vis-à-vis an important partner, Germany, are regressed on labour and capital intensities on the one hand, and R&D on the other hand. Another explanatory variable is price differentiation, measuring vertical product differentiation.

If the variable measuring R&D intensity is significant, it can be explained by two possible channels: either, as just explained, by the strategic use of R&D, or by the more usual explanation of the effect of R&D on productivity and product quality (theories of technology gap, i.e. endogenous growth). But that coefficient of R&D intensity does not prove significant in our first estimates.

The variable price differentiation is significant, that is, the higher quality of the products as reflected by the ability to charge higher prices than the foreign competitors has a positive effect on market share of Belgian industrial firms.

We then added a second equation: the price differentiation is itself positively influenced by R&D expenditures, tat is, the higher the R&D expenditures in a Belgian industry the higher are the export prices of that industry relative to the export prices of the German competitors: a unit increase of the ratio of the R&D intensity in a Belgian industry to the corresponding German R&D intensity allows a 4% increase of the Belgian export price (relative to the German export price). This ability to price differentiate despite the small open economy position, and to increase market share despite the higher prices, is ascribed to vertical product differentiation.

This hypothesis of vertical product differentiation has also been tested along another line of empirical research, namely the kind of work done by Beccarello (1997) for major manufacturing industries of leading OECD countries and by Bughin and Huveneers (1998) for the Belgian chemical sector. They analyse empirically the long-run relationship between selling prices and costs in order to formulate the dynamics of price-setting behavior. By dynamics of price-setting, we mean the distinction between short-term and long-term effects on prices of for example cost increases. This allows us to know more about the persistence or short life of market power.

The result obtained by Bughin and Huveneers can be summarized as follows:

1. though Belgium is a small open economy and the largest Belgian chemical firms' turnover is just a fraction of the largest German companies' turnover, market power of Belgian firms, in the form of price differentiation vis-à-vis German prices, is apparent albeit only in the short term. Belgian companies are able to depart from the price constraint of Germany and pass through some of the evolution of their costs to the prices charged to their customers;
2. in the long term, however, there is a cointegration (price-taking) relationship between Belgian output prices, German prices, and costs (wages and oil input prices);
3. there is a sufficiently long lag for adjustment to cointegrated price-taking behaviour of between six to eleven quarters. This is in line

with the literature on the persistence of profits (Encaoua, D. *et al.* 1986).

This is in line with work by Sutton (1991) which suggests that sunk costs in the industry make chemical companies prone to price differentiation.

This is confirmed by Bughin and Copeland (1997), by Davies and Lyons (1996), who show, for chemicals, the role of some types of intangible assets, especially R&D and advertisement, as a source of product and price differentiation, and of value creation (European Commission, 1996, p. 121).

As stressed also by Gambardella *et al.*, the high exogenous and endogenous fixed, sunk costs of the chemical industry, explain the success of the chemical sector which takes a special place in European industry.

This is even the case in a small open economy like Belgium. As casual business cases suggest, Belgian chemical companies, despite strong international competition, have performed quite well, being in the list of top capital market performers, based on metrics such as market value added, return on invested capital, or total returns to shareholders.

By revealing that a short-term wedge exists in relative prices between Belgian and German companies, the empirical results of Bughin and Huveneers help understand that part of the high market-to-book value experienced by some Belgian chemical companies, might come not only from above-average efficiency, but also from short-term price differentiation relying on R&D investment.

References

Beccarello, M. (1997), "Time series analysis of market power: evidence from G-7 manufacturing", *International Journal of Industrial Organization (IJIO)*, 15,1, 123-136.

Brander, J. and Spencer, B. (1983), "Strategic commitment with R&D: the symmetric case", *Bell Journal of Economics*, 14, 225-235.

Bughin, J. (1996), "Capacity constraints and export performance - theory and evidence from Belgian manufacturing", *Journal of Industrial Economics*, 44, 2, 187-204, June.

Bughin, J. and Copeland, T.E. (1997), "The virtuous cycle of shareholder value creation", *McKinsey Quarterly*, 2.

Bughin, J. and Huveneers, C. (1997), "Cointegrated price behavior in the Belgian chemical industry", Paper presented at the 25th E.A.R.I.E. Conference, Copenhagen, September.

Davies, S. and Lyons, B., (1996), "Industrial organization in the European Union: Structure, strategy and competitive mechanism", University Press, Oxford.

Encaoua, D., Geroski, P. and Jacquemin, A. (1986), "Strategic competition and the persistence of dominant firms: a survey", in Stiglitz, J.E and Mathewson, G.F., ed., *New developments in the analysis of market structure: Proceedings of a conference held by the International Economic Association in Ottawa, Canada*. Cambridge, MA: MIT Press; London: Macmillan Press, 1986, 55-86.

Engle, R. and Granger, C. (1987), "Co-integration and error correction: representation, estimation and testing", *Econometrica*, 55, 2, March, 251-276.

European Commission (1996), "Economic evaluation of the internal market", *European Economy*, 4.

Geroski, P. and Jacquemin, A. (1988), "The persistence of profits: a european comparison", *Economic Journal*, 98 (391), June, 375-389.

Huveneers, C. (1996), "Modèles de formation des prix en Économie industrielle internationale: application aux mesures de compétitivité pour une petite Économie ouverte", *Bulletin de l'IRES*, 188, UCL (Louvain-la-Neuve), April.

Lemaire, F. (1991), "Etude de la structure et du comportement en prix du secteur chimique belge - Référence à un sous-secteur particulier: les cosmétiques et parfums", Bachelor's thesis UCL, Louvain-la-Neuve.

Mahieu, G. (1997), "Technologie, innovation, recherche et développement au travers des différents courants d'Économie internationale et d'Économie industrielle - Etude de leur influence sur la part de marché belge en Allemagne", Bachelor's thesis, University of Louvain-la-Neuve, 152 pages, July.

Sutton, J. (1991), *Sunk Costs and Market Structure*, Cambridge MA, MIT Press.

Thiran, J.M. (1993), "Les importations belges de produits manufacturés allemands sous l'angle de l'Économie industrielle", Master's thesis, University of Louvain-la-Neuve.

Yamawaki, H. and Audretsch, D. (1988), "Import share under international oligopoly with differentiated products : Japanese imports in U.S. manufacturing", *Review of Economics and Statistics*, 70, 569-579.

PART III

INTANGIBLES: ANALYSIS OF INPUTS

12. Human Capital Stock and Productivity:
The Case of Dutch Manufacturing Firms
Martin Boon

Introduction

Increasing competition and technological changes force firms to invest more in the training of their employees, which contributes to the human capital stock of the firms. Investment in training directed to higher product quality is of utmost importance for Dutch firms that have to compete with firms in low-wage countries. It is generally assumed that productivity is higher in firms with a better-trained work force. The argument is that skilled employees are able to adapt more easily to new production processes and new products.

The issue of productivity growth has attracted much attention from economic science. Recent contributions to growth theory emphasise that the concept of capital has to be broadened to include physical capital as well as human capital and R&D capital. Human capital depends on the number of years and type of education and on in-company training, while R&D capital concerns knowledge not directly embodied in labour. The effects of education and R&D on productivity growth have already been measured by other researchers. OECD (1994) reviews a number of studies on the influence of initial skills of workers on firm performance. An example of a study on the effects of education (vocational qualifications of the labour force) on productivity growth is O'Mahony and Wagner (1996). Mairesse and Sassenou (1991) have given an overview of econometric studies on R&D productivity. However, there is little empirical evidence to assess the quantitative impact of further training provided by the employers on productivity performance.

Most empirical work on the link between training and productivity has been based on employee-level surveys to focus on the characteristics of those who have been trained. The majority of these studies, for instance Groot (1994) and Bishop (1994), used a subjective measure of the individual productivity of workers such as the answer to the following question: on a scale of 0-100 how has your productivity changed because of training? Groot (1994) found that after participation in a formal training program employees are on average 16 percent more productive than before. Bishop (1994) concludes that formal off-the-job training raises worker productivity by 16 percent. The problem with subjective measures of productivity is that they are not comparable across firms or even within firms over time.

Other studies used objective micro-data on firm characteristics to estimate the magnitude of the returns earned by the firms that train their employees. Using longitudinal firm-level data Bartel (1991) found that training programs resulted in increases in firm productivity of the order of 17 percent. Lynch and Black (1995) saw, using cross-sectional firm-level data, that significantly positive effects on firm productivity are associated with certain types of employer-provided training. Tan and Batra (1995) showed by using cross-sectional data for individual firms that employer investment in formal training has a large and significant impact on value added.

The findings of the above-mentioned firm-level studies are subject to some limitations. The most important one is that they did not use a quantitative measure of the accumulated stock of human capital over time within a firm. In other words, they did not consider the fact that training expenditure accumulates into a stock of human capital. Both Bartel and Tan and Batra used as a training measure a dummy variable indicating whether or not the firm provided any formal training to its employees. Lynch and Black considered the numbers of workers trained, time spent in training and dummies for specific training types for a given year.

Another limitation of both Lynch and Black and Tan and Batra is that their estimates could be biased because of unobservable firm characteristics.

This chapter examines the impact that employee training has on firm output in the Dutch manufacturing sector, using a production function framework. Our empirical analysis uses linked firm-level data of the training surveys, the production surveys, and the wage and employment surveys for the years 1990 and 1993. The chapter is organised as follows. The second section summarises the data and discusses some descriptive statistics. In the third section we outline the production function framework within which human capital is considered as a separate input.

The fourth section presents different estimates for the production model and the fifth section contains some concluding remarks.

Data description and summary statistics

The data used in this study concern information on individual firms in the Dutch manufacturing sector for the years 1990 and 1993. The data are created at Statistics Netherlands by joining micro—data of the production survey, the training survey and the wage and employment survey.

In the annual production survey (PS) firms in the manufacturing sector are asked for detailed information on inputs and outputs. This information contains, amongst other things, sales, gross output, gross value added, wage costs, number of employees, materials, electricity use and capital consumption allowances (depreciation costs). Since 1987 all firms with twenty or more employees are surveyed and from the firms with less than twenty employees a sample is drawn.

The training survey (TS) asks firms in the private sector with five or more employees to provide information on formal training that is financed wholly or partly by firms. Formal training in this survey is defined as courses that take place away from the work floor (i.e. class room, training centre), at which a group of persons receive instruction for a period of time specified in advance. The sampling design has two phases. This implies that first a large sample of firms is surveyed with a limited set of questions about the training activity. In the second phase a sub-sample was drawn from the responding firms which were active in training. The sub-sampled firms received a comprehensive questionnaire about training expenditure, training participation, number of hours worked for training staff and number of training days (during working time). Training expenditure is disaggregated into wage costs of lost working time and of training staff, and material costs (which consist of fees of training institutes, compensation of study fees, travelling and lodging expenses). See Slagter (1995) for more details.

The wage and employment survey (WES) contains information on number of hours worked and wages for firms which have employees. The survey is based on a two-stage sample design. First a stratified sample of firms is drawn and then each sampled firm takes a simple random sample of its employees.

The nominal variables in the data set are all deflated to 1990 guilders. Output and materials are deflated by applying three-digit SIC[1] product and material price index numbers to all firms within the corresponding industry. Training expenditures are deflated by a composite index of wages of trainers and trainees, and of material prices. The wage change for trainers and trainees was computed for industry groups at the two-digit SIC level as the change in average hourly compensation for employees between 1990 and 1993. Using firm-specific labour and material expenditure shares, the appropriate wage change was averaged with the material price change to construct training expenditure deflators.

The individual firms belonging to the cross-sectional data sets for 1990 and 1993 are linked to each other. This link results in a balanced panel consisting of 173 firms. Summary statistics of the key variables for this data set are given and compared with those for the linked PS90-PS93 panel in Table 12.1. The linked PS90-PS93 panel contained 4834 firms that existed in both 1990 and 1993. At these firms, gross output decreased by 0.9 percent per year, employment decreased by 2.5 percent per year and labour productivity decreased by 1.0 percent per year. The second column presents data for the linked PS90-PS93-TS90-TS93-WES90-WES93 panel (in this section referred to as panel A). It can be inferred that value added declined less strongly for panel A than for the PS90-PS93 panel, while employment declined more strongly, resulting in labour productivity growth of 4.6 percent per year.

We have looked at the representativeness of panel A. It appears that firms in panel A are larger than in the PS90-PS93 panel. The larger average firm size reflects the design for the training survey and the sample selection from survival caused by linking the 1990 and 1993 production survey. Further, in 1993 all manufacturing firms together spent 971 million guilders on formal employee training and employed 725.000 workers. The firms belonging to panel A contribute to 30 percent of total manufacturing training expenditure and cover 17 percent of total manufacturing employment in 1993.

---

[1] SIC denotes Standard Industrial Classification of Statistics, Netherlands.

Table 12.1: Summary statistics[a]

Data set	PS90-PS93	PS90-PS93-TS90-TS93-WES90-WES93
1990		
Number of employees	136	879
Gross output[c]	48	298
Value added[c]	14	96
Labour productivity[b]	103	112
Average annual growth 1990-1993 (in %)		
Number of employees	-2.54	-5.78
Gross output	-0.92	-5.17
Value added	-3.50	-1.98
Labour productivity[b]	-1.03	4.60
Number of firms	4834	173

Notes: [a] Means
[b] Value added per employee in thousands of 1990 guilders.
[c] In millions of 1990 guilders.

Production function framework

Next, we describe the framework for analysing the impact of employee training on firm output. Investment in employee training accumulates into a firm's stock of human capital, similar to the formation of physical capital through investment in fixed assets. The theoretical framework will be a production function with human capital as a separate input.[2] We adopt the log-linear specification of the Cobb-Douglas production function:

$$q_{it} = \alpha + \beta h_{it} + \gamma c_{it} + \varphi l_{it} + \omega m_{it} + \theta d_t + \varepsilon_{it} \qquad (1)$$

---

[2] It can be argued that training is embodied in the particular employees receiving the training. As these workers leave the firm, presumably they take their human capital with them. However, in the short run labour turnover can be neglected.

where q_{it} is the (log of) output of firm i in year t, α is a constant, h_{it} is the (log of) human capital stock at the beginning of year t,[3] c_{it} is the (log of) physical capital in year t, l_{it} is the (log of) labour, m_{it} is the (log of) materials, d_t is a year dummy which is a time-specific indicator of the level of disembodied technology, and ε_{it} is a disturbance term. If output is measured by gross output then the input set consists of the above-mentioned factors, and if it is measured by value added then material input is excluded from this set. The parameters β, γ, φ and ω are the elasticities of output with respect to the inputs.

We can estimate equation (1) with OLS on pooled cross-sectional data, under the assumption that the disturbance term ε_{it} has mean zero and a constant variance. However, it is likely that the error term ε_{it} comprises heterogeneity across firms in their technologies and type of output and this will introduce a firm-specific effect τ_i. In symbols

$$\varepsilon_{it} = \tau_i + \upsilon_{it} \qquad (2)$$

where υ_{it} denotes the random disturbance. Under error-component model (2) the pooled estimates of the standard errors of the coefficients are biased. To allow for the firm-specific effects, we use fixed effects and random effects panel estimators. To be precise, in the fixed effects specification the firm-specific effects are assumed to be fixed parameters which have to be estimated, while in the random effects specification the firm-specific effects are assumed to be random variables.[4] It can be shown that if the data consist of only two years the fixed effects approach gives the same result as estimating the model on the first differences.

It is difficult to measure the accumulated stock of human capital of a firm. The situation for human capital is comparable with R&D capital. Just as training expenditure enhances the stock of human capital, R&D expenditure accumulates into the stock of R&D capital of a firm. Hall and Mairesse (1995), followed by Bartelsman et al. (1996), have applied two alternative methods for measuring R&D capital as a separate input into the production function. We will use one of these methods, the so-called stock approach, for estimating the production function with human capital as input.

---

[3] Ideally, the human capital input measure to estimate the production function is the flow of services which are added from the human capital stock. However, in practice there is no data available on the utilisation rate of the human capital stock. We assume that the utilisation rate is constant over time.

[4] We can obtain the fixed effects estimates by performing OLS on the deviations from its mean over time, while the random effects estimator is equivalent to the GLS estimator.

The stock approach calculates the human capital stock at the beginning of this year as the sum of last year's investment in training and the human capital stock at the beginning of last year (minus depreciation). In symbols:

$$H_{it} = E_{i,t-1} + (1-\delta)H_{i,t-1} \qquad (3)$$

where H_{it} is the stock of human capital of firm i at the beginning of year t, E_{it} represents training expenditures in year t and δ is the rate of depreciation. This implies that past training continues to have spillover effects on output in the present, although the effect may diminish over time through depreciation. The depreciation is supposed to reflect the obsolescence of skills with age. The content of formal training can vary, from courses related to specific firm's activities (such as machinery operation and quality control) to courses related to the firm's general operation (management techniques, accounting, foreign languages, etc.). The magnitude of depreciation differs between the various formal training programs. Know-how of computer systems, for instance, becomes obsolete faster than knowledge of management techniques. The magnitude of yearly depreciation is usually chosen in the 1 to 12 percent range (see De Mooij, 1997).

In our data set, training expenditure is observed only in the years 1990 and 1993 and no initial human capital stock measure is available. Training expenditure for the intervening years is interpolated using the observed growth rate for each firm. Following Hall and Mairesse (1995), the human capital stock for the year 1990 can be written as:

$$H_{i,90} = \frac{E_{i,90}}{(g+\delta)} \qquad (4)$$

where g is the pre-sample annual growth rate of training expenditure, which is assumed constant across firms. From equation (3) we can derive the following expression for the human capital stock in year 1993:

$$H_{i,93} = (1-\delta)^3 H_{i,90} + \sum_{s=0}^{2}(1+e_i)^{2-s}(1-\delta)^s E_{i,90} \qquad (5)$$

with e_i the annual growth rate of training expenditure for firm i in the period 1990-1993.

From the estimate of the output elasticity for human capital (β) we can derive an estimate for the rate of return of human capital (ρ) in the following way. For the Cobb-Douglas specification the marginal product of the human capital stock, ρ, is equal to the output elasticity of human capital times the ratio of output (Q) to the human capital stock (H):

$$\rho \equiv \frac{\partial Q_{it}}{\partial H_{it}} = \beta \frac{Q_{it}}{H_{it}} \qquad (6)$$

The parameter ρ can be interpreted as the amount by which output increases with an increase in training expenditure, that is, as the private, gross (i.e. including depreciation) rate of return of human capital. In actual estimation it is assumed that for every firm both the output and the human capital stock is equal to the corresponding average over the firms in our data set.

Estimation results for the production function

We have assessed the effects of investment in training on output by providing estimates of the output elasticity of the human capital stock. We have adopted production function (1) in which human capital is measured using the stock approach. We have calculated human capital for 1990 and 1993 according to (4) and (5) for two different depreciation rates ($\delta=5$ and 15 percent), using a pre-sample annual growth rate of training expenditure (g) of 5 percent. In addition, we have also used this year's training expenditure as a measure of human capital. We have applied different estimation methods depending on the assumption concerning the error term, i.e. the pooled, fixed effects and random effects method. Next to the factor inputs, we have included in the specifications dummies for four sectors of economic activity: 1) food, beverages and tobacco, 2) petroleum, chemical industry and allied, 3) metal industries and 4) other industries (textiles, apparel, paper and paper products, and building materials).[5]

The capital input measure required to estimate the production function is proxied by the depreciation costs. Variations in the utilisation of the capital stock can cause differences between the depreciation data and the desired measure of the flow of capital services. When the fixed effects specification of the production function is estimated, changes in the capital inputs are proxied by changes in electricity use. This measure should better correct for fluctuations in capital usage over time. There are differences between firms and within firms over time in shares of full-time

---

[5] The fixed effects estimator cannot estimate the effect of any time-invariant variable like the SIC dummies. These time-invariant variables are wiped out by the 'deviations from means' transformation.

and part-time employees and in the incidence of short-time working and holidays. In order to take into account these differences, the input of labour is measured by total hours actually worked per year instead of total number of employees.

The training expenditure is separated from the other operating expenses of the firm, since the training inputs do not produce current output but are used to increase the stock of human capital. In this way we can avoid the biases in estimation of the production function caused by 'double-counting' of resource inputs (see Mairesse and Sassenou, 1991). In the production function, labour and material input variables are adjusted for the amounts used in training endeavour. This implies that labour input is defined exclusive of hours worked by (in-firm) trainers and of lost working time of trainees and that material inputs contain only non-training inputs. Value added is measured as gross output less non-training materials.

In Tables 12.2 and 12.3 production function estimates are presented using real gross output and real gross value added respectively as measures of the volume of output. The estimated coefficients of the production function are elasticities, that is, they denote the percentage rise in output which results from a one percentage rise in the given input factor. The estimates for the elasticities of the factor inputs are reasonably close to the corresponding factor shares in the output value as these should be under the hypothesis of perfect competition.

For both output measures the pooled estimates show that the output elasticity with respect to human capital is positive and statistically significant at the 10 percent level. A problem with the pooled estimates is that under error-components model (2) the standard errors are biased. This problem can be solved by applying the fixed effects estimator. Before having estimated the fixed effects estimators, we performed the F-test for the joint significance of firm-specific effects. The test results indicate the presence of firm-specific effects. We find that the elasticity of human capital becomes insignificant when we control for permanent differences between firms.

Table 12.2: Estimates of the gross output elasticity with respect to human capital[a]

	Specification[b]		
Coefficient of	(1)	(2)	(3)
Pooled (OLS)			
Labour	0.172 (0.014)**	0.179 (0.014)**	0.178 (0.014)**
Material inputs	0.764 (0.010)**	0.766 (0.010)**	0.766 (0.010)**
Physical capital	0.059 (0.008)**	0.059 (0.008)**	0.059 (0.008)**
Human capital	0.015 (0.006)**	0.007 (0.006)	0.008 (0.006)*
R^2	0.991	0.991	0.991
Fixed effects (OLS on deviations from means over time)			
Labour	0.179 (0.035)**	0.180 (0.035)**	0.179 (0.035)**
Material inputs	0.763 (0.030)**	0.763 (0.030)**	0.763 (0.030)**
Physical capital	0.051 (0.022)**	0.051 (0.023)**	0.051 (0.023)**
Human capital	0.004 (0.007)	0.043 (0.075)	0.025 (0.040)
R^2	0.998	0.998	0.998
Random effects (GLS)			
Labour	0.189 (0.015)**	0.189 (0.016)**	0.188 (0.016)**
Material inputs	0.776 (0.012)**	0.776 (0.012)**	0.775 (0.012)**
Physical capital	0.039 (0.008)**	0.039 (0.008)**	0.039 (0.008)**
Human capital	0.009 (0.005)*	0.009 (0.008)	0.010 (0.008)
R^2	0.997	0.997	0.997
Number of firms	173	173	173
Number of years	2	2	2

Notes: [a] Based on the linked panel PS90-PS93-TS90-TS93-WES90-WES93. We have included dummies for four sectors of economic activity (except in the fixed effect specification). Numbers in parentheses are standard errors.
[b] Specification:
(1) human capital is equal to training expenditures.
(2) human capital constructed according to (4) and (5) with $g=0.05$ and $\delta=0.05$.
(3) human capital constructed according to (4) and (5) with $g=0.05$ and $\delta=0.15$.
** denotes significance at the 5 percent level.
* denotes significance at the 10 percent level.

Table 12.3: Estimates of the value added elasticity with respect to human capital[a]

Coefficient of	Specification[b]		
	(1)	(2)	(3)
Pooled (OLS)			
Labour	0.682 (0.043)**	0.701 (0.045)**	0.696 (0.045)**
Physical capital	0.265 (0.026)**	0.270 (0.026)**	0.270 (0.026)**
Human capital	0.072 (0.020)**	0.053 (0.020)**	0.057 (0.021)**
R^2	0.898	0.896	0.896
Fixed effects (OLS on deviations from means over time)			
Labour	0.712 (0.127)**	0.710 (0.127)**	0.711 (0.127)**
Physical capital	0.255 (0.085)**	0.256 (0.085)**	0.256 (0.085)**
Human capital	0.027 (0.025)	0.304 (0.285)	0.159 (0.152)
R^2	0.976	0.976	0.976
Random effects (GLS)			
Labour	0.757 (0.046)**	0.748 (0.051)**	0.743 (0.051)**
Physical capital	0.215 (0.028)**	0.214 (0.028)**	0.214 (0.028)**
Human capital	0.056 (0.019)**	0.062 (0.024)**	0.066 (0.025)**
R^2	0.947	0.947	0.947
Number of firms	173	173	173
Number of years	2	2	2

[a] Based on the linked panel PS90-PS93-TS90-TS93-WES90-WES93. We have included dummies for four sectors of economic activity (except in the fixed effect specification). Numbers in parentheses are standard errors.
[b] Specification:
(1) human capital is equal to training expenditures.
(2) human capital constructed according to (4) and (5) with $g=0.05$ and $\delta=0.05$.
(3) human capital constructed according to (4) and (5) with $g=0.05$ and $\delta=0.15$.
** denotes significance at the 5 percent level.
* denotes significance at the 10 percent level.

In the fixed effects specification a model parameter is estimated for every firm in the balanced panel. Because of the extra parameters the fixed effects estimator results in a large loss of degrees of freedom. Since our sample size of firms and years is rather small, this can easily lead to insignificant regression coefficients. As already mentioned, there exists another approach to control for the firm-specific effects, namely the random effects method. The random effects estimate of the value added elasticity of human capital differs significantly from zero. The disadvantage of the random effects model is that estimates will be biased if the firm-specific effects are correlated with the explanatory variables. By comparing the 95 percent confidence intervals of the fixed effects and the random effects estimates we can test whether there exist correlated effects. We find that the fixed effects estimate of the human capital elasticity does not differ significantly from the random effects estimate. This implies that in our case the firm-specific effects and the human capital variable are not correlated and the random effects estimator is (approximately) unbiased. Then the random effects estimator is the preferred one, because it has a smaller variance than the fixed effects estimator. According to the random effects estimates the output elasticity of human capital is insignificantly different from zero for gross output and 0.06-0.07 for value added.

Next, we turn to the effect of the human capital measure on the estimation results. Using a higher depreciation rate when constructing the human capital variable (compare columns (2) and (3)) makes no difference to the pooled and the random effects estimates, but gives slightly lower coefficients for the fixed effects estimates. To underline the insensitivity of the results to the choice of depreciation rate, we note that the human capital measure based solely on training expenditures gave coefficients with the same order of magnitude as the measure constructed with a depreciation rate of 15 percent.

Using formula (6) we derive an estimate for the rate of return of human capital (ρ) from the estimate of the output elasticity for human capital (β). It is assumed that for every firm both the output and the human capital stock is equal to the corresponding average over the firms in our data set.[6] We carry out this exercise only for the random effects estimates but for different human capital measures (except the measure solely based on training expenditures). Then, we find that with a depreciation rate of 5 percent (15 percent) the rate of return is insignificantly different from zero for the gross output specification and 23 percent (50 percent) with a standard error of 9 percent (19 percent) for the value added specification.

---

[6] We have also calculated the rate of return from the output elasticity for human capital using (6), under the assumption that for every firm the output to human capital ratio is equal to the average over the firms in our data set. However, in this case the calculated rate of return appear to be implausibly high, i.e. three times as large as the rate of return under the first-mentioned assumption.

Finally, we want to point out some limitations of the results presented. We have only considered the influence of expenditures on formal training programs on the output of firms. However, informal training is also an important form of employer-provided training. If informal training is positively correlated with formal training, then the estimated coefficient for human capital will reflect the returns not only to formal but also to informal training. Thus, presumably the estimated rate of return to human capital is upward biased.

Another source of bias in the estimated coefficients of the production model is the simultaneity between changes in output and investment in human capital, driven either by demand shocks or liquidity shocks. This phenomenon casts doubt on the assumption of exogeneity of the human capital variable. Unfortunately we lack good instruments to take endogeneity into account by econometric methods. This implies that we cannot quantify the simultaneity bias.

Concluding remarks

We have examined the impact of employer-provided formal training programs on output using firm-level data for the Dutch manufacturing sector. With different estimation methods and different measures for human capital, we have estimated a production function. The data are derived from training surveys for 1990 and 1993, which are linked to the production surveys, and the wage and employment surveys.

After correction for unobservable firm-specific effects, we find that the output elasticity of human capital is insignificantly different from zero for gross output and 0.06-0.07 for value added. From the estimated output elasticities we can derive that with a depreciation rate of 5 percent (15 percent) the private rate of return to human capital is insignificantly different from zero for gross output and 23 percent (50 percent) for value added. The empirical results show that investment in human capital has a significant and positive effect on value added for manufacturing firms.

Finally, we may compare our findings for human capital with the results recently published for R&D capital for the Netherlands by Bartelsman et al. (1996). They found that the output elasticity of R&D capital is about 0.06 for gross output and 0.08 for value added, while the private rate of return to R&D varies between 12 percent for gross output and 30 percent for value added. This means that the rate of return to human capital is of the same order of magnitude as that of R&D capital.

References

Bartel, A.P., 1991, Productivity gains from the implementation of employee training programs. Working paper no. 3893 (National Bureau of Economic Research, Cambridge).

Bartelsman, E., G. van Leeuwen, H. Nieuwenhuijsen and K. Zeelenberg, 1996, R&D and productivity growth: evidence from firm-level data for The Netherlands. *Netherlands Official Statistics*, 11 (3), 52-69.

Bishop, J.H., 1994, The impact of previous training on productivity and wages. In: L.M. Lynch, ed., *Training and the Private Sector: International Comparisons* (University of Chicago Press, Chicago), 161-199.

De Mooij, R.A., 1997, Belastingheffing en de vorming van menselijk kapitaal (Taxation and human capital accumulation), *Maandschrift Economie*, 61, 224-240.

Groot, W., 1994, Bedrijfsopleidingen: goed voor produktiviteit en loon (Employer-sponsored training: positive effects on productivity and wages). Economisch-Statistische Berichten (7 December 1994), 1108-1111.

Hall, B.H. and J. Mairesse, 1995, Exploring the relationship between R&D and productivity in French manufacturing firms. *Journal of Econometrics*, 65, 263-293.

Lynch, L.M. and S.E. Black, 1995, Beyond the incidence of training: evidence from a national employers survey. Working paper no. 5231 (National Bureau of Economic Research, Cambridge).

Mairesse, J. and M. Sassenou, 1991, R&D and productivity: a survey of econometric studies at the firm-level. *Science-Technology-Industry Review*, 8 (OECD, Paris).

OECD, 1994, *The OECD Jobs Study: Evidence and Explanations* (OECD, Paris), 125-126.

O'Mahony, M., and K. Wagner, 1996, Anglo German productivity performance: 1960-1989. In: K. Wagner and B. van Ark (eds.), *International Productivity Differences: Measurement and Explanations* (Elsevier, Amsterdam), 143-194.

Slagter, H.C.A., 1995, A survey on employer sponsored training. *Netherlands Official Statistics* (Summer 1995), 23-27.

Tan, H. and G. Batra, 1995, *Enterprise Training in Developing Countries: Incidence, Productivity Effects and Policy Implications* (World Bank, Washington DC).

13. Patents and Trademarks as Indicators of International Competitiveness: The VAR versus the Hysteresis Approach
Wim Meeusen and Glenn Rayp

Introduction

With European integration reaching the stage of a unified market and a monetary union, the degree of openness of the EU countries, and indeed also of the countries in the wider OECD context, has made a qualitative leap. As a result, their governments have become more attentive to issues of international competitiveness and to identifying the determinants of the latter. One important reason out of many is the fear that the high levels of social protection and security that many countries enjoy may be at stake.

However, is this social pessimism actually justified? After all, the industrialised countries with historically the highest degrees of openness (i.e. the small open economies of Northwest Europe) apparently did combine external exposure and highly developed social provisions rather well. Moreover, some of these countries (e.g. Denmark and the Netherlands) succeeded recently in improving their economic performances, without jeopardising at least the core of their welfare state. It would seem that considerations other than price are more important. Frequently, one points to the impact of technological innovation, as one of the major determinants of international competitiveness.

Research along the lines of the technological gap approach of international trade already provided some quite substantial and robust results (see e.g. Soete (1981), Fagerberg (1988), Greenhalgh (1990), Greenhalgh et al. (1994) and Amendola et al. (1993)) and contributed to the more general acceptance of the technological hypothesis of international competitiveness. Yet, in all these studies, the concept of technological innovation was typically proxied by indicators relating to one or other "upstream" link in the chain of successful innovation, such as the share of R&D expenditures in GDP or the national share of patent applications. The aspects of innovation pertaining to marketing and commercial efforts required by a successful innovation were neglected. Hence, the innovation concept used in the literature on the determinants of international competitiveness might be too narrow.

In this contribution we propose an empirical proxy allowing the extension of the innovation concept to include its commercial aspects and the determination of the respective importance of production costs, technological and commercial innovation for international competitiveness.

Besides the conceptual considerations concerning the relevance of the variables used, some attention has also to be paid to model specification issues. Most examples of the technology gap approach to competitiveness rely explicitly or implicitly on an equilibrium framework, where long-run export market shares are determined by national technological efforts or results, or do not dwell on the ultimate theoretical meaning of a possible absence of long-run equilibria. Recent developments in international trade theory, in an attempt to explain the rather peculiar evolution of the US trade and current account balance deficit, explore however hysteresis phenomena in trade (see e.g. Baldwin (1990), Dixit (1989) and Grossman and Helpman (1993)). Seen from this angle, one might wonder to what extent an equilibrium (market share) model is still appropriate. Since the choice of an adequate model for competitiveness is an unsettled issue, the least one can do is to check if results and conclusions with respect to the relative importance of different types of determinants are reasonably robust for different model specifications. Hence, we will perform our estimations for two kinds of rather different specifications, the first inspired by an equilibrium (market share) approach, the second using a model based upon the hysteresis hypothesis.

The next section digresses on the concept of international competitiveness, its potential determinants and the stylised facts one can discern for industrialised countries in particular. The third and fourth sections present the results of our estimations according to the two model approaches mentioned above. Conclusions are drawn in the last section.

The stylised facts of international competitiveness

International competitiveness of the manufacturing industry of twelve OECD countries is examined over the period 1970-1995. As a measure of international competitiveness, we took the value share of exports in a 12-country total, that is, a so-called "output indicator" of competitiveness in Turner and Van't Dack's (1993) terminology, instead of "input indicators" of competitiveness (real effective exchange rates or unit labour costs) because we want to investigate how much the latter weigh in the international economic "success" of a country. The value of exports is preferred above the volume of exports as a target variable so as not to lose track of price-related quality effects in the explanation of changes in trade flows. Export shares are considered rather than net exports as we want to focus on the *relative* importance of countries on world markets. In order to correct for the "natural" loss of export market shares due to the progress of trade liberalisation and globalisation, export positions are considered within a group of countries assumed to be homogeneous with respect to the influence of the latter effects. Within group market-share dynamics indicate net changes of position, implicitly adjusted for the global geo-economical trend. Despite the increasing tradability of the services, the open sector of the economy studied was limited to manufacturing industry, for obvious reasons of potential measurement error when attempting to include them.

We identify five major direct determinants of country share on a particular industrial market:

1. relative price or cost according to whether firms operate as price-makers or price-takers; relative unit labour cost can be used as a proxy for the price variable (in the first case), or as an indicator of gross profit margins (in the second);
2. relative quality;
3. relative marketing efforts;
4. relative "capacity to deliver";
5. "reputation".

We limit ourselves to the consideration of data at the level of the aggregate manufacturing industry sector. We implicitly therefore treat this sector as being homogeneous, and discard possible composition effects in the evolution of global export shares.

We define relative unit labour costs as follows:

$$RelULC_{it} = \frac{(1-\omega_{it})ULC_{it}}{\sum_{\substack{j=1 \\ j \neq i}}^{n} \omega_{jt} ULC_{jt}} \qquad [1]$$

where

$$ULC_{it} = \frac{W_{it}L_{it}/e_{it}}{y_{it}/\hat{e}_{i0}} \cdot \frac{N_{it}}{L_{it}} \qquad [2]$$

W_i is the (nominal) wage cost per worker in the currency of country i, L_i is the number of workers, N_i is total employment (including the self-employed), y_i is real output at constant 1985 domestic prices, e_{it} is the current exchange rate for the currency of country i with respect to a common currency, $\hat{e}_{i0}$ is the purchasing power exchange rate of the currency of country i in 1985, and ω_t is the OECD export share (*Xsh*), used as weights for converting ULC's into *relative* unit labour costs. Equation [2] makes it clear that due account is taken of the fact that part of the industry output is attributable to non-salaried employment (we implicitly assume that the self-employed operate at the same average productivity as wage-earners).[1]

Lack of precision in the definition of the "non-price" product quality component of competitiveness explains why it is commonly reduced to production cost considerations. Direct measures of product quality are indeed scarcely available and it is therefore proxied by indicators of the efforts which result in product quality differences, innovation efforts in the first place, of which we get an idea from the proportion of R&D outlays to output (*RelRDY*) relative to the average proportion in the other

---

[1] Some have argued that labour costs per unit of output may produce an underestimation of the effect of the labour cost factor on competitiveness (see e.g. instance Turner and Van 't Dack, 1993). If the rise of labour costs per unit of labour were "excessive" in comparison with other countries, this might lead to a relatively more rapid substitution of labour by capital, and a relatively more important destruction or delocalisation of domestic firms. This would entail an artificial, not a real, increase in labour productivity and create a situation where an underestimated increase or even decrease in unit labour cost would possible correlate with a decrease in market share. The problem reduces to the question whether the unit labour cost variable is correctly measured (i.e. absence of a bias introduced by the contemporaneous influence of wage cost increases on labour productivity). We believe it is, because of the time lags involved in the influence of labour costs per unit of labour on labour productivity. One may indeed safely assume that excessive wage cost increases will only give rise to extra labour-saving investment or to shut-downs or delocalisations after at least a number of years. This obviously implies that wage costs corrected for the average labour productivity at that moment reflect an average reality and can be used as a basis for inter-country comparisons.

countries (again using export shares as weights) or by the share of patent applications in the US (*PATsh*).

Measurement problems of the same kind and order as with product quality arise concerning marketing efforts for which it is not easy to compose internationally comparable data series for a sufficiently long time period.[2] However, disregarding the matter by assuming a priori that there exists a good correlation between marketing and technical innovation efforts might also be rather hazardous. First, even if this correlation were high, the indicators of innovation of which one disposes are imperfect and biased. R&D expenditures constitute an indicator of innovation effort, not of its result, and are generally considered to underestimate innovation outside formal research departments. Patenting decisions are conditioned by commercial considerations about the costs and (expected) benefits of the protection of an innovation offered by the patent, that is, its adequacy as a strategy against imitation. This is generally regarded as sector and country specific. Geroski (1995), who finds a rather weak relationship between directly measured innovation and patenting in the UK, confirms this. Second, how well should marketing efforts and technological innovation be correlated in order to be able to neglect relative marketing efforts altogether in the list of determinants to be included in the right-hand side (RHS) of a market-share equation?

Technological innovation is not identical with commercial innovation and excelling in the first does not imply straightforward success in the latter. Patenting may be considered an aspect of commercial strategy, but it reflects more the *intention* of the commercial exploitation of an innovation rather than the *extent* to which this is effectively done: a technologically successful firm might easily fail in its efforts to commercialise its potentially superior goods. Moreover, commercial innovation does not necessarily require a technological breakthrough.

Ideally, one would like to dispose of data for the commercial efforts of firms on their foreign markets, but these are not readily available. Usual breakdowns of marketing data (which are anyway of rather recent date) neither include the nationality of the spending firms nor the origin of the amounts spent. As a substitute, we could turn to the importance of the national advertising market, as an indicator of the global commercial dynamism of firms. One might indeed assume that firms that are

---

[2] To our knowledge, the only attempt to include marketing efforts in explaining international trade flows (import penetration in this case) is Tharakan et al. (1978), who used advertising expenditures from national data sources.

compelled to important marketing efforts in their home markets will be more sensitive and will pay more attention to their marketing mix in general.

Internationally comparable figures on national advertising expenditures exist for a large number of countries, but have only been systematically collected since the beginning of the 1980s (Euromonitor 1983 to 1993a and b. For previous periods, data are only sporadically provided, in various forms and for different aggregates.

We do dispose however of rather long and complete data on trademark applications at the different national patent and trademark offices, including the US Patent and Trademark Office. A foreign firm which takes the trouble to go through the lengthy and costly procedure of applying for, say, a US trademark, may also reasonably be assumed to invest seriously in marketing efforts on international markets. In this sense trademark applications could serve as an indicator of commercial efforts. We remain however conscious of its shortcomings. Foremost, marketing efforts for the promotion of existing brand names are neglected. Next, as with patents, not all traded goods qualify for potential protection by trademarks. Trademark protection is mainly relevant for consumer goods and much less so for investment goods.

The high values of the Pearson correlation coefficient that we found between patent and trademark shares in the US (contemporaneously, for different lag specifications and for different countries) come as no surprise. On the other hand, we noticed also a rather important correlation of annual trademark application shares in the US with national advertising expenditures. Especially when Japan was discarded, the Pearson correlation coefficient amounted to 0.7-0.8.[3] [4] Apparently, the trademark share variable contains sufficient information when it comes to measuring marketing efforts and therefore, though potentially affected with similar sins to the patent measure, we decided to use the national shares in the foreign trademark applications in the US (*TMsh*) as a statistical proxy of commercial innovativity.

Concerning the fourth and fifth determinants of competitiveness that we distinguished, we used relative capacity use in industry and the lagged

---

[3] Correlation coefficients including Japan have a comparable value for the beginning of the 1980s but show a gradual decline over the decade to 0.4-0.5. The same phenomenon is present when correlating trademark and patent shares.

[4] Allegrezza and Guarda-Rauchs (1998), using firm-level data coming from a survey of small and medium-sized enterprises (SMEs) conducted by the Benelux Trademark Office, surprisingly however, do not find a significant relation between trademark applications and the size of the advertising budget.

value of the market share as their respective empirical measures. The data used come mainly from OECD sources: the International Sectoral Database (ISDB), containing data for internationally comparable sector definitions (Meyer zu Schlochtern and Meyer zu Schlochtern (1994)), was used for trade, production and labour rewards and the Basic Science and Technology Statistics (BSTS) provided the R&D expenditures and patent applications data. Trademark applications data are to be found in the databank of the World Intellectual Property Organisation (WIPO).

Table 13.1 summarises the observed relation between OECD competitiveness and its main determinants. We omitted to report the summary statistics in the table on relative "capacity do deliver". No clear causal pattern emerged from these data. Neither did we find evidence of the role of this variable in the econometric exercises on which we will report in the third and fourth sections. For the manufacturing industry taken as a whole, international goods markets do not seem to be supply constrained. The situation may of course be different if we look at specific sectors (see Greenhalgh (1990) and Greenhalgh et al. (1994)).

One notices on the one hand that in five of the twelve countries examined the relation between movements in the export share and movements in relative unit labour cost is "perverse". In Belgium, France, the Netherlands, Sweden and Canada, a loss of export shares in the period considered coincided with a gain in cost competitiveness. In Japan the opposite holds. Only Germany, Italy, Denmark, the UK, Finland and the US confirm the expectations generated by traditional economic theory, albeit in many cases only marginally. This is particularly true in the two most important cases. Germany only very slightly lost market share although in the same period labour cost competitivity deteriorated by more than 28%. Something equivalent holds for the US. This country witnessed only a very small increase in market share against a very serious gain in cost competitiveness (more than 23%).[5]

The reason for the apparent lack of influence of wage costs is that, as we shall see in the next section, although – in terms of partial rather than

---

[5] An analysis for six major sectoral aggregates (steel and non-ferrous metals, paper, food, textiles, machinery and chemical industry) did not add to more clarity with respect to the role of labour costs. In none of the cases did the number of countries which saw a decline of their cost competitiveness and export share or an improvement of cost competitiveness and export share, dominate the number of countries which combined the opposite, i.e. a decline in their cost competitiveness and an improvement in their export share or an improvement in their cost competitiveness and a decline in their export share (Meeusen and Rayp, 1995).

simple correlations – the relation between labour costs and export shares carries often the right (negative) sign, the influence of labour costs is relatively weak and in most cases compensated by the influence of technology shifts. The picture of this negative net influence of labour costs is for that matter probably also blurred by reverse causation of opposite sign: as countries grow more competitive (for technology reasons) and their wealth increases, more room is created for wage increases (cf. the so-called Kaldor paradox). This last argument is at present nothing more than a conjecture: Granger causality tests did not prove to be conclusive one way or another.

While the cost factor does not seem to be decisive in the struggle for market shares, the quality and marketing factors apparently do. The countries which lost market share in the period considered also saw their relative share of R&D expenditures in GDP decrease, and/or lost patent or trademark share. Obviously the picture which emerges is not sufficiently clear when it comes to distinguishing the relative importance of each of these factors. For this, we need to turn to an econometric analysis.

Table 13.1: Export-shares, relative unit labour cost, relative R&D intensities, patent shares and trademark shares in manufacturing industry in twelve OECD countries (average shares and proportions per period, and relative differences), 1970-95

	Belgium	Germany	France	Italy	The Netherlands	Denmark	UK	Sweden	Finland	US	Canada	Japan
Export-shares (Xsh)												
1970-79 (1)	0.0610	0.1889	0.0967	0.0723	0.0610	0.0158	0.0899	0.0333	0.0119	0.1693	0.0547	0.1211
1980-89 (2)	0.0580	0.1826	0.0919	0.0768	0.0580	0.0148	0.0805	0.0292	0.0134	0.1672	0.0562	0.1579
1988-94 (3)	0.0575	0.1872	0.0952	0.0800	0.0575	0.0150	0.0804	0.0270	0.0122	0.1701	0.0514	0.1577
(3)-(1) (%)	-5.74	-0.90	-1.55	10.65	-5.74	-5.06	-10.57	-18.92	2.52	0.47	-6.03	30.22
Relative unit labour cost (RelULC)												
1970-79 (1)	1.3970	0.9432	0.9102	0.9150	1.0813	1.2955	0.8161	1.5794	1.1174	1.0401	1.0369	0.7999
1980-89 (2)	0.9777	0.9917	0.8994	0.8399	0.9188	1.1457	1.0482	1.3179	1.1344	1.0746	1.0051	0.9888
1990-95 (3)	1.0045	1.2091	0.9054	0.8402	0.8771	1.3247	0.9748	1.2579	0.9949	0.8001	0.8364	1.2010
(3)-(1) (%)	-28.10	28.19	-0.53	-8.17	-18.88	2.25	19.45	-20.36	-10.96	-23.07	-19.34	50.14
Relative share of R&D expenditures in GDP (BERD)												
1970-79 (1)	0.7328	1.4286	1.1371	0.4473	1.0842	0.5175	0.6696	0.9537	0.5313	1.6422	0.5774	1.0558
1980-89 (2)	0.6888	1.3813	1.1180	0.4862	0.9281	0.5677	0.9430	1.0393	0.6830	1.5145	0.5924	1.2371
1987-92 (3)	0.6755	1.3550	1.0583	0.5155	0.8048	0.6166	0.9229	1.0069	0.7651	1.2543	0.5395	1.2693
(3)-(1) (%)	-7.82	-5.15	-6.93	15.24	-25.77	19.15	37.83	5.58	44.01	-23.62	-6.56	20.22
Patent share, average over the periods t-5 to t-1 [1]												
1970-79 (1)	0.0183	0.3638	0.1363	0.0527	0.0432	0.0110	0.2257	0.3157	0.0526	**0.7130**	0.0898	**0.2370**
1980-89 (2)	0.0166	0.3885	0.1386	0.0592	0.0443	0.0131	0.1821	0.6095	0.0591	**0.6057**	0.0859	**0.3739**
1988-93 (3)	0.0178	0.3753	0.1441	0.0618	0.0462	0.0152	0.1758	0.8596	0.0528	**0.5525**	0.0906	**0.4626**
(3)-(1) (%)	-2.73	3.16	5.72	17.27	6.94	38.18	-22.11	172.28	0.38	**-22.51**	0.89	**95.19**
Trademark share, average over the periods t-3 to t [2]												
1970-79 (1)	0.0126	0.1925	0.1598	0.0668	0.0333	0.0179	0.1886	0.0369	0.0061	**0.9311**	0.1403	0.1452
1980-89 (2)	0.0125	0.1993	0.1716	0.0990	0.0315	0.0137	0.1211	0.0367	0.0098	**0.9021**	0.1659	0.1390
1990-95 (3)	0.0133	0.1540	0.1786	0.1130	0.0412	0.0135	0.1362	0.0261	0.0094	**0.8694**	0.1954	0.1194
(3)-(1) (%)	5.56	-20.00	11.76	69.16	23.72	-24.58	-27.78	-29.27	54.10	**-6.63**	39.27	-17.77

Source: Own computations on the basis of ISDB-OECD, International Labor Statistics (Bureau of Labor Statistics), Basic Science and Technology Statistics (OECD) and World Organisation for Industrial Property (WIPO).

Notes: [1] The patent shares relate to national shares in the total number of applications of foreign origin in the US, Japan not included. The figures for the US are the share of domestic applications in the total number of applications, regardless of origin. The figures for Japan are the share of Japanese applications in the total number of foreign applications.
[2] The trademark shares are computed as the national shares in the total number of applications of foreign origin in the US. The figures for the US are the share of domestic applications in the total number of applications, regardless of origin.
BERD stands for "Business Enterprise Expendediture on R&D".

A VAR model of OECD export market shares of the manufacturing industry

The choice of an appropriate theoretical framework for modelling exports is not an obvious one. A first decision concerns the degree of detail of the model. A complete structural model of international competitiveness would require that the variables that in turn determine cost factors, product quality etc., or their proxies, are taken into account, together with the feedbacks involved. This would mean, among other things, that the determinants of economic growth, the balance of payments, the exchange rate and the government budget constraint in each of the countries considered are to be included in such a model. Yet, for the purpose of identifying the respective weights of the determinants of competitiveness, shortcuts in modelisations using the reduced form composed of export shares and its final intervening determinants, seem justified.

A second choice relates to the possible existence of long-run equilibrium export shares. If such is thought to be the case, an error-correction model (ECM) specification is warranted (Greenhalgh (1990) and Greenhalgh et al. (1994); see also Meeusen and Rayp (1995)). We are interested primarily in the long-run relationships of competitiveness. These could in principle be straightforwardly inferred from the export shares and their potential determinants, provided that the national economies are close to their steady state equilibrium, or adjust 'almost immediately' to it. But, though international trade equilibrium might constitute a reasonable a priori assumption in the long run (because of current account feedbacks, which normally exclude a permanent disequilibrium), nothing guarantees a quick adjustment. The variables may well show considerable persistence and autocorrelation, due to for example the interference of international commodity and capital flows, of transaction or sunk costs and the rather long time lags involved in the effects of some determinants of competitiveness, in the first place innovation effects. These can be coped with by distinguishing in a consistent way long-run relationships and short-term adjustments, as in an ECM. In this analysis we focus on the long-run aspect of the model.

Whether variables show but limited deviations from or quick correction to their equilibrium values or not (in which case they would be stationary) can be verified by means of (Augmented) Dickey-Fuller unit root tests, along the lines of Perron's (1988) sequential procedure, in order to control for test power losses when the deterministic trend of the variable is wrongly (i.e. over- as well as insufficiently) specified. However, as

Xsh, *PATsh* and *TMsh* are by definition variables between 0 and 1, and *RelULC* fluctuates around 1, we may reasonably assume them to be processes without drift. Hence, we only have to check whether the variables might be generated by processes of the form $x_t = x_{t-1} + u_t$, (u_t is a white noise process), against the alternative that they would be stationary around a fixed mean. The table in the appendix indicates that stationarity is rejected for the majority of the variables, though first order integration may be accepted.[6]

While specifying our model, we must keep in mind the Kaldor-paradox pattern potentially present in the stylised facts. The positive association between export shares and relative unit labour costs would point in any case to the potential endogeneity of these variables. Consequently, caution is required when imposing a causal relation a priori. Moreover, other feedback effects might be discerned which may induce reverse causation, for example, from export share, over profits and government policy, on private and public investment and hence on innovation efforts.[7] Considering this potential simultaneity between the variables, it might be preferable to renounce any a priori division between endogenous and exogenous variables at all and to identify the long-run relationships in a vector autoregressive model, following the Johansen-Juselius approach to co-integration

with $$Y = \begin{bmatrix} Xsh \\ PATsh \\ TMsh \\ RelULC \end{bmatrix}$$

as the vector of endogenous variables.

In the case of driftless variables, the constant terms, common to all equations, are included in the co-integration space. We use the maximum eigenvalue and trace test statistics in order to determine the co-integration rank. To avoid potential problems of power to which both statistics are known to be subject and which may cause an overstatement of the number of long-run relationships between the variables, we required a rejection of the null hypothesis concerning the rank of the matrix of the structural coefficients of the jointly dependent variables Π at a 99% confidence level for at least one test. The results for the countries for which at least one

---

[6] We retained only 11 of the 12 countries in the analysis and excluded the US, in view of the somewhat specific meaning of *PATsh* and *TMsh*, not comparable to that of the other countries.
[7] See Hughes (1986) for an early attempt to take account of simultaneity between innovation and international trade.

co-integration vector could be identified, are summarised in Table 13.2.

The VAR estimation results were acceptable for each country, despite occasional rejection (for a 95% confidence interval) of absence of residual autocorrelation or normality of residuals at the level of the individual variables (but not for the system as such). The lag length of the VAR systems was determined as the shortest length for which we obtained a statistically sound system. In the case of Italy, rank(Π) = 0 was not rejected by any of the two tests even for a 90% confidence interval, and we concluded that there was no long-run relationship. Except for the UK, the number of co-integration vectors we can accept amounts to two or three, the latter number being especially typical for the smaller countries in the sample. This might refer to the more compelling current account constraint to which small countries are subject, in which case the indications for the existence of long-run equilibrium relationships would remain typically limited for the larger (i.e. G7) countries. Indeed, the relations between the variables for these countries are unbounded in at least two dimensions and are characterised by two I (1) common trends.

The long-run relationships between the variables that were found were determined exclusively according to statistical criteria and do not necessarily warrant a meaningful economic interpretation (Johansen and Juselius (1994)). The latter may require the imposition of (over) identifying zero restrictions on the parameter space, by means of which we try to identify the relationship between the export share, the patent and trademark application share and the relative unit labour costs as a *competitiveness equation*. This we accept if the following restrictions are not rejected:[8]

$$\beta_{PATsh} \geq 0; \quad \beta_{TMsh} \geq 0; \quad \beta_{RelULC} \leq 0.$$

Apart from Italy where no long-run relation was found at all, the

---

[8] Because of the presence of more than one long-run stationary relationship between the variables for almost all countries, we need to identify the whole system instead of just one equation, for which we applied the following method. A wage equation was determined if the estimated parameters satisfied the constraints:

$$\beta_{Xsh} \geq 0; \quad \beta_{PATsh} \leq 0; \quad \beta_{TMsh} \leq 0.$$

If

$$\beta_{Xsh} \geq 0; \quad \beta_{RelULC} \geq 0,$$

the relation was identified as an innovation equation (with arbitrary sign of the commercial innovation variable).

presence of more than one co-integration vector (1) is not rejected, for all other countries but one (the UK). Additional restrictions had to be imposed to identify the CI vectors structurally. Problems with the identification of the system of long-run equilibrium relationships arose in the case of Germany and Japan. Concerning the first, we did not succeed in finding an intelligible economic interpretation of the system of estimated vectors, as for each of the three relations that we defined (that is, a competitiveness, a wage or labour cost, and an innovation equation), at least one coefficient restriction had to be rejected. In the case of Japan, the interpretation of the co-integration vectors seemed to be 'path-dependent', that is, sensitive to the order of elimination of insignificant variables in the system (*RelULC* or *PATsh* respectively) and hence, not fully unambiguous. For all other countries, identification the system of co-integration vectors was possible, yet in the case of the UK and Finland, in the apparent absence of a competitiveness equation. This implies that, of the ten OECD countries initially considered in the analysis, we were capable of determining a system of long-run equilibrium relationships including a competitiveness equation in six of them. These countries and the particular form of their competitiveness equation(s) are shown in Table 13.3.

Concerning the specification of the competitiveness equation and, hence, the importance of the determinants of competitiveness that we distinguished, the following observations can be made:

1. In all the countries, for which we succeeded in identifying a competitiveness relation, except Canada, innovation efforts *sensu stricto* constitute a significant determinant of the long-run export market share.
2. The shares in the trademark applications in the US, which we proposed as a proxy of marketing efforts, is significant in all competitiveness equations we obtained except for France and Sweden, independent from the innovation efforts *sensu stricto*. This may be seen as a confirmation of the assumption that they do indeed measure something other than patent shares (innovation efforts, in other words), and can be interpreted as a significant independent indicator of competitiveness.
3. The indicators of product quality (i.e. technical innovation and marketing efforts) form a significant determinant of long run competitiveness. For Canada, this took the particular and divergent form of significant commercial but not innovation efforts. On the other hand, we find no indications of a significant influence of relative unit

labour costs on competitiveness within the OECD in the long run. On the contrary, for five out of six countries, a positive long-run relation between OECD export market shares (i.e. competitiveness) and relative unit labour costs was found which pointed to a causal link in the opposite direction as it usually stated, but in agreement with a Kaldor paradox interpretation.

Table 13.2: Results of the co-integration analysis of eleven OECD countries, $Y^{*'} = (Xsh, PATsh, TMsh, RelULC, 1)$

	Rank	Rank tests	Standardised co-integration vectors				
	Max.	Trace	Xsh	PATsh	TMsh	RelULC	Constant
Germany	0	46.45***	101.40***				
	1	32.28***	54.97***	1.000	-0.142	0.40	0.031	-0.26
	2	12.30	22.69**	-2.33	0.81	1.18	1	-0.90
France	0	30.89**	71.24**				
	1	23.08**	40.35***	1	0.792	0.036	-0.452	0.245
	2	10.18	17.27	-7.806	0.573	-0.652	1	-0.08
Italy	0	18.11	43.49				
NL*	0	53.54***	111.90***				
	1	29.79***	58.40***	1.000	0.652	0.372	-0.034	-0.058
	2	21.13***	28.61***	1.64*10^4	-	-3420	1	-425.9
	3	7.48	7.48	-0.1	1	0.23	0.01	0.02
Belgium	0	84.23***	148.90***				
	1	31.11***	64.62***	1.000	-23.19	-49.39	0.26	0.54
	2	25.81***	33.51***	-27.98	-76.13	-48.61	1	1.90
	3	7.70	7.70	-0.65	1	-0.45	0.002	0.03
Denmark	0	59.06***	118.90***				
	1	41.10***	59.88***	1	-0.19	-0.22	0.0006	-0.01
	2	11.96	18.78	-29.35	-76.74	-9.2670	1	-0.03
UK	0	48.79***	77.21				
	1	15.63	28.41	1.000	0.26	-0.10	0.04	-0.14
Canada	0	66.28***	138.10***				
	1	40.68***	71.82***	1	0.41	0.15	-0.038	-0.067
	2	20.17***	31.14***	-12.63	0.27	3.42	1	-0.89
	3	10.97	10.97	3.37	1	0.80	-0.28	-0.09
Japan	0	39.31***	80.29***				
	1	23.03***	40.97***	1.000	-0.22	3.6	-0.075	-0.59
	2	13.30	17.94	-9.80	1.80	10.82	1	-1.78
Sweden	0	42.87***	86.54***				
	1	26.04**	43.67***	1	-0.39	0.007	0.002	-0.02
	2	12.47	17.63	-36.99	-5.824	-0.2031	1	0.07
Finland	0	50.87***	97.49***				
	1	31.32***	46.62***	1	0.11	0.02	-0.02	0.005
	2	9.33	15.29	157	26.24	-71.16	1	-2.77

Note: Own computations (PCFIML), using ISDB (OECD) and WIPO. One, two and three stars refer to rejection for a 90, 95 and 99% confidence interval respectively (Osterwald-Lenum (1992) table values).

The order of the lagged first differences was determined, starting again from an arbitrary specification with three lags, which were reduced as long as the error terms remain normally and independently distributed and the F-test for model reduction was not significant.

*: NL stands for The Netherlands.

Table 13.3: Long-run competitiveness (C) and labour cost (W) equations for seven OECD countries

Country		Competitiveness equation	System of co-integration vectors
France	C	$Xsh = 0.06 + 0.47\ PATsh$	C, W
	W	$RelULC = 0.34 + 5.84\ Xsh$	
NL*	C	$Xsh = 1.79\ PATsh + 0.64\ TMsh$	C, W, I
	W	$RelULC = -0.99 + 27.23\ Xsh$	
Belgium	C	$Xsh = 0.85\ PATsh + 1.27\ TMsh$	C, W, I
	W	$RelULC = -1.9 + 107.5\ Xsh$	
Denmark	C	$Xsh = 0.011 + 0.14\ PATsh + 0.22\ TMsh$	C, I
Canada	C	$Xsh = 0.09 + 0.8\ TMsh$	C, W, I
	W	$RelULC = 0.75 + 4.99\ Xsh$	
Sweden	C	$Xsh = 0.02 + 0.34\ PATsh$	C, W
	W	$RelULC = -0.46 + 57.8\ Xsh$	
Finland	W	$RelULC = 0.25 + 74.76\ Xsh$	W, I

Note: Own computations, using ISDB (OECD) and WIPO. C, W and I in the last column refer respectively to the competitiveness, the wage or labour cost and innovation equations of which are defined in order to identify the system of co-integration vectors of the countries.
*: NL stands for The Netherlands.

We can conclude that the estimation of the present vector autoregression, that is, simultaneous equation, version of the error-correction model of international competitiveness does not yield convincing global evidence for the existence of long-run equilibria. First, long-run competitiveness equations were only found for half of the countries. Second, none of the long-run competitiveness equations that we did obtain contained an indicator of cost-competitiveness. Although the latter result is not completely surprising in a "technology gap" interpretation of international competitiveness, it is certainly a result that needs additional confirmation.

Another conclusion is that the examination of an alternative approach, where the idea of adjustment to a long-run trade equilibrium is abandoned, is called for. This is the starting point of the next section.

A hysteresis approach to international competitiveness

While the VAR-ECM approach, which assumes a stable long-run relationship between competitiveness and its determinants, product quality and relative costs especially, does seem to lead to some meaningful results, at least for a number of countries, we cannot ignore the fact that the indications of long-run equilibrium (be it determined by relative costs, innovation or both) remain limited, especially for the larger OECD countries, possibly because of the weaker current account constraints to which they are subject. In one important case (Italy) we had to reject explicitly the existence of any long-run relationship, and in the overwhelming majority of the other countries, we couldn't accept more than two. In addition, almost half of the systems of long-run relationships do not seem to include a competitiveness equation, at least in a rigorous, that is, non-benevolent interpretation of the results.[9] Moreover, as available time series are rather short and cover 25 years at the most, small changes in data availability appeared to have important consequences for the pattern of long-run relationships we may discern. Reducing the series by one or two observations results in a situation where at most one cointegration vector remains present for all countries but one (Sweden), and this even when zero rank of the Π matrix is rejected benevolently (i.e. despite disagreement between the indications of the trace and maximum eigenvalue test for a number of countries). Hence, the variables are at best bounded to a rather limited extent. How sensible then is a long-run equilibrium approach to competitiveness at all?

Suppose that trade hegemonies were continuously shifting, and world trade would therefore always be seen to adjust to new targets, then international markets would show permanent disequilibrium conditions, which econometric specifications should reflect. An increasing number of trade theorists believe that technological change is the main driving force behind these shifts in trade positions, at least within an OECD context, given the fact that there obviously is diversity in the rate of change of technological innovation. The leads from which innovating firms, sectors and therefore indeed countries can profit give them a competitive edge which very often will have durable effects. The following equation provides a natural modelisation of these "persistence" effects:

$$Xsh_t = \lambda Xsh_{t-1} + B(L)Z_t + u_t \qquad [3]$$

where Z is a vector of exogenous variables, $B(L)$ is the corresponding vector polynomial in the lag operator I and $0 < \lambda \leq 1$ is the parameter expressing the "persistence" effect. In the case where $\lambda = 1$, we obtain a model of hysteresis. The long-run equilibrium is then no longer unambiguously defined, and loosely speaking "where you get will depend on how you get there".[10]

---

[9] In an "accommodating" interpretation of the results, it is possible to discern a competitiveness equation for the UK, Japan and Finland too. These confirm our initial observations, except for the presence of a significant relative unit cost variable in the case of the UK.

[10] We use the term "hysteresis" in the usual, somewhat loose, way. Hysteresis in the strict sense as it is applied in the physical sciences implies not only "persistence", but also "remanence", meaning that there are permanent output effects following a transitory change of inputs in the process considered. Remanence is always a result of some form of non-linearity. See Amable et al. (1995).

Baldwin (1990) is one of the authors who makes a convincing theoretical case for hysteresis in trade. He cites three possible mechanisms: fixed selling costs that are sunk and durable; consumers who are imperfectly informed about the quality of the goods and, finally, multiple equilibria in the presence of increasing returns to scale. He illustrates the first mechanism by considering the effect of a prolonged overvaluation of the currency of a country. Profits and market shares of foreign firms will increase, and this in turn may induce these firms to make the necessary investment in the country considered to increase selling there. Since however the investment costs are sunk, not all new entrants will exit when the exchange rate returns to its "fundamental" level.

The same kind of mechanism may be presumed to be at work when a country enjoys the benefits of a market lead due to technological innovation. After the diffusion phase the gain in market share may easily remain. Grossman and Helpman (1991, ch. 8 and 1993) show, under conditions of (strictly) national technological spillovers, how a temporary headstart in R&D results in a permanent advantage in the production and exports of technology intensive activities. Exchange rate or production cost considerations could be combined with the acquisition of a technological lead, for example, along the lines of Brezis et al. (1993), where technological "leapfrogging" is caused by a sufficiently low wage, which makes a new technology profitable.

The second mechanism relates to the risk-reducing strategy of the representative consumer: confronted with the choice between tried and untried products of the same quality, he will be willing to pay more for the known brand since it involves no uncertainty. Clearly this mechanism refers to the last determinant of export shares ("reputation") and to which we paid no explicit attention so far.

If, as it turned out, λ is not significantly different from unity in regressions like [3], and if *RelULC*, *PATsh* and *TMsh* are I (1), as indeed it appears (see the table in the appendix), then [3] can be reduced to the following hysteresis model:

$$\Delta Xsh_t = B_1(L)\Delta RelULC_t + B_2(L)\Delta PATsh_t + B_3(L)\Delta TMsh_t + u_t \qquad [4]$$

with $B_1(L)$, $B_2(L)$ and $B_3(L)$ representing lag polynomials.

One may object that by allowing for hysteresis in our approach, we grant too much weight to 'history', that is, temporary occurrences with lasting consequences, in the determination of competitiveness. After all, while it is true that hysteresis has been much neglected in this context so far, comparative advantage may form an equally important element of competitiveness and specialisation, and natural feedback effects from the current account position may be present. Hence one might be more inclined to take an intermediate modelling position which accounts for hysteresis phenomena as well as comparative advantage influences. But, by distinguishing somewhat more radically between the two possible approaches, we can at least check to what extent it really matters, that is, how sensitive our results and our main conclusions are to variations in model specification.

Equation [4] was estimated for each country by OLS in a general-to-specific framework, starting with orders 3, 7 and 4 respectively for the polynomials B_i. No attempts were made at this stage, as in the estimation of the vector autoregression model in the previous section, to account for the inherently simultaneous nature of the equations: the implicit cross-equations restrictions on the parameters turn out to be data-dependent and some of them are highly non-linear. Moreover an intuitively appealing GTS strategy to be pursued in the case of the application of a SURE method is not readily available.

The reduction strategy used was as follows: first we eliminated the terms, one by one, which had the wrong signs, beginning with those which were statistically most "significant"; then we eliminated, again one by one, the terms whose coefficients had t-values lower than 1 in absolute value. Finally we accepted those resulting equations which passed the unit root tests on the regression errors and which were significant as a whole (the Wald χ^2-test). We failed to arrive at a meaningful result only in the case of the Netherlands and Canada. Table 13.4 summarises our findings.

As can be seen, the earlier impression that labour costs play only a minor role has to be qualified: for Denmark, the US, Japan, Finland and the UK the coefficient for the labour cost variable carries a significantly negative sign, although only marginally so for the latter country. But equally important is the result that for all countries, except Germany (where the influence of labour costs was anyway not significant) and the UK, the patent share and/or the trademark share variables turned out to be statistically significant. For Italy, Belgium and Denmark both variables were significant.

It should be noted too that there is a remarkable consistency with respect to the lag structure of the *PATsh* and *TMsh* variables. The patent lag is nearly always between five and seven years for the countries where this variable was significant. Exceptions are Italy and Finland where the lags are less important. The same consistency holds for the trademark lag. The lag is nearly always between two and four years.

When we compare the results of the alternative models, the parameter estimates for *RelULC* show the highest variability in sign and significance. There is nevertheless a good general consistency between the results of both models with respect to the parameter estimates (in sign and size) of the product quality component of competitiveness (technological innovation and commercial efforts), except for the somewhat lesser extent to which the two components of product quality are both individually significant in the hysteresis model. Despite these differences, the conclusions remain qualitatively identical for the two approaches: in the co-integration as well as in the hysteresis model one would conclude that the product quality component of competitiveness that dominates over the component of cost competitivity, either technological or commercial, or both.

Conclusion

In this chapter a double extension of the technology approach to international competitiveness was attempted. First, the notion of innovation was extended to its commercial aspects, and next we tried to assess how differences in the underlying theoretical framework matter, namely the choice between an equilibrium model and a "pure" hysteresis model. One sees indeed that both approaches may have some justification, theoretically and empirically. Indications of long-run equilibrium relations between the variables were indeed found but only to a limited extent (certainly when tests were rigorously interpreted), and seem to concern competitiveness relationships in only a small number of cases. As such, which model to choose may still be subject to discussion. Yet, we noticed in both approaches the minor weight of the production cost component of competitiveness in comparison to product quality (confirming further the importance of innovation for competitiveness), and the independent and significant influence of the commercial aspects of innovation, as measured by trademark shares. This indicates the relevance of the use of an extended statistical notion of innovation.

Table 13.4: First difference regression results for OECD export shares (1970-1995)

	t-adf(0) Xsh	t-adf(0) ΔXsh	RelULC	PATsh	TMsh	Wald χ^2	LM AR F-test	t-adf(0) u
Germany	-2.149	-4.931***	-0.042 (1) (0.028)	-	0.317 (3,4) (0.156)	7.096*	2.5373	-4.165**
France	-2.010	-5.829***	-0.025 (1) (0.017)	0.238 (7) (0.180)	**0.075** (3) (0.038)*	8.113**	1.0285	-6.172***
Italy	-2.038	-5.979***	-0.013 (1) (0.011)	**0.525** (3) (0.289)*	**0.125** (1) (0.054)**	11.283**	1.2643	-7.266***
Belgium	-1.920	-3.822***	-	**1.709** (5,6) (0.675)**	**0.918** (1,2,4) (0.280)**	12.712***	0.9482	-9.057***
UK	-2.685	-6.559***	**-0.021** (1) (0.012)*	-	0.205 (1,2,3) (0.084)	8.862**	0.9515	-7.973***
Denmark	-2.676	-7.452***	**-0.0035** (3) (0.0012)**	**0.422** (7) (0.153)**	**0.164** (1,2) (0.055)***	18.859***	0.0747	-6.668***
US	-2.015	-3.409**	**-.058** (1,2) (0.016)***	0.189 (5,6) (0.109)	**0.319** (3,4) (0.140)**	16.470***	2.5473	-4.134**
Canada	-2.282	-3.158**	-	**0.441** (7) (0.185)**	0.052 (2) (0.048)	5.861*	1.1712	-2.962*
Japan	-1.778	-5.024***	**-0.090** (1,2) (0.027)**	**0.265** (7) (0.108)**	0.618 (2,3,4) (0.287)	13.426***	0.2248	-6.456***
Finland	-1.931	-3.428**	**-0.0051** (2) (0.0012)***	**0.258** (2,3) (0.110)*	0.031 (2) (0.029)	30.790***	0.6037	-3.865*

Note: Own computations, using ISDB (OECD) and WIPO. Standard errors of estimates between brackets; ***, **, * means respectively 99%, 95% and 90% statistical significance.
The estimates are the sums $B_i(1)$ over the different lags of the coefficients in the final form of equation [4]; the lags are given in brackets. The unit root tests on Xsh and ΔXsh are performed in a model with intercept.

References

Allegrezza, S. and A. Guarda-Rauchs (1998), "Trademarks and innovation", paper presented at the AEA conference 'Innovation and Patents: Industrial Property Econometrics', Lyon 14-15 May 1998.

Amable, B., J. Henry, F. Lordon and R. Topol (1995), "Hystereris revisited: a methodological approach", in: R. Cross (ed.), *The Natural Rate of Unemployment: Reflections on 25 Years of the Hypothesis*, Cambridge University Press, Cambridge, 153-180.

Amendola, G., G. Dosi and E. Papagni (1993), "The dynamics of International Competitiveness", *Weltwirtschaftliches Archiv*, 129(3): 451-471.

Baldwin, R. (1990), "Hysteresis in Trade", *Empirical Economics*, 15: 127-142.

Brezis, E.S., P. Krugman and D. Tsiddon (1993), "Leapfrogging in international competition: a theory of cycles in national technological leadership", *American Economic Review*, 83(5): 1211-1219.

Dixit, A. (1989), "Hysteresis, import penetration and exchange rate pass-through", *Quarterly Journal of Economics*, 105(2): 205-228.

Euromonitor (1982a-1993a), *European Marketing Data and Statistics*, London.

Euromonitor (1982b-1993b), *International Marketing Data and Statistics*, London.

Fagerberg, J. (1988), "International Competitiveness", *Economic Journal*, 98: 355-374.

Geroski, P. (1995), "Innovation and Competitive Advantage", *Economics Department Working Papers*, 159, OECD.

Greenhalgh, C. (1990), "Innovation and trade performance in the United Kingdom", *Economic Journal*, 100: 105-118.

Greenhalgh, C., P. Taylor and R. Wilson (1994), "Innovation and export volumes and prices - a disaggregated study", *Oxford Economic Papers*, 46(1): 102-135.

Grossman, G. and E. Helpman (1991), *Innovation and Growth in the Global Economy*, MIT Press, Cambridge, Mass.

Grossman, G. and E. Helpman (1993), "Hysteresis in the trade pattern", in: W. Ethier, E. Helpman and P. Neary (eds.), *Theory, Policy and Dynamics in International Trade. Essays in honour of Ronald W. Jones*, Cambridge University Press, Cambridge, 268-290.

Hughes, K. (1986), "Exports and innovation, a simultaneous model", *European Economic Review*, 30: 383-399.

Johansen, S. and K. Juselius (1994), "Identification of the long-run and the short-run structure. An application to the ISLM model", *Journal of Econometrics*, 63: 7-36.

Meeusen, W. and G. Rayp (1995), "Sociale zekerheid en concurrentievermogen", in: M. Despontin and M. Jegers (eds.), *De Sociale Zekerheid Verzekerd?*, VUBPress, Brussels, 169-212.

Meyer zu Schlochtern, F.M.J. and J.L. Meyer zu Schlochtern (1994), "An International Sectoral Data Base for fourteen OECD countries (2nd ed.)", *Economics Department Working Papers*, 145, OECD, Paris.

Osterwald-Lenum, M. (1992), "A note with quantiles of the asymptotic distribution of the maximum likelihood co-integration rank test statistics: four causes", *Oxford Bulletin of Economics and Statistics*, 54, 461-472.

Perron, P. (1988), "Trends and random walks in macroeconomic time series. Further evidence from a new approach", *Journal of Economic Dynamics and Control*, 12: 297-332.

Soete, L. (1981), "A general test of the technological gap trade theory", *Weltwirtschaftliches Archiv*, 117(4): 638-660.

Tharakan, P.K.M., L. Soete and J. Busschaert (1978), "Heckscher-Ohlin and Chamberlin determinants of comparative advantage", *European Economic Review*, 11: 221-239.

Turner, P. and J. Van't Dack (1993), "Measuring international price and cost competitiveness", *BIS Economic Papers*, 39, Bank for International Settlements, Basle.

Table 13.A.1: Results of the (Augmented) Dickey-Fuller unit root tests

	(A)DF	Lag	Variable	(A)DF	Lag
Export share (*Xsh*)					
Xsh12	-2.2218	0	DXsh12	-3.9347***	1*
				-4.0495***	0
Xsh14	-2.0337	0	DXsh14	-5.0952***	0
Xsh16	-2.5063	0	DXsh16	-5.1996***	1
Xsh18	-2.0153	0	DXsh18	-4.9773***	0
Xsh22	-1.5095	0	DXsh22	-4.7654***	1
Xsh26	-2.2181	0	DXsh26	-5.8602***	0
Xsh30	-2.1917	0	DXsh30	-6.0765***	0
Xsh44	-2.6918	1	DXsh44	*-2.8923****	0
Xsh46	-1.8559	1	DXsh46	-5.0859***	0
Xsh60	-0.5464	0	DXsh60	-3.8365***	0
Xsh64	-1.5241	0	DXsh64	-5.4112***	0
Patent share (*PATsh*)					
PATsh12	0.8687	0	DPATsh12	-6.4106***	0
PATsh14	-1.2853	1	DPATsh14	-7.5940***	0
PATsh16	-1.7858	0	DPATsh16	-3.4878**	0
PATsh18	-1.9595	1	DPATsh18	-9.5743***	0
PATsh22	-1.2853	0	DPATsh22	-6.5038***	0
PATsh26	-3.0074**	0			
PATsh30	-2.6983*	0			
PATsh44	-2.7016*	0			
PATsh46	-1.2853	0	DPATsh46	-5.9425***	0
PATsh60	-1.3456	0	DPATsh60	-7.1196***	0
PATsh64	-0.4037	3	DPATsh64	-7.0093***	2
Trade mark share (*TMsh*)					
TMsh12	-2.5247	0	DTMsh12	-4.8849***	0
TMsh14	-3.1489**	0			
TMsh16	-1.9416	0	DTMsh16	-6.0214***	2*
				-6.9745***	0
TMsh18	-2.2856	1	DTMsh18	-9.3344***	0
	-3.7308***	0			
TMsh22	-8.0601***	0			
TMsh26	-1.3956	1	DTMsh26	-7.7885***	0
	-2.0510	0			
TMsh30	-3.9440***	0			
TMsh44	-1.0167	1	DTMsh44	-3.6496**	3
TMsh46	-3.4194**	0			
TMsh60	-3.4699**	0			
TMsh64	-2.3793	1	DTMsh64	-9.4233***	0
Relative unit labour cost (*RelULC*)					
RelULC12	-0.8612	0	DRelULC12	-9.0585***	0
RelULC14	-3.0129**	0			
RelULC16	-1.7362	0	DRelULC16	*-6.0587****	2
RelULC18	-1.5589	0	DRelULC18	-3.5899***	0
RelULC22	-1.8701	1	DRelULC22	*-1.9582***	0
RelULC26	-2.4219	1	DRelULC26	*-2.9202****	0
RelULC30	-1.1576	0	DRelULC30	-3.5404**	0
RelULC44	-3.3439**	1			
RelULC46	-2.4172	0	DRelULC46	-5.2828***	0
RelULC60	-2.3433	0	DRelULC60	-1.6627	2*
				-3.9380***	1
RelULC64	-3.3493**	1			

Note: Own computations using ISDB (OECD) and WIPO.
One, two and three stars indicate the rejection of the unit root tests at respectively 90, 95 and 99%. The significance of the lag length of the variable was determined for a 95% confidence interval except for the values followed by a star (90% confidence interval), from a lag reduction procedure starting from a default specification with three lags.
The values in bold and italic for the first differences of the variables refer to a test specification without constant term.
OECD country codes were used: 12 (Germany), 14 (France), 16 (Italy), 18 (the Netherlands), 22 (Belgium), 26 (UK), 30 (Denmark), 44 (Canada), 46 (Japan), 60 (Sweden) and 64 (Finland).

14. Research and Development as a Source of Technological Change
Dominique Guellec

1. R&D and other types of expenditure in relation to technological innovation

Economists are interested in R&D as one major source of inventions, therefore of technical change and economic efficiency.

R&D is defined in the *Frascati Manual* (OECD 1993) as follows: "Research and experimental development [R&D] comprise creative work undertaken on a systematic basis in order to increase the stock of knowledge, including knowledge and the use of this stock of knowledge to devise new applications. R&D is a term covering three activities: basic research, applied research and experimental development." Basic research is undertaken with the aim of improving knowledge, without any particular application in view. Applied research creates new knowledge, with a practical objective. Development draws on existing knowledge to create new applications. Moreover, R&D is broken down by two further criteria: the source of funding and the place of performance, which can be either government or business.

The European Union performs less than one third of OECD countries, R&D expenditure (28 per cent, around US dollars 140 billion in 1997), as compared with 43 per cent for the US (US dollars 212 billion) and 18 per cent for Japan (US dollars 90 billion). The ratio of R&D on GDP is substantially lower for the EU, at 1.8 per cent, versus 2.6 in the United States and 2.8 in Japan. Within the EU there is large dispersion of R&D intensity, from a high 3.5 per cent in Sweden to a low 0.6 per cent in Portugal and Greece, with most large countries between 2 and 2.4 per cent. The share of public sources in the funding of R&D is 47 per cent, as compared with 35 per cent in the United States and 26 per cent in Japan.

These indicators point to two problems in EU R&D expenditure: it is low, and the share of business is low.

The relative decline of the EU in the 1990s in business R&D is due mainly to slow GDP growth, to a relative reduction in government spending (pressures on budgetary policy, reduction in defence), and to high real interest rates.

2. The levelling off in R&D

Business expenditure on R&D (BERD) has grown on average by 1 per cent a year since 1990, as compared with more than 5 per cent per annum in the 1980s and 3 per cent per annum in the 1970s (Table 14.1). This sharp slowdown is a feature of almost all OECD countries, with the exception of Iceland, Australia and Ireland (in Ireland, the growth of BERD accelerated sharply over this period). In some countries, notably Japan, Germany, Italy and the United Kingdom, BERD decreased in the 1990s. The levelling-off started in the mid-1980s in a first group of countries (including the United States, Canada, Netherlands and Sweden), and in the early 1990s in a second group (including Japan, Germany, France, the United Kingdom, Italy).

The empirical analysis reported here (from Guellec and Ioannidis 1999) allows for an influence on R&D expenditures from the business cycle (fluctuations of GDP), government funding, interest rates and industry structure.

The sensitivity of R&D to GDP, giving rise to "cyclicality" can be explained by both supply and demand factors. Case studies and statistical evidence show that R&D expenditures are financed primarily by the firm's cash flow (Hall 1992; Himmelberg and Petersen 1994). A firm gets little external funding for R&D projects, due to the difficulty of providing collateral, and to the difficulty for an external party to assess the value of a project and the ability of the firm to carry it out. Cash flow is very pro-cyclical, since it is generated by the current activity of the firm. A further reason why R&D might be pro-cyclical is that a large share of research is oriented towards short-term needs: it is devoted to adapting existing goods to new requirements or new markets and hence follows demand fluctuations. Finally, there are static as well as dynamic increasing returns to scale in R&D, implying that a downturn in economic activity will reduce the rate of return on R&D.

Table 14.1: Growth of R&D expenditures in the business sector: average annual growth rate at 1990 GDP prices

	Total				Financed by the business sector				1990s1980s	
	1960s[1]	1970s	1980s	1990s[2]	1960s[1]	1970s	1980s	1990s[2]	Total	Financed by business
United States	2.0	2.0	4.9	0.8	6.2	3.8	5.7	2.6	-4.1	-3.1
Canada	3.9	5.0	7.7	6.1	4.9	5.6	6.2	6.0	-1.5	-0.2
Japan	..	6.4	9.2	-0.6	..	6.4	9.2	-0.7	-9.8	-9.9
France	5.7	4.3	5.2	0.7	9.9	5.2	5.2	2.5	-4.5	-2.7
Germany	10.5	4.5	3.9	-1.5	11.1	4.1	4.7	-1.0	-5.4	-5.7
Italy	10.4	3.3	8.2	-4.0	9.6	2.6	6.5	-2.6	-12.2	-9.1
United Kingdom	2.4	2.6	3.3	-1.2	2.2	2.5	4.2	-0.8	-4.5	-5.0
Australia	..	6.9	11.0	13.1	..	2.9	12.8	12.5	2.1	-0.3
Austria	16.5	10.2	4.5	2.5	17.6	10.0	4.6	..	-2.1	..
Belgium	..	6.3	3.1	0.9	..	6.4	3.2	0.7	-2.2	-2.5
Denmark	13.1	4.1	7.6	5.6	12.7	3.1	7.5	4.2	-2.0	-3.3
Finland	19.3	6.6	10.4	3.9	..	6.5	10.5	4.1	-6.5	-6.4
Iceland	..	..	15.2	17.6	..	..	20.4	17.3	2.4	-3.1
Ireland	14.5	5.1	10.0	20.5	14.3	3.7	10.7	20.6	10.5	9.9
Netherlands	0.0	1.7	3.7	1.2	0.0	1.1	3.8	0.0	-2.5	-3.8
Norway	9.2	8.1	5.7	3.5	10.3	6.4	7.0	5.0	-2.2	-2.0
Spain	22.7	11.9	11.8	-1.7	21.7	11.9	9.7	-0.7	-13.5	-10.4
Sweden	4.9	5.6	5.8	7.3	8.1	6.2	6.0	7.3	1.5	1.3
Switzerland	2.4	1.2	3.7	-4.8	3.1	1.4	3.5	..	-8.5	..

Notes: 1. First year available: 1963 for France, Ireland, Italy, Norway, Switzerland, United States; 1964 for Austria, Germany, Spain, Sweden, United Kingdom; 1966 for Canada and 1967 for Denmark.
2. Last year available: 1966 for Canada, France, Germany, Iceland, Italy, Spain, United States; 1995 for Australia, Denmark, Finland, Ireland, Japan, Netherlands, Norway, Sweden, United Kingdom; 1993 for Austria.

Source: OECD, Economic Outlook 60 and STIU databases, January 1998.

Government funding is a second obvious factor in determining business R&D expenditure. Governments of most OECD countries spend much money on R&D, either by supporting their own facilities (universities and public laboratories) or by funding firms. Beyond fulfilling certain public needs (defence or health), a rationale for government support is that the social rate of return on R&D is higher than the private rate of return. Subsidisation reduces the private cost, therefore increasing the private return. Although a positive relationship between public funding and private funding might be expected, it is sometimes argued that government support essentially substitutes for, or even crowds out, business funding.

Interest rates should influence R&D expenditures since they constitute an investment. As with physical investment, research is profitable only in the future, and expected profits have to be discounted. Moreover R&D must be financed, and interest rates reflect the actual cost of external funds or the opportunity cost of internal funds.

Finally, changes in industry structure may play a prominent role since the distribution of R&D across sectors is very skewed. Some sectors, such as aerospace or drugs, are highly research intensive, whereas others, such as food or wood products, perform nearly no research. Thus, even if research remains stable at the industry level, changes in the pattern of demand can have important aggregate effects.

Econometric estimates are reported in Table 14.2. The model has been estimated on two fitted panels of countries. The largest one ("G12") includes 12 OECD countries: the United States, Canada, Japan, France, Germany, the United Kingdom (this sub-group is labelled "G6"), Italy, the Netherlands, Denmark, Finland, Norway, and Sweden. Isolating the G6 is justified by the fact that it includes the largest R&D spenders in the OECD. The period of estimation is 1972-1996 (or the latest year available).

Table 14.2: Estimated results: sample period 1972-1995

Models	G6 countries				G12 countries			
	GDP,GOV IR(-3)	GDP,GOV IR(-3) trend	GDP,GOV IR(-3), STRUC	GDP,GOV IR(-3) STRUC, trend	GDP,GOV IR(-3)	GDP,GOV IR(-3) trend	GDP,GOV IR(-3), STRUC	GDP,GOV IR(-3) STRUC, trend
Adjustment to long term	-0.26 t(-4.80)**	-0.42 t(-7.26)**	-0.31 t(-5.43)	-0.44 t(-7.08)**	-0.06 t(-3.75)**	-0.07 t(-3.80)**	-0.10 t(-5.39)**	-0.12 t(-5.67)**
GDP long term	1.68 t(28.82)**	0.70 t(4.70)**	1.84 t(25.81)**	0.98 t(5.96)**	1.67 t(7.23)**	0.64 t(1.07)	1.94 t(15.51)**	0.69 t(2.22)**
GOV long term	0.33 t(5.75)**	0.35 t(10.27)**	0.13 t(2.42)**	0.24 t(5.37)**	0.60 t(3.80)**	0.52 t(3.69)**	0.24 t(4.15)**	0.19 t(4.02)**
STRUC long term			1.00 t(3.95)**	0.58 t(3.60)**			2.09 t(5.81)**	1.94 t(6.55)**
IR(-3) long term	-0.012 t(-1.65)*	0.001 t(0.22)	-0.006 t(-0.94)	0.004 t(0.99)	-0.077 t(-3.18)**	-0.070 t(-3.18)**	-0.035 t(-3.09)**	-0.027 t(-3.00)**
Trend		0.02 t(6.76)**		0.02 t(5.32)**		0.03 t(1.84)*		0.03 t(4.40)**
D(GDP)	0.88 t(8.45)**	0.61 t(6.41)**	0.75 t(6.50)**	0.55 t(4.63)**	0.69 t(9.97)**	0.65 t(8.68)**	0.60 t(9.07)**	0.49 t(6.66)**
D(GOV)	0.03 t(1.14)	0.07 t(3.01)**	-0.01 t(-0.36)	0.03 t(1.45)	-0.01 t(-0.51)	0.00 t(-0.31)	-0.01 t(-1.03)	-0.01 t(-1.03)

Notes: The response variable is the volume of R&D performed and financed by the business enterprise sector; GOV is the volume of R&D performed by the business enterprise sector but financed by government; STRUC is an indicator reflecting the industry structure of the economy; IR are real long-term interest rates.

Source: Guellec and Ioannidis (1999).

Table 14.2 cont'd

Models	G6 countries					G12 countries				
	GDP,GOV IR(-3)	GDP,GOV IR(-3) trend	GDP,GOV IR(-3), STRUC	GDP,GOV IR(-3) STRUC, trend		GDP,GOV IR(-3)	GDP,GOV IR(-3) trend	GDP,GOV IR(-3), STRUC	GDP,GOV IR(-3) STRUC, trend	
D(STRUC)			0.45 t(4.77)**	0.44 t(4.77)**				0.38 t(7.50)**	0.40 t(7.73)**	
D(IR(-3))	0.001 t(0.44)	0.001 t(0.59)	0.001 t(0.73)	0.002 t(0.95)		-0.003 t(-3.10)**	-0.003 t(-3.18)**	-0.002 t(-1.73)*	-0.001 t(-1.12)	
D(GDP) (-1)	0.26 t(2.21)**	0.14 t(1.39)	0.33 t(2.82)**	0.29 t(2.56)**		0.11 t(1.31)	0.07 t(0.83)	0.17 t(2.35)**	0.14 t(1.78)*	
D(GOV) (-1)	0.05 t(1.69)*	0.10 t(3.89)**	0.01 t(0.29)	0.06 t(2.12)**		0.02 t(2.10)**	0.02 t(2.00)**	0.01 t(1.11)	0.01 t(0.90)	
D(STRUC) (-1)			0.33 t(3.07)**	0.27 t(2.62)**				0.19 t(3.29)**	0.21 t(3.60)**	
D(IR(-3)) (-1)	-0.001 t(-0.59)	0.000 t(0.22)	-0.002 t(-1.06)	-0.001 t(-0.30)		-0.003 t(-3.17)**	-0.003 t(-3.19)**	-0.003 t(-3.10)**	-0.003 t(-2.60)**	
D(RD) (-1)	0.14 t(1.78)*	0.00 t(0.02)	0.03 t(0.41)	-0.06 t(-0.73)		0.15 t(2.69)**	0.16 t(2.78)**	0.06 t(1.08)	0.06 t(1.06)	
R² Adjusted	33%	38%	39%	45%		25%	25%	31%	33%	
DW	2.05	1.99	2.01	2.06		2.22	2.24	2.11	2.15	
Modified LM test	0.03 t(0.14)	-0.09 t(-0.49)	0.11 t(0.46)	-0.14 t(-0.71)		-0.22 t(-1.03)	-0.22 t(-1.08)	-0.03 t(-0.09)	0.02 t(0.08)	
Number of observations	140	140	140	140		274	274	274	274	
Model fit for the 1990s²	-0.005 t(-0.62)	-0.003 t(-0.34)	0.003 t(0.41)	0.004 t(0.53)		-0.009 t(-1.30)	-0.009 t(-1.31)	0.002 t(0.29)	0.001 t(0.10)	

GDP appears to play the most significant role in both the long and short run. The long-run elasticity of GDP ranges from 1.7 to 2 depending on the panel, reflecting the fact that over the estimation period R&D expenditures grew – on average – faster than GDP, in all countries. In the above estimate this phenomenon is picked up by the long-run coefficient of GDP. However, when a time trend and the structure variable are introduced, the long-run elasticity of GDP is not significantly different from unity. An increase in the share of R&D in GDP might reflect the transition towards the knowledge-based economy, an economy in which knowledge in all its forms (technology, but also human capital, high-tech equipment and software) plays a crucial role. The knowledge base of all OECD economies has been expanding for years, more rapidly than their tangible base. Whether this is better captured by an elasticity higher than unity or by a positive time trend and a unit elasticity is an open question: the first approach assumes that it is GDP growth which has led to the emergence of the knowledge-based economy, because when an economy gets richer it increases its knowledge base (probably related to the relative cost of physical and intangible assets, to demand patterns and to competition with low wage-low technology countries); the second approach assumes that the growth of R&D intensity is partly autonomous, and should grow independently of GDP.

Over the recent period and particularly in the first half of the 1990s, most OECD economies have experienced slower economic growth and also a sharp slowdown or reduction in R&D expenditures. The upturn of economic growth in the United States since 1993 has been followed by an upturn in R&D expenditures, and similar signals have been reported in European countries more recently. The positive impact of GDP on R&D at a macroeconomic level is therefore strongly supported by recent developments. On the other hand, the various estimates of the short-run elasticity of business R&D to GDP are not significantly different from unity, which means that business R&D does not *overreact* to fluctuations in GDP. In other words, the economic downturn of the 1990s has generated a slowdown in R&D, but it cannot explain by itself the decrease in R&D *intensity* that was observed in many OECD countries. It played a prominent role, but other factors must be taken into account when it comes to explaining the levelling-off of R&D expenditures.

Government funding of research is the second most important factor in the explanation of R&D fluctuations: it exhibits a long-run elasticity of about 0.3 to 0.6 in the basic equations, and around 0.2 when a time trend and structure variable are introduced. Over the short run, government funding seems to have a much weaker effect, around 0.1 in most equations (with a zero contemporaneous effect in all except one equation). Therefore the impact of government funding is mainly a long-term one. It takes years for firms to adjust their R&D expenditures to the change in conditions generated by a change in government funding. The delayed adjustment of private funding to subsidies may signal that government funding is rather concerned with projects of a long duration, or that the research generated by government funds may open new, long-lasting opportunities to firms.

High real interest rates are usually taken to have contributed to the reduction in physical investment experienced by European countries in the 1990s. When interest rates are introduced in the R&D equation the results differ across the panels. In the G12 countries, they have a strong impact on business R&D: a rise in real interest rates of 100 base points reduces the level of business R&D by 3 per cent in the long run (when a time trend and a structure variable are introduced); but the effect is significant in only one equation in the G6 panel.

Changes in the cross-industry structure of the economy also seem to play an important role in R&D fluctuations. In order to capture these multi-dimensional changes quantitatively, an indicator (STRUC) which – basically – reflects the share of high-technology sectors in GDP is constructed. More precisely, this is defined as the weighted average across sectors of their shares in GDP, where the weights are the sectors' respective R&D shares at a specific point in time. For the G12, the long-term elasticity of this factor is around 2, whether there is a time trend or not and its short-term elasticity (contemporaneous plus one year lag) is close to 0.6. For the G6, the long-term value is 1 without a time trend, 0.6 with a time trend, and the short-term value is 0.7 to 0.8.

3. R&D and economic performance

The existence of substantial rewards from performing R&D is not in question. However, measuring these rewards, estimating a rate of return on R&D, is very difficult. In most cases, R&D is mixed with other inputs for producing innovations - manufacturing, marketing, training etc.- and these various inputs are complementary, so that disentangling their respective contribution to the production of value is a real challenge, even for firms.

The econometric approach tries to make up for the lack of precise information on each firm or each project by using many of them, looking for variance in their economic return. The rate of return is defined as the value generated by one euro of R&D. It is estimated by regressing the production or value added of the economic unit, or an indicator of productivity, on its R&D expenditure (possibly cumulated over time) and some control variables (physical capital, skills of the labour force). When the considered unit is a firm, this is the private rate of return. A second concept is the "social rate of return", which captures the external effects (spillovers) associated with R&D expenditure.

More precisely, there are two distinct types of externalities:

- Knowledge spillovers, related to the intangible nature of information and the difficulty of restricting other firms' access to anyone's discoveries. Patents are one way of dealing with this issue. They seem to be especially important in the chemicals industry, where discoveries (chemical formula) are highly codified, therefore easy to imitate if not patented.
- Pecuniary externalities, coming from the difficulty for an innovator of capturing all the value generated by its innovation, the rest of which goes to competitors, customers or the society as a whole. This may be due to competition, to market power of customers, etc. This applies also to the chemicals industry, which produces mainly intermediate goods, and whose customers are other firms, some of which may be big enough to exert pressure on prices.

On the other hand, there are also sources of negative externalities, owing to creative destruction (innovation by one firm reduces the market value of competing, substitutable products). One study only has succeeded in capturing these negative spillovers.

Estimates of the rate of return are very diverse across studies. They depend on:

- the economic unit (firm, industry, country);
- the sample and period of estimate;
- the econometric method (endogeneity and collinearity issues constrain to use sophisticated methods, which are not in general very robust);
- the underlying theoretical framework (estimated equation).

Overall, according to an exhaustive survey by Mairesse and Mohnen (1999), estimates of the private rate of return (firm level) are in the range of 10-20 per cent, and the social return is 50 to 100 per cent higher.

There is a presumption of a diversity of rates of return across industries, with science-based sectors ranking high. Recall that usual estimates of the rate of return on physical capital are in the range of 5-10 per cent. Why is the rate of return on R&D so much higher? Two explanations at least come to mind: first, there is a risk premium; second, R&D is only one component of expenditure on innovation, and taking into account the whole cost would lead to lower estimates of the rate of return.

Table 14.3: Average results from available estimates of internal rate of return to R&D at the industry level (40 observations)

C	SPILL.	VA	Panel	R2 (F-test)
0.347*	-0.100*	0.073	-0.221*	0.071
(0.077)	(0.046)	(0.050)	(0.046)	(34.89)

Note: Estimation method is weighted least squares (number of industries), standard errors between parentheses are White Heteroskedastic-Consistent. The dependent variable is the rate of return to R&D, SPILL. is a dummy which takes the value of one for the studies that measure the rates of return to both internal and external R&D, zero otherwise; VA is a dummy which takes the value of one for the studies that proxy output by value added; Panel is a dummy which takes a value of one for the panel data studies; Year is the average period of estimation defined as the average year covered by the sample (mean year less 1950); UP65 and UP75 are dummies which take a value of one if the average year is above 1965 and 1975, respectively.
Source: Bruno van Pottelsberghe (1998).

Finally, let's go back to spillovers. Beyond estimating a social rate of return, it is key for policy makers and industry analysts to identify the actual channels and mechanisms supporting the diffusion of knowledge. A simple abstract view, such as the one taken in macroeconomic models, is of no use for policy makers in the field. Just knowing that there are substantial spillovers provides a legitimacy to government policy, it does not give an indication of how, and in which domains, such an intervention should be performed. Microeconomic studies, theoretical as well as empirical, have identified some of the mechanisms which encourage the circulation of knowledge between firms:

- technological proximity (can be measured by a distance between patent portfolio); they support the idea of "clusters" of innovative firms (sharing some common costs, competing etc.);
- geographical proximity ("technopoles");
- financial links (support the development of technological links).

Conclusion

Technological change stands as the major source of productivity growth in the long run. Technological change consists both in innovation and diffusion. In turn, there are various sources of technological change: research and development (R&D), education and training, investment in software, and various types of investment in innovation (product design, uptooling, marketing, etc.). This chapter focuses on R&D, while examining its complementary relationships with other sources of technological change. R&D can be either basic, generating knowledge useful in the medium or long run, or applied, with a direct commercial result. The European Union as a whole turns out to spend relatively less than the United States and Japan in R&D, although most advanced EU countries are large spenders. The share of business in the performance of research is lower in the EU than in the United States and Japan.

R&D expenditure levelled off in most OECD countries in the late 1980s to early 1990s, after several decades of steady growth. Four factors are identified as the main causes of the levelling-off: the economic downturn of the early 1990s, the reduction in government funding (due mainly to shrinking defence budgets), high real interest rates and a shift in industry structure (the growth in services and a slowdown in certain high tech industries). However, whereas R&D expenditure has picked up in the United States since 1995 (5 per cent a year), it is still sluggish in the EU (2 per cent a year). Slow economic growth in Europe is the first explanation of this growing gap, but there is a case also for deepening the structural reform engaged in European countries (e.g. increasing the industry/university linkages).

The social rate of return on R&D seems to far exceed the private rate of return (by 50 to 100 per cent). However, before engaging in R&D policy, government may well identify the channels that spillovers take: targeting the wrong projects, or the wrong firms or using ill-designed instruments may have detrimental effects on R&D itself or on its outcome.

References

Guellec, D. and E. Ioannidis (1999), "Causes of fluctuations in R&D: a quantitative analysis". *OECD Economic Studies*, N°. 29, 123-138. Paris.

Hall, B. H. (1992), "Investment and R&D at the firm level: Does the source of financing matter?" *NBER Working Paper*, No. 4096, Cambridge, MA.

Himmelberg, C. and B. Petersen (1994), "R&D and internal finance: a panel study of small firms in high-tech industries", *Review of Economics and Statistics*, 76(1), 38-51.

Mairesse, J. and P. Mohnen (1999), "Econométrie de l'innovation", *Working Paper CNRS*, Paris.

OECD (1993), *Frascati Manual*.

van Pottelsberghe, B. (1998), "The efficiency of science and technology policy inside the Triad", PhD. Dissertation, Université Libre de Bruxelles.

15. Education and Information Society
Jacques Lesourne

The growing importance of intangible assets is only one aspect of a deeper evolution, which has been mentioned before, the progressive transformation of industrial societies into information societies.

Such societies are not post-industrial societies in which the importance of industry would decrease, but they are dominated by a bundle of technologies which are generally called "the information technologies".

Therefore, it is necessary to stress at first a few of the characteristics of the information technology before considering the role of education in such a society.

The Information Society

Most of our concepts, which are related to the industrial society, will no longer be valid for an information society. Let us take a few examples.

The change in the concept of investment is the main topic of this book. Investment in the industrial society is in building machines, roads, airports and so on. But if we define investment as a present expenditure for a future profit, the creation of intangible assets now becomes a very significant part of investment.

Another example: unions. In the industrial societies, they protect workers' interests. Their development comes from the fact that many people have very similar situations and problems, and therefore want to cooperate in order to fight for their common interests. This homogeneity of the working class is no longer true in an information society.

Consider pensions: the French pensions system is built on the idea that you have a career, and therefore in the public service for instance, you get a pension related to your last salary because it is the highest in your career. But, what will a career be in an information society? More generally, many statistical concepts, GNP, industrial sectors, investment, budgets, etc. will have to be rethought because of the characteristics of the information society. A very urgent task for Eurostat would be to commission a report on the future statistical system in an information society.

For our present purpose, it is necessary to stress five features of the information society.

1. The first one is the *change in working relations*. Remember that in the agricultural society, the relations between the owners and the farmers, or people who exploit the land, have nothing to do with the payment of salary in exchange for work. And in the industrial society, labour is characterised by a *location* - people have to work in the plant or in the office -; *length of working time* - in the day, in the week, in the year, in the life; the fact that, generally, the *work contract is on an indefinite period of time* and also that, at the climax of industrial society, you receive generally fixed wages. If you discuss each of these points, you find that they are, at least in the margin, transformed in the information society.

    Location: it is not necessary to have one if you are a consultant, an architect, a man working in advertising, a man or a woman working at cleaning offices. Tomorrow, the location will not really be associated with work.

    The length of working days, weeks or years may be different from one person to another. In many sectors, you may work very hard for one week or one month, and moderately for the rest of the year. The fact that the *nature of the contract* expresses the idea of an *indefinite length of time*, and of a *career in a specific sector* will no longer be usual. And of course, in many sectors, the income you will get will depend on the profitability of the unit in which you operate.

2. A second aspect is "*Where will the jobs be?*". We see already that jobs which were mainly concentrated in production units are migrating upstream or downstream, downstream in the intermediaries and upstream in research, training, writing software programmes and so on, so that the distribution of jobs in future economies will be very different from what we knew. And of course, it will also be related to the structure of the industry. For instance, the importance of outsourcing will give rise to so-called "hollow" corporations. The hollow corporation may, in fact,

control many jobs, but these will be distributed in different corporations, and the centre of the network will keep only the workers who are necessary to hold the key segment in the added value chain.

3. A third point is the *number of jobs*. A very crucial transformation which has been developing inside our societies for twenty years is the change in the relative scarcity of the various capabilities of individuals under the impact of globalisation and of information technologies. Capabilities, which were essential and demanded in the industrial society, are now less demanded, so that the firms are not able to pay the same cost for these capabilities, while they are ready to pay very high or higher costs for other capabilities. As a consequence, the distribution of direct income becomes more and more unequal in almost all our societies. In the information society, the problem will be to find means to make compatible a not too unequal distribution of income and a great dispersion of labour costs according to capabilities (in order to make people with low capabilities employable).

4. A fourth point is the progressive *modification of social groups*. People favoured by the information society are engineers, university professors, scientists, interpreters, teachers, programmers and many other types of technicians. Of course, they may have highly different incomes, but they marry each other and live in the same districts. On the contrary, blue and white collar workers, who were characteristic groups of the industrial societies, tend to be dispersed and smaller in numbers, while farmers represent a marginal fraction of society. But beside the central group, of course, you have all the groups of people who are excluded to some extent from society. There remain also the remnants of groups corresponding to the past social structures, among them retired persons.

5. Finally, a fifth aspect is that *the information society is a society in which, in the various segments of culture, the systemic approach becomes more and more important*. It becomes important in thinking, it becomes important in the models of science, it is important in management because managers have to master complex systems with technical, economic and sociological features.

So, if we enter such an information society, what are the problems it raises for education? It is not worth spending much time on the problems of education and information technologies. Everybody knows how childish it was, in the 1960s or the 1970s, to think that to reform the educational system, the problem was just to buy computers and to give computers to schools and universities. In France, such a program had as a consequence the transfer of unused computers either to cellars or to attics. We should remember that the competition between teachers and books - though books had been invented a few centuries ago - was still prevailing ten years ago. Education is based on a very simple technology, which relates the teacher and the pupil. If we except the training of the teacher, it does not need much investment. So, to introduce new technologies is a much deeper and more profound change than just putting computers in classrooms.

Therefore, it seems more important to consider the general problem of education in an industrial society.

The Issues for Education

1. To begin with, let us ask ourselves what will be demanded in the labour market? It's *capability*. And what is capability? A mixture of knowledge, practice and behaviour. The words are important. For instance, in France, if you look at agreements between unions and entrepreneurs, you will always find the word "qualification", with this idea that what is demanded on the labour market is a qualification. And the qualification is defined by a diploma or tests given through anonymous procedures. But such a diploma does not at all guarantee ability in practice and adequate behaviour. For instance, Martine Aubry, the French labour minister, was very happy to announce that she was creating fifteen or twenty new qualifications for careers in the education public service. She forgot that the market invented hundreds of new capabilities every year and attached importance not only to knowledge but to practice and behaviour.

    What are the "dimensions" of appropriate behaviour?
    - *Autonomy*. The ability of a person to master situations within the firm or out of the firm. Autonomy protects workers against an adverse evolution of their firm, since such workers have an ability to adapt to a new situation. So, autonomy is important and the firms have an interest in having people who can quit the firm

without too many difficulties because a firm is not an institution forever.
- *Ability to cooperate with other people in a team.* These two dimensions have not really been integrated in many educational systems. In the French educational system, for instance, you never give value to cooperation. Preference is given to individualistic competition, but this competition is not in real situations, but in abstracts situations defined by examination.

2   A second point which has to be stressed is that *general education has to cater for the totality of the population.*

There is always a difficult part of the population, representing maybe 30% of an age cohort, which may have problems in their basic education. So, it remains essential for these people not only to master the "3 R's" of the British, but to acquire the ability to use information technologies and also, a fourth category, to understand what it means to be a citizen in a democratic society and what his or her duties and rights are.

We should not forget that information technologies will have immense political consequences for the functioning of democracies. Imagine for instance a society in which the Head of State was questioning people every night on what he should decide the day after. Such a democracy would be very different from the one in which a vote is organised every five years for a party which has as an emblem a snake, or an apple or an elephant. It might be an unstable political system, but information technology makes it feasible.

3.   After general education, let us consider *professional education*. Obviously, there are two challenges. The first one is that professional education has to be broader than in the past in order for persons to be able to retrain themselves in the course of their lives. To avoid unemployment and remain "employable", they must be adaptable and cover a broad range of skills. A classical example is the case of workers in public works. If a flat has to be restored by painters, electricians, plumbers and so on, each of them generally destroys part of the man before has done. And they have to be closely supervised. But you may imagine that in the future, for some tasks, people will be able to master a few of the basic skills.

The second challenge may seem contradictory to the first, but in practice it is not. People must have a high degree of professional reliability, which is another way of expressing their ability to be autonomous.

4. A fourth point concerns *higher education*. In the system of higher education, you have two obvious poles, one centred on specific knowledge and another centred on the mastering of complexity.

The existence of these two poles is illustrated by an anecdote concerning the French system. You may at the end of your studies receive a diploma as a doctor or as an engineer. But now, engineers may in addition obtain, after additional studies, a doctor's degree. And the question was: "With a doctor's degree, do the engineers have better recruitment prospects?". To which the answer was "Oh yes! if they don't tell anyone about it.". Why? Because part of the demand of the firms is for people whom they thought, rightly or wrongly, able to master complex systems, and they were afraid that people with doctor's degrees were too specialised in a narrow segment. They also thought they had internalised the values of research and not the values of a firm in competitive markets.

5. The last point to stress is *the importance of continuous training*. The information society implies that, in the course of your life, you will have to train yourself in order to improve your capability. But it's not so easily done as said. I remember at the beginning of my career, I decided that in my firm - it was a consulting firm - a significant share of the time of the consultants be spent every week on training themselves. But what did I find after a while? That they were specialists of training, people who were always ready to be trained. After a doctorate in physics, they were ready to start a doctorate in chemistry, and after that, to acquire some knowledge of economics. On the contrary, other people, but not necessarily the worst, were totally resisting and, in fact, after a while, did not attend any training session.

The big firms tend to attach more and more importance to continuous training. The attitude of small firms is different. Does it matter?. I'm not sure. It's only that the process is not organised, not formalised, not approved in a committee with the unions. But in many small firms, especially in firms in advanced technology, training is absolutely inherent to the operation of the firm. If you are writing and selling software, the training is almost continuous, but it is not declared as a training expenditure.

Concluding remarks

Two concluding remarks:

1. It is urgent to adapt the educational system to the needs of the information society because such a system is responding very slowly.

    If we recruit a teacher now, an elementary school teacher that is, the last pupil he or she will train will retire in 2100, so that somebody retiring at the end of the next century will have in his mind some of the biases of the European teacher aged around 25, recruited in 2000.

    The educational system is also made up of institutions which are very difficult to adapt. In France, the teachers' unions always believe that the solution is a higher budget, more expenditure. They think they would reach the ideal if 100% of a generation were to end with a PhD. Of course, this was not too bad an aim when there were a few percent of PhDs, but is it still an objective when 65% of a generation have a baccalaureate?

2. The aims of the education system of the future, the nature of relations that should exist between the government, the firms and this system have to be rethought for the information society.

16. Discussion
Elisabeth Waelbroeck-Rocha

Intangible Investments and Empirical Links: Implications for Decision Makers

At a time when many talk about the "New [Economic] Paradigm" or the "New [US] Economy", an important debate has been launched on the role of ICT investments in fostering productivity enhancements and changing society. According to the *New Economy* theory, the intelligence revolution and the shift to a knowledge-based economy have changed society in such a way that continued rapid growth can go hand in hand with low inflation and low unemployment. Proponents of the *New Economy* theory attribute much of the US economy's recent success to information technology, one of the forms of "intangible investments". Information technology is transforming the way companies do business, revealing new opportunities for growth, new markets, new ways to serve customers and new channels of distribution, and is helping companies to lower their costs. As a result, economies can grow faster than before without igniting inflation.

As shown in the chapters presented in this book and particularly in the third part, there are many forms of intangible investments that are liable to foster non-inflationary long-term growth in the economy, among which are research and development efforts, innovation, education and training, improvements in software and in the organization of supplier and customer networks. All play an important role in fostering competitiveness and growth through productivity enhancements. There is a problem with "intangible investments", however, which lies in their very name: being "intangible", they are difficult to quantify or measure. The number of new patent registrations and/or copyrights can be used as a measure of the output of investments in R&D, and trademarks can provide a measure of commercial (marketing and advertising) efforts – though with obvious shortcomings. "Measuring" the quality of education or training, in contrast, is another matter. As a result, it is difficult to assess the impact of intangible investments on the economy, or the link between intangibles and competitiveness, with traditional economic methods. Attempts to measure this have thus been of two types: the first is more descriptive in nature, while the second is quantitative but starts from a more limited definition of intangibles than would be ideal.

The chapters in this book describe, each in their own way, how intangible investments, or some forms thereof, have contributed to improving economic growth and/or competitiveness. Martin Boon examines the impact of employer-provided training on firm output and value added in the Dutch manufacturing sector, and shows that investments in human capital have a significant positive effect on value added for manufacturing firms. Wim Meeusen and Glenn Rayp show that, in most of the countries they analysed, innovation efforts *stricto sensu* constitute a significant determinant of long-run export market share. The same applies to the country shares in trademark applications, which are used as a proxy for marketing efforts, and which were significant in all competitiveness equations independently of the innovation efforts *stricto sensu*. The authors also find indicators of product quality to be important determinants of long-term competitiveness. Even more important, they find that innovation efforts, marketing efforts and quality, appear to be more important in explaining competitiveness than production costs. Dominique Guellec tries to link R&D expenditure and technological change, the latter being a major source of productivity growth in the long term, and explores why R&D expenditure in Europe increasingly lags expenditures in the US. Slower growth in the EU is one factor, different sources and structure of financing is another.

Even if at present, we have at our disposal very limited instruments for measuring intangible assets and their impact on competitiveness, they can still tell us that intangibles matter. Whether from the private or the public sphere, decision makers that are able to perceive the importance of a new "paradigm" already gain a prime mover advantage, to the benefit of many others.

Thus, to come back to "Research and Development as a Source of Technological Change", Dominique Guellec reminds us that case studies and statistical evidence show that R&D expenditures are primarily financed from the firm's cash flow, which is pro-cyclical. The financial system (banks, stock markets) provides little funding for R&D projects, due to the difficulty of providing collateral or the difficulty for external parties assessing the value of a given project and the ability of the firm to carry it out. This "inefficiency" of capital markets can and has to be corrected. Both the private and the public sector have a role to play here. In the US, corporate venturing – involving large (private) companies' investing in and assisting smaller high-growth businesses – has proved to be at the root of the US's vibrant venture capital markets. In Europe, venture capitalists tend to focus on too narrow segments, and are reluctant to lend to truly small (or new) businesses.

But the move to information-based societies reaches far beyond economic aspects and touches deeply on social values. At the outset, education systems have a challenge: ensure that all future citizens will have the chance to prosper in competitive, knowledge-based economies. As J. Lesourne rightly stresses, what is demanded in the labour market today is not a "qualification" but a "capability", that is, knowledge, practice and adequate behaviour (the latter meaning autonomy and ability to cooperate with other people in a team). Adapting the education system in order to increase the "capabilities" of people of working age – all of them, not just those "in the labour market" today – is an essential contribution that governments can make to the development of intangibles. This requires improvements in the general education system – where people learn to have a proper "attitude to work" or behaviour – as well as in the professional education system (where people improve their knowledge and learn to put this knowledge into practice) – and in the higher education system. The provision of continuous training – or, better, encouraging the private sector to do so – is also essential. Under the Amsterdam Treaty, the European Union is committed to promoting the highest possible level of knowledge. Programmes such as Socrates (European programme for education), Leonardo da Vinci (for vocational training) and the new Youth Programme are particularly important in this context, especially in terms of their contributions to enhancing mobility and work force flexibility.

For the social system however, the development of the information society may be favouring certain types of individuals – that is, individuals with certain skill sets (engineers, scientists, teachers, programmers and many types of technicians) while neglecting others, who risk being excluded from active life (working society) as a result. Increased emphasis on intangible investments, whilst necessary, carries the risk of further increasing imbalances, unless explicitly dealt with through adequate social policy. Providing appropriate training to those at risk of being excluded from society, and organizing society in such a way as to minimize the risk of exclusion, are essential to preserve the benefits of such investments on competitiveness. Imagine a "high-tech" society, presumably highly competitive, but in which half the population were excluded from wealth creation. The social implications would be unacceptable, challenging the very successes of the "information society".

It is therefore most important that efforts by all decision makers aimed at promoting investment in intangibles be implemented in a consistent and coordinated way, so that all their potential benefits be reaped by all the citizens of Europe.

17. Conclusion
Pierre Buigues, Alexis Jacquemin and Jean-François Marchipont

Intangibles and European Policies

This conference[1] has considered the impact of tangible investments, mainly defined as plant, machinery and equipment, versus intangible investments, mainly defined as research and development, marketing, advertising software and training, on economic performance at the level of companies, sectors and the economy as a whole. One of the first conclusions reached by the studies presented here is that the importance of intangible investment is growing. The estimates presented by J. Mortensen in his chapter show that the proportion of the total stock of capital in the US economy accounted for by conventional tangible capital fell from 58% in 1948 to 46% in 1990, as the share of intangible capital rose from 42% in 1948 to 54% in 1990. In 1990, that is, the estimated value of intangible capital was higher than that of tangible fixed capital, and in the 1990s the trend towards the intangible has been growing even faster.

The growing importance of intangibles has transformed the sources of competitiveness, and should therefore lead to significant shifts in the content of public policies. This applies equally, of course, to national, European and international policies. This chapter will concentrate on European policies and will try to pinpoint the changes which have already taken place as well as those which might be envisaged for the future.

---

[1] Conference on 'Intangible Assets and the Competitiveness of the European Economy', held in Louvain-la-Neuve on 29-30 April 1999. The studies presented at the Conference were funded and monitored by the European Commission's Directorate General for Research and Development, the Directorate General for Industry and the Forward Studies Unit.

As far back as its White Paper on "Growth, Competitiveness, Employment", the European Commission encouraged investment in intangibles, to support the dissemination of R&D results into products and processes and to foster collaboration and exchange networks so as to develop clusters.

More generally, the considerations which have the greatest effect on competitiveness are no longer related solely to the direct costs of the various production factors. They include, to name the key elements, standards of education and training, the degree of efficiency of corporate organisation, the capacity to make continuous improvements in production processes, the focus on R&D and its practical application for industrial purposes, and the fluidity of the conditions under which markets operate.

Government policies must in future accord at least the same priority to these intangible factors as they do to physical investment. This type of investment is becoming the key element in bringing about growth that is durable, creates skilled jobs and is economical in its use of resources. Even more crucial is the capacity to incorporate all of these elements into coherent strategies.

Conversely, several studies show that size or technology are not sufficient in themselves to guarantee success in industrial activity. According to Jacquemin and Pench (1999), new forms of competitive advantage derive from *knowledge-based factors* - branding and advertising, innovation and patent protection and control of standards - which were previously of marginal significance and are still largely unrecognised in Europe. Traditionally, firms, institutions, national statistical bodies and governments have focused primarily on investment in physical assets, such as machinery and equipment, and have been slow to acknowledge the crucial importance of intangible assets. At the individual business level, the gap is particularly evident in financial statements and reports to shareholders, where information on intangibles is either absent or difficult to interpret. Within firms, knowledge about intangibles and the ability to manage them effectively varies, despite evidence that these assets are key resources for future growth and profitability. In addition, the benefits of investment in intangibles are often difficult for firms to grasp, and this exacerbates problems of underinvestment and poor resource allocation.

Furthermore, despite the increasing importance of intangible assets, government support programmes for industry have so far mainly been targeted on physical investment (OECD, 1997). The approach based on individual industrial sectors, too, is becoming more and more difficult to apply, as the distinction between goods and services is less and less clear: industries such as telecommunications, electronics and information technology, which had high individual profiles a few years ago, are now interpenetrating, while new types of activities, such as those related to the internet, are developing at exponential growth rates.

Official authorities, whether at the national or the European level, still have a long way to go to assimilate these changes. They are still structured on the traditional industry segmentation pattern. The time has probably come for a drastic reorganisation of these structures.

Lastly, activities based on intangible investment and activities based on tangible investment differ in term of externalities, sunk cost and economies of scale, with the result that the types of competition in which both categories engage also diverge widely. Table 17.1 shows the main differences between intangible activities and tangible activities from the economic point of view. The analyses by Sutton (1991) and by Davies and Lyons (1996) show that there are significant differences in the way industries are organised internationally, depending on whether or not they are characterised by intangible investment and therefore by product differentiation.

In sectors where the level of tangible investment is high, firms enjoy economies of scale based on production. Products are homogeneous and competition is based fundamentally on price. Markets of this type are steel, wood and paper, cement, shipbuilding, wool and cotton. We call these industries "tangible activities".

In sectors where intangible investment is high, research and development directed at new products and processes or advertising to establish brand names and reputation are used by the firms involved as strategic tools to improve their market position. Vertical differentiation based on R&D and advertising spending enhances consumers' perception of quality and their willingness to pay. Raising the profile of the firm is therefore a major objective which entails high sunk cost. In markets of this kind, a substantial degree of price spread occurs, since non-price competition is essential. Examples of markets with high levels of spending on both R&D and advertising are pharmaceuticals, soaps, motor vehicles and consumer electronics. Markets with a high level of spending only on R&D are chemicals, machine-tools, aerospace and telecommunication, while the chief markets which spend heavily only on advertising are parts of the food industry, tobacco and confectionery.

Table 17.1: Tangible versus intangible activities and market structure

	Existence of statistical indicators	Existence of positive externalities	Sunk cost	Economies of scale or scope	Type of competition
Intangible activities	Low	High (in RD, training)	High (reputation)	Economies of scope	Differentiated services, non-price competition
Tangible activities	High	Depends, but generally low	Depends	Economies of scale	Price competition

Finally, as Peneder shows in his chapter, industries characterised by major intangible investment perform much more competitively than traditional tangible investment activities.

If we define the "knowledge economy" using the broader OECD approach as in G. Vickery's chapter (as consisting of sectors with high R&D activity, high ICT use and/or a significant proportion of highly skilled workers), the proportion of the economy held by these sectors accounted for nearly 55% of value added in the business sector in the USA as against 48% in the EU.

Against this background, emphasis needs to be given to various official initiatives designed to fit into the new context of competitiveness. These would be:

- developing a new set of indicators to monitor the development of the new knowledge-based industries. This involves giving the requisite resources to Statistical Offices in the Member States and at the European level. A system of generally accepted best practice is a second best;
- reinforcing public support for investments characterised by strong positive externalities, ranging from R&D to training, so that these activities are appropriate from the societal point of view;
- increasing the scale and enhancing the cooperative nature of precompetitive research efforts. If the efforts of public authorities are to bear fruit, firms must do something to correct the excessively low level of their own investment in technological research, development and innovation;
- promoting generic technologies, such as new materials, biotechnology or information technology, whose characteristic is that they do not only concern specific firms or sectors but the whole industry (A. Jacquemin and J.-F. Marchipont, 1992);

- promoting an active innovation policy, based on the rapid transfer of know-how from basic research to industrial application, by ensuring that small businesses and start-up firms have access to this know-how and the ability to make the best use of it. This should, as a result, focus on the circulation of information and scientists, from both inside and outside the Community, and on encouraging the transferral of university research results to the fields of production and marketing.
- putting more emphasis on training, through specialised centres of higher education and by pursuing best practice in learning models.

All this implies that our traditional policies need to be converted into policies which enhance competitiveness and are consistent with each other (Buigues, Jacquemin and Sapir, 1995). To illustrate what can be done at the European level to deal with these new priorities. we will take the examples of the policies developed in relation to industry, R&D, competition and trade.

Industrial Policy

It is a well known fact that the macroeconomic environment has a key part to play in the development of an efficient industrial policy. In particular, a stable macroeconomic environment, which calls for monetary stability, is vitally important for intangible investment since technological progress is a long-term activity. The effect of any monetary uncertainty is that industrial firms become unsure of the future and thus work on a shorter-term basis, because they cannot predict the long-term profitability of their investments. Monetary uncertainties make long-term investment and savings decisions more hazardous and economic players become less willing to take risks and prefer to concentrate on the short-term during such periods (Caracostas and Muldur, 1998).

The 1990 communication on "Industrial policy in an open and competitive environment" underlined the central role played by the provision of a supportive environment for industry and stable macroeconomic conditions. The general approach adopted by the communication was intended to establish the basis for an industrial policy going beyond the traditional and conflict-generating debate between a purely non-interventionist policy in the industrial field and the disputed practices of sector targeting. The 1994 communication on "An industrial competitiveness policy for the European Union", argues for across-the-board measures, given that the new dynamics of competitive advantage disrupt past patterns of sectoral and industrial organisation.

The 1994 communication very clearly takes on board the concept of intangibles. The "action priorities" it contains specifically mention "intangible investment". They give higher priority to non-physical investment in the general measures to encourage investment, promote quality more effectively, take better account of market needs in RDT and develop an integrated approach as regards intellectual property.

There is confirmation of this approach in *Agenda 2000* (1997), which says: "Community action aims at speeding up adjustment to structural change, encouraging an environment favourable to initiative, to the development of undertakings throughout the Community, and to industrial co-operation, and fostering better exploitation of the industrial potential of policies of innovation, research and technological development." It is, however, still the case that the EU is lagging behind the United States in intangible activities, as emphasised in the Competitiveness Report: "Compared to the USA, structural differences arise primarily from *poor performance in creating lead-time in the fast moving markets*, where competitive advantage is based on intangible investment in research and marketing. Since first mover advantages create substantial benefits in terms of growth and employment, the USA seems to have a greater ability to benefit from the particularly high growth dynamics in these activities."

R&D policy

Far from being a top-down approach, the Fifth Framework Programme of Research, Development and Demonstration is intended to help establish in Europe an environment favourable to innovation. That means encouraging technology transfer, ensuring venture capital is available, helping to protect intellectual property rights and developing human resources. In Europe today, the drive belt connecting research to economic development is still too loose. This is precisely the point on which the EU's new programmes will focus: putting research and innovation to work.

In short, the European Union's programmes stimulate mobility among those involved and encourage the movement of ideas. This is of fundamental importance, as technical and scientific knowledge is the main raw material of modern industry ("The Fifth Framework Programme", European Commission, 1999). From that point of view, the key actions, as they are called, are important instruments. The aim is to focus the resources and skills of all the relevant disciplines, technologies and people on a series of well-defined socioeconomic problems. The spirit underlying the key actions is thus quite different from the traditional way of organising research by separating it into different disciplines.

This means that resources have to be targeted so that they are not wasted on measures that are unlikely to have a significant impact. At the same time, allocations may be stepped up at a rate faster than GNP growth in the case of certain programmes which have been given priority because of the added value they derive from Community-level action, in terms, for instance, of growth, employment and the development and dissemination of new forms of technology. This would essentially mean the trans-European networks such as research, education and training, the introduction of environment-friendly technologies and measures to support SMEs, many of the actions being focused on intangible investment.

Competition Policy

Where competition policy is concerned, tougher, tighter action needs to be taken, since identifying restrictions on competition deriving from a dominant position, cartel or merger means looking not only at tangible assets but also at intangibles such as intellectual property, patents, cross-licensing technologies and brands, knowing that there are huge differences between the market values of companies and their book assets.

These aspects are accentuated by the growing number of cases involving software and the internet-based industry. A strategy of restricting competition in operating software and Internet products could slow the development of new technology and increase the prices to consumers. Intangibles constitute a wide field, and new types of restrictions on competition are emerging. A thoroughgoing analysis of the various complex practices used to control markets is required.

The fact is that regulation becomes harder to apply where output is knowledge-driven and the regulated body increasingly has more information than the regulator. This makes it more difficult for the regulator to assess the position of the regulated with any accuracy and consequently to make policy that is economically efficient (DTI, 1998).

Clarifying the relationship between the competition authorities and these markets is a major task.

For example, an abuse of a dominant position in the intensive, intangible-investment areas of activity such as the software industries, training organisations, research and development organisations, business services and patenting is clearly more difficult to demonstrate than it is in relation to intensive, tangible-investment activities such as machinery and equipment manufacture. By its very nature, intangible-investment activity is intrinsically different from physical-investment activity, with the result that there tend to be substantial differences between the types of competition in which manufacturing and services activities become involved.

To begin with, the need for suppliers to be close to buyers in knowledge-based activities means that competition tends to be localised. Secondly, as the quality of knowledge-based activities cannot be assessed before consumption takes place (because of the imbalance in the information available as between buyers and sellers), in most knowledge-based activities there is non-price competition. Thirdly, knowledge-based activities are highly differentiated services and tend to involve high fixed intangible costs, such as reputation, which is likely to be irreversible (representing a high sunk cost). So, in knowledge-based activities, businesses tend to enjoy a certain degree of market power, their reputation serving to reduce the degree of competition. This generally makes analysing competition cases in the anti-trust sphere a much more complex matter, the Microsoft case in the USA being one of the best examples. Consequently, the analytical capacity which anti-trust bodies can apply to dealing with the new challenge of cartels and abuse of dominant position in knowledge-based activities needs to be strengthened.

There is also a question mark over the matter of making checks on State aid. The approach which the Commission's competition policy takes towards State aid is to prohibit it, but the Commission may consider aid compatible with the common market if it is intended "to facilitate the development of certain economic activities where such aid does not adversely affect trading conditions to an extent contrary to the common interest" (Art. 3(c)). In practice, aid will be allowed if the positive effects outweigh the adverse effects on competition and trade, for example if aid achieves objectives which market forces alone would not secure. In the past, however, the exemption schemes focused on the tangible investment dimension. For example, under the 1992 guidelines on State aid for small and medium-sized enterprises, the Commission may grant exemptions for SMEs' investment where the degree of aid to investment as a proportion of the costs is below a certain threshold, but the investment "must be in fixed assets".

It was only with the new 1996 guidelines on SMEs that the definition of investment was extended to "intangible investment in the form of transfers of technology". The Commission decided then that "the test of acceptability of aid to industry was reviewed in order to eliminate the bias in favour of tangible investment". Aid for R&D, training, consultancy or technology transfer were treated as tangible investment.

Trade policy

In the field of trade policy, the latest international rounds of negotiations as well as the development in the priorities of the World Trade Organisation clearly show that there is a move under way towards a better understanding and more effective treatment of problems linked to intangibles, such as the trade in services, intellectual property, public tenders and non-tariff barriers.

Nevertheless, most of the instruments available for implementing trade policy, such as anti-dumping and anti-subsidy regulations, customs duties and quantitative restrictions, were set up at a time when trade consisted almost exclusively of exchanges of products between independent geographic regions.

These instruments are difficult to apply to the trade in services or intangible products. In fact, many of the problems faced in attempting to ensure fair competition under competition rules are just as difficult to solve when it comes to ensuring fair trade under international rules. This is increasingly the case as the link between the site of production and the nationality of the producers becomes more and more complicated.

For instance, as far as the anti-dumping instrument is concerned (except for maritime transport), there is no legal basis for applying it to services or intangibles. And even if there were a legal basis, the existing rules covering physical products would be hard to apply: in industries such as the audiovisual or software sectors, it would be extremely difficult to analyse "normal values", "dumping margins" or "injury" under such rules.

The combination of "dematerialisation" and the globalisation of production is leading to a situation where the terms of reference and implementing rules for many trade instruments have lost most of their efficiency. In the future, instead of dealing with exchanges of goods and services between geographical areas, we are likely to be dealing more and more with the commercial practices of companies operating worldwide, whatever the geographical origin of their products. This is already true of electronic commerce. Production, storage, administration, advertising, ordering, delivery, accounting and billing, payment, even quality control and customer care – all of these can be and are being done by electronic means, using information and communication support structures.

Conclusion

We are clearly at the outset of a process which could last a very long time and will undoubtedly require a serious rethinking of the way Europe's policies are organised and the tools which are used to incorporate the intangible dimension. What is more, the European policies on intangibles covered here (competition, R&D, trade and industrial policies) are strongly interrelated and they all contribute together to shaping a "global competitiveness policy" on intangible activities.

The transformation of our economies into an information-based economy is a fundamental new development. This reaches far beyond the economic aspects and touches deeply on social values, ranging from maintaining the basic concepts of a public service provided to every citizen, to freedom of speech and protection against intrusion into privacy. With a radical economic transformation of society such as this, a new economic paradigm is emerging. More than ever, governments have an important role to play in promoting the development of human capital and ensuring access to new knowledge for the whole of society. Conversely, these changes must not be used as an excuse for discriminating against the disadvantaged, be they individuals or specific categories. Everyone must be given *equal opportunities* in the new economy.

References

Buigues, P., Jacquemin, A. and Sapir, A. (1993), European Competition Policy in Manufacturing and Services: A Two-speed approach?, *Oxford Review of Economic Policy*, Vol. 9, n° 2.

Buigues, P., A. Jacquemin and A. Sapir (1995), European Policies on Competition, Trade and Industry. Conflicts and Complementarities, Edward Elgar.

Caracostas, P. and U. Muldur (1998), "Society, the Endless Frontier", *European Commission, DG.XII*.

Davies, S and B. Lyons (1996), Industrial Organisation in the European Union, Oxford University Press.

UK - Department of Trade and Industry (DTI), (1998), "Our Competitive Future - Building the Knowledge Driven Economy", *The 1998 Competitiveness White Paper*.

European Commission (1993), *White Paper on "Growth, Competitiveness, Employment"*.

European Commission (1999), *The Fifth Framework Programme*.

Jacquemin, A. and J.F. Marchipont (1992), "De nouveaux enjeux pour la politique industrielle de la Communauté", *Revue d'économie politique*, 102, n° 1.

Jacquemin, A. and L. Pench (ed.) (1997), *Europe Competing in the Global Economy*, Edward Elgar Publishing, London.

Marchipont J-F. (1995), Les nouveaux réseaux de l'information, *Continent "Europe"*.

OECD (1997), "New directions for industrial policy", *OECD Policy Brief*, N° 3.

Sutton, J. (1991), *Sunk Costs and Market Structure*, Cambridge MA, MIT Press.

Index

Advertising 21, 74, 113, 115-7, 124, 128-30, 136-42, 167-71, 181-4, 190-2, 198, 200-203, 215, 220, 277-9, 310, 316, 320-2, 328

Assets 7, 15, 19-22, 25, 33-4, 47-8, 59-61, 111, 113, 201, 207-8, 231-3, 235-7, 238-40, 251-3, 255, 263, 303, 309, 317, 321, 326-7

Barriers 21, 32, 189, 193, 251, 328

Benchmarking 29, 31-2, 34, 47, 83

Best practices 83, 323-4

Brand 21-2, 25, 27, 30-4, 86, 89, 91, 94, 103-5, 110, 114, 119, 123, 125-6, 128-31, 140, 189, 196-8, 278, 289, 321-2, 326

Business 4, 14-5, 24-5, 34-5, 42-5, 49, 51-4, 57, 59, 62, 66-8, 72-3, 76, 80-3, 85-6, 103, 105-10, 119-21, 141, 158-9, 165-75, 181-4, 200, 202, 215-6, 218-20, 297-8, 303-4, 307, 316, 318, 321, 323-4, 326-7

Capital 3-9, 17-18, 21, 25-6, 29, 34, 42-55, 58-68, 83-4, 91, 103, 116, 123, 128-130, 138-142, 146-7, 150, 160, 167, 189-191, 194-5, 199, 203-22, 224-7, 231-3, 238, 244, 246, 248, 253, 255, 282, 317-8, 320, 325, 329

Capital markets 11, 14-5, 87, 89, 110, 198

Cluster 106, 159, 166, 169, 189-91, 193, 195-7, 306, 321

Cluster analysis 159, 176

Clustering 171, 181, 189-91, 196-7

Commercial 57, 65-6, 107, 116, 274, 277-9, 285, 291, 307, 316, 328

Company 14-5, 19, 22, 25, 29, 33-4, 66, 116, 120, 141, 151, 199, 205-6, 215, 219

Company performance 82, 86, 95, 199-201, 219, 233

Competition 9, 44, 50-1, 55, 67, 84, 107, 127, 138, 156, 187, 189, 193, 195, 253, 255, 259, 267, 303, 305, 312-3, 322-4, 326-9

Competitive 26, 30, 35, 38, 44, 81, 103-4, 116-26, 128, 141, 143, 148-50, 156, 188, 193, 210, 220, 230, 314, 318, 324-5

Competitive advantage 18, 20, 23, 27, 37, 106-16, 117, 121

Competitiveness 3-4, 17, 26-7,

32, 36, 42, 47, 82, 85, 103, 116, 120, 154, 156, 181, 183, 187, 194, 229-30, 249, 253, 273-6, 278-9, 282, 284-93, 316-8, 320-1, 323-5, 329
Corporate performance 17, 29, 31, 35, 228, 251
Corporate strategy 22, 118-9, 125, 151, 189
Corporations 22, 88, 113-5, 310-1
Culture 4, 22, 25, 30, 83, 104, 108-9, 115, 163-5, 311

Differentiation 104, 110, 116, 120, 125, 127-8, 130-1, 143, 146, 152, 181, 189-90, 193, 251, 253-5, 322
Diffusion 51, 73, 76, 79, 289, 306-7

Economic performance 3, 14, 27, 117, 119, 150, 155, 187, 199, 202, 228, 231, 248, 252, 273, 304, 320
Economy 3, 8-9, 11, 13-4, 19, 43-4, 46-7, 49-50, 52, 54-5, 62-3, 68, 109, 116, 118, 154, 157, 163-7, 182-3, 191, 194, 197, 200, 202, 204, 206, 228, 254-5, 275, 303-4, 316-7, 320, 323, 329
Education 6-7, 10, 25, 32, 43, 51, 61, 63, 72-3, 76, 79, 113, 161, 168-71, 194, 259, 307, 309, 312-6, 318, 321, 324, 326
Eurostat 13, 117, 119, 154, 181-4, 197, 310
Expert 3, 13, 64-6

Expertise 21, 67, 82-3, 116, 190
Externality 193, 202, 208

Finance 21-2, 24-5, 32-3, 35, 45, 48, 50, 57-8, 61, 64, 74, 76, 84-91, 95, 104, 108, 112, 156, 167-77, 180, 205, 230, 231, 240-1, 252
Firm organisation 20, 22-3, 37, 73, 90, 103-4, 107-10

Globalisation 103, 107-8, 110, 112-3, 115, 156, 183, 237, 243, 246, 249, 275, 311, 328
Goodwill 33, 35, 90-2, 94, 201
Growth 4-7, 10, 13-4, 17-8, 42-3, 57, 68, 72-8, 82-3, 85, 91, 95, 104, 106, 111, 113, 144, 170, 182, 187, 189-90, 192-3, 195, 202-6, 216-7, 220, 224, 228, 231, 234-5, 237-46, 248-9, 252-3, 259, 262-3, 265-6, 282, 298, 300, 303, 307, 316-8, 321-2, 325-6

High-technology 9, 89, 155, 162, 180, 193, 200, 304
Horizontal policies 17, 194
Human capital 4, 9-11, 15, 25-6, 29, 34-6, 69, 79, 88, 303, 317, 329
Human resources 21-2, 32, 34, 38-9, 72, 79-82, 86, 88, 90-1, 94, 97, 118, 120, 125-7, 129, 135, 143, 160-1, 166, 169, 182, 325

Industry 25, 32, 43, 45, 47, 55-6, 58, 62-3, 65-7, 82, 85, 103-4, 106-8, 112-3, 115-6, 116-

Index

21, 125-6, 128-34, 136-7, 139, 141-3, 146, 148, 150, 151, 165, 167, 174, 175, 188, 191-2, 194-6, 203-4, 206, 226-5, 228-37, 246, 248-9, 251, 253-5, 262, 264, 275-6, 278-9, 281-2, 304-10, 321-8

Information 3-4, 14, 18, 25, 43, 45-54, 59, 63-4, 66-8, 72-3, 76-8, 81-2, 85-9, 91, 95-6, 103-6, 112, 115-6, 117, 119, 131, 134, 154, 159-61, 170, 183, 189, 196, 206, 234, 305, 309-15, 318-21, 326-7, 329

Information technologies 3, 18, 22, 24, 44-6, 72, 86, 103, 105-6, 309, 313, 316, 322-3

Innovation 3-4, 7, 12-3, 26, 30, 32, 37, 49, 51, 55-9, 63, 72-3, 81, 91, 105-6, 109, 111-2, 118-9, 121-2, 133, 137, 155, 158, 160, 170, 172-3, 175-7, 180-1, 183, 189, 190, 192-4, 196, 228-33, 235, 241, 246, 248, 252, 273-7, 282-3, 285, 287-9, 291, 297, 304-7, 316-7, 321, 323-5

Inputs 26, 134, 146, 150, 261-2, 263-4, 267-70, 275, 304

Intangible assets 14, 17, 21, 27, 32, 34, 37, 81-3, 85, 90-1, 94-6, 116-7, 122-8, 149, 154, 187, 189, 195-7, 303, 309, 317, 321

Intangible capital 8-9, 42-5, 64-8, 72-5, 199, 206-7, 209, 213, 216, 220

Intangible investment 7, 9, 38, 73, 91, 116-8, 121, 128, 141, 154-7, 159-60, 164, 167, 169, 173, 181, 184, 187-9, 191-4, 196, 199, 202, 205, 209-10, 213, 215, 219-20, 226

Intellectual capital 3-4, 7, 9, 13-7, 24-5, 27-8, 32-3, 35, 37-8, 72, 75, 83, 84-9, 95, 103

Intellectual property 25, 84, 112, 155, 157, 325-6, 328

Know-how 9, 22, 25, 194, 265, 324

Knowledge base information economy 12, 23, 35, 73, 75-6, 80-2, 84, 95, 184, 303, 323

Labour 4-6, 12, 14-5, 75-6, 82-3, 88, 110-3, 116, 118, 121-9, 134-40, 146-8, 150, 155, 166, 168-70, 189-91, 196, 199, 207-9, 215, 253, 259, 262-4, 267-9, 275-6, 279-81, 283-7, 290, 295, 305, 310-2, 318

Location 116-7, 159, 189, 310

Management 3-4, 13-5, 17, 22, 24-5, 27, 36-7, 47, 50-1, 57-9, 65, 81-6, 88, 95-6, 103, 105-6, 109, 114, 157, 161, 185, 265, 311

Manufacturing firms 110-1, 200, 206, 252-4, 259, 262, 271, 317

Manufacturing industry 29, 62, 65, 114, 156-7, 177, 205, 230, 275, 279, 281-2

Manufacturing sectors 106, 110, 154, 159, 175, 205, 213-4, 215-6, 221, 260-1, 271, 317

Market 4, 9, 17, 20, 23, 27, 32, 36, 42-4, 49, 51-2, 56-8, 61-8,

72-3, 75, 80-2, 85-7, 89-90, 95, 103-8, 111-6, 126, 131, 138, 141, 158, 176-7, 181, 184, 189, 193-5, 215, 221, 229, 243, 252-5, 273-5, 277, 279-82, 285-6, 289, 298, 312-8, 321-3, 325-7
Market organisation 110, 119, 121, 149, 189
Market value 15, 19, 33, 61, 65, 87, 231-4, 238-44, 248-50, 305
Marketing 7, 18, 43, 55-7, 59, 61, 67, 82, 86, 90-1, 116-8, 120-1, 123-8, 131, 133-5, 146-7, 150, 182, 188, 199, 213, 217, 219, 220, 241, 274-5, 277-8, 280, 285, 304, 307, 316-7, 320, 324-5

Networks 3-4, 25, 27, 32, 36, 47, 57, 72, 86, 109, 112, 311, 316, 321, 326

OECD 8, 12-3, 73-8, 81-2, 84, 86, 91, 120, 154-5, 161-6, 169, 172-5, 181-2, 190-2, 194, 197, 199, 254, 259, 273-6, 281-2, 285-8, 292, 297-8, 300, 303, 307, 321, 323

Patents 21, 25, 27, 32, 34, 48, 84, 86, 91, 94, 111, 114, 157, 228, 231-3, 235-8, 251, 273-4, 277-81, 284-5, 290, 305-6, 316, 321, 326-7
Physical capital 48, 73, 75-6, 117-8, 134-5, 204, 208, 210-2, 214, 216-9, 226-7, 259, 263-4, 268-9, 305-6

Product differentiation 119-20, 121, 125, 135

R&D 4, 7, 13, 17, 19, 21-2, 26, 32, 43, 59, 62, 72-4, 76, 87, 89, 90-2, 94-5, 118, 139-41, 155-7, 169-70, 171-7, 180-1, 189-91, 193-5, 199-218, 224-33, 237, 239-41, 243-4, 246, 248, 274, 276-7, 279-81, 289, 297-8, 300, 303-7, 316-7, 321-5, 328-9
Reputation 21-3, 27, 33-4, 86, 104-6, 112, 114, 116, 128, 275, 289, 322-3, 327
Resource 7, 9, 14, 17, 19-30, 32, 35-8, 43-4, 47, 49-53, 57-9, 73, 76, 83, 92, 96, 321, 323, 325-6
Return 9-12, 21, 48, 60, 87-8, 92, 112, 200, 203, 208-10, 213, 217, 228-9, 231-3, 238, 243-4, 248, 255, 260, 265-6, 270, 289, 298, 300, 304-7

Service sector 13-4, 18, 20, 22, 24-5, 29-30, 32, 34, 36-7, 47, 51, 62-3, 76, 78, 81-3, 85, 91, 104, 106, 108, 110, 112, 114, 116, 119-21, 127, 131, 150, 155-7, 161-7, 169-76, 179, 181-4, 189-91,
SMEs 31, 156, 173, 326-7
Social 13, 104, 106, 109, 158, 163-5, 183, 193, 232, 273, 300, 305-7, 311, 318-9, 329
Software 7, 9, 24, 33-4, 60-1, 72-4, 80, 82, 86, 90-2, 94, 114, 156, 159, 161, 172, 174-6, 181-2, 200, 303, 307, 310,

314, 316, 320, 326, 328
Specialisation 11-2, 81, 83, 119, 121, 127, 141, 143-51, 187, 189, 193-4, 237, 290
Spillover 55, 194, 203, 206, 219, 232, 265, 289, 305-7
Strategy 14, 22-3, 25, 35-6, 38, 45, 56, 75, 80-2, 84-6, 89, 117, 119-20, 122-6, 148, 150, 157, 188-9, 229, 233, 236-8, 240, 247, 249, 277, 289-90, 326

Tangible capital 7, 199, 207-9, 210, 215-6, 219-220
Technology 3-4, 6-7, 11-3, 21, 26, 32, 45, 54, 56, 62-3, 66, 72-3, 76-82, 85-7, 89, 95, 103, 105, 107-8, 116, 118-20, 123-31, 133-5, 138, 142, 146-7, 150, 155-7, 160, 166, 175-7, 179-80, 183, 191, 193-7, 202-3, 253, 264, 274, 279-80, 287, 289, 291, 303-4, 309, 312, 314, 316, 321-3, 325-6, 328
Trade 21, 25, 47-9, 62, 66, 106, 112-3, 128, 130, 155, 158, 161-5, 174-5, 180-4, 187, 189, 190-5, 200, 251-3, 273-5, 279, 282, 287-9, 316-7, 324, 327-9
Training 4, 7, 10-1, 24, 72-3, 79, 86, 88, 90-1, 94-5, 166, 176-7, 259-71, 304, 307, 310, 312, 314, 316-8, 320-4, 326, 328
Transaction 15, 34, 54, 59, 63, 105, 182, 188, 282

WTO - World Trade Organisation 182, 187, 190, 195, 328